SOME HONORABLE MEN
Political Conventions 1960 -1972

BOOKS BY NORMAN MAILER

Norman Mailer

SOME HONORABLE MEN
Political Conventions 1960-1972

LITTLE, BROWN AND COMPANY — BOSTON – TORONTO

FIRST EDITION

T 04/76

The photographs in this book
are by United Press International.

The author is grateful to the following publishers for permission
to reprint previously copyrighted materials:

The New American Library, Inc., New York, New York, for *Miami
and the Siege of Chicago* by Norman Mailer, copyright © 1968 by
Norman Mailer; and for *St. George and the Godfather* by Norman
Mailer, copyright © 1972 by Norman Mailer.

G. P. Putnam's Sons, for "The Existential Hero" from *Presidential
Papers* by Norman Mailer. Copyright © 1960, 1961, 1962, 1963 by
Norman Mailer.

The New York Times, for material quoted on pages 146–147, 236,
and 244. Copyright © 1968 by *The New York Times* Company.

The Village Voice, for material quoted on pages 228–230 and 245–
246. Copyright © 1968 by *The Village Voice.*

The Washington Post, for material quoted on pages 226–227. Copyright © 1968 by *The Washington Post.*

Material from *Miami and the Siege of Chicago* previously appeared
in *Harper's* magazine.

LIBRARY OF CONGRESS CATALOGING IN PUBLICATION DATA

Mailer, Norman.
    Some honorable men.

    1. Political conventions. 2. Political parties —
United States. 3. United States — Politics and
government — 1945–   I. Title.
JK2255.M243   329'.0221'0973   75-8595
ISBN 0-316-54415-9

Designed by Susan Windheim

*Published simultaneously in Canada
by Little, Brown & Company (Canada) Limited*

PRINTED IN THE UNITED STATES OF AMERICA

CONTENTS

To the memory of my father

In particular appreciation —

Willie Morris
Midge Decter
Tom Griffith
Ralph Graves
Jack Newcombe
Molly Malone Cook
Mary Oliver
Suzanne Nye

PREFACE

Ever since Tom Wolfe began to write those self-serving encomiums to the New Journalism, it has become a literary reflex to point to the convention pieces printed here as objects of the new art, and it is possible I received more praise as a new journalist than ever as a novelist. That is an irony which tempts me to spit to the wind: I never worked as a journalist and dislike the profession. It is a promiscuous way to live. Just as a lawyer has no love of truth comparable to his attachment to the interests of his client, so a reporter has no respect for nuance. The feel of a situation is not what he explores, indeed he often avoids atmosphere since that is difficult to capture in a quickly written piece. His youthful attempts at looking for the mood of an event were all beheaded years ago on the copy editor's desk; he has since been drilled to look for facts even if invariably he gets those facts wrong. He is subtly encouraged when working on a story to depend on everything but his writing. That is because few reporters write well.

Actually, it is worse than that. Centuries from now, the moral intelligence of another time may look in horror on the history implanted into Twentieth Century people by way of newsprint. A deadening of the collective brain has been one consequence. Another is the active warping of consciousness in any leader whose actions are consistently in the papers, for he has been obliged to learn how to speak only in quotable and self-protective remarks. He has also had to learn not to be too interesting since his ideas would then be garbled and his manner criticized. Some men could never learn, Gene McCarthy for one, and so their careers did not prosper in proportion to their courage and their abilities. Of course, those heroes who learned how to respect the limitations of the reporter may never have had a serious thought again. In order to communicate with the communicators, they gave up any hint of a private philosophy.

It could be said, however, that sour remarks about journalists are not new for me. I thought even less of the profession eleven years ago. If my bitterness at the conformity of the Eisenhower years gives its special tone to the prose, still no improvement in the press has been so great that I would withdraw the words.

> The reporter hangs in a powerless-power — his voice directly, or
> via the rewrite desk indirectly, reaches out to millions of readers;

the more readers he owns, the less he can say. He is forbidden by a hundred censors, most of them inside himself, to communicate notions which are not conformistically simple, simple like plastic is simple, that is to say, monotonous. Therefore a reporter forms a habit equivalent to lacerating the flesh: he learns to write what he does not naturally believe. Since he did not start presumably with the desire to be a bad writer or a dishonest writer, he ends by bludgeoning his brain into believing that something which is half true is in fact — since he creates a fact each time he puts something into a newspaper — nine-tenths true. A psyche is debauched — his own; a false fact is created. For which fact, sooner or later, inevitably, inexorably, the public will pay. A nation which forms detailed opinions on the basis of detailed fact which is askew from the subtle reality becomes a nation of citizens whose psyches are skewed, item by detailed item, away from *any* reality.

So great guilt clings to reporters. They know they help to keep America slightly insane. As a result perhaps they are a shabby-looking crew . . . and suffer each day from the damnable anxiety that they know all sorts of powerful information a half hour to twenty-four hours before anyone else in America knows it, not to mention the time clock ticking away in the vault of all those stories which cannot be printed or will not be printed. It makes for a livid view of existence. It is like an injunction to become hysterical once a day. Then they must write at lightning speed. It may be heavy-fisted but true, it may be slick as a barnyard slide, it may be great, it may be fill — what does it matter? The matter rides out like oats in a conveyor belt, and the unconscious takes a ferocious pounding. Writing is of use to the psyche only if the writer discovers something he did not know he knew in the act itself of writing. That is why a few men will go through hell in order to keep writing — Joyce and Proust, for example. Being a writer can save one from insanity or cancer; being a bad writer can drive one smack into the center of the plague. Think of the poor reporter who does not have the leisure of the novelist or the poet to discover what he thinks. The unconscious gives up, buries itself, leaves the writer to his cliché, and saves the truth, or that part of it the reporter is yet privileged to find, for his colleagues and his friends. A good re-porter is a man who must still tell you the truth privately; he has bright harsh eyes and can relate ten good stories in a row standing at a bar.

Still, they do not quit. That charge of adrenalin once a day, that hysteria, that sense of powerless-power close to the engines of his-tory — they can do without powerless-power no more than a gen-tleman junkie on the main line can do without his heroin, doctor. You see, a reporter is close to the action. He is not *of* the action, but he is close to it, as close as a crab louse to the begetting of a child. One may never be President, but the photographer working for his paper has the power to cock a flashbulb and make the eyes of JFK go blink! *

* "Ten Thousand Words a Minute," *The Presidential Papers* (New York, Putnam, 1963).

While that passage happened to be written two years after the Democratic Convention of 1960, it could as fairly have been put on paper two years before. So it should be evident I began these forays into the nature of the political convention with prejudices for how the materials of such history were gathered. I also possessed the large advantage that I had weeks to ponder over what I had seen and nearly enough days in which to do the writing. I also had a literary heritage to remind me that the world is not supposed to be reassembled by panels of prefabricated words. Rather, I was a novelist. It was expected of me to see the world with my own eyes and own words. See it by the warp or stance of my character. Which if it could collect into some kind of integrity might be called a style. I was enlisted then on my side of an undeclared war between those modes of perception called journalism and fiction. When it came to accuracy, I was on the side of fiction. I thought fiction could bring us closer to the truth than journalism, which is not to say one should make up facts when writing a story about real people. I would endeavor to get my facts as scrupulously as a reporter. (At least!) The difference would be found elsewhere. Journalism assumes the truth of an event can be found by the use of principles which go back to Descartes. (A political reporter has a fixed view of the world: you may plot it on axes which run right to left on the horizontal and down from honesty to corruption on the vertical.) Indeed, the real premise of journalism is that the best instrument for measuring history is a faceless, even a mindless, recorder. Whereas the writer of fiction is closer to that moving world of Einstein. There the velocity of the observer is as crucial to the measurement as any object observed. For fiction probably makes the secret assumption that we learn the truth through a comparison of the lies, since we are obliged to receive the majority of our experience at second hand through parents, friends, mates, lovers, enemies, and the journalists who report it to us. So our best chance of improving those private charts of our own most complicated lives, our unadmitted maps of reality, our very comprehension, if you will, of the way existence works — seems to profit most if we can have some little idea, at least, of the warp of the observer who passes on the experience. Fiction, as I use the word, is then that reality which does not cohere to anonymous axes of fact but is breathed in through the swarm of our male and female movements about one another, a novelistic assumption, for don't we perceive the truth of a novel as its events pass through the personality of the writer? We tend to know, in our unconscious at least, by the time we have finished a story where we think the author is most to be trusted, and where in secret we suspect he is more ignorant than ourselves. That is the flavor of fiction. We observe the observer. Maybe that is why there is less dead air in fiction and usually more light. It is because we have the advantage of seeing around a corner, and that is aesthetically analogous to a photograph of a range of hills when the sunset offers its back-lighting to the contours. Be certain the journalistic flashbulb is better for recording the carnage of an auto crash. But little else.

Very well. These convention pieces written by most novelists' measure in a great hurry, yet by a journalist's schedule in real leisure, are pieces which range themselves on the side of fiction, a remark, to repeat, that ought not to encourage a reader to assume my facts are the fiction — no, many good and great novelists take pains with the details of their facts which would put the average of journalists (with their slovenly habits) to shame, no, my facts were as good as I could get, but my prose lived in the relative world of fiction where I, the author, was a presence in this gathering-up of what I had seen of some history being made. I was proud of that, proud of the method I used, and would do it again — what, indeed, are these four small histories worth if the reader cannot now interpret them with his own fine notion of my strengths and comic lacks as an observer; what, we could inquire, would be here worth rereading if it had not been done with the confidence of the novelist?

Speaking at the MacDowell Colony a while ago, I found myself saying: "There is no reason to believe the novelist is not better equipped to deal with the possibilities of a mysterious and difficult situation than anyone else, since he or she is always trying to discover what the nature of reality might be. It's as if the novelist is out there, sprung early, with something most people never contemplate — which is 'How and what is the nature of this little reality before me.' The novelist is the first to ask, 'Do I love my wife? Does she love me? What is the nature of love? Do we love our child? How do we love? Would we die for our child? Or do we let the child die for us?' The novelist has to deal with these questions because living with them is the only way to improve his or her brain. Without improving that brain, without refining the edge of one's perception, it's almost impossible to continue to work as a writer. Because if there is one fell rule in art it is that repetition kills the soul. So the novelist is out there early with a particular necessity that may become the necessity of us all. It is to deal with life as something God did not give us as eternal and immutable but rather as something half-worked because it was our human destiny to enlarge what we were given, to forge (I might have said, to *clarify*) a world which was always before us in a manner different from the way we had seen it the day before."

It is likely that in trying to write about political conventions my undeclared emotion may have been similar to the speech just quoted. Certainly I must have had the confidence I could do it. For in the years from 1960 to 1972 there was some easy marriage between my literary desires and my ability to perceive a fair amount of what was happening in those clouds of moral ambiguity where politics itself existed. So it may be right to put these four pieces together now into a book. They may even justify my confidence that the world (not the techniques but the *world*) of fiction can be brought to the facts of journalism.

Of course, we are now in the years which follow Watergate. So we are obliged to recognize that much of what we look on as our history is, in fact, not much related to the facts. At least, those facts we supposed were facts. Who can now read what I wrote about the Democratic and Republican conventions of 1972 without searching for everything I did not see? How much we did not know at the time of all the secret history being made.*

Of course I wrote these pieces at a time when one could try to believe in history as the product of forces more or less open to the vision of skilled observers. One could still believe in the mood generated by a clash of forces — the Kennedys versus Stevenson in 1960, the Goldwater Republicans against the emergence of a revolutionary youth in '64, the open view America was given of the wounds of the Democratic Party in '68, even the play of idealisms, fresh, hysterical, and inept against the brilliantly covert manipulations of Nixon's own convention in '72 — they were the stuff of the novelist. Observing such forces offered direct literary confidence and a method of writing, a mode of perceiving. If the observations were probably not as accurate as one thought at the time — how many of the fights in the streets of Chicago came flowering for instance out of the departments of the dirtiest tricks? — still, it was a stimulating way to work.

---

* How, for instance, is it possible not to consider the possibility that secret files of the FBI open to the White House had all the details of Eagleton's medical history? Since no other Democrat could do more for the Republicans as a candidate than the Senator from Missouri, it is fair to wonder if anyone in the room with McGovern on the panicky afternoon when Eagleton was selected may actually have been working undercover for the Republicans. Not all political agents are obligatorily as clumsy as Segretti.

Yet now I have to wonder if we are entering an era in which everyday dead-air journalism will be preeminent again. For if our history is not an interplay of open forces so much as a game between some forces partially open and some which are altogether closed, then the confidence to seize a mood on the fly and read history into the sound of bagpipes at four in the morning * is ready to dissipate.

Living with such thoughts, one grew more depressed during much of a hot summer in Washington while listening to the proceedings of the Ervin Committee. For it felt as if an old magic had disappeared. Magic is confidence, and there was no longer any certainty that one saw details to observe no one else might notice, or even that one had things to say and others were not ready to. The mood was, instead, jurisdictional. It called for a lawyer. When a friend came by and whispered, "Who do you think is lying?" the answer was that one did not know who was lying. The process of Watergate went deep, and the truth existed far beneath the mood, lived indeed in those Washington vaults where secret forces conducted war, and on the hot street outside, as one left the Old Senate Caucus Room, no youth were demonstrating on the street, no slogans were shouted, the history of the republic had gone down into the mines again, and the novelist was left with his fiction. Watergate would have to be divided between the daily reporters and the scholars and documents to come, the revelations of the legal process.

So, too, might the politics of the future live in electronic solid-states of power and televised communication. If the pessimism is just, then these convention writings assembled here are vintage and done. But a writer does well not to make prophecies. Let us see if 1972 was the conclusion of one fair attempt to perceive our history through our conventions, or if we are witnessing an ongoing process some of us first became connected to in the promising and not so uncrazy summer of 1960, that first of the Kennedy years, in which we became a nation royal with triumphs, tragedies, and ongoing obsessive fears. How much America becomes the character, no, the protagonist of that novel no genius is large enough to write. Shakespeare would grow modest before America.

---

* Only years later did the writer learn that the bagpipers were professional musicians practicing for a very early morning television show. See p. 70.

Superman Comes to the Supermarket

FOR ONCE let us try to think about a political convention without losing ourselves in housing projects of fact and issue. Politics has its virtues, all too many of them — it would not rank with baseball as a topic of conversation if it did not satisfy a great many things — but one can suspect that its secret appeal is close to nicotine. Smoking cigarettes insulates one from one's life, one does not feel as much, often happily so, and politics quarantines one from history; most of the people who nourish themselves in the political life are in the game not to make history but to be diverted from the history which is being made.

If that Democratic Convention which has now receded behind the brow of the Summer of 1960 is only half-remembered in the excitements of moving toward the election, it may be exactly the time to consider it again, because the mountain of facts which concealed its features last July has been blown away in the winds of High Television, and the man-in-the-street (that peculiar political term which refers to the quixotic voter who will pull the lever for some reason so salient as: "I had a brown-nose lieutenant once with Nixon's looks," or "that Kennedy must have false teeth"), the not so easily estimated man-in-the-street has forgotten most of what happened and could no more tell you who Kennedy was fighting against than you or I could place a bet on who was leading the American League in batting during the month of June.

So to try to talk about what happened is easier now than in the days

3

of the convention, one does not have to put everything in — an act of writing which calls for a bulldozer rather than a pen — one can try to make one's little point and dress it with a ribbon or two of metaphor. All to the good. Because mysteries are irritated by facts, and the 1960 Democratic Convention began as one mystery and ended as another.

Since mystery is an emotion which is repugnant to a political animal (why else lead a life of bad banquet dinners, cigar smoke, camp chairs, foul breath, and excruciatingly dull jargon if not to avoid the echoes of what is not known), the psychic separation between what was happening on the floor, in the caucus rooms, in the headquarters, and what was happening in parallel to the history of the nation was mystery enough to drown the proceedings in gloom. It was on the one hand a dull convention, one of the less interesting by general agreement, relieved by local bits of color, given two half hours of excitement by two demonstrations for Stevenson, buoyed up by the class of the Kennedy machine, turned by the surprise of Johnson's nomination as Vice-President, but, all the same, dull, depressed in its overall tone, the big fiestas subdued, the gossip flat, no real air of excitement, just moments — or as they say in bullfighting — details. Yet it was also, one could argue — and one may argue this yet — it was also one of the most important conventions in America's history, it could prove conceivably to be the most important. The man it nominated was unlike any politician who had ever run for President in the history of the land, and if elected he would come to power in a year when America was in danger of drifting into a profound decline.

ONE

A DESCRIPTIVE OF THE DELEGATES
Sons and Daughters of the Republic in a Legitimate Panic;
Small-time Practitioners of
Small-town Political Judo in the Big Town and the Big Time

DEPRESSION OBVIOUSLY HAS its several roots: it is the doubtful protection which comes from not recognizing failure, it is the psychic burden of exhaustion, and it is also, and very often, that discipline of the will or the ego which enables one to continue working when one's unadmitted emotion is panic. And panic it was I think which sat as the largest single sentiment in the breast of the collective delegates as they came to convene in Los Angeles. Delegates are not the noblest sons and daughters of the Republic; a man of taste, arrived from Mars, would take one look at a convention floor and leave forever, convinced he had seen one of the drearier squats of Hell. If one still smells the faint living echo of a carnival wine, the pepper of a bullfight, the rag, drag, and panoply of a jousting tourney, it is all swallowed and regurgitated by the senses into the fouler cud of a death gas one must rid oneself of — a cigar-smoking, stale-aired, slack-jawed, butt-littered, foul, bleak, hard-working, bureaucratic death gas of language and faces ("Yes, those *faces*," says the man from Mars: lawyers, judges, ward heelers, *mafiosos*, Southern goons and grandees, grand old ladies, trade unionists and finks), of pompous words and long pauses which lay like a leaden pain over fever, the fever that one is in, over, or is it that one is just behind history? A legitimate panic for a delegate. America is a nation of experts without roots; we are always creating tacticians who are blind to strategy and strategists who cannot take a step, and when the culture has finished its work the institutions handcuff the infirmity. A delegate is a man who

5

picks a candidate for the largest office in the land, a President who must live with problems whose borders are in ethics, metaphysics, and now ontology; the delegate is prepared for this office of selection by emptying wastebaskets, toting garbage and saying yes at the right time for twenty years in the small political machine of some small or large town; his reward, one of them anyway, is that he arrives at an invitation to the convention. An expert on local catch-as-catch-can, a small-time, often mediocre practitioner of small-town political judo, he comes to the big city with nine-tenths of his mind made up, he will follow the orders of the boss who brought him. Yet of course it is not altogether so mean as that: his opinion is listened to — the boss will consider what he has to say as one interesting factor among five hundred, and what is most important to the delegate, he has the illusion of partial freedom. He can, unless he is severely honest with himself — and if he is, why sweat out the low levels of a political machine? — he can have the illusion that he has helped to choose the candidate, he can even worry most sincerely about his choice, flirt with defection from the boss, work out his own small political gains by the road of loyalty or the way of hard bargain. But even if he is there for no more than the ride, his vote a certainty in the mind of the political boss, able to be thrown here or switched there as the boss decides, still in some peculiar sense he is reality to the boss, the delegate is the great American public, the bar he owns or the law practice, the piece of the union he represents, or the real-estate office, is a part of the political landscape which the boss uses as his own image of how the votes will go, and if the people will like the candidate. And if the boss is depressed by what he sees, if the candidate does not feel right to him, if he has a dull intimation that the candidate is not his sort (as, let us say, Harry Truman was his sort, or Symington might be his sort, or Lyndon Johnson), then vote for him the boss will if he must; he cannot be caught on the wrong side, but he does not feel the pleasure of a personal choice. Which is the center of the panic. Because if the boss is depressed, the delegate is doubly depressed, and the emotional fact is that Kennedy is not in focus, not in the old political focus, he is not comfortable; in fact it is a mystery to the boss how Kennedy got to where he is, not a mystery in its structures; Kennedy is rolling in money, Kennedy got the votes in primaries, and, most of all, Kennedy has a jewel of a political machine. It is as good as a crack Notre Dame team, all discipline and savvy and go-go-go, sound, drilled, never dull, quick as a knife, full of the salt of hipper-dipper, a beautiful machine; the boss could adore it if only a sensible candidate were driving it, a Truman, even a Stevenson, please God a Northern Lyndon Johnson, but it is run by a man who looks young enough to be coach of the Freshman team, and that is not comfortable at all. The boss knows political machines, he knows issues, farm parity, Forand health bill, Landrum-Griffin, but this is not all so adequate after all to revolutionaries in Cuba who look like beatniks, competitions in missiles, Negroes looting whites in the Congo, intricacies of nuclear fallout, and NAACP men one does well to call Sir. It is all out of hand, everything important is off the center, foreign affairs is now the lick of the heat, and senators are candidates instead of governors, a disaster to the old family style of political measure where a political boss knows his governor and knows who his governor knows. So the boss is depressed, profoundly depressed. He comes to this convention resigned to nominating a man he does not understand, or let us say that, so far as he understands the candidate who is to be nominated, he is not happy about the secrets of his appeal, not so far as he divines these secrets; they seem to have too little to do with politics and all too much to do with the private madnesses of the nation which had thousands — or was it hundreds of thousands — of people demonstrating in the long night before Chessman was killed, and a movie star, the greatest, Marlon the Brando out in the night with them. Yes, this candidate for all his record, his good, sound, conventional liberal record has a patina of that other life, the second American life, the long electric night with the fires of neon leading down the highway to the murmur of jazz.

TWO

AN APPARENT DIGRESSION
A Vivid View of the "City of Lost Angels"; The
Democrats Defined; A Pentagon of Traveling Salesmen;
Some Pointed Portraits of the Politicians

> I was seeing Pershing Square, Los Angeles, now for the first time
> ... the nervous fruithustlers darting in and out of the shadows, fu-
> gitives from Times Square, Market Street SF, the French Quarter
> — masculine hustlers looking for lonely fruits to score from, any-
> thing from the legendary $20 to a pad at night and breakfast in the
> morning and whatever you can clinch or clip; and the heat in their
> holy cop uniforms, holy because of the Almighty Stick and the
> Almightier Vagrancy Law; the scattered junkies, the small-time
> pushers, the queens, the sad panhandlers, the lonely, exiled
> nymphs haunting the entrance to the men's head, the fruits with
> the hungry eyes and the jingling coins; the tough teen-age
> chicks — 'dittybops' — making it with the lost hustlers . . . all amid
> the incongruous piped music and the flowers — twin fountains
> gushing rainbow colored: the world of Lonely America squeezed
> into Pershing Square, of the Cities of Terrible Night, downtown
> now trapped in the City of lost Angels . . . and the trees hang over it
> all like some type of apathetic fate.
> — JOHN RECHY, *Big Table 3*

Seeing Los Angeles after ten years away, one realizes all over again that America is an unhappy contract between the East (that Faustian thrust of a most determined human will which reaches up and out above the eye into the skyscrapers of New York) and those flat lands of compromise and mediocre self-expression, those endless half-pretty repetitive small towns of the Middle and the West, whose spirit is forever horizontal and whose marrow comes to rendezvous in the pastel monotonies of Los Angeles architecture.

8

So far as America has a history, one can see it in the severe heights of New York City, in the glare from the Pittsburgh mills, by the color in the brick of Louisburg Square, along the knotted greedy façades of the small mansions on Chicago's North Side, in Natchez' antebellum homes, the wrought-iron balconies off Bourbon Street, a captain's house in Nantucket, by the curve of Commercial Street in Provincetown. One can make a list; it is probably finite. What culture we have made and what history has collected to it can be found in those few hard examples of an architecture which came to its artistic term, was born, lived and so collected some history about it. Not all the roots of American life are uprooted, but almost all, and the spirit of the supermarket, that homogenous extension of stainless surfaces and psychoanalyzed people, packaged commodities and ranch homes, interchangeable, geographically unrecognizable, that essence of the new postwar SuperAmerica is found nowhere so perfectly as in Los Angeles' ubiquitous acres. One gets the impression that people come to Los Angeles in order to divorce themselves from the past, here to live or try to live in the rootless pleasure world of an adult child. One knows that if the cities of the world were destroyed by a new war, the architecture of the rebuilding would create a landscape which looked, subject to specifications of climate, exactly and entirely like the San Fernando Valley.

It is not that Los Angeles is altogether hideous, it is even by degrees pleasant, but for an Easterner there is never any salt in the wind; it is like Mexican cooking without chile, or Chinese egg rolls missing their mustard; as one travels through the endless repetitions of that city which is the capital of suburbia with its milky pinks, its washed-out oranges, its tainted lime-yellows of pastel on one pretty little architectural monstrosity after another, the colors not intense enough, the styles never pure, and never sufficiently impure to collide on the eye, one conceives the people who live here — they have come out to express themselves. Los Angeles is the home of self-expression, but the artists are middle-class and middling-minded; no passions will calcify here for years in the gloom to be revealed a decade later as the tessellations of a hard and fertile work, no, it is all open, promiscuous, borrowed, half bought, a city without iron, eschewing wood, a kingdom of stucco, the playground for mass men — one has the feeling it was built by television sets giving orders to men. And in this land of the pretty-pretty, the virility is in the barbarisms, the vulgarities, it is in the huge billboards, the screamers of the neon lighting, the shouting farm-utensil colors of the gas stations and the monster drugstores, it is in the swing of the sports cars, hot rods, convertibles. Los Angeles is a city to drive in, the boulevards are wide, the traffic is nervous and fast, the radio stations play bouncing, blooping, rippling tunes, one digs the pop in a pop tune, no one of character would make love by it but the sound is good for swinging a car, electronic guitars and Hawaiian harps.

So this is the town the Democrats came to, and with their unerring instinct (after being with them a week, one thinks of this party as a crazy, half-rich family, loaded with poor cousins, traveling always in caravans with Cadillacs and Okie Fords, Lincolns and quarter-horse mules, putting up every night in tents to hear the chamber quartet of Great Cousin Eleanor invaded by the Texas-twanging steel-stringing geetarists of Bubber Lyndon, carrying its own mean high-school princi-pal, Doc Symington, chided for its manners by good Uncle Adlai, told the route of march by Navigator Jack, cut off every six months from the rich will of Uncle Jim Farley, never listening to the mechanic of the caravan, Bald Sam Rayburn, who assures them they'll all break down unless Cousin Bubber gets the concession on the garage; it's the Snopes family married to Henry James, with the labor unions thrown in like a Yankee dollar, and yet it's true, in tranquility one recollects them with affection, their instinct is good, crazy family good) and this instinct now led the caravan to pick the Biltmore Hotel in downtown Los Angeles for their family get-together and reunion.

The Biltmore is one of the ugliest hotels in the world. Patterned after the flat roofs of an Italian Renaissance palace, it is eighty-eight times as large, and one-millionth as valuable to the continuation of man, and it would be intolerable if it were not for the presence of Pershing Square, that square block of park with cactus and palm trees, the three-hun-dred-and-sixty-five-day-a-year convention of every junkie, pot-head, pusher, queen (but you have read that good writing already). For years Pershing Square has been one of the three or four places in America famous to homosexuals, famous not for its posh, the chic is round-heeled here, but because it is one of the avatars of the good old mas-turbatory sex, dirty with the crusted sugars of smut, dirty rooming houses around the corner where the score is made, dirty book and photograph stores down the street, old-fashioned out-of-the-Thirties burlesque houses, cruising bars, jukeboxes, movie houses; Pershing Square is the town plaza for all those lonely, respectable, small-town homosexuals who lead a family life, make children, and have the Phil-brick psychology (How I Joined the Communist Party and Led Three

Lives). Yes, it is the open-air convention hall for the small-town inverts who live like spies, and it sits in the center of Los Angeles, facing the Biltmore, that hotel which is a mausoleum, that Pentagon of traveling sales.nen the Party chose to house the headquarters of the Convention.

So here came that family, cursed before it began by the thundering absence of Great-Uncle Truman, the delegates dispersed over a run of thirty miles and twenty-seven hotels: the Olympian Motor Hotel, the Ambassador, the Beverly Wilshire, the Santa Ynez Inn (where rumor has it the delegates from Louisiana had some midnight swim), the Mayan, the Commodore, the Mayfair, the Sheraton-West, the Hunt-ington-Sheraton, the Green, the Hayward, the Gates, the Figueroa, the Statler Hilton, the Hollywood Knickerbocker — does one have to be a collector to list such names? — beauties all, with that up-from-the-farm Los Angeles décor, plate-glass windows, patio and terrace, foam-rub-ber mattress, pastel paints, all of them pretty as an ad in full-page color, all but the Biltmore where everybody gathered every day — the news-men, the TV, radio, magazine, and foreign newspapermen, the dele-gates, the politicos, the tourists, the campaign managers, the runners, the flunkies, the cousins and aunts, the wives, the grandfathers, the eight-year-old girls, and the twenty-eight-year-old girls in the Kennedy costumes, red and white and blue, the Symingteeners, the Johnson Ladies, the Stevenson Ladies, everybody — and for three days before the convention and four days into it, everybody collected at the Bilt-more, in the lobby, in the grill, in the Biltmore Bowl, in the elevators, along the corridors, three hundred deep always outside the Kennedy suite, milling everywhere, every dark-carpeted gray-brown hall of the hotel, but it was in the Gallery of the Biltmore where one first felt the mood which pervaded all proceedings until the convention was almost over, that heavy, thick, witless depression which was to dominate every move as the delegates wandered and gawked and paraded and set for a spell, there in the Gallery of the Biltmore, that huge depressing alley with its inimitable hotel color, that faded depth of chiaroscuro which unhappily has no depth, that brown which is not a brown, that gray which has no pearl in it, that color which can be described only as hotel-color because the beiges, the tans, the walnuts, the mahoganies, the dull blood rugs, the moaning yellows, the sick greens, the grays and all those dumb browns merge into that lack of color which is an over-large hotel at convention time, with all the small-towners wearing their set, starched faces, that look they get at carnival, all fever and suspicion, and proud to be there, eddying slowly back and forth in that high block-long tunnel of a room with its arched ceiling and square recesses filling every rib of the arch with art work, escutcheons and blazons and other art, pictures I think, I cannot even remember, there was such a hill of cigar smoke the eye had to travel on its way to the ceiling, and at one end there was galvanized-pipe scaffolding and workmen repairing some part of the ceiling, one of them touching up one of the endless squares of painted plaster in the arch, and another worker, passing by, yelled up to the one who was working on the ceiling: "Hey, Michelangelo!"

Later, of course, it began to emerge and there were portraits one could keep, Symington, dogged at a press conference, declaring with no conviction that he knew he had a good chance to win, the disappointment eating at his good looks so that he came off hard-faced, mean, and yet slack — a desperate dullness came of the best of his intentions. There was Johnson who had compromised too many contradictions and now the contradictions were in his face: when he smiled the corners of his mouth squeezed gloom; when he was pious, his eyes twinkled irony; when he spoke in a righteous tone, he looked corrupt; when he jested, the ham in his jowls looked to quiver. He was not convincing. He was a Southern politician, a Texas Democrat, a liberal Eisenhower; he would do no harm, he would do no good, he would react to the machine, good fellow, nice friend — the Russians would understand him better than his own.

Stevenson had the patina. He came into the room and the room was different, not stronger perhaps (which is why ultimately he did not win), but warmer. One knew why some adored him; he did not look like other people, not with press lights on his flesh; he looked like a lover, the simple truth, he had the sweet happiness of an adolescent who has just been given his first major kiss. And so he glowed, and one was reminded of Chaplin, not because they were the least alike in features, but because Charlie Chaplin was luminous when one met him and Stevenson had something of that light.

There was Eleanor Roosevelt, fine, precise, hand-worked like ivory. Her voice was almost attractive as she explained in the firm, sad tones of the first lady in this small town why she could not admit Mr. Kennedy, who was no doubt a gentleman, into her political house. One had the impression of a lady who was finally becoming a woman, which is to say that she was just a little bitchy about it all; nice bitchy, charming, it had a touch of art to it, but it made one wonder if she were not now satisfying the last passion of them all, which was to become physically attractive, for she was better-looking than she had ever been as she spurned the possibilities of a young suitor.

Jim Farley. Huge. Cold as a bishop. The hell he would consign you to was cold as ice.

Bobby Kennedy, that archetype Bobby Kennedy, looked like a West Point cadet, or, better, one of those unreconstructed Irishmen from Kirkland House one always used to have to face in the line in Harvard house football games. "Hello," you would say to the ones who looked like him as you lined up for the scrimmage after the kickoff, and his type would nod and look away, one rock glint of recognition your due for living across the hall from one another all through Freshman year, and then bang, as the ball was passed back, you'd get a bony king-hell knee in the crotch. He was the kind of man never to put on the gloves with if you wanted to do some social boxing, because after two minutes it would be a war, and ego-bastards last long in a war.

Carmine DeSapio and Kenneth Galbraith on the same part of the convention floor. DeSapio is bigger than one expects, keen and florid, great big smoked glasses, a suntan like Mantan — he is the kind of heavyweight Italian who could get by with a name like Romeo — and Galbraith is tall-tall, as actors say, six foot six it could be, terribly thin, enormously attentive, exquisitely polite, birdlike, he is sensitive to the stirring of reeds in a wind over the next hill. "Our gray eminence," whispered the intelligent observer next to me.

Bob Wagner, the Mayor of New York, a little man, plump, groomed, blank. He had the blank, pomaded, slightly worried look of the first barber in a good barbershop, the kind who would go to the track on his day off and wear a green transparent stone in a gold ring,

And then there was Kennedy, the edge of the mystery. But a sketch will no longer suffice.

THREE

PERSPECTIVE FROM THE BILTMORE BALCONY
The Colorful Arrival of the Hero with the Orange-brown Suntan and Amazingly White Teeth; Revelation of the Two Rivers Political Theory

> ... it can be said with a fair amount of certainty that the essence of his political attractiveness is his extraordinary political intelligence. He has a mind quite unlike that of any other Democrat of this century. It is not literary, metaphysical and moral, as Adlai Stevenson's is. Kennedy is articulate and often witty, but he does not seek verbal polish. No one can doubt the seriousness of his concern with the most serious political matters, but one feels that whereas Mr. Stevenson's political views derive from a view of life that holds politics to be a mere fraction of existence, Senator Kennedy's primary interest is in politics. The easy way in which he disposes of the question of Church and State — as if he felt that any reasonable man could quite easily resolve any possible conflict of loyalties — suggests that the organization of society is the one thing that really engages his interest.
>
> — RICHARD ROVERE, *The New Yorker*, July 23, 1960

The afternoon he arrived at the convention from the airport, there was of course a large crowd on the street outside the Biltmore, and the best way to get a view was to get up on an outdoor balcony of the Biltmore, two flights above the street, and look down on the event. One waited thirty minutes, and then a honking of horns as wild as the getaway after an Italian wedding sounded around the corner, and the Kennedy cortege came into sight, circled Pershing Square, the men in the open and leading convertibles sitting backwards to look at their leader, and finally came to a halt in a space cleared for them by the police in the crowd. The television cameras were out, and a Kennedy band was playing some circus music. One saw him immediately. He had the deep orange-brown suntan of a ski instructor, and when he smiled at the crowd his teeth were amazingly white and clearly visible at a distance of fifty yards. For one moment he saluted Pershing Square, and Pershing Square saluted him back, the prince and the beggars of glamour staring at one another across a city street, one of those very special moments in the underground history of the world, and then with a quick move he was out of the car and by choice headed into the crowd instead of the lane cleared for him into the hotel by the police, so that he made his way inside surrounded by a mob, and one expected at any moment to see him lifted to its shoulders like a matador being carried back to the city after a triumph in the plaza. All the while the band kept playing the campaign tunes, sashaying circus music, and one had a moment of clarity, intense as a *déjà vu,* for the scene which had taken place had been glimpsed before in a dozen musical comedies; it was the scene where the hero, the matinee idol, the movie star comes to the palace to claim the princess, or what is the same, and more to our soil, the football hero, the campus king, arrives in the dean's home surrounded by a court of open-singing students to plead with the dean for his daughter's kiss and permission to put on the big musical that night. And suddenly I saw the convention, it came into focus for me, and I understood the mood of depression which had lain over the convention, because finally it was simple: the Democrats were going to nominate a man who, no matter how serious his political dedication might be, was indisputably and willy-nilly going to be seen as a great box-office actor, and the consequences of that were staggering and not at all easy to calculate.

Since the First World War Americans have been leading a double life, and our history has moved on two rivers, one visible, the other underground; there has been the history of politics which is concrete, factual, practical and unbelievably dull if not for the consequences of the actions of some of these men; and there is a subterranean river of untapped, ferocious, lonely and romantic desires, that concentration of ecstasy and violence which is the dream life of the nation.

The Twentieth Century may yet be seen as that era when civilized man and underprivileged man were melted together into mass man, the iron and steel of the Nineteenth Century giving way to electronic circuits which communicated their messages into men, the unmistakable tendency of the new century seeming to be the creation of men as interchangeable as commodities, their extremes of personality singed out of existence by the psychic fields of force the communicators would impose. The loss of personality was a catastrophe to the future of the imagination, but billions of people might first benefit from it by having enough to eat — one did not know — and there remained citadels of resistance in Europe where the culture was deep and roots were visible in the architecture of the past.

Nowhere, as in America, however, was this fall from individual man to mass man felt so acutely, for America was at once the first and most prolific creator of mass communications, and the most rootless of countries, since almost no American could lay claim to the line of a family which had not once at least severed its roots by migrating here. But, if rootless, it was then the most vulnerable of countries to its own homogenization. Yet America was also the country in which the dynamic myth of the Renaissance — that every man was potentially extraordinary — knew its most passionate persistence. Simply, America was the land where people still believed in heroes: George Washington; Billy the Kid; Lincoln, Jefferson; Mark Twain, Jack London, Hemingway; Joe Louis, Dempsey, Gentleman Jim; America believed in athletes, rum-runners, aviators; even lovers, by the time Valentino died. It was a country which had grown by the leap of one hero past another — is there a county in all of our ground which does not have its legendary figure? And when the West was filled, the expansion turned inward, became part of an agitated, overexcited, superheated dream life. The film studios threw up their searchlights as the frontier was finally sealed, and the romantic possibilities of the old conquest of land turned into a vertical myth, trapped within the skull, of a new kind of heroic life, each choosing his own archetype of a neo-renaissance man, be it Barrymore, Cagney, Flynn, Bogart, Brando or Sinatra, but it was almost as if there were no peace unless one could fight well, kill well (if always with honor), love well and love many, be cool, be daring, be dashing, be wild, be wily, be resourceful, be a brave gun. And this myth, that each of us was born to be free, to wander, to have adventure and to grow on the waves of the violent, the perfumed, and the unexpected, had a force which could not be tamed no matter how the nation's regulators — politicians, medicos, policemen, professors, priests, rabbis, ministers, *idéologues,* psychoanalysts, builders, executives and endless communicators — would brick-in the modern life with hygiene upon sanity, and middle-brow homily over platitude; the myth would not die. Indeed a quarter of the nation's business must have depended upon its existence. But it stayed alive for more than that — it was as if the message in the labyrinth of the genes would insist that violence was locked with creativity, and adventure was the secret of love.

Once, in the Second World War and in the year or two which followed, the underground river returned to earth, and the life of the nation was intense, of the present, electric; as a lady said, "That was the time when we gave parties which changed people's lives." The Forties was a decade when the speed with which one's own events occurred seemed as rapid as the history of the battlefields, and for the mass of people in America a forced march into a new jungle of emotion was the result. The surprises, the failures, and the dangers of that life must have terrified some nerve of awareness in the power and the mass, for, as if stricken by the orgiastic vistas the myth had carried up from underground, the retreat to a more conservative existence was disorderly, the fear of communism spread like an irrational hail of boils. To anyone who could see, the excessive hysteria of the Red wave was no preparation to face an enemy, but rather a terror of the national self: free-loving, lust-looting, atheistic, implacable — absurdity beyond absurdity to label communism so, for the moral products of Stalinism had been Victorian sex and a ponderous machine of material theology.

Forced underground again, deep beneath all *Reader's Digest* hospital dressings of Mental Health in Your Community, the myth continued to flow, fed by television and the film. The fissure in the national psyche widened to the danger point. The last large appearance of the myth was the vote which tricked the polls and gave Harry Truman his victory in '48. That was the last. Came the Korean War, the shadow of the H-bomb, and we were ready for the General. Uncle Harry gave way to Father, and security, regularity, order, and the life of no imagination were the command of the day. If one had any doubt of this, there was Joe McCarthy with his built-in treason detector, furnished by God, and the damage was done. In the totalitarian wind of those days, anyone who worked in Government formed the habit of being not too original, and many a mind atrophied from disuse and private shame. At the summit there was benevolence without leadership, regularity without vision, security without safety, rhetoric without life. The ship drifted on, that enormous warship of the United States, led by a Secretary of State whose cells were seceding to cancer, and as the world became more fantastic — Africa turning itself upside down, while some new kind of machine man was being made in China — two events occurred which stunned the confidence of America into a new night: the Rus-

17

sians put up their Sputnik, and Civil Rights — that reluctant gift to the American Negro, granted for its effect on foreign affairs — spewed into real life at Little Rock. The national Ego was in shock: the Russians were now in some ways our technological superiors, and we had an internal problem of subject populations equal conceivably in its difficulty to the Soviet and its satellites. The fatherly calm of the General began to seem like the uxorious mellifluences of the undertaker.

Underneath it all was a larger problem. The life of politics and the life of myth had diverged too far, and the energies of the people one knew everywhere had slowed down. Twenty years ago a post-Depression generation had gone to war and formed a lively, grousing, by times inefficient, carousing, pleasure-seeking, not altogether inadequate army. It did part of what it was supposed to do, and many, out of combat, picked up a kind of private life on the fly, and had their good time despite the yaws of the military system. But today in America the generation which respected the code of the myth was Beat, a horde of half-begotten Christs with scraggly beards, heroes none, saints all, weak before the strong, empty conformisms of the authority. The sanction for finding one's growth was no longer one's flag, one's career, one's sex, one's adventure, not even one's booze. Among the best in this newest of the generations, the myth had found its voice in marijuana, and the joke of the underground was that when the Russians came over they could never dare to occupy us for long because America was too Hip. Gallows humor. The poorer truth might be that America was too Beat, the instinct of the nation so separated from its public mind that apathy, schizophrenia, and private beatitudes might be the pride of the welcoming committee any underground could offer.

Yes, the life of politics and the life of the myth had diverged too far. There was nothing to return them to one another, no common danger, no cause, no desire, and, most essentially, no hero. It was a hero America needed, a hero central to his time, a man whose personality might suggest contradictions and mysteries which could reach into the alienated circuits of the underground, because only a hero can capture the secret imagination of a people, and so be good for the vitality of his nation; a hero embodies the fantasy and so allows each private mind the liberty to consider its fantasy and find a way to grow. Each mind can become more conscious of its desire and waste less strength in hiding from itself. Roosevelt was such a hero, and Churchill, Lenin and de Gaulle; even Hitler, to take the most odious example of this thesis, was a hero, the hero-as-monster, embodying what had become the monstrous fantasy of a people, but the horror upon which the radical mind and liberal temperament foundered was that he gave outlet to the energies of the Germans and so presented the twentieth century with an index of how horrible had become the secret heart of its desire. Roosevelt is of course a happier example of the hero; from his paralytic leg to the royal elegance of his geniality he seemed to contain the country within himself; everyone from the meanest starving cripple to an ambitious young man could expand into the optimism of an improving future because the man offered an unspoken promise of a future which would be rich. The sexual and the sex-starved, the poor, the hard-working and the imaginative well-to-do could see themselves in the President, could believe him to be like themselves. So a large part of the country was able to discover its energies because not as much was wasted in feeling that the country was a poisonous nutrient which stifled the day.

Too simple? No doubt. One tries to construct a simple model. The thesis is after all not so mysterious; it would merely nudge the notion that a hero embodies his time and is not so very much better than his time, but he is larger than life and so is capable of giving direction to the time, able to encourage a nation to discover the deepest colors of its character. At bottom the concept of the hero is antagonistic to impersonal social progress, to the belief that social ills can be solved by social legislating, for it sees a country as all-but-trapped in its character until it has a hero who reveals the character of the country to itself. The implication is that without such a hero the nation turns sluggish. Truman for example was not such a hero, he was not sufficiently larger than life, he inspired familiarity without excitement, he was a character but his proportions came from soap opera: Uncle Harry, full of salty common-sense and small-minded certainty, a storekeeping uncle.

Whereas Eisenhower has been the anti-Hero, the regulator. Nations do not necessarily and inevitably seek for heroes. In periods of dull anxiety, one is more likely to look for security than a dramatic confrontation, and Eisenhower could stand as a hero only for that large number of Americans who were most proud of their lack of imagination. In American life, the unspoken war of the century has taken place between the city and the small town: the city which is dynamic, orgiastic, unsettling, explosive and accelerating to the psyche; the small town which is rooted, narrow, cautious and planted in the life-logic of the family. The need of the city is to accelerate growth; the pride of the small town is to retard it. But since America has been passing through a period of enormous expansion since the war, the double-four years of Dwight Eisenhower could not retard the expansion, it could only denude it of color, character, and the development of novelty. The small-town mind is rooted — it is rooted in the small town — and when it attempts to direct history the results are disastrously colorless because the instrument of world power which is used by the small-town mind is the committee. Committees do not create, they merely proliferate, and the incredible dullness wreaked upon the American landscape in Eisenhower's eight years has been the triumph of the corporation. A tasteless, sexless, odorless sanctity in architecture, manners, modes, styles has been the result. Eisenhower embodied half the needs of the nation, the needs of the timid, the petrified, the sanctimonious, and the sluggish. What was even worse, he did not divide the nation as a hero might (with a dramatic dialogue as the result); he merely excluded one part of the nation from the other. The result was an alienation of the best minds and bravest impulses from the faltering history which was made. America's need in those years was to take an existential turn, to walk into the nightmare, to face into that terrible logic of history which demanded that the country and its people must become more extraordinary and more adventurous, or else perish, since the only alternative was to offer a false security in the power and the panacea of organized religion, family, and the FBI, a totalitarianization of the psyche by the stultifying techniques of the mass media which would seep into everyone's most private associations and so leave the country powerless against the Russians even if the denouement were to take fifty years, for in a competition between totalitarianisms the first maxim of the prizefight manager would doubtless apply: "Hungry fighters win fights."

FOUR

THE HIPSTER AS PRESIDENTIAL CANDIDATE
Thoughts on a Public Man's Eighteenth-Century Wife;
Face-to-Face with the Hero; Significance of a Personal
Note, or the Meaning of His Having Read an Author's Novel

SOME PART of these thoughts must have been in one's mind at the moment there was that first glimpse of Kennedy entering the Biltmore Hotel; and in the days which followed, the first mystery — the profound air of depression which hung over the convention — gave way to a second mystery which can be answered only by history. The depression of the delegates was understandable: no one had too much doubt that Kennedy would be nominated, but if elected he would be not only the youngest President ever to be chosen by voters, he would be the most conventionally attractive young man ever to sit in the White House, and his wife — some would claim it — might be the most beautiful first lady in our history. Of necessity the myth would emerge once more, because America's politics would now be also America's favorite movie, America's first soap opera, America's best-seller. One thinks of the talents of writers like Taylor Caldwell or Frank Yerby, or is it rather *The Fountainhead* which would contain such a fleshing of the romantic prescription? Or is it indeed one's own work which is called into question? "Well, there's your first hipster," says a writer one knows at the convention, "Sergius O'Shaugnessy born rich," and the temptation is to nod, for it could be true, a war hero, and the heroism is bona-fide, even exceptional, a man who has lived with death, who, crippled in the back, took on an operation which would kill him or restore him to power, who chose to marry a lady whose face might be too imaginative for the taste of a democracy which likes its first ladies to be executives of home-management, a man who courts political suicide by choosing to go all out for a nomination four, eight, or twelve years before his political elders think he is ready, a man who announces a week prior to the convention that the young are better fitted to direct history than the old. Yes, it captures the attention. This is no routine candidate calling every shot by safety's routine book ("Yes," Nixon said, naturally but terribly tired an hour after his nomination, the TV cameras and lights and microphones bringing out a sweat of fatigue on his face, the words coming very slowly from the tired brain, somber, modest, sober, slow, slow enough so that one could touch emphatically the cautions behind each word, "Yes, I want to say," said Nixon, "that whatever abilities I have, I got from my mother." A tired pause . . . dull moment of warning, ". . . and my father." The connection now made, the rest comes easy, ". . . and my school and my church." Such men are capable of anything.)

One had the opportunity to study Kennedy a bit in the days that followed. His style in the press conferences was interesting. Not terribly popular with the reporters (too much a contemporary, and yet too difficult to understand, he received nothing like the rounds of applause given to Eleanor Roosevelt, Stevenson, Humphrey, or even Johnson), he carried himself nonetheless with a cool grace which seemed indifferent to applause, his manner somehow similar to the poise of a fine boxer, quick with his hands, neat in his timing, and two feet away from his corner when the bell ended the round. There was a good lithe wit to his responses, a dry Harvard wit, a keen sense of proportion in disposing of difficult questions — invariably he gave enough of an answer to be formally satisfactory without ever opening himself to a new question which might go further than the first. Asked by a reporter, "Are you for Adlai as Vice-President?" the grin came forth and the voice turned very dry, "No, I cannot say we have considered *Adlai* as a Vice-President." Yet there was an elusive detachment to everything he did. One did not have the feeling of a man present in the room with all his weight and all his mind. Johnson gave you all of himself, he was a political animal, he breathed like an animal, sweated like one, you knew his mind was entirely absorbed with the compendium of political fact and maneuver; Kennedy seemed at times like a young professor whose manner was adequate for the classroom, but whose mind was off in some intricacy of the Ph.D. thesis he was writing. Perhaps one can give a sense of the discrepancy by saying that he was like an actor who had been cast as the candidate, a good actor, but not a great one — you were aware all the time that the role was one thing and the man another — they did not coincide, the actor seemed a touch too aloof (as, let us say, Gregory Peck is usually too aloof) to become the part. Yet one had little sense of whether to value this elusiveness, or to beware of it. One could be witnessing the fortitude of a superior sensitivity or the detachment of a man who was not quite real to himself. And his voice gave no clue. When Johnson spoke, one could separate what was fraudulent from what was felt, he would have been satisfying as an actor the way Broderick Crawford or Paul Douglas are satisfying; one saw into his emotions, or at least had the illusion that one did. Kennedy's voice, however, was only a fair voice, too reedy, near to strident, it had the metallic snap of a cricket in it somewhere, it was more impersonal than the man, and so became the least-impressive quality in a face, a body, a selection of language, and a style of movement which made up a better-than-decent presentation, better than one had expected.

With all of that, it would not do to pass over the quality in Kennedy which is most difficult to describe. And in fact some touches should be added to this hint of a portrait, for later (after the convention), one had a short session alone with him, and the next day, another. As one had suspected in advance the interviews were not altogether satis-factory, they hardly could have been. A man running for President is altogether different from a man elected President: the hazards of the campaign make it impossible for a candidate to be as interesting as he might like to be (assuming he has such a desire). One kept advancing the argument that this campaign would be a contest of personalities, and Kennedy kept returning the discussion to politics. After a while one recognized this was an inevitable caution for him. So there would be not too much point to reconstructing the dialogue since Kennedy is hardly inarticulate about his political attitudes and there will be a li-brary vault of text devoted to it in the newspapers. What struck me most about the interview was a passing remark whose importance was invisible on the scale of politics, but was altogether meaningful to my particular competence. As we sat down for the first time, Kennedy smiled nicely and said that he had read my books. One muttered one's pleasure. "Yes," he said, "I've read . . ." and then there was a short pause which did not last long enough to be embarrassing in which it was yet obvious no title came instantly to his mind, an omission one was not ready to mind altogether since a man in such a position must be obliged to carry a hundred thousand facts and names in his head, but the hesitation lasted no longer than three seconds or four, and then he said, "I've read *The Deer Park* and . . . the others," which startled me for it was the first time in a hundred similar situations, talking to someone whose knowledge of my work was casual, that the sentence did not come out, "I've read *The Naked and the Dead* . . . and the others." If one is to take the worst and assume that Kennedy was briefed for this interview (which is most doubtful), it still speaks well for the striking instincts of his advisers.

What was retained later is an impression of Kennedy's manners which were excellent, even artful, better than the formal good manners of Choate and Harvard, almost as if what was creative in the man had been given to the manners. In a room with one or two people, his voice improved, became low-pitched, even pleasant — it seemed obvious that in all these years he had never become a natural public speaker and so his voice was constricted in public, the symptom of all orators who are ambitious, throttled, and determined.

His personal quality had a subtle, not quite describable intensity, a suggestion of dry pent heat perhaps, his eyes large, the pupils gray, the whites prominent, almost shocking, his most forceful feature: he had the eyes of a mountaineer. His appearance changed with his mood, strikingly so, and this made him always more interesting than what he was saying. He would seem at one moment older than his age, forty-eight or fifty, a tall, slim, sunburned professor with a pleasant weathered face, not even particularly handsome; five minutes later, talking to a press conference on his lawn, three microphones before him, a television camera turning, his appearance would have gone through a metamorphosis, he would look again like a movie star, his coloring vivid, his manner rich, his gestures strong and quick, alive with that concentration of vitality a successful actor always seems to radiate. Kennedy had a dozen faces. Although they were not at all similar as people, the quality was reminiscent of someone like Brando whose expression rarely changes, but whose appearance seems to shift from one person into another as the minutes go by, and one bothers with this comparison because, like Brando, Kennedy's most characteristic quality is the remote and private air of a man who has traversed some lonely terrain of experience, of loss and gain, of nearness to death, which leaves him isolated from the mass of others.

> The next day while they waited in vain for rescuers, the wrecked
> half of the boat turned over in the water and they saw that it would
> soon sink. The group decided to swim to a small island three miles

away. There were other islands bigger and nearer, but the Navy officers knew that they were occupied by the Japanese. On one island, only one mile to the south, they could see a Japanese camp. McMahon, the engineer whose legs were disabled by burns, was unable to swim. Despite his own painfully crippled back, Kennedy swam the three miles with a breast stroke, towing behind him by a life-belt strap that he held between his teeth the helpless McMahon . . . it took Kennedy and the suffering engineer five hours to reach the island.

The quotation is from a book which has for its dedicated unilateral title *The Remarkable Kennedys,* but the prose is by one of the best of the war reporters, the former *Yank* editor, Joe McCarthy, and so presumably may be trusted in such details as this. Physical bravery does not of course guarantee a man's abilities in the White House — all too often men with physical courage are disappointing in their moral imagination — but the heroism here is remarkable for its tenacity. The above is merely one episode in a continuing saga which went on for five days in and out of the water, and left Kennedy at one point "miraculously saved from drowning (in a storm) by a group of Solomon Island natives who suddenly came up beside him in a large dugout canoe." Afterward, his back still injured (that precise back injury which was to put him on crutches eleven years later, and have him search for "spinal-fusion surgery" despite a warning that his chances of living through the operation were "extremely limited") he asked to go back on duty and became so bold in the attacks he made with his PT boat "that the crew didn't like to go out with him because he took so many chances."

It is the wisdom of a man who senses death within him and gambles that he can cure it risking his life. It is the therapy of the instinct, and who is so wise as to call it irrational? Before he went into the Navy, Kennedy had been ailing. Washed out of Freshman year at Princeton by a prolonged trough of yellow jaundice, sick for a year at Harvard, weak already in the back from an injury at football, his trials suggest the self-hatred of a man whose resentment and ambition are too large for his body. Not everyone can discharge their furies on an analyst's couch, for some angers can be relaxed only by winning power, some rages are sufficiently monumental to demand that one try to become a hero or else fall back into that death which is already within the cells. But if one succeeds, the energy aroused can be exceptional. Talking to a man who had been with Kennedy in Hyannis Port the week before the convention, I heard that he was in a state of deep fatigue.

25

SUPERMAN COMES TO THE SUPERMARKET

"Well, he didn't look tired at the convention," one commented.

"Oh, he had three days of rest. Three days of rest for him is like six months for us."

One thinks of that three-mile swim with the belt in his mouth and McMahon holding it behind him. There are pestilences which sit in the mouth and rot the teeth — in those five hours how much of the psyche must have been remade, for to give vent to the bite in one's jaws and yet use that rage to save a life: it is not so very many men who have the apocalyptic sense that heroism is the First Doctor.

If one had a profound criticism of Kennedy it was that his public mind was too conventional, but that seemed to matter less than the fact of such a man in office because the law of political life had become so dreary that only a conventional mind could win an election. Indeed there could be no politics which gave warmth to one's body until the country had recovered its imagination, its pioneer lust for the unexpected and incalculable. It was the changes that might come afterward on which one could put one's hope. With such a man in office the myth of the nation would again be engaged, and the fact that he was Catholic would shiver a first existential vibration of consciousness into the mind of the White Protestant. For the first time in our history, the Protestant would have the pain and creative luxury of feeling himself in some tiny degree part of a minority, and that was an experience which might be incommensurable in its value to the best of them.

FIVE

A VIGNETTE OF ADLAI STEVENSON;
THE SPEECHES
What Happened When the Teleprompter Jammed: How
U.S. Senator Eugene McCarthy Played the Matador. An
Observation on the Name Fitzgerald

As YET we have said hardly a word about Stevenson. And his actions must remain a puzzle unless one dares a speculation about his motive, or was it his need?

So far as the people at the convention had affection for anyone, it was Stevenson, so far as they were able to generate any spontaneous enthusiasm, their cheers were again for Stevenson. Yet it was obvious he never had much chance because so soon as a chance would present itself he seemed quick to dissipate the opportunity. The day before the nominations, he entered the Sports Arena to take his seat as a delegate — the demonstration was spontaneous, noisy and prolonged; it was quieted only by Governor Collins' invitation for Stevenson to speak to the delegates. In obedience perhaps to the scruple that a candidate must not appear before the convention until nominations are done, Stevenson said no more than: "I am grateful for this tumultuous and moving welcome. After getting in and out of the Biltmore Hotel and this hall, I have decided I know whom you are going to nominate. It will be the last survivor." This dry reminder of the ruthlessness of politics broke the roar of excitement for his presence. The applause as he left the platform was like the dying fall-and-moan of a baseball crowd when a home run curves foul. The next day, a New York columnist talking about it said bitterly, "If he'd only gone through the motions, if he had just said that now he wanted to run, that he would work hard, and he hoped the delegates would vote for him. Instead he made that lame joke." One wonders. It seems almost as if he did not wish to win unless victory came despite himself, and then was overwhelming. There are men who are not heroes because they are too good for their time, and it is natural that defeats leave them bitter, tired, and doubtful of their right to make new history. If Stevenson had campaigned for a year before the convention, it is possible that he could have stopped Kennedy. At the least, the convention would have been enormously more exciting, and the nominations might have gone through half-a-dozen ballots before a winner was hammered into shape. But then Stevenson might also have shortened his life. One had the impression of a tired man who (for a politician) was sickened unduly by compromise. A year of maneuvering, broken promises, and detestable partners might have gutted him for the election campaign. If elected, it might have ruined him as a President. There is the possibility that he sensed his situation exactly this way, and knew that if he were to run for President, win and make a good one, he would first have to be restored, as one can indeed be restored, by an exceptional demonstration of love — love, in this case, meaning that the Party had a profound desire to keep him as their leader. The emotional truth of a last-minute victory for Stevenson over the Kennedy machine might have given him new energy; it would certainly have given him new faith in a country and a party whose good motives he was possibly beginning to doubt. Perhaps the fault he saw with his candidacy was that he attracted only the nicest people to himself and there were not enough of them. (One of the private amusements of the convention was to divine some of the qualities of the candidates by the style of the young women who put on hats and clothing and politicked in the colors of one presidential gent or another. Of course, half of them must have been hired models, but someone did the hiring and so it was fair to look for a common denominator. The Johnson girls tended to be plump, pie-faced, dumb sexy Southern; the Symingteeners seemed a touch mulish, stubborn, good-looking pluggers; the Kennedy ladies were the handsomest; healthy, attractive, tough, a little spoiled — they looked like the kind of girls who had gotten all the dances in high school and/or worked for a year as an airline hostess before marrying well. But the Stevenson girls looked to be doing it for no money; they were good sorts, slightly horsy-faced, one had the impression they played field hockey in college.) It was indeed the pure, the saintly, the clean-living, the pacifistic, the vegetarian who seemed most for Stevenson, and the less humorous in the Kennedy camp were heard to remark bitterly that Stevenson had nothing going for him but a bunch of Goddamn Beatniks. This might even have had its sour truth. The demonstrations outside the Sports Arena for Stevenson seemed to have more than a fair proportion of tall, emaciated young men with thin, wry beards and three-string guitars accompanied (again in undue proportion) by a contingent of ascetic, face-washed young Beat ladies in sweaters and dungarees. Not to mention all the Holden Caulfields one could see from here to the horizon. But of course it is unfair to limit it so, for the Democratic gentry were also committed half en masse for Stevenson, as well as a considerable number of movie stars, Shelley Winters for one: after the convention she remarked sweetly, "Tell me something nice about Kennedy so I can get excited about him."

What was properly astonishing was the way this horde of political half-breeds and amateurs came within distance of turning the convention from its preconceived purpose, and managed at the least to bring the only hour of thoroughgoing excitement the convention could offer.

But then nominating day was the best day of the week and enough happened to suggest that a convention out of control would be a spectacle as extraordinary in the American scale of spectator values as a close seventh game in the World Series or a tied fourth quarter in a professional-football championship. A political convention is after all not a meeting of a corporation's board of directors; it is a fiesta, a carnival, a pig-rooting, horse-snorting, band-playing, voice-screaming medieval get-together of greed, practical lust, compromised idealism, career-advancement, meeting, feud, vendetta, conciliation, of rabble-rousers, fist fights (as it used to be), embraces, drunks (again as it used to be) and collective rivers of animal sweat. It is a reminder that no matter how the country might pretend it has grown up and become tidy in its manners, bodiless in its legislative language, hygienic in its separation of high politics from private life, that the roots still come grubby from the soil, and that politics in America is still different from politics anywhere else because the politics has arisen out of the immediate needs, ambitions, and cupidities of the people, that our politics still smell of the bedroom and the kitchen, rather than having descended to us from the chill punctilio of aristocratic negotiation.

So. The Sports Arena was new, too pretty of course, tasteless in its design — it was somehow pleasing that the acoustics were so bad for one did not wish the architects well; there had been so little imagination in their design, and this arena would have none of the harsh grandeur of Madison Square Garden when it was aged by spectators' phlegm and feet over the next twenty years. Still it had some atmosphere; seen from the streets, with the spectators moving to the ticket gates, the bands playing, the green hot-shot special editions of the Los Angeles newspapers being hawked by the newsboys, there was a touch of the air of promise that precedes a bullfight, not something so good as the approach to the Plaza Mexico, but good, let us say, like the entrance into El Toreo of Mexico City, another architectural monstrosity, also with seats painted, as I remember, in rose-pink, and dark, milky sky-blue.

Inside, it was also different this nominating day. On Monday and Tuesday the air had been desultory, no one listened to the speakers, and everybody milled from one easy chatting conversation to another — it had been like a tepid Kaffeeklatsch for fifteen thousand people. But today there was a whip of anticipation in the air, the seats on the floor were filled, the press section was working, and in the gallery people were sitting in the aisles.

Sam Rayburn had just finished nominating Johnson as one came in, and the rebel yells went up, delegates started filing out of their seats and climbing over seats, and a pullulating dance of bodies and bands began to snake through the aisles, the posters jogging and whirling in time to the music. The dun color of the floor (faces, suits, seats and floor boards), so monotonous the first two days, now lit up with life as if an iridescent caterpillar had emerged from a fold of wet leaves. It was more vivid than one had expected, it was right, if felt finally like a convention, and from up close when one got down to the floor (where your presence was illegal and so consummated by sneaking in one time as demonstrators were going out, and again by slipping a five-dollar bill to a guard) the nearness to the demonstrators took on high color, that electric vividness one feels on the sidelines of a football game when it is necessary to duck back as the ballcarrier goes by, his face tortured in the concentration of the moment, the thwomp of his tackle as acute as if one had been hit oneself.

That was the way the demonstrators looked on the floor. Nearly all had the rapt, private look of a passion or a tension which would finally be worked off by one's limbs, three hundred football players, everything from seedy delegates with jowl-sweating shivers to livid models, paid for their work that day, but stomping out their beat on the floor with the hypnotic adulatory grimaces of ladies who had lived for Lyndon these last ten years.

Then from the funereal rostrum, whose color was not so rich as mahogany nor so dead as a cigar, came the last of the requests for the delegates to take their seats. The seconding speeches began, one minute each; they ran for three and four, the minor-league speakers running on the longest as if the electric antenna of television was the lure of the Sirens, leading them out. Bored cheers applauded their concluding Götterdämmerungen and the nominations were open again. A favorite son, a modest demonstration, five seconding speeches, tedium.

Next was Kennedy's occasion. Governor Freeman of Minnesota made the speech. On the second or third sentence his television prompter jammed, an accident. Few could be aware of it at the moment; the speech seemed merely flat and surprisingly void of bravura. He was obviously no giant of extempore. Then the demonstration. Well run, bigger than Johnson's, jazzier, the caliber of the costumes and decorations better chosen: the placards were broad enough, LET'S BACK JACK, the floats were garish, particularly a papier-mâché or plastic balloon of Kennedy's head, six feet in diameter, which had nonetheless the slightly shrunken, over-red, rubbery look of a toy for practical jokers in one of those sleazy off–Times Square magic-and-gimmick stores; the band was suitably corny; and yet one had the impression this demonstration had been designed by some hands-to-hip interior decorator who said, "Oh, joy, let's have fun, let's make this *true* beer hall."

Besides, the personnel had something of the Kennedy *élan,* those paper hats designed to look like straw boaters with Kennedy's face on the crown, and small photographs of him on the ribbon, those hats which had come to symbolize the crack speed of the Kennedy team, that Madison Avenue cachet which one finds in bars like P. J. Clarke's, the elegance always giving its subtle echo of the Twenties so that the raccoon coats seem more numerous than their real count, and the colored waistcoats are measured by the charm they would have drawn from Scott Fitzgerald's eye. But there, it occurred to one for the first time that Kennedy's middle name was just that, Fitzgerald, and the tone of his crack lieutenants, the unstated style, was true to Scott. The legend of Fitzgerald had an army at last, formed around the self-image in the mind of every superior Madison Avenue opportunist that he was hard, he was young, he was In, his conversation was lean as wit, and if the work was not always scrupulous, well the style could aspire. If there came a good day . . . he could meet the occasion.

The Kennedy snake dance ran its thirty lively minutes, cheered its seconding speeches, and sat back. They were so sure of winning, there had been so many victories before this one, and this one had been scouted and managed so well, that hysteria could hardly be the mood. Besides, everyone was waiting for the Stevenson barrage which should be at least diverting. But now came a long tedium. Favorite sons were nominated, fat mayors shook their hips, seconders told the word to constituents back in Ponderwaygot County, treacly demonstrations tried to hold the floor, and the afternoon went by; Symington's hour came and went, a good demonstration, good as Johnson's (for good cause — they had pooled their demonstrators). More favorite sons, Governor Docking of Kansas declared "a genius" by one of his lady speakers in a tense go-back-to-religion voice. The hours went by, two, three, four hours, it seemed forever before they would get to Stevenson. It was evening when Senator Eugene McCarthy of Minnesota got up to nominate him.

The gallery was ready, the floor was responsive, the demonstrators were milling like bulls in their pen waiting for the *toril* to fly open — it would have been hard not to wake the crowd up, not to make a good speech. McCarthy made a great one. Great it was by the measure of convention oratory, and he held the crowd like a matador, timing their *olés!*, building them up, easing them back, correcting any sag in attention, gathering their emotion, discharging it, creating new emotion on the wave of the last, driving his passes tighter and tighter as he readied for the kill. "Do not reject this man who made us all proud to be called Democrats, do not leave this prophet without honor in his own party." One had not heard a speech like this since 1948 when Vito Marcantonio's voice, his harsh, shrill, bitter, street urchin's voice screeched through the loudspeakers at Yankee Stadium and lashed seventy thousand people into an uproar.

"There was only one man who said let's talk sense to the American people," McCarthy went on, his muleta furled for the *naturales*. "There was only one man who said let's talk sense to the American people," he repeated. "He said the promise of America is the promise of greatness. This was his call to greatness. . . . Do not forget this man. . . . Ladies and Gentlemen, I present to you not the favorite son of one state, but the favorite son of the fifty states, the favorite son of every country he has visited, the favorite son of every country which has not seen him but is secretly thrilled by his name." Bedlam. The kill. "Ladies and Gentlemen, I present to you Adlai Stevenson of Illinois." Ears and tail. Hooves and bull. A roar went up like the roar one heard the day Bobby Thomson hit his home run at the Polo Grounds and the Giants won the pennant from the Dodgers in the third playoff game of the 1951 season. The demonstration cascaded onto the floor, the gallery came to its feet, the Sports Arena sounded like the inside of a marching drum. A tidal pulse of hysteria, exaltation, defiance, exhilaration, anger and roaring desire flooded over the floor. The cry which had gone up on McCarthy's last sentence had not paused for breath in five minutes, and troop after troop of demonstrators jammed the floor (the Stevenson people to be scolded the next day for having collected floor passes and sent them out to bring in new demonstrators) and still the sound mounted. One felt the convention coming apart. There was a Kennedy girl in the seat in front of me, the Kennedy hat on her head, a dimpled healthy brunette; she had sat silently through McCarthy's speech, but now, like a woman paying her respects to the power of natural thrust, she took off her hat and began to clap herself. I saw a writer I knew in the next aisle; he had spent a year studying the Kennedy machine in order to write a book on how a nomination is won. If Stevenson stampeded the convention, his work was lost. Like a reporter at a mine cave-in I inquired the present view of the widow. "Who can think," was the answer, half frantic, half elated, "just watch it, that's all." I found a cool one, a New York reporter, who smiled in rueful respect. "It's the biggest demonstration I've seen since Wendell Willkie's in 1940," he said, and added, "God, if Stevenson takes it, I can wire my wife and move the family on to Hawaii."

"I don't get it."

"Well, every story I wrote said it was locked up for Kennedy."

Still it went on, twenty minutes, thirty minutes, the chairman could hardly be heard, the demonstrators refused to leave. The lights were turned out, giving a sudden theatrical shift to the sense of a crowded church at midnight, and a new roar went up, louder, more passionate than anything heard before. It was the voice, it was the passion, if one insisted to call it that, of everything in America which was defeated, idealistic, innocent, alienated, outside and Beat, it was the potential voice of a new third of the nation whose psyche was ill from cultural malnutrition, it was powerful, it was extraordinary, it was larger than the decent, humorous, finicky, half-noble man who had called it forth, it was a cry from the Thirties when Time was simple, it was a resentment of the slick technique, the oiled gears, and the superior generals of Fitzgerald's Army; but it was also — and for this reason one could not admire it altogether, except with one's excitement — it was also the plea of the bewildered who hunger for simplicity again, it was the adolescent counterpart of the boss's depression before the unpredictable dynamic of Kennedy as President, it was the return to the sentimental dream of Roosevelt rather than the approaching nightmare of history's oncoming night, and it was inspired by a terror of the future as much as a revulsion of the present.

Fitz's Army held; after the demonstration was finally down, the convention languished for ninety minutes while Meyner and others were nominated, a fatal lapse of time because Stevenson had perhaps a chance to stop Kennedy if the voting had begun on the echo of the last cry for him, but in an hour and a half depression crept in again and emotions spent, the delegates who had wavered were rounded into line. When the vote was taken, Stevenson had made no gains. The brunette who had taken off her hat was wearing it again, and she clapped and squealed when Wyoming delivered the duke and Kennedy was in. The air was sheepish, like the mood of a suburban couple who forgive each other for cutting in and out of somebody else's automobile while the country club dance is on. Again, tonight, no miracle would occur. In the morning the papers would be moderate in their description of Stevenson's last charge.

SIX

A SKETCH OF THE REPUBLICANS GATHERED IN CONVENTION
The Choice Between the Venturesome and the Safe; What May Happen at Three O'Clock in the Morning on a Long Dark Night

ONE DID NOT GO to the other convention. It was seen on television, and so too much cannot be said of that. It did however confirm one's earlier bias that the Republican Party was still a party of church ushers, undertakers, choirboys, prison wardens, bank presidents, small-town police chiefs, state troopers, psychiatrists, beauty-parlor operators, corporation executives, Boy Scout leaders, fraternity presidents, tax-board assessors, community leaders, surgeons, Pullman porters, head nurses and the fat sons of rich fathers. Its candidate would be given the manufactured image of an ordinary man, and his campaign, so far as it was a psychological campaign (and this would be far indeed), would present him as a simple, honest, dependable, hard-working, ready-to-learn, modest, humble, decent, sober young man whose greatest qualification for president was his profound abasement before the glories of the Republic, the stability of the mediocre, and his own unworthiness. The apocalyptic hour of Uriah Heep.

It would then be a campaign unlike the ones which had preceded it. Counting by the full spectrum of complete Right to absolute Left, the political differences would be minor, but what would be not at all minor was the power of each man to radiate his appeal into some fundamental depths of the American character. One would have an inkling at last if the desire of America was for drama or stability, for adventure or monotony. And this, this appeal to the psychic direction America would now choose for itself was the element most promising

35

about this election, for it gave the possibility that the country might be able finally to rise above the deadening verbiage of its issues, its politics, its jargon, and live again by an image of itself. For in some part of themselves the people might know (since these candidates were not old enough to be revered) that they had chosen one young man for his mystery, for his promise that the country would grow or disintegrate by the unwilling charge he gave to the intensity of the myth, or had chosen another young man for his unstated oath that he would do all in his power to keep the myth buried and so convert the remains of Renaissance man as rapidly as possible into mass man. One might expect them to choose the enigma in preference to the deadening certainty. Yet one must doubt America's bravery. This lurching, unhappy, pompous and most corrupt nation — could it have the courage finally to take on a new image for itself, was it brave enough to put into office not only one of its ablest men, its most efficient, its most conquistadorial (for Kennedy's capture of the Democratic Party deserves the word), but also one of its more mysterious men (the national psyche must shiver in its sleep at the image of Mickey Mantle-cum-Lindbergh in office, and a First Lady with an eighteenth-century face). Yes, America was at last engaging the fate of its myth, its consciousness about to be accelerated or cruelly depressed in its choice between two young men in their forties who, no matter how close, dull, or indifferent their stated politics might be, were radical poles apart, for one was sober, the apotheosis of opportunistic lead, all radium spent, the other handsome as a prince in the unstated aristocracy of the American dream. So, finally, would come a choice which history had never presented to a nation before — one could vote for glamour or for ugliness, a staggering and most stunning choice — would the nation be brave enough to enlist the romantic dream of itself, would it vote for the image in the mirror of its unconscious, were the people indeed brave enough to hope for an acceleration of Time, for that new life of drama which would come from choosing a son to lead them who was heir apparent to the psychic loins? One could pause: it might be more difficult to be a President than it ever had before. Nothing less than greatness would do.

Yet if the nation voted to improve its face, what an impetus might come to the arts, to the practices, to the lives and to the imagination of the American. If the nation so voted. But one knew the unadmitted specter in the minds of the Democratic delegates: that America would go to sleep on election eve with the polls promising Kennedy a victory on the day to come, yet in its sleep some millions of Democrats and

Independents would suffer a nightmare before the mystery of un-charted possibilities their man would suggest, and in a terror of all the creativities (and some violences) that mass man might now have to dare again, the undetermined would go out in the morning to vote for the psychic security of Nixon the way a middle-aged man past adventure holds to the stale bread of his marriage. Yes, this election might be fearful enough to betray the polls and no one in America could plan the new direction until the last vote was counted by the last heeler in the last ambivalent ward, no one indeed could know until then what had happened the night before, what had happened at three o'clock in the morning on that long dark night of America's search for a security cheaper than her soul.

Former President Harry S. Truman explaining his resignation as a delegate to the Democratic National Convention.

Robert F. Kennedy with records of theme songs from
the Kennedy campaign.

Left to right: Frank Sinatra, Stuart Symington, Lyndon Johnson,
John F. Kennedy, Adlai Stevenson.

Kennedy and Johnson before the Texas delegation.

Mrs. Franklin D. Roosevelt addressing the
Democratic National Convention.

Shaking hands after one of the Nixon-Kennedy debates.

The Eisenhowers and the Nixons.

John F. Kennedy with Frank D. Reeves, National Committeeman
from Washington, D.C.

Senator and Mrs. Kennedy at New York's Columbus Day parade.

Richard M. Nixon learns of his nomination as Republican Presidential candidate by the party Convention in Chicago.

John F. Kennedy with Hubert Humphrey.

In the Red Light:
A History of the Republican
Convention in 1964

... He had drawn the burning city, a great bonfire of architectural styles, ranging from Egyptian to Cape Cod colonial. Through the center, winding from left to right, was a long hill street and down it, spilling into the middle foreground, came the mob carrying baseball bats and torches. For the faces of its members, he was using the innumerable sketches he had made of the people who come to California to die; the cultists of all sorts, economic as well as religious, the wave, airplane, funeral and preview watchers — all those poor devils who can only be stirred by the promise of miracles and then only to violence. A super "Dr. Know-All Pierce-All" had made the necessary promise of miracles and they were marching behind his banner in a great united front of screwballs and screwboxes to purify the land. No longer bored, they sang and danced joyously in the red light of the flames.

— NATHANAEL WEST, *The Day of the Locust*

Now, THE CITY was beautiful, it was still the most beautiful city in the United States, but like all American cities it was a casualty of the undeclared war. There had been an undisclosed full-scale struggle going on in America for twenty years — it was whether the country would go mad or not. And the battle line of that war (which showed that yes slowly the country was losing the war, we were indeed going mad) was of course the progress of the new roads, buildings, and supermarkets which popped out all over the cities of the nation. San Francisco was losing her beauty. Monstrous corporations in combine with monstrous realtors had erected monstrous boxes of Kleenex ten, twenty, thirty stories high through the downtown section, and the new view from Telegraph Hill had shards of glass the size of a mountain wall stuck into the soft Italian landscape of St. Francis' City. The San Francisco Hilton, for an example, while close to twenty stories high, was near to a square block in size and looked from the street to have the proportions and form of a cube of sugar. It was a dirty sugar-white in color and its windows were set in an odd elongated checkerboard, a harlequin pattern in which each window was offset from the one above and beneath like the vents in a portable radio.

The Hilton was only six weeks old, but already it was one of the architectural wonders of the world, for its insides were composed in large part of an automobile ramp on which it was possible to drive all the way up to the eleventh floor, open a door and lo! you were in your hotel corridor, twenty feet from your own room door. It was a startling way to exhaust the internal space of a hotel, but it had one huge American advantage: any guest at the Hilton could drive all the way to his room without ever having to steer a lady through the lobby. Of course, after all those automobile ramps, there was not much volume left, so the rooms were small, the rooms were very small for seventeen dollars a day, and the windows were placed to the extreme left or right of the wall and ran from ceiling to floor, in order to allow the building to appear to the outside eye like a radio being carried by a model who worked in the high nude. The carpets and wallpapers, the drapes and the table tops were plastic, the bathroom had the odor of burning insecticide. It developed that the plastic cement used to finish the tiling gave off this odor during the months it took to dry. Molecules were being tortured everywhere.

Well, that was American capitalism gainfully employed. It had won the war. It had won it in so many places you could picture your accommodations before you arrived. Such is the nature of the promiscuous. Flying out, way out on the jet, on the way West, not yet at the Hilton but knowing it would be there, I got into a conversation with the man who sat at the window, an Australian journalist named Moffitt, a short fellow with a bushwhacker's moustache; and he scolded me for reading Buchanan's book, *Who Killed Kennedy?* He wanted to know why a man of my intelligence bothered with trash. Well, the country had never been the same since Kennedy was assassinated, courtesy was ready to reply; some process of derailment, begun with Hemingway's death and the death of Marilyn Monroe, had been racing on now through the months, through the heavens, faster than the contrails of our jet across the late afternoon mind of America; so one looked for clues where they could be found. It would be easier to know that Oswald had done it all by himself, or as an accomplice to ten other men, or was innocent, or twice damned; anything was superior to that sense of the ship of state battering its way down swells of sea, while in the hold cargo was loose and ready to slide.

This conversation did not of course take place — an Astrojet is not the vehicle for metaphorical transactions, it is after all still another of the extermination chambers of the century — slowly the breath gives up some microcosmic portion of itself, green plastic and silver-gray plastic, the nostrils breathe no odor of materials which existed once as elements of nature, no wood, no stone, no ore, time molders like a sponge in the sink. But Moffitt was Australian and fascinated with America, and had his quick comments to make, some provincial, some pure shrewd; finally he poked his finger on something I had never put together for myself, not quite: "Why is it," he asked, "that all the new stuff you build here, including the interior furnishings of this airplane, looks like a child's nursery?"

And that is what it was. The inside of our airplane was like a child's plastic nursery, a dayroom in the children's ward, and if I had been Quentin Compson, I might have answered, "Because we want to go back, because the nerves grew in all the wrong ways. Because we developed habits which are suffocating us to death. I tell you, man, we do it because we're sick, we're a sick nation, we're sick to the edge of vomit and so we build our lives with materials which smell like vomit, polyethylene and bakelite and fiberglas and styrene. Yes, our schools look like nurseries, and our factories and our temples, our kitchens and our johns, our airports and our libraries and our offices, we are one great big bloody nursery attached to a doctor's waiting room, and we are sick, we're very sick, maybe we always were sick, maybe the Puritans carried the virus and were so odious the British were right to drive them out, maybe we're a nation of culls and weeds and half-crazy from the start."

Nobody of course was Quentin Compson, nobody spoke that way any more, but the question was posed by a ghost and so had to linger: was there indeed a death in the seed which brought us here? was the country extraordinary or accursed, a junkyard where even the minnows gave caviar in the filthy pond in the fierce electric American night?

ONE

I must see the things; I must see the men.
— BURKE, *Reflections on the Revolution in France*

AT THE MARK HOPKINS on Saturday morning two days before the convention would begin, the atmosphere had the same agreeable clean rather healthy excitement (that particular American excitement) one picks up on the morning of a big football game. The kids were out, the children who were for Goldwater and those who were for Scranton, and they milled about in the small open courtyard of the hotel, and in the small hopelessly congested lobby where lines one hundred long were waiting for each of the three overworked elevators beating up to the twelfth and fourteenth floors, Scranton and Goldwater Headquarters respectively. It was a clear day outside, one of those cool sunny days in July when San Francisco is as nice as New York on a beautiful day in October, and the city fell away from Nob Hill in a perfect throw. There were apples in the air. It was a perfect football day. There was even wistfulness to be eighteen and have a date for lunch before the game. So the teams lined up first this way in one's mind, the children, adolescents, and young men and women for Goldwater to one side, the Scrantons to the other, and you could tell a lot about the colleges and the teams by looking at the faces. The Goldwater girls and boys were for the most part innocent, and they tended to have large slightly protruded jaws, not unlike Big Barry himself, and blue eyes — an astonishing number had blue eyes (was the world finally coming to the war of the blue-eyed versus the brown-eyed?) — and they were simple, they were small-town, they were hicky, the boys tended to have a little acne, an introspective pimple or two by the corner of the mouth or the side of the chin, a lot of the boys looked solemn and serious, dedicated but slightly blank — they could fix a transistor radio, but a word like "Renaissance" would lay a soft wound of silence, stupefaction in their brain. They were idealists, nearly every last one of them, but they did not speak of the happier varieties of idealism; one thought of Lutherans from North Dakota, 4-H from Minnesota, and Eagle Scouts from Maine. Many of them wore eyeglasses. They were thrifty young men, hardworking young men, polite, slightly paralyzed before the variety of life, but ready to die for a cause. It was obvious they thought Goldwater was one of the finest men ever to be born into American life. And they were stingy, they wore store-bought ready-mades, skinny kids in twenty-dollar suits and that pinch of the jaw, that recidivism of the gums which speaks of false teeth before you are fifty.

The Goldwater girls ran to two varieties. There were the models who had been hired for the purpose, and they were attractive but not very imaginative, they looked like hookers on horses, and then there were the true followers, the daughters of delegates, the California children who belonged to one Goldwater club or another. They were younger than the models of course, they were most of them fifteen, sixteen, not even seventeen, wearing cowboy hats and white vests and shirts with fringes, white riding boots; nearly all of them were blonde and they had simple rather sweet faces, the sort of faces which television commercials used to use for such product fodder as biscuit batter before the commercials turned witty; these Goldwater girls had the faces of young ladies who listened to their parents, particularly to their fathers, they were full of character, but it was the character of tidiness, industry, subservience — unlike the Goldwater boys who looked on the whole not unintelligent though slightly maniacal in the singularity of their vision (the way young physicists look slightly maniacal) the girls seemed to be just about all quite dumb. There was one blonde little girl who was lovely, pretty enough to be a starlet, but she left a pang because her eyes when open were irremediably dim. Taken altogether, boys and girls, they were like the graduating class of a high school in Nebraska. The valedictorian would write his speech on the following theme: Why is the United States the Greatest Nation on Earth?

Whereas the kids who were for Scranton were prep-school or

country-day. Some of the boys were plump and merry, some were mildly executive, but they shared in common that slightly complacent air of success which is the only curse of the fraternity president or leader of the student council. They were keen, they tended to be smooth, they had a penchant for bow ties and they were the kind to drive Triumphs or Pontiac convertibles, while the Goldwater boys would be borrowing their father's Dodge Dart (except for the one in a hundred who was automotive in his genius and so had built a dragster to top out at one-six-five). Then there were the Scranton boys who were still the descendants of Holden Caulfield. Faces like theirs had been seen for Stevenson in '60 in L.A. against JFK, and faces like theirs might appear (one would hope) in '68 for still another, but for now they were for the nearest candidate with wit, class, and the born foreknowledge of defeat. Slim, slightly mournful, certainly acerb, and dubious of the fraternity presidents with whom they had made cause, the Holden Caulfields were out for Scranton, and looked a size overmatched by the girls who were for Scranton, good-looking most of them, slightly spoiled, saucy, full of peeves, junior debs doing their best to be cool and so wearing their hair long with a part down the center in such a way that the face, sexy, stripped of makeup (except for some sort of white libidinous wax on the lips) was half-concealed by a Gothic arch of falling tresses. Such were Scranton's parts, such were Goldwater's, as the children shaped up for the game.

> In this state of . . . warfare between the noble ancient landed interest and the new monied interest, the . . . monied interest is in its nature more ready for any adventure; and its possessors more disposed to new enterprises of any kind. Being of a recent acquisition, it falls in more naturally with any novelties. It is therefore the kind of wealth which will be resorted to by all who wish for change.
> — BURKE, *Reflections on the Revolution in France*

Among the young industrial and financial monopolies of the West and Southwest that want a "bigger slice of the capitalist profit pie," Mr. Vasilyev listed H. L. Hunt, the Texas multimillionaire, the Lockheed Aircraft Corporation, the Douglas Aircraft Company, the Boeing Company and the Northrop Corporation and the Giannini "financial empire" headed by the Bank of America.

These are the forces, Mr. Vasilyev said, that overcame the last-minute effort by "Wall Street, the Boston financial group and the Pennsylvania industrial complex" to promote the candidacy of Governor William W. Scranton of Pennsylvania at the Republican convention last month.

"But the 'new money' of the West proved to be stronger than the old money of the Northeast," the Soviet commentator said.
— *New York Times*, August 13, 1964

For a time it had been interesting history. You will remember that Scranton decided to run for nomination after a talk in Gettysburg on June 6 with President Eisenhower. He left with the solid assumption he would receive Eisenhower's support, solid enough for Governor Scranton's public-relations machine to announce this fact to the nation. That night or early next morning President Eisenhower received a phone call from George Humphrey. Eisenhower had been planning to visit Humphrey in Cleveland during the week of the Governors' Conference. But it developed Barry Goldwater had already been invited to be at Humphrey's home as well. A social difficulty thus presented itself. Humphrey resolved it in this fashion: Eisenhower would understand if, under the circumstances, Goldwater having been invited first...

Ike knew what that meant. If his old friend, crony, subordinate and private brain trust George Humphrey was willing to let the old gander-in-chief come out second on a collision of invitations, then Ike had picked a loser, Ike was in danger of being a loser himself. Well, Ike hadn't come out of Abilene, Kansas, all those years ago *ever* to end on the losing side. So he waddled back to the middle. He phoned Bill Scranton you will remember but an hour before Scranton was ready to announce his candidacy at the Governors' Conference on June 7, and told Scranton he could not be party to a "cabal." It was obvious to everybody in America that the old man had not labored through the night and through the day to make the truth of his first conversation with the young man stand out loud and clear in the high sun of ten A.M.

Still, one could not feel too sorry for the young man. It is never easy to grieve for a candidate of the Establishment, particularly the Republican Establishment of the East, which runs a spectrum from the Duke of Windsor to Jerome Zerbe, from Thomas E. Dewey to Lowell Thomas, from Drue Heinz to Tex and Jinx, from Maine to Nassau, New York to South of France, from Allen Dulles to Henry Luce, Igor Cassini to Joe Alsop, from Sullivan & Cromwell to Cartier's, and from Arthur Krock to Tuxedo Park.

Well, the last two years, all the way from Arthur Krock to Tuxedo Park, you could hear that Bill Scranton was going to be the Republican candidate in '64. Attempts might be made to argue: Goldwater looks strong, somebody could say at a dinner table; hasn't got a chance, the Establishment would give back — it's going to be Scranton. What was most impressive is that the Establishment did not bother to photograph their man, immerse him in publicity, or seek to etch his image. It was taken for granted that when the time came, doors would open, doors would shut, figures would be inserted, heads would be removed, a whiff of incense, a whisk of wickedness — Scranton would be the candidate.

Of course, Goldwater, or the Goldwater organization, or *some* organization, kept picking up delegates for Goldwater, and from a year away there was a bit of sentiment that it might be easier to make a deal with Goldwater, it might be easier to *moderate* him than to excise him. Once upon a time, J. P. Morgan would doubtless have sent some bright young man out on the Southern Pacific with a bag full of hundred-dollar bills. Now, however, possessing a mass media, the buyoff could take place in public. Last November, three weeks before JFK was assassinated, *Life* magazine put Goldwater on their cover wearing a pearl-gray Stetson and clean, pressed, faded blue work shirt and Levi's while his companion, a Palomino named Sunny, stood with one of the Senator's hands on his bridle, the other laid over the vein of his nose. It was Hopalong Cassidy all baby fat removed, it gave promise of the campaign to come: the image of Kennedy was now to be combated by Sheriff B. Morris Goldwater, the Silver Gun of the West. It was one of those pictures worth ten thousand speeches — it gave promise of delivering a million votes. It was also a way of stating that the Establishment was not yet unalterably opposed to Goldwater, and could yet help him, as it had with this cover. But inside the magazine across the heads of seven million readers, another message was delivered to the Senator.

> Financial interests in Ohio, Illinois, Texas, Los Angeles and San Francisco — all centers of wealth independent of eastern ties — have been lining up money and intense local pressure for Goldwater. But . . . people fail to realize there's a difference in kinds of money. . . . Old money has political power but new money has only purchasing power. . . . When you get to a convention, you don't buy delegates. But you do put the pressure on people who control the delegates — the people who owe the old money for their stake.

Which was a way to remind Goldwater there were concessions to make. It was in foreign affairs that Goldwater had the most to explain about his policies.

> Barry Goldwater [went *Life's* conclusion] represents a valuable impulse in the American politics of '64. He does not yet clearly represent all that a serious contender for the Presidency should. "Guts without depth" and "a man of one-sentence solutions" are the epithets of his critics. The time has come for him to rebut them if he can.

Two months later Goldwater announced his formal candidacy for the Republican nomination, and issued a pamphlet called "Senator Goldwater Speaks Out on the Issues." Written in that milk-of-magnesia style which is characteristic of such tracts, one could no longer be certain what he thought — he had moved from being a man of "one-sentence solutions" to a man who showed a preference for many imprecise sentences. Barry was treading water. As he did, his people, his organization, kept picking up delegates. It was not until he voted against the Civil Rights Bill that the open battle between old money and new was at last engaged. Too late on the side of the East. To anyone who knew a bit about the workings of the Establishment, a mystery was present. For unless the Establishment had become most suddenly inept, there was a buried motive in the delay, a fear, as if the Eastern money were afraid of some force in the American mind racing to power in defiance of them, some mystique from out the pure accelerating delirium of a crusade which would make cinder of the opposition. So they had waited, all candidates but Rockefeller had waited, none willing to draw the fires of the Right until Scranton was flushed by the ebb and flow, the mystery or murmur, in an old man's throat.

Somewhat later that morning, one saw Scranton in a press conference at the San Francisco Hilton. The Corinthian Room on the ballroom floor (Press Headquarters) was a white room, perhaps forty-five feet by forty feet with a low ceiling and a huge puff of a modern chandelier made up of pieces of plastic which looked like orange candy. The carpet was an electric plastic green, the bridge seats (some two hundred of them) were covered in a plastic the color of wet aspirin, and the walls were white, a hospital-sink white. The practical effect was to leave you feeling like a cold cut set in the white tray of a refrigerator.

The speaker, however, was like a fly annealed on the electric-light bulb of the refrigerator. The banks of lights were turned on him, movie lights, TV lights, four thousand watts in the eye must be the average price a politician pays for his press conference. It gives them all a high instant patina, their skin responding to the call of the wild; there is danger, because the press conference creates the moment when the actor must walk into the gears of the machine. While it is a hundred-to-one or a thousand-to-one he will make no mistake, his career can be extinguished by a blunder. Unless one is making news on a given day — which is to say an important announcement is to be made — the press conference is thus a virtuoso price to be paid for remaining in the game, since there are all too many days when it is to the interest of the speaker, or of his party, or his wing of the party, to make no particular news, but rather to repress news. Still, the speaker must not be too dull, or he will hurt his own position, his remarks will be printed too far back in the paper. So he must be interesting without being revealing. Whereas it is to the interest of the press to make him revealing. A delicate game of balance therefore goes on. Nixon used to play well until the day of his breakdown. Eisenhower was once good at it. Goldwater was considered bad at this game, sufficiently bad that at the convention he held but one press conference before his nomination, and in the six preceding weeks had given but two.

An opportunity to observe the game in operation came with Melvin Laird who tried to convince the Press Corps that the Republican platform was liberal, strong on civil rights, critical of extremists, and yet true to Goldwater. Laird, a smooth vigorous man with a bald domelike head, held the breach for half an hour, ducking questions with grace the way Negroes used once to duck baseballs in a carnival. When he got into trouble (it was after all a most untenable position), he called on one of the most necessary rules of the game, which is that you don't insult the good character of the speaker. So Laird would finally say, "We worked hard on this platform, it's a good platform, I'm proud of it." That made the questioners retreat and regroup for a new attack.

Now Scranton's press conferences were of course different — because no one could be certain if Scranton was part of the game or a wild hare diverting the chase from every true scent. The result was a choppiness to the questioning, a sense of irritation, a hint of vast contempt from the Press Corps; a reporter despises a politician who is not professional, for the game then becomes surrealistic, and it is the function of games to keep dreams, dread and surrealism out in the night where they belong. They would dog at Scranton, they would try to close: *Governor, Governor, could you give the name of any delegate who has moved over from Goldwater to you?* No, we are not prepared to say at this time, would come the answer. *Are there any?* (Titter from the audience.) Certainly. *But you do not care to say?* Not at this time. *Governor* (a new man now) *is there any truth to the rumor you are going to concede before the convention begins?* None whatsoever. *Governor, is it not true that you may be willing to run for Vice-President?* For the eighty-eighth time, it is certainly not true. *Unqualifiedly?* Yes (said Scranton sadly) unqualifiedly.

He stood there like a saint, a most curious kind of saint. If he had been an actor he would have played the Dauphin to Ingrid Bergman's Joan of Arc. He was obviously, on superficial study, a weak and stubborn man. One felt he had been spoiled when he was young by a lack of testing. It was not that he lacked bravery, it was that he had lacked all opportunity to be brave for much too long, and now he was not so much engaged in a serious political struggle as in a puberty rite. It was incredible that this pleasant urbane man, so self-satisfied, so civilized, so reasonable, so innocent of butchers' tubs and spleens and guts (that knowledge which radiates with full ceremony off Khrushchev's halo), should be now in fact the man the Eastern Establishment had picked as their candidate for President. He had a fatal flaw to his style, he was just very slightly delicate the way, let us say, a young Madison Avenue executive will seem petulant next to the surly vigor of a president of a steel corporation. Scranton had none of the heft of a political jock-strapper like Goldwater; no, rather he had the big wide thin-lipped mouth of a clown — hopeless! If the roles had been reversed, if it had been Scranton with six hundred delegates and Goldwater who led a rush in the last four weeks to steal the land, why Goldwater might still have won. Scranton was decent but some part of his soul seemed to live in the void. Doubtless he had been more formidable when he began, but he had been losing for four weeks, one loss after another, delegates, delegations, caucuses, he had been losing with Eisenhower, he had lost with Dirksen, he had lost Illinois, he was losing Ohio, his wheeler-dealers stood by idle wheels; you cannot deal when you are losing delegates, there is nothing to offer the delegate but the salvation of his soul, and the delegate has put salvation in hock a long time ago. So Scranton had begun with the most resistant of missions — there are few works in life so difficult as to pry delegates loose from a man who has a nomination virtually won. To be a delegate and stick with the loser is a kind of life, but no delegate can face the possibility of going from a winner to a loser; the losses are not measurable. People are in politics to win. In these circumstances, consider the political weight lifting required of Scranton. He announces his candidacy four weeks before the convention, Goldwater within fifty votes of the nomination. Is Scranton to pull delegates loose from such a scene by an unhappy faculty for getting pictures taken with his legs in the air doing polkas,

RCAF exercises, and backhands in tennis? One knows Scranton's the product of a good many evenings when Eastern gentry circled around cigars and brandy and decided on poor Bill because he was finally not offensive to any. But it would have taken Paul Bunyan to claw into Goldwater's strength from four weeks out. His two hundred plus of Southern delegates were firm as marble, firm as their hatred of Civil Rights. And there was much other strength for Barry from the Midwest and the West, a hard core of delegates filled with hot scalding hatred for the Eastern Establishment. They were (unlike the children who were for Goldwater) this hard core of delegates, composed in large part of the kind of tourists who had been poisoning the air of hotel lobbies for twenty years. You could see them now with their Goldwater buttons, ensconced in every lobby, a Wasp Mafia where the grapes of wrath were stored. Not for nothing did the White Anglo-Saxon Protestant have a five-year subscription to *Reader's Digest* and *National Geographic,* high colonics and arthritis, silver-rimmed spectacles, punched-out bellies, and that air of controlled schizophrenia which is the merit badge for having spent one's life on Main Street. Indeed there was general agreement that the basic war was between Main Street and Wall Street. What was not seen so completely is that this war is the Wagnerian drama of the Wasp. For a century now the best of the White Protestants have been going from the farm to the town, leaving the small city for the larger one, transferring from Shaker Heights High to Lawrenceville, from Missouri State Teachers to Smith, from Roast Turkey to Cordon Rouge, off rectitude onto wickedness, out of monogamy into *Les Liaisons Dangereuses,* from *Jane Eyre* to *Candy;* it's a long trip from the American Legion's Annual Ball to the bustouts of Southampton. There's the unheard cry of a wounded coyote in all the minor leagues of the Junior League, in all the tacky doings of each small town, the grinding rasp of envy rubs the liver of each big frog in his small pond, no hatred like hatred for the East in the hearts of those who were left behind: the horror in the heart of social life in America is that one never knows whether one is snubbed for too much or too little, whether one was too fine or not fine enough, too graceless or too possessed of special grace, too hungry for power or not ambitious enough — the questions are burning and never answered because the Establishment of the East rarely rejects, it merely yields or ignores, it promises and forgets, it offers to attend your daughter's party and somehow does not quite show up, or comes that fraction too late which is designed to spoil the high anticipation of the night. (Or worse, leaves a fraction too early.) The Wasps who were for Goldwater were the social culls of that Eastern Society which ran the land, yes, the Goldwater Wasps were the old doctors of Pasadena with their millions in stock and their grip on the AMA, the small-town newspaper editors, the president of the second most important bank, the wives of Texas oil, yes the wives and family of all the prominent and prosperous who had a fatal touch of the hick, all the Western ladies who did the Merengue at El Morocco on a trip to New York, and did it not quite well enough, you could just hear the giggles in the throat of Archie or Lightning Dick or Sad One-Eye, the Haitian and/or Jamaican who had taught them how. Yes the memory of those social failures is the saliva of intellectual violence. The old Goldwater Wasps, the ones who had been sitting in the hotel lobbies, had an insane sting to their ideas — they were for birching America's bare bottom where Come-you-nisms collected: white and Negro equality; sexual excess; Jew ideas; dirty linen, muddled thinking, lack of respect for the Constitution. The Right in America had an impacted consistency of constipation to their metaphor. Small wonder they dreamed of a Republican purge. The Wasps were full of psychic wastes they could not quit — they had moved into the Middle West and settled the West, they had won the country, and now they were losing it to the immigrants who had come after and the descendants of slaves. They had watched as their culture was adulterated, transported, converted into some surrealist mélange of public piety *cum* rock and roll, product of the movies and television, of the mass media where sons of immigrants were so often king, yes the Wasps did not understand what was going on, they were not so ready after all to listen to those of their ministers who would argue that America had a heritage of sin and greed vis-à-vis the Negro, and those sins of the blood must be paid; they were not at all ready to listen to the argument that America's industry had been built out of the hardworking hard-used flesh of five generations of immigrants, no, they were Christian but they did not want to hear any more about the rights of others, they suffered from the private fear they were not as good, not as tough, not as brave as their great-grandfathers, they suffered from the intolerable fear that they were not nearly so good nor so tough as those other Christians close to two thousand years ago who faced Romans, so they were now afraid of the East which had dominated the fashion and style of their life, they were ready to murder the East, the promiscuous adulterous East — in a good fast nuclear war they might allow the Russians a fair crack at New York — yes they were loaded with one hatred: the Eastern Establishment was not going to win again, this time Main Street was going to take Wall Street. So Barry had his brothers, three or four hundred of the hardest delegates in the land, and they were ready to become the lifelong enemy of any delegate who might waver to Scranton.

That was the mood. That was the inner condition of the Goldwater delegates about the time Scranton announced he was going all out for the nomination and would pry these people loose from Barry. Henry Cabot Lodge came in from Vietnam. He was, you remember, going to help. Cynics in the Establishment were quick to inform you that Lodge was actually getting the hell out before the roof fell in, but Lodge gave this message to reporters:

> . . . One of the things that always used to please me about being in Vietnam was the thought that I might as an older man be able to do something to help our soldiers who were out risking their lives.
>
> Well, a couple of weeks ago I ran into this captain who was one of the battalion advisors and he said, "Are you going back to help Governor Scranton?" And I said, "No." Well, he said, "You're not?" He said, "I think you ought to."
>
> Well, that gave me quite a — that startled me, rather, because his attitude was: "I'm doing my duty out here, you'd better get back and do your duty pretty fast."

Obviously, no one had ever told Henry Cabot Lodge he might not necessarily be superb. So he came in, kingpin, boy, and symbol of the Establishment, and for two weeks he worked for Scranton (although most curiously — for Lodge was back in America a week before he even made arrangements to meet with Scranton). Still, Lodge announced his readiness to be the first target of the Wasp Mafia. At the end of two weeks of picking up the telephone to call old friends only to have the telephone come back in the negative, Lodge looked like a man who had been handsome once. His color was a dirty wax yellow, his smile went up over the gums at the corner of his mouth and gave a hint of the skull the way ninety-year-old men look when their smile goes past the teeth. He looked like they had been beating him in the kidneys with his own liver. It was possible something had been beaten out of him forever.

Of course this was Sunday night — the first session of the convention was not ten hours off on Monday morning — and Scranton and Lodge had had a ferocious bad Sunday; the particular letter inviting Goldwater to debate Scranton before the convention had gone out earlier that day above the Governor's signature and it had gone so far as this:

> Your managers say in effect that the delegates are little more than a flock of chickens whose necks will be wrung at will. . . . Goldwaterism has come to stand for a whole crazy-quilt collection of absurd and dangerous positions that would be soundly repudiated by the American people in November.

Denison Kitchel, Goldwater's General Director of the National Goldwater for President Committee, issued a statement:

> Governor Scranton's letter has been read here with amazement. It has been returned to him.
> Perhaps, upon consideration, the Governor will recognize the intemperate nature of his remarks. As it stands, they tragically reflect upon the Republican Party and upon every delegate to the convention.

Then Kitchel sent out mimeographed copies of Scranton's letter and his own reply to every Republican delegate. The Scranton mine caved in. Flooding at one end of the shaft, it was now burning at the other. Delegates do not like to be told they are a flock of chickens. It is one of those metaphors which fit like a sliver of bone up the nostril. Scranton was to repudiate his letter the following day; he accepted responsibility but disowned the letter — the language was not his — which is to say he admitted he could not run a competent organization. Nor, it developed, could he protect his own people: the name of the assistant who had actually written the letter slipped out quick enough.

Thus, one night before the convention, the letter public, Scranton may just conceivably have moved from deep depression to outright agony. The Republicans were having a Gala that night, five hundred dollars a plate for funds, the press not admitted, although many, some from the front, some from the rear, found a way in, and all the Republican luminaries were there, Eisenhower, and the Luces, Mrs. Eisenhower, Henry Cabot Lodge, Thruston Morton, George Murphy, Ray Bliss, Mrs. Goldwater, Scranton. All but Barry. In a much-announced rage about the letter, Goldwater was boycotting the Gala. Of course, it was essentially an Establishment Gala, that slowly came clear, and therefore was in degree a wake — news of the letter was passing around. The dance floor was not to be crowded this night.

Scranton came in. He walked down the center aisle between the tables looking like one of the walking wounded. People came up to greet him and he smiled wanly and sadly and a little stiffly as if he were very weary indeed, as if he had just committed hara-kiri but was still walking. When introduced, he said with wan humor, "I've read your books" — something finally splendid about Scranton.

A minute later, Scranton and Eisenhower came together. It was their first meeting in San Francisco; the General had just arrived that day, come into the Santa Fe depot after crossing the country by train. He was Scranton's last hope; he might still give momentum to the bogged-down tanks of Scranton's attack — what, after all, was the measure of magic? So Scranton must have looked for every clue in Eisenhower's greeting. There were clues running all over. Ike stood up from his table, he pumped Scranton's hand, he held his elbow, he wheeled about with him, he grinned, he smiled widely, he grinned again, his face flushed red, red as a two-week-old infant's face, his eyes twinkled, he never stopped talking, he never took his hands off Scranton, he never looked him in the eye. It was the greeting of a man who is not going to help another man.

Next day, Eisenhower dropped William Warren Scranton. He had a press conference at the Hilton in which he succeeded in saying nothing. It was obvious now he would not come out for anyone, it was also obvious he would not join the Moderates' call for a stronger civil-rights plank. "Well," he said, "he [Melvin Laird] came to see me, and the way he explained it to me, it sounded all right." Asked about an amendment the Moderates wished to put in the plank, "The authority to use America's nuclear weapons belongs to the President of the United States," Eisenhower thought "this statement was perfectly all right with me because it reaffirms what the Constitution means." Still he would not fight for it. Asked how he reacted to the idea of a debate before the entire convention between Senator Goldwater and Governor Scranton, a reference directed to Scranton's now famous letter of the day before, Eisenhower said, "This, of course, would be a precedent, and I am not against precedents. I am not particularly for them." A little earlier he had said, "I really have no feeling of my own." He didn't. He was in a private pond. He had been in one for years. Something had been dying in him for years, the proportions and magnitude of his own death no doubt, and he was going down into the cruelest of fates for an old man, he was hooked on love like an addict, not large love, but the kind of mild tolerant love which shields an old man from hatred. It was obvious that Eisenhower had a deep fear of the forces which were for Gold-water. He did not mind with full pride any longer if people felt contempt for him, but he did not want to be hated hard by anyone. So he could not declare himself, not for anything, and as he made his lapses in syntax, in word orders, in pronunciations, they took on more prominence than ever they had. At times, they were as rhythmic as a tic, or a dog scratching at a bite. He would say, "We must be objec*tive,* I mean *obj*ec*tive, we must be objective . . ." and on he would go as if he were sinking very slowly and quietly into the waters of his future death which might be a year away or ten years away but was receiving him nonetheless like a marsh into which he disappeared twitch by twitch, some beating of wet wings against his fate.

> . . . Looke, Lord, and finde both Adams met in me.
>
> — JOHN DONNE

Now, as for Goldwater, he had dimensions. Perhaps they were no more than contradictions, but he was not an easy man to comprehend in a hurry. His wife, for example, had been at the Gala, sitting with some family and friends, but at one of the less agreeable tables on the floor, off to the side and sufficiently back of the stage so that you could not see the entertainer. It seemed a curious way for the Establishment to treat the wife of the leading contender, but I was assured by the young lady who brought me over for the introduction that Mrs. Goldwater preferred it that way. "She hates being the center of attention," I was told. Well, she turned out to be a shy attractive woman with a gentle not altogether happy but sensual face. There was something nice about her and very vulnerable. Her eyes were moist, they were luminous. It was impossible not to like her. Whereas her daughters were attractive in a different fashion. "I want the best ring in this joint, buster," I could hear them say.

Goldwater's headquarters, however, were at a remove from the ladies. Occupying the fourteenth and fifteenth floors of the Mark Hopkins, they were not easy to enter. The main elevators required a wait of forty-five minutes to go up. The alternate route was off the mezzanine through a pantry onto a service car. A half-filled twenty-gallon garbage can stood by the service-elevator door. You went squeezed up tight with high and low honchos for Goldwater, plus waiters with rolling carts working room service. Once there, the fourteenth and fifteenth floors were filthy. A political headquarters is never clean — stacks of paper, squeezed-out paper cups, typewriter carbons on the floor, jackets on wire hangers all angles on a rack — a political headquarters is like the City room of a newspaper. But Goldwater's headquarters were filthier than most. There was a general detritus like the high-water mark on a beach. The armchairs were dusty and the sofas looked like hundred-dollar newlywed sofas dirty in a day. The air had the beat-out cigar smell of the waiting room in a large railroad station. It had nothing to do with the personnel. No one on the fourteenth or fifteenth floor had anything to do with his surroundings. You could have dropped them in Nymphenburg or a fleabag off Eighth Avenue — the rooms would come to look the same. A room was a place with a desk where the work got out.

They had something in common — professional workers for Gold-water — something not easy to define. They were not like the kids out in the street, nor did they have much in common with the old cancer-guns in the lobby; no, the worst of these workers looked like divinity students who had been expelled from the seminary for embezzling class funds and still felt they were nearest to JC — there was a dark blank fanaticism in their eyes. And the best of the Goldwater profes-sionals were formidable, big rangy men, some lean, some flabby, with the hard distasteful look of topflight investigators for fire-insurance companies, field men for the FBI, or like bright young district at-torneys, that lean flat look of the hunter, full of moral indignation and moral vacuity. But the total of all the professional Goldwater people one saw on the fourteenth and fifteenth floors was directly reminiscent of a guided tour through the FBI in the Department of Justice Build-ing in Washington, that same succession of handsome dull faces for guide, hair combed straight back or combed straight from a part, eyes lead shot, noses which offered nothing, mouths which were functional, good chins, deft moves. A succession of these men took the tourists through the halls of the FBI and read aloud the signs on the exhibits for us and gave short lectures about the function of the FBI (guard us from the enemy without, the enemy within, Communism and Crime — the statements offered in simple organizational prose of the sort used in pamphlets which welcome new workers to large corporations, soldiers to new commands, freshmen to high school, and magazine readers to editorials). The tourists were mainly fathers and sons. The wives were rugged, the kind who are built for dungarees and a green plaid hunting jacket, the sisters and daughters plain and skinny, no expression. They all had lead shot for eyes, the lecturers and the

66

tourists. Most of the boys were near twelve and almost without exception had the blank private faces which belong to kids who kill their old man with a blast, old lady with a butcher knife, tie sister with telephone cord and hide out in the woods for three days. The climax of the tour was a demonstration by the FBI agent how to use a tommy gun. For ten minutes he stitched targets, using one shot at a time, bursts of three, full magazine, he did it with the mild grace of a body-worker hitting small rivets, there was solemn applause after each burst of shots.

That was a part of the Republic, and here it was at Headquarters for Goldwater. The faces in these rooms were the cream of the tourists and the run of the FBI; there was a mood like the inside of a prison: enclosed air, buried urgency. But that was not altogether fair. The sense of a prison could come from the number of guards and the quality of their style. They were tough dull Pinkertons with a tendency to lean on a new visitor. One desire came off them. They would not be happy if there were no orders to follow. With orders, they were ready to put the arm on Bill Scranton, Nelson Rockefeller, or General Eisenhower (if told to). Probably they would put the arm on Johnson if he appeared and was ordered out. Naturally they were not there for that, they were there to defend Headquarters from mobs (read: niggers) and the Senator from Black assassination. It made sense up to a point: Goldwater was in more danger than Scranton, at least so long as Scranton showed no sign of winning; just that day, Sunday, there had been a civil-rights anti-Goldwater march down Market Street. The heavy protection was nonetheless a fraud. No mob was getting to the fourteenth floor, nor to Goldwater's fort on the fifteenth (a separate barricade of Pinkertons guarded the twenty-odd steps), no mob was going to get all the way up with just those three elevators and a wait of forty-five units of sixty seconds each, no assassin was likely to try Headquarters when there were opportunities on the street; no, the atmosphere was created to create atmosphere, the aura at Headquarters was solemnity, debris underfoot, and grave decisions, powers put to the service of order, some conspiracy of the vault, a dedication to the necessity of taking power. That was Headquarters. One never got to see Goldwater in the place.

There was opportunity, however, to come within three feet of him later that day, once at the caucus of the Florida delegation in the Beverly Plaza, once on the street moving from hotel to hotel (Pinkertons no longer in evidence now — just cops) and again at the Clift, where he talked to the Washington delegation. There was excitement watching Barry go to work with a group, an intensity in the air, a religious devotion, as if one of the most urbane priests of America was talking at a Communion breakfast, or as if the Principal-of-the-Year was having a heart-to-heart with honor students. The Florida delegation, meeting in a dingy little downstairs banquet room, was jammed. The afternoon had turned hot for San Francisco. Eighty degrees outside, it may have been ninety in the room. Everybody was perspiring. Barry sat in the front, a spotlight on him, a silver film of perspiration adding to his patina, and the glasses, those black-framed glasses, took on that odd life of their own, that pinched severity, that uncompromising idealism which made Goldwater kin to the tight-mouthed and the lonely. Talking in a soft modest voice, he radiated at this moment the skinny boyish sincerity of a fellow who wears glasses but is determined nonetheless to have a good time. Against all odds. It was not unreminiscent of Arthur Miller: that same mixture of vast solemnity and unspoiled boyhood, a sort of shucks and aw shit in the voice. "Well, you see," said Goldwater, talking to the Florida delegation, "if I was to trust the polls right now, I'd have to say I didn't have a chance. But why should I trust the polls? Why should any of us trust the polls? They've been wrong before. They'll be wrong again. Man is superior to the machine. The thing to remember is that America is a spiritual country, we're founded on belief in God, we may wander a little as a country, but we never get too far away. I'm ready to say the election is going to give the Democrats a heck of a surprise. Why, I'll tell you this," Goldwater said, sweating mildly, telling the folks from Florida just as keen as if he was alone with each one of them, each one of these elderly gents and real-estate dealers and plain women with silver-rimmed eyeglasses, "tell you this, I'm doing my best not to keep this idea a secret, but I think we're not only going to give the Democrats a heck of a surprise, I think we're going to win. [Applause, cheers.] In fact I wouldn't be in this if I didn't think we were going to win. [Applause.] Why, as I sometimes tell my wife, I'm too young to retire and too old to go back to work. [Laughter, loud cheers.]" Goldwater was done. He smiled shyly, his glasses saying: I am a modest man, and I am severe on myself. As he made his route to the door, the delegates were touching him enthusiastically.

Back on the street — he was walking the blocks to the Hotel Clift where the Washington State delegation was having a Goldwater reception — his tail consisted of fifty or sixty excited people, some Florida delegates who didn't wish to lose sight of the man, plus a couple of cops glad to have the duty. Cars slowed down to look at him; one stopped. A good-looking woman got out and cheered. There was something in the way she did it. Just as strange Negroes scattered at random through a white audience may act in awareness of one another, so the Goldwater supporters in their thirties and forties gave off a similar confidence of holding the secret. This very good-looking woman yelled, "You go, Barry, you go, go." But there was anger and elation in her voice, as if she were declaring, "We're going to get the country back." And Goldwater smiled modestly and went on. He looked a little in fever. Small wonder. He could be President of the United States in less than half a year, he could stop a sniper's bullet he never knew when, he was more loved and hated than any man in America, and inside all this was just *him,* the man who adjusted radio knobs in the early morning in order to transmit a little better, and now conceivably adjusted a few knobs. . . .

At the Hotel Clift he talked to the Washington delegates. We were definitely back in high school. That was part of Goldwater's deal — he brought you back to the bright minted certitudes of early patriotism when you knew the U.S. was the best country on earth and there was no other. Yes, his appeal would go out to all the millions who were now starved and a little sour because some part of their life had ended in high school, and the university they had never seen. But then Barry had had but one year of college — he had indeed the mind of a powerful Freshman. "I want to thank you folks from Washington for giving me this warm greeting. Of course, Washington is the name of a place I often like to get the heck out of, but I'm sure I won't confuse the two right here. [Laughter.]" He was off, a short political speech. In the middle, extremism. "I don't see how anybody can be an extremist who believes in the Constitution. And for those misguided few who pretend to believe in the Constitution, but in secret don't, well they may be extremists, but I don't see any necessity to legislate against them. I just feel sorry for them. [Cheers. Applause. Happiness at the way Barry delivered anathemas.]" At a certain point in the speech, he saw a woman in the audience whom he recognized, and stopped in the middle of a phrase. "Hi, honey," he sang out like a traveling salesman, which brought a titter from the delegation, for his voice had shifted too quickly, the codpiece was coming off, *Rain* and the Reverend Davidson. Something skinny, itchy, hard as a horselaugh, showed — he was a cannoneer with a hairy ear. Goldwater went on, the good mood continued; then at the end, speech done, he turned down a drink but said in his best gee-whizzer, "I'm sorry I have to leave because gosh I'd like to break a few with you." Laughter, and he took off head down, a little modest in the exit, a little red in the neck.

There was entertainment at the Republican Gala on Sunday night. The climax was a full marching band of bagpipers. They must have been hired for the week since one kept hearing them on the following days, and at all odd times, heard them even in my hotel room at four A.M., for a few were marching in the streets of San Francisco, sounding through the night, giving off the barbaric evocation of the Scots, all valor, wrath, firmitude, and treachery — the wild complete treachery of the Scots finding its way into the sound of the pipes. They were a warning of the fever in the heart of the Wasp. They are sounds which seem to pass through all the protective gates in the ear and reach into some nerve where the eschatology is stored. Few parents have failed to hear it in the cry of their infant through the morning hours of a bad night — stubbornness, fury, waste, and the promise of revenge come out of a flesh half-created by one's own flesh; the knowledge is suddenly there that seed is existential, no paradise resides in seed, seed can be ill-inspired and go to a foul gloomy end. Some find their part of the truth in listening to jazz — it is moot if any white who had no ear for jazz can know the passion with which some whites become attached to the Negro's cause. So, too, listening to the bagpipes, you knew this was the true music of the Wasps. There was something wild and martial and bottomless in the passion, a pride which would not be exhausted, a determination which might never end, perhaps should never end, the Faustian rage of a white civilization was in those Highland wails, the cry of a race which was born to dominate and might never learn to share, and never learning, might be willing to end the game, the end of the world was in the sound of the pipes. Or at very least the danger one would come closer to the world's end. So there was a vast if all-private appeal in listening to the pipes shrill out the herald of a new crusade, something jagged, Viking, of the North in the air, a sense of breaking ice and barbaric shields, hunters loose in the land again. And this had an appeal which burrowed deep, there was excitement at the thought of Goldwater getting the nomination, as if now finally all one's personal suicides, all the deaths of the soul accumulated by the past, all the failures, all the terrors, could find purge in a national situation where a national murder was being planned (the Third World War) and one's own suicide might be lost in a national suicide. There was that excitement, that the burden of one's soul (always equal to the burden of one's personal responsibility) might finally be lifted — what a release was there! Beauty was inspired by the prospect. For if Goldwater won, and the iron power of the iron people who had pushed him forth — as echoed in the iron of the Pinkertons on the fourteenth and fifteenth floor — now pushed forth over the nation an iron regime with total-itarianism seizing the TV in every frozen dinner, well then at last a true underground might form; and liberty at the thought of any catalyst which could bring it on. Yes, the Goldwater movement excited the depths because the apocalypse was brought more near, and like mil-lions of other whites, I had been leading a life which was a trifle too pointless and a trifle too full of guilt and my gullet was close to nausea with the endless compromises of an empty liberal center. So I followed the four days of the convention with something more than simple apprehension. The country was taking a turn, the colors were deepen-ing, the knives of the afternoon were out, something of the best in American life might now be going forever; or was it altogether to the opposite? and was the country starting at last to take the knots of its contradictions up from a premature midnight of nightmare into the surgical terrains of the open skin? Were we in the beginning, or turn-ing the middle, of our worst disease? One did not know any longer, you simply did not know any longer, but something was certain: the country was now part of the daily concern. One worried about it for the first time, the way you worried about family or work, a good friend or the future, and that was the most exceptional of emotions.

TWO

   . . . When men are too much confined to professional and faculty habits, and as it were inveterate in the recurrent employment of that narrow circle, they are rather disabled than qualified for whatever depends on the knowledge of mankind, on experience in mixed affairs, on a comprehensive, connected view of the various, complicated, external and internal interests, which go to the formation of that multifarious thing called a state.
        — BURKE, *Reflections on the Revolution in France*

IF THE DETAILS of the Republican Convention of 1964 were steeped in concern, it was nonetheless not very exciting, not technically. As a big football game, the score might have been 76 to 0, or 76 to 3. (There were sentimentalists who would claim that Rockefeller kicked a field goal.) Compared however to the Republican Convention of 1940 when Wendell Willkie came from behind to sweep the nomination on the sixth ballot, or the 1952 convention when Eisenhower defeated Taft on the second roll call of the states, compared even to the Democratic Convention of 1960, there were few moments in this affair, and nothing even remotely comparable in excitement to the demonstration for Adlai Stevenson four years ago when Eugene McCarthy put him in nomination. Yet this convention of 1964 would remain as one of the most important in our history; it took place with religious exaltation for some, with dread for others, and in sheer trauma for the majority of the press and television who were present on the scene. For them it offered four days of anxiety as pure and deep as a child left alone in a house. The purpose of the press in America has been to tinker with the machine, to adjust, to prepare a seat for new valves and values, to lubricate, to excuse, to justify, to serve in the maintenance of the Establishment. From I. F. Stone on the left, going far to the right of Joseph Alsop, over almost so far as David Lawrence, the essential understanding of the mass media is that the machine of the nation is a muddle which is endlessly grateful for ministrations of the intellect; so a game is played in which the Establishment always forgives the mass media for its excesses, and the mass media brings its sense of civilization (adjustment, psychoanalysis, responsibility, and the milder shores of love) to the service of the family Establishment. Virtually everything is forgiven by both sides. The contradictory remarks of politicians are forgotten, the more asinine predictions of pundits are buried with mercy. The Establishment for example would not remind Joe Alsop that in March 1964 he had written, "No serious Republican politician, even of the most Neanderthal type, any longer takes Goldwater seriously." No, the Press was not to be twitted for the limits of their technique because half their comprehension of the nation derived after all from material supplied by the Establishment; the other half came from conversations with each other. All too often the Press lives in the investigative condition of a lover who performs the act for two minutes a day and talks about it for twenty hours of the twenty-four. So a daisy chain like the *National Review* proves to be right about Goldwater's strength and the intellectual Establishment with its corporate resources is deep in error.

An explanation? Those who hold power think the devil is best contained by not mentioning his name. This procedure offers a formidable shell in which to live, but its cost is high; the housing is too ready to collapse when the devil decides to show. There has been no opportunity to study him. Just as a generation of the Left, stifled and ignored through the McCarthyism of the Fifties and the Eisenhowerism of the Fifties, caused panic everywhere when they emerged as the Beat Generation, so another generation, a generation of the Right, has been stifled, their actions reported inaccurately, their remarks distorted, their ideals (such as they are) ignored, and their personal power underestimated. The difference however is that the Beat Generation was a new flock of early Christians gathered prematurely before the bomb, an open-air asylum for the gentle and the mad, where in contrast the underground generation of the Right is a frustrated posse, a convention of hangmen who subscribe to the principle that the executioner has his rights as well. The liberal mind collapses before this notion but half of nature may be contained in the idea that the weak are happiest when death is quick. It is a notion which since the Nazis has been altogether detestable, but then the greatest intellectual damage the Nazis may have done was to take a few principles from nature and pervert them root and nerve. In the name of barbarism and a return to primitive health they accelerated the most total and surrealistic aspects of civilization. The gas chamber was a full albino descendant of the industrial revolution.

But that is a digression. To return to the as yet milder political currents of the Left and the Right in America, one could say the Beat Generation was a modest revolution, suicidal in the center of its passion. At its most militant it wished for immolation rather than power, it desired only to be left free enough to consume itself. Yet in the mid-Fifties liberals reacted with a profound terror, contumely, and ridicule to its manifestations as if their own collective suicide (the private terror of the liberal spirit is invariably suicide, not murder) was to be found in the gesture of the Beat. What then the panic of the liberal Establishment before a revolution of the Right whose personal nightmare might well be their inability to contain their most murderous impulse, a movement of the Right whose ghost is that unlaid blood and breath of Nazism which has hovered these twenty years like a succubus over the washed-out tissues of civilization. Consider but one evidence of the fear: that part of the Press called Periodicals sat in a section of the gallery to the left of the speakers in the Cow Palace. There were one hundred writers in this Periodical section of the gallery and six passes to get down to the floor where one could talk to delegates and in turn be looked at by them. Of those six passes, one or two were always available. Which meant that the majority of writers did not try to get down to the floor very often. Sitting next to one another the writers were content to observe — there were killers on the floor.

There were. It was a convention murderous in mood. The mood of this convention spoke of a new kind of society. Chimeras of fascism hung like fogbank. And high enthusiasm. Some of the delegates were very happy. "*Viva*," would shout a part of the gallery. "*Olé*," would come the answer. There was an éclat, a bull roar, a mystical communion in the sound even as *Sieg Heil* used to offer its mystical communion. *Viva-Olé*. Live-Yay! Live-Yay! It was the new chic of the mindless. The American mind had gone from Hawthorne and Emerson to the

Frug, the Bounce, and Walking the Dog, from *The Flowering of New England* to the cerebrality of professional football in which a quarterback must have not only heart, courage, strength and grace but a mind like an IBM computer. It marks the turn we have taken from the Renaissance. There too was the ideal of a hero with heart, courage, strength, and grace, but he was expected to possess the mind of a passionate artist. Now the best heroes were — in the sense of the Renaissance — mindless: Y. A. Tittle, John Glenn, Tracy, Smiling Jack; the passionate artists were out on the hot rods, the twist band was whipping the lovers, patriotism was a football game, a fascism would come in (if it came) on Live-Yay! Let's live-yay! The hype had made fifty million musical-comedy minds; now the hype could do anything; it could set high-school students to roar *Viva-Olé,* and they would roar it while victims of a new totalitarianism would be whisked away to a new kind of camp — hey, honey, do you twist, they would yell into the buses.

> When men of rank sacrifice all ideas of dignity to an ambition without a distinct object, and work with low instruments and for low ends, the whole composition becomes low and base.
> — BURKE, *Reflections on the Revolution in France*

First major event of the convention was Eisenhower's appearance at the Cow Palace to give a speech on Tuesday afternoon. The arena was well chosen for a convention. Built in the Thirties when indoor sports stadiums did not yet look like children's nurseries, the Cow Palace offered echoes — good welterweights and middleweights had fought here, there was iron in the air. And the Republicans had installed the speaker's platform at one end of the oval; the delegates sat therefore in a file which was considerably longer than it was wide, the speaker was thus installed at the handle of the sword. (Whereas the Democrats in 1960 had put the speaker in the middle of the oval.) But this was the party after all of Republican fathers rather than Democratic mothers. If there were any delegates to miss the psychic effect of this decision, a huge banner raised behind the speaker confronted them with the legend: Of the people, By the people, For the people. "Of the people" was almost invisible; "By the people" was somewhat more clear; "For the people" was loud and strong. This was a party not much "of the people" but very much "for the people," it presumed to know what was good for them.

And for fact, that had always been Ike's poor lone strength as a speaker, he knew what was good for you. He dipped into his speech, "here with great pride because I am a Republican," "my deep dedication to Republicanism" — he had not been outward bound for five minutes before the gallery was yawning. Ike had always been a bore, but there had been fascination in the boredom when he was President — this, after all, was *the* man. Now he was just another hog wrassler of rhetoric; he pinned a few phrases in his neat determined little voice, and a few phrases pinned him back. Ike usually fought a speech to a draw. It was hard to listen. All suspense had ended at Monday morning's press conference. Ike would not come out in support of Scranton. So the mind of the Press drifted out with the mind of the gallery. If Ike said a few strong words about the Civil Rights Bill — "Republicans in Congress to their great credit voted far more overwhelmingly than did our opponents to pass the Civil Rights Bill" — it meant nothing. The Moderates tried to whoop it up, the Goldwater delegations looked on in ranked masses of silence. Ike went on. He gave the sort of speech which takes four or five columns in *The New York Times* and serves to clot the aisles of history. He was still, as he had been when he was President, a cross between a boy and an old retainer. The boy talked, earnest, innocent, a high-school valedictorian debating the affirmative of, Resolved: Capitalism Is the Most Democratic System on Earth; and the old retainer quavered into the voice, the old retainer could no longer live without love.

Ike had bored many a crowd in his time. He had never bored one completely — he had always known how to get some token from a mob. Ever since 1952, he had been giving little pieces of his soul to draw demonstrations from the mob. You could always tell the moment. His voice shifted. Whenever he was ready to please the crowd, he would warn them by beginning to speak with a brisk little anger. Now it came, now he said it. ". . . Let us particularly scorn the *divisive* efforts of those outside our family, including sensation-seeking columnists and commentators [beginning of a wild demonstration] because," said Ike, his voice showing a glint of full spite, "I assure you that these are people who couldn't care less about the good of our party." He was right, of course. That was not why he said it, however; he said it to repay the Press for what they had said about him these last three weeks; the sensation they had been seeking was — so far as he was concerned — to arouse needles of fury in an old man's body — he said what he said for revenge. Mainly he said it to please the Goldwater crowd, there was the hint of that in his voice. The Goldwater delegations and the gallery went into the first large demonstration of the convention. Trumpets sounded, heralds of a new crusade: cockroaches, columnists, and Communists to be exterminated. There were reports in the papers next day that delegates shook their fists at newspapermen on the floor, and at the television men with their microphones. The mass media is of course equipped for no such war. Some of the men from the mass media looked like moon men: they wore red helmets and staggered under the load of a portable camera which must have weighed fifty pounds and was packed on their back; others of the commentators had portable mikes and hats with antennae. To the delegates they must have looked like insects grown to the size of a man. Word whipped in to the delegations from the all-call telephone in the office trailer of the Goldwater command post back of the Cow Palace. Cut the demonstration, was the word from F. Clifton White. The demonstration subsided. But the Press did not, the rest of the mass media did not. They remain in a state of agitation: if Ike was ready to accuse, anyone could serve as hangman. Anyone would. Anyone they knew.

Much later that Tuesday, after the full reading of the full platform, came a debate between the Moderates and the Conservatives. Success in politics comes from putting one's seat to a chair and sitting through dull wrangles in order to be present after midnight when the clubhouse vote is cast. Playboys do not go far in these circumstances, nor adventurers; the mediocre recognized early that a society was evolving which would enable them to employ the very vice which hitherto had made life intolerable — mediocrity itself. So the cowardly took their place in power. They had the superior ability to breathe in hours of boredom.

Politics was now open however to the disease of the bored — magic. Magic can sweep you away. Once a decade, once every two decades, like a big wind which eludes the weather charts and seems to arise from the caverns of the ocean itself, so does a hurricane sweep a convention. It happened with Wendell Willkie in 1940; it flickered on the horizon with Stevenson in '60; it was Scranton's hope to work a real debate on the last session before the balloting. If he could win even once on some small point, rumors of magic could arise. The Moderates had forced therefore a floor fight to propose a few amendments to the Republican platform of '64. One: that only the President have the authority to use America's nuclear weapons. Two: repudiate the John Birch Society. Three: introduce a language of approval for the Civil Rights Act. The

77

chances of success were small at best: only an extraordinary assault on the emotions of the Goldwater delegations could sway them to vote yes for the amendments.

The Moderates however went to battle moderately. Their speakers were impressive (as such a quality is measured in the *Times*). They were Christian Herter, Hugh Scott, Clifford Case, George Romney, Lindsay, Javits, Rockefeller. They were not, however, lively speakers, not this night. Lindsay and Javits were presentable in professional groups; devoted to detailed matters, they spoke with reason; Case spoke like a shy high-school teacher; Christian Herter was reminiscent of Mr. Chips; Hugh Scott owned no fire. Carlino (Majority Leader in the New York Assembly) sounded like a successful restaurant owner. And Governor Romney of Michigan had his own special amendments, he was a moderation of the moderates. As he spoke, he looked like a handsome version of Boris Karloff, all honesty, big-jawed, soft-eyed, eighty days at sea on a cockeyed passion. He spoke in a loud strong voice yet one sensed a yaw at the center of his brain which left his cerebrations as lost as Karloff's lost little voice. No, the only excitement had come at the beginning. Rockefeller was not a man who would normally inspire warmth. He had a strong decent face and something tough as the rubber in a handball to his makeup, but his eyes had been punched out a long time ago — they had the distant lunar glow of the small sad eyes you see in a caged chimpanzee or gorilla. Even when hearty he gave an impression the private man was remote as an astronaut on a lost orbit. But Rockefeller had his ten minutes at the podium and as he talked of suffering "at first hand" in the California primary from the methods of "extremist elements," threatening letters unsigned, bomb threats, "threats of personal violence," telephone calls, "smear and hate literature," "strong-arm and goon tactics," the gallery erupted, and the boos and jeers came down. Rockefeller could have been Leo Durocher walking out to the plate at Ebbets Field to protest an umpire's decision after Leo had moved from the Dodgers to the Giants. Again the all-call in the Goldwater trailer outside the Cow Palace was busy, again the delegations were told to be silent, and obeyed. But the gallery would not stop, and Thruston Morton, the Chairman, came forward like one of the sweepers in *Camino Real* to tell Kilroy his time was up. Rockefeller had his moment. "You quiet them," he said to Morton. "That's your job. I want my time to speak." And there was a conception of Rockefeller finally — he had few ideas and none of them were his own, he had a personality which was never in high focus (in the sense that Bobby

Kennedy and Jimmy Hoffa are always in high focus) but he had an odd courage which was profound — he could take strength from defying a mob. Three hundred thousand years ago, a million years ago, some gorilla must have stood up to an enraged tribe and bellowed back and got away alive and human society was begun. So Rocky finally had his political moment which was precisely right for him.

But the other Moderates did not. There was in their collective voice a suggestion of apology: let-us-at-least-be-heard. Speakers who were opposed to the amendments sounded as effective, sometimes more. Ford from Michigan spoke after Rockefeller, and had better arguments. It was not, he suggested, the purpose of a party which believed in free speech to look for formulas to repress opinion. He was right, even if he might not be so ready to protect Communists as Reactionaries. And Senator Dominick of Colorado made a bright speech employing an editorial from *The New York Times* of 1765 which rebuked Patrick Henry for extreme ideas. Delegates and gallery whooped it up. Next day Dominick confessed. He was only "spoofing." He had known: there was no *New York Times* in 1765. Nor was there any editorial. An old debater's trick. If there are no good facts, make them up. Be quick to write your own statistics. There was some umbilical tie between the Right Wing and the psychopathic liar.

More speakers came on. After four or five speakers for each side, a vote would come. Each time the amendment was voted down. Eight hundred and ninety-so-many to four hundred-and-a-few went the votes. Hours went by, three hours of debate. After a while, the Moderates came collectively to seem like a club fighter in still another loser. A vacuum hung over empty cries for civil rights. One wondered why a Negro delegate loyal to the Party for thirty years had not been asked by the Moderates to make a speech where he could say: *You are sending me home to my people a mockery and a shame. My people have been saying for thirty years that the Republican Party has no love for the colored man, and I have argued back. Tonight you will tell me I was wrong. You are denying me the meaning of my life.*

Such a speech (and there were Negro delegates to give it) might not have turned the vote, doubtless it would not have turned the vote, but it was the Moderates' sole chance for an explosion which could loose some petrified emotion, some magic. They did not take it. Probably they did not take it because they did not care that much if they lost. By now, it might be better to lose decisively than come nearer to winning and divide the party more. So they accepted their loser's share of the

79

purse, which is that they could go back East and say: I campaigned at the convention for civil rights. Tomorrow was nominating day. The last chance in a hundred had been lost.

> *The Bleat, the Bark, Bellow & Roar —*
> *Are Waves that Beat on Heaven's Shore.*
> — WILLIAM BLAKE, *Auguries of Innocence*

Everett Dirksen gave the nominating speech for Goldwater, Dirksen from Illinois, the Silver Fox of the Senate, the Minority Leader, the man who had done the most, many would claim, to pass the Civil Rights Bill, for it was his coalition with Hubert Humphrey on cloture which had carried the day. "I guess Dirksen finally got religion," Humphrey said, and Dirksen, making his final speech for the bill, declared, "There is no force so powerful as an idea whose time has come." It was said that when Goldwater voted against the bill, Dirksen would not speak to him. Two weeks later, Dirksen agreed to nominate Goldwater. "He's got it won, that's all," Dirksen said of Goldwater, "this thing has gone too far."

This day, nominating day, any orator could have set fire to the Cow Palace. The gallery and Goldwater delegations were as tense and impatient as a platoon of Marines going down to Tijuana after three weeks in the field. But this day Dirksen had no silver voice. He made a speech which contained such nuggets as, "In an age of do-gooders, he was a good doer." Dirksen was an old organist who would play all the squeaks in all the stops, rustle over all the dead bones of all the dead mice in all the pipes. He naturally made a large point that Barry Goldwater was "the grandson of the peddler." This brought no pleasure to the crowd. Main Street was taking Wall Street; Newport Beach, California, would replace Newport; and General Goldwater, Air Force Reserve, possessed sufficient cachet to negotiate the move; but not the grandson of the peddler. Dirksen however went on and on, making a sound like the whir of the air conditioning in a two-mile tunnel.

When he was done, they blew Dirksen down, the high screams of New Year's Eve went off, a din of screamers, rattles, and toots, a clash of bands, a dazzle of posters in phosphorescent yellow and orange and gold, the mad prance of the state standards, wild triumphant pokes and jiggles, war spears, crusaders' lances, an animal growl of joy, rebel cries, eyes burning, a mad nut in each square jaw, *Viva-Olé, Viva-Olé,* bugle blasts and rallying cries, the call of heralds, and a fall from the rafters of a long golden rain, pieces of gold foil one inch square, hundreds of thousands of such pieces in an endless gentle shimmer of descent. They had put a spot on the fall — it was as if sunlight had entered every drop of a fine sweet rain. I ran into Mike Wallace on the floor. "The guy who thought of this was a genius," said Mike. And the sounds of the band went up to meet the rain. There was an unmistakable air of beauty, as if a rainbow had come to the field of war, or Goths around a fire saw visions in a cave. The heart of the beast had loosed a primitive call. Civilization was worn thin in the center and to the Left the black man raised his primitive cry; now to the far Right were the maniacal blue eyes of the other primitive. The jungles and the forests were readying for war. For a moment, beauty was there — it is always there as tribes meet and clans gather for war. It was certain beyond certainty now that America was off on a ride which would end — was it God or the Devil knew where.

But the ride did not begin for another seven hours and seven nominations. Knowland seconded Goldwater's nomination; and Clare Boothe Luce, Charlie Halleck, Senator Tower. Then Keating nominated Rockefeller, a twenty-two-minute demonstration, decent in size but predictably hollow. More seconding speeches. Next came Scranton's turn. Dr. Milton Eisenhower, Ike's younger brother, did the nominating. It was good, it was clear, but there was not much excitement any more. One knew why the older Eisenhower had wanted the younger Eisenhower to be President. One also knew why he had not come very near — he gave a hint of Woodrow Wilson. Then the demonstration for Scranton. It was respectable, it let loose a half hour of music, it had fervor, the Scranton supporters died pure, an enjoyable demonstration. But the music was softer. Instead of *Viva-Olé* and the bugle blasts and rallying cries of the crusaders, one now heard "Boys and Girls Together," or "Hail, Hail, the Gang's All Here." And the Scranton posters did not have the deep yellow and deep orange of the phalanxes who had jammed the gorge for Goldwater; no, they bore blue and red letters on white, or even black on white, a gray photograph of Scranton on a white background with letters in black — the sign had been designed by Brooks Brothers, you may bet. Even some of the lapel buttons for Scranton revealed a camp of understatement, since they were five inches in diameter, yet Scranton's name was in letters one-eighth of an inch high. It made one think of *The New Yorker* and the blank ordered harmoniums of her aisles and text.

Now went the nominations hour after hour like the time between four in the morning and breakfast at a marathon dance. Here came the nominating speeches and the pumped-up state demonstrations on the floor which spoke of plump elderly tourists doing the hula in Hawaii. Then would come a team of seconding speeches, the weepers and the wringers, the proud of nose and the knotty of nose, the kickers and the thumpers, the ministerial bores and the rabbinical drones, the self-satisfied, the glad-to-be-there, the self-anointed, the unctuous, the tooth suckers, the quaverers.

Fong was nominated, and Margaret Chase Smith, first woman ever to be nominated for President. Now she had a lock on the footnotes in the history books. Romney was nominated, and Judd, defeated Congressman Walter H. Judd of Minnesota, given a grand-old-man-of-the-party nominating speech. The band played "Glory, Glory, Hallelujah." Just after World War II, early in 1946, Judd had been one of the first to talk of war with Russia. Last came Lodge who scratched himself. The nominations were done. The balloting could begin. They cleared the floor of the Press.

We had been there off and on for seven hours, circling the delegations, talking where we could, a secondary sea of locusts. All through the seven hours of this afternoon and evening, there was the California delegation. They could not be ignored. They sat in the front rows off the center aisle just beneath the speaker on the podium. They wore yellow luminescent Goldwater shirts, the sort of sleeveless high-colored shirts which highway workers wear to be phosphorescent at night. On the floor there were a thousand sights and fifty conversations those seven hours, but there was nothing like the California delegation. In California, Rockefeller had lost to Goldwater by less than three percent of the vote, and losing, had lost all the delegates. California had eighty-six delegates — all eighty-six by the rules of the victory were for Goldwater. So there were eighty-six yellow shirts right down front. Winning California, the Right had also won the plums of the convention, the distribution of tickets in the gallery, central placement on the floor, the allegiance of the Cow Palace cops. They had won the right to have their eighty-six faces at the center of the convention.

Most of the California delegation looked like fat state troopers or prison guards or well-established ranchers. A few were thin and looked like Robert Mitchum playing the mad reverend in *Night of the Hunter*. One or two were skinny as Okies, and looked like the kind of skinny wild-eyed gas-station attendant who works in a small town, and gets his picture in the paper because he has just committed murder with a jack handle. Yes, the skinny men in the California delegation leered out wildly. They looked like they were sitting on a body — the corpse of Jew Eastern Negritudes — and when the show was over, they were gonna eat it. That was it — half the faces in the California delegation looked like geeks. They had had it and now they were ready to put fire to the big tent.

There was one man who stood out as their leader — he had the face to be a leader of such men. Of course he looked not at all like a robber baron, the pride of Pinkerton, and a political boss all in one, no, nor was he in the least like an amalgam of Wallace Beery and fat Hermann Goering, no he was just Bill Knowland, ex-Senator William F. Knowland, Lord of the China Lobby, and honcho number one for Barry in Northern and Southern Cal.

So began the balloting. In twenty minutes there was another demonstration. The California standard, a white silk flag with a beast, some mongrel of bear and wild boar, danced in the air as if carried by a knight on a horse. The chairman for South Carolina intoned, "We are humbly grateful that we can do this for America. South Carolina casts sixteen votes for Senator Barry Goldwater." Barry was in. Four years of work was over. Final score: 883 for Goldwater. Scranton, 214. Rockefeller had 114, Romney 41. Smith received 27, Judd 22, Lodge 2, and Fong had 5.

When the voting was done, when the deliriums were down, an ooh of pleasure came up from the crowd, like the ooh for an acrobat. For Scranton accompanied by his wife was walking down the ramp to the podium, down the high ramp which led from the end-arena exits to the speaker's stand. It was a walk of a hundred feet or more, and Scranton came down this ramp with a slow measured deferential step, like a boy carrying a ceremonial bowl.

He made a clear speech in a young rather vibrant voice. He was doing the thing he was best at. He was making a gesture his elders would approve. He called on Republicans "not to desert our party but to strengthen it."

They cheered him modestly and many may have thought of his comments about Goldwater. On different days through June and July he had said: "dangerously impulsive," "spreading havoc across the national landscape," "a cruel misunderstanding of how the American economy works," "injurious to innumerable candidates," "chaos and uproar," "talking off the top of his head." "Hypocrisy . . ." says our friend Burke, "delights in the most sublime speculations; for never intending to go beyond speculation, it costs nothing to have it magnificent." "I ask . . .," Scranton said. He asked his delegates to make Goldwater's nomination unanimous.

Anywhere but in politics the speed with which the position had been shifted would be sign of a monumental instability. But politics was the place where finally nobody meant what they said — it was a world of nightmare; psychopaths roved. The profound and searing conflicts of politicians were like the quarrels between the girls in a brothel — they would tear each other's hair one night, do a trick together the next. They had no memory. They had no principles but for one — you do not quit the house. You may kill each other but you do not quit the house.

One could imagine the end of an imaginary nightmare: some time in the future, the Iron Ham (for such had become the fond nickname attached to President Barry Goldwater) would be told, thinking back on it all, that Billy-boy Scranton should be removed for some of the things he had said, and old Eisenhower, our General Emeritus, would find it in himself to say at a press conference on TV that while removal could not in itself be condoned, that is for high political figures, still it was bad, of course, policy, for people to have gotten away with insulting the President even if it was in the past and in the guise of free speech which as we all know can be abused. They would shave Scranton's head. Like a monk would he take the walk. And Old Ike would walk with him, and tell Willy S. a joke at the end, and have his picture taken shaking hands. Then, back to the White House for a two-shot drinking beer with Barry, the Iron Ham. After it was over, Barry would go back to the people who had put the ring in his nose.

> . . . They should not think it amongst their rights to cut off the entail, or commit waste on the inheritance, by destroying at their pleasure the whole original fabric of their society; hazarding to leave to those who come after them a ruin instead of a habitation.
> — BURKE, *Reflections on the Revolution in France*

> Goldwater: "There have been several suggestions made. I don't think we would use any of them. But defoliation of the forests by low-yield atomic weapons could well be done. When you remove the foliage, you remove the cover."
> — *New York Post,* May 27, 1964

Driving away from the Cow Palace after the nomination, I could hear Goldwater on the car radio. He was celebrating. He was considerably more agreeable than Dick Nixon celebrating — no all-I-am-I-owe-to-my-mother-and-father-my-country-and-church; no, Goldwater was off instead on one of his mild rather tangy excursions, "I feel very humble," he said, and you could feel the itch in the long johns and the hair in the nose, a traveling salesman in an upper berth, belt of bourbon down the hatch — as Mrs. Goldwater entered the room, he cried out, "Hi, honey," and added just a touch mean and small-town, "You didn't cry very much tonight."

"No," said Mrs. Goldwater, "wait till tomorrow."

The questioning went back and forth. He was all voice and very little mind, you could tell he had once been so bright as to invent and market a novelty item called Antsy Pants, men's white shorts with red ants embroidered all over them. But he had a voice! It made up for the mind. Lyndon Johnson's hambone-grits-and-turnip-greens was going to play heavy to this; Goldwater on radio was sweet and manly, clean as Dad in the show of new shows, One Man's Dad. They asked him, *Senator, you said that you would not wage a personal campaign against the President.* Yes, said Goldwater. *Well, sir,* said the interviewer now, *today you called President Johnson the biggest faker in the U.S.* Butters of ecstasy in the interviewer's mouth. *It's going to be a hard-hitting campaign, I assume then?* "Oh," said Goldwater, "I think you'll find some brickbats flying around."

The dialogue went on: *Could you tick off just a few of the major issues you think will be in the campaign against the Democrats?* "I think," said Goldwater, "law and dis — the abuse of law and order in this country, the total disregard for it, the mounting crime rate is going to be another issue — at least I'm going to make it one, because I think the responsibility for this has to start someplace and it should start at the Federal level with the Federal courts enforcing the law.

"I noticed one tonight in the evening paper, for example — a young girl in New York who used a knife to attack a rapist is now getting the worst of the deal and the rapist is probably going to get the Congressional Medal of Honor and sent off scot-free," said Goldwater, neglecting to tell us that the girl had had her indictment dismissed, and the alleged rapist was already up on a charge of attempted rape. Goldwater now said in the sort of voice Daddy employs when he is ready to use the strap, "That kind of business has to stop in this country and as the President, I'm going to do all I can to see that women can go out in the streets of this country without being scared stiff." Yes, he would. He was a Conservative and he was for States' Rights. It was just that he wasn't for *local* rights.

> By this wise prejudice we are taught to look with horror on those children of their country, who are prompt rashly to hack that aged parent in pieces, and put him into the kettle of magicians, in hopes that by their poisonous weeds, and wild incantations, they may regenerate the paternal constitution, and renovate their father's life.
>
> — BURKE, *Reflections on the Revolution in France*

Next day was the last day of the convention. Bill Miller was nominated for Vice-President. He was not a very handsome man nor did his manner seem particularly agreeable, but then the thought obtruded itself that the President of the United States was now in a more dramatic statistical relation to violent death than a matador. So a candidate would not necessarily look for too appealing a Vice-President — it might encourage notions of succession in the mind of an assassin. One would look instead for deterrents. William Miller was a deterrent.

THREE

A LITTLE LATER on the last day, Nixon made the speech of introduction for Goldwater. In the months ahead, when the bull in Barry
swelled too wild and he gave promise of talking again of Negro assail-
ants getting Medals of Honor, they would send in Nixon to calm him
down. The Eastern Establishment, hydra head, was not dead after all;
they still had Nixon. He was the steer to soothe the bull. Poor Barry. He
tried to lose Nixon in Cleveland, he had said, "He's sounding more like
Harold Stassen every day." Nixon however was as easy to lose as a plain
wife without prospects is easy to divorce.

"My good friend and great Republican, Dick Nixon . . ." was how
Goldwater began his historic acceptance speech. It had come after a
rich demonstration of happiness from the delegates. A boxcar of small
balloons was opened in the rafters as Goldwater came down the ramp
with his wife, his sons, his daughters. The balloons tumbled in thousands to the floor where (fifty balloons being put out each second by
lighted cigarettes) a sound like machine-gun fire popped its way
through the cheers. Fourth of July was here once more. He looked
good, did Goldwater. Looking up at him from a position just beneath
the speaker's stand, not twenty feet away, it was undeniable that Barry
looked as handsome as a man who had just won the five-hundred-mile
race in Indianapolis, had gone home to dress, and was now attending a
party in his honor. He was even, protect the mark, elegant.

Then he began his speech. Today, the voice for large public gatherings had dignity. It was not a great voice, as Churchill's voice was great; there were no majesties nor storms of complexity, no war of style between manner and the obligation to say truth; but it was a balanced manly voice which would get votes. His speech was good in its beginning.

> Now my fellow Americans, the tide has been running against freedom. Our people have followed false prophets. . . . We must, and we shall, set the tide running again in the cause of freedom. . . . Every breath and every heartbeat has but a single resolve, and that is freedom. . . . Tonight there is violence in our streets, corruption in our highest offices, aimlessness among our youth, anxiety among our elderly . . . despair among the many who look beyond material success toward the inner meaning of their lives.

As the speech went on, the mind went out again on a calculation that this candidate could win. He was humbug — H. L. Hunt's idea of freedom would not be very close to the idea of freedom in the minds of the children who were for Barry, no, nor William Knowland's idea, either, no, nor the Pinkertons, the Hawkshaw *Geist* of the FBI, nor the fourteenth and fifteenth floor. Goldwater was a demagogue — he permitted his supporters to sell a drink called Gold Water, twenty-five cents a can for orange concentrate and warm soda — let no one say it went down like piss — he was a demagogue. He was also sincere. That was the damnable difficulty. Half-Jew and blue-eyed — if you belonged in the breed, you knew it was manic-depressive for sure: a man who designed his own electronic flagpole to raise Old Glory at dawn, pull her down at dusk — he had an instinct for the heart of the disease — he knew how to bring balm to the mad, or at least to half the mad; Goldwater would have much to learn about Negroes. But one thing was certain: he could win. He would be breadwinner, husband and rogue to the underprivileged of the psyche, he would strike a spark in many dry souls for he offered release to frustrations deeper than politics. Therefore, he could beat Lyndon Johnson, he could beat him out of a variety of cause, out of natural flood or hurricane, in an epidemic of backlash, or by an epidemic of guilt — how many union workers fed to the nose with exhortations that Johnson was good for take-home pay might rise and say to themselves, "I've been happy with less." Indeed I knew Goldwater could win because something in me leaped at the thought; a part of me, a devil, wished to take that choice. For if Goldwater were President, a new opposition would form, an underground — the time for secret armies might be near again. And when in sanity I thought, Lord, give us twenty more years of Lyndon Johnson, nausea rose in some cellar of the throat, my stomach was not strong enough to bear such security; and if true for me, true for others, true perhaps for half or more of a nation's vote. Yet what of totalitarianism? What of war? But what of war? And the answer came back that one might be better a little nearer to death than the soul dying each night in the plastic encirclements of the new architecture and the new city, yes better, if death had dimension and one could know the face of the enemy and leave a curse. What blessing to know the face of the enemy by the end of the second third of the twentieth century.

And what of the Negro if Goldwater won? What of all the small-town Southern sheriffs who wished to wipe their hands in the Black man's hair? And a fury, a white fury, burst out of the mind and said, "No white sheriff is necessarily so very much worse than the worst Negro," no, the mad light of the Black hoodlum might be getting equal geek to geek to the worst of the California delegation. Then came a memory of James Baldwin and Diana Sands on a show called "Night Line" where television viewers could make a telephone call to the guests. Baldwin had received a call from a liberal which went, "I'd like to help, and I'm asking you how." "Don't ask me, baby," said Baldwin, "ask yourself." "You don't understand," said the liberal, "I know something about these matters, but it's getting confusing for me. I'm asking you in all sincerity where you think my help could be best offered." "Well, baby," said Baldwin, "that's *your* problem." And Diana Sands, pinky extended in total delicate Black-lady disgust, put the receiver back in the cradle. "You see," said Baldwin, talking to Les Crane, the master of ceremonies, "I remember what an old Negro woman told me once down South. She said, 'What the white man will someday learn is that there is no remission of sin.' That I never forgot," said Jimmy, "because you see it's perfectly possible the white will not be forgiven, not for a single cut or whipping or lynch mob or rape of a Black woman," his voice now as soft and reminiscent of the wind as some African man of witchcraft. And I had to throttle an impulse to pick up the phone and call Baldwin, and say, "You get *this*, baby. There's a shit storm coming like nothing you ever knew. So ask yourself if what you desire is for the white to kill every Black so that there be total remission of guilt in your Black soul." And the mind went out still again.

The country was in disease, it was conceivably so ill that a butcher could operate with dirty hands and have magic sufficient to do less harm than the hospital with its wonder drugs and the new pestilence.

(As the oil goes out, the earth turns cold, an arid used-up space, a ground for jumping off Texas to the used-up pits of the moon.) Still, you could not keep Americans from madness; our poetry was there, our symbolic logic: $AuH_2O+GOP+64=Victory!$ color of orange juice, Go, Go, Goldwater. Mrs. Goldwater's maiden name was Johnson, a portent of triumph to Barry? *Viva-Olé.* Eager to slay.

The country was in disease. It had been in disease for a long time. There was nothing in our growth which was organic. We had never solved our depression, we had merely gone to war, and going to war had never won it, not in our own minds, not as men, no, we had won it but as mothers, sources of supply; we did not know that we were equal to the Russians. We had won a war but we had not really won it, not in the secret of our sleep. So we had not really had a prosperity, we had had fever. *Viva-Olé.* We had grown rich because of one fact with two opposite interpretations: there had been a cold war. It was a cold war which had come because Communism was indeed a real threat to freedom, or it had come because capitalism would never survive without an economy geared to war; or was it both — who could know? who could really know? The center of our motive was the riddle wrapped in the enigma — was the country extraordinary or accursed? No, we had not even found our Communist threat. We had had a secret police organization and an invisible government large enough by now to occupy the moon, we had hunted Communists from the top of the Time-Life Building to the bottom of the Collier mine; we had not found that many, not that many, and had looked like Keystone cops. We had even had a Negro Revolution in which we did not believe. We had had it, yes we had had it, because (in the penury of our motive) we could not afford to lose votes in Africa and India, South America and Japan, Vietnam, the Philippines, name any impoverished place: we were running in a world election against the collective image of the Russ, and so we had to give the Black man his civil rights or Africa was so much nearer to Marx. But there had not been much like love in the civil rights. Just Dirksen. So we were never too authentic. No.

We had had a hero. He was a young good-looking man with a beautiful wife, and he had won the biggest poker game we ever played, the only real one — we had lived for a week ready to die in a nuclear war. Whether we liked it or not. But he had won. It was our one true victory in all these years, our moment; so the young man began to inspire a subtle kind of love. His strength had proved stronger than we knew.

Suddenly he was dead, and we were in grief. But then came a trial which was worse. For the assassin, or the man who had been arrested but was not the assassin — we would never know, not really — was killed before our sight. In the middle of the funeral came an explosion on the porch. Now, we were going mad. It took more to make a nation go mad than any separate man, but we had taken miles too much. Certainties had shattered. Now the voice of our national nerves (our arts, our events) was in a new state. Morality had wed itself to surrealism, there were cockroaches in all the purple transistors, we were distractable. We had an art of the absurd; we had moral surrealism. Our best art was *Dr. Strangelove* and *Naked Lunch, Catch-22; Candy* was our heroine; Jack Ruby our aging juvenile; Andy Warhol, Rembrandt; our national love was a corpse in Arlington; and heavyweight champion turned out to be Cassius Clay; New York was the World's Fair plus the Harlem bomb — it would take a genius to explain they were the same — and Jimmy Baldwin said, "That's *your* problem," on the Les Crane show at one A.M. Even the reverends were salty as the sea.

Yes, our country was fearful, half mad, inauthentic. It needed a purge. It had a liberal Establishment obeisant to committees, foundations, and science — the liberal did not understand that the center of science was as nihilistic as a psychopath's sense of God. We were a liberal Establishment, a prosperous land — we had a Roman consul among us — the much underrated and much disliked Lyndon Johnson was become a power in the land and doubtless a power upon the land; civilization had found its newest helmsman in the restraints, wisdom, and corruption of a major politician, of an organization boss to whom all Mafias, legit and illegit, all syndicates, unions, guilds, corporations and institutions, cadres of conspiracy and agents for health, Medicare, welfare, the preservation of antibiotics, and the proliferation of the Pentagon could bend their knee. The Establishment (the Democratic Establishment and the reeling columns of the Republican Establishment, falling back upon the center in the thundering confusion of Barry Goldwater's breakthrough) had a new leader, a mighty Caesar had arisen, Lyndon Johnson was his name, all hail, Caesar. Caesar gave promise to unify the land. But at what a cost. For if the ideology were liberal, the methodology was total — to this political church would come Adlai Stevenson and Frank Sinatra, the President of U.S. Steel and the President of the Steel Workers' Union, there would be photographs of Johnson forty feet high in Atlantic City — Big Bubber

Lyndon — and parties in which minority groups in native costume would have their folk dance: could one see the ghost of Joe Stalin smiling on his pipe?

Yes, if we all worked to beat Barry, and got behind Lyndon and pushed, radicals and moderate Republicans, Negroes and Southern liberals, college professors and Cosa Nostra, café society and Beatniks-for-Johnson, were we all then going down a liberal superhighway into the deepest swamp of them all? For Johnson was intelligent enough to run a total land, he had vast competence, no vision, and the heart to hold huge power, he had the vanity of a Renaissance prince or a modern dictator, whereas Barry might secretly be happier with his own show daily on radio. If Goldwater were elected, he could not control the country without moving to the center; moving to the center he would lose a part of the Right, satisfy no one, and be obliged to drift still further Left, or moving back to the Right would open schisms across the land which could not be closed. Goldwater elected, America would stand revealed, its latent treacheries would pop forth like boils; Johnson elected, the drift would go on, the San Francisco Hiltons would deploy among us. Under Goldwater, the odds were certainly greater that nuclear war would come, but under Johnson we could move from the threat of total war to war itself with nothing to prevent it; the anti-Goldwater forces which might keep the country too divided to go to war would now be contained within Johnson. Goldwater promised to lead the nation across the edge of a precipice, Johnson would walk us through the woods, perchance to quicksand itself. Goldwater would open us to the perils of our madness, Johnson would continue our trip into the plague. Goldwater could accelerate the Negro Revolution to violence and disaster — Johnson might yet be obliged to betray it from within. And what a job could be done! Who in such a pass should receive the blessing of a vote — the man who inspired the deepest fear, or the man who encouraged us to live in a lard of guilt cold as the most mediocre of our satisfied needs?

Still, the more Goldwater talked, the less impressive became his voice. When he went on too long, his voice grew barren. One could never vote for him, one could not vote for a man who made a career by crying Communist — that was too easy: half the pigs, bullies, and cowards of the twentieth century had made their fortune on that fear. I had a moment of rage at the swindle. I was tired of hearing about Barry Goldwater's high fine courage. Yesterday, on the floor, talking to a young delegate from Indiana, I had said, "Did it ever occur to you that Fidel Castro might have more courage than Barry Goldwater?"

"Yes, but Castro is a criminal mentality," said the boy.

I had cut off the argument. I was too close to losing my temper. Would the best of the young in every hick town, washed by the brainwater of the high school and the Legion, come to join this conservative crusade because Goldwater made an appeal to freedom, to courage, to change? What a swindle was in the making, what an extinction of the best in Conservative thought. They were so righteous, these Republicans. Goldwater might end with more warfare, security, and statism than any Democrat had ever dared; as a conservative, he would fail altogether (doubtless!) but certain he was to do one thing: he would march into Cuba. That was too much. One could live with a country which was mad, one could even come to love her (for there was agony beneath the madness), but you could not share your life with a nation which was powerful, a coward, and righteously pleased because a foe one-hundredth our size had been destroyed. So one got up to leave at this — we would certainly be strong enough to march into Cuba.

Then Goldwater uttered his most historic words: "Extremism in the defense of liberty is no vice. . . . Moderation in the pursuit of justice is no virtue," and I sat down and took out my notebook and wrote in his words, since I did not know how famous they would become. And thought: Dad, you're too much. You're really too much. You're too hip, baby, I have spent my life seeking to get four-letter words into U.S. magazines, and now you are ready to help me.

And as I left the arena, there was a fire engine and the cry of a siren and the police with a gaunt grim look for the end of the week. There had been a fire burning, some small fire.

On the way out, outside the Cow Palace, a wet fog was drifting, and out beyond the exits, demonstrators from CORE were making a march. They had been out there every day of the convention: Monday, Tuesday, Wednesday, and Thursday now, each day had demonstrated, carrying their placards, marching in a circle two abreast, singing "We Shall Overcome," shouting "Goldwater Must Go," marching round and round like early Christians in the corrals waiting to be sent to the arena, while about them, five, six, ten deep, was a crowd of the Republican curious, some with troubled faces, some with faces troubled by no more than appetite, hounds staring at the meat, these white girls and Negro boys walking side by side, the girls pale, no lipstick, nunlike,

93

disdainful, wearing denim shirts and dungarees; the Negroes tall and sometimes handsome, not without dignity, bearded almost all, the wild Negro girl in the center screaming savage taunts at the watching crowd, rude as Cassius Clay with a high-yaller mouth, and the crowd dreaming of an arena where lions could be set on these cohabiting Blacks and whites, and the Blacks and whites in the marching circle with their disdainful faces. Yes, kill us, says the expression on the face of the nunlike girl with no lipstick, you will kill us but you will never digest us: I despise you all. And some of the old Wasps are troubled in their Christian heart, for the girl is one of theirs, no fat plain Jewess with a poor nose is this one, she is part of the West, and so their sense of crisis opens and they know like me that America has come to a point from which she will never return. The wars are coming and the deep revolutions of the soul.

Governor William Scranton waits to address GOP platform committee.

Dwight D. Eisenhower with Senator Barry Goldwater.

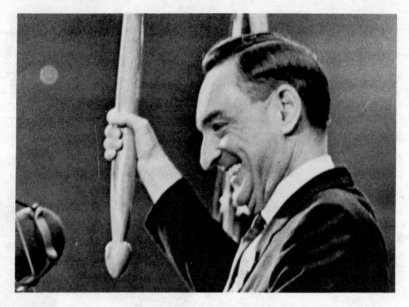

Representative William Miller, Chairman of the
Republican National Committee.

Senator Kenneth Keating and Governor Nelson Rockefeller.

Goldwater girls.

Nixon arriving at Fisherman's Wharf, San Francisco tourist attraction.

Mrs. Barry Goldwater.

Senator Everett Dirksen of Illinois.

Barry Goldwater, Jr., is congratulated by former Senator William
Knowland of California (left) and Peter Pitchers (right)
of the California delegation.

Republican Presidential candidate Barry Goldwater and Vice-Presidential
candidate William Miller with their wives.

Robert F. Kennedy receives ovation at the
Democratic National Convention.

President Johnson and running mate Hubert Humphrey.

Miami and the Siege of Chicago

ONE

NIXON IN MIAMI

Miami Beach, August 3–9

THEY SNIPPED THE RIBBON in 1915, they popped the cork, Miami Beach was born. A modest burg they called a city, nine-tenths jungle. An island. It ran along a coastal barrier the other side of Biscayne Bay from young Miami — in 1868 when Henry Lum, a California forty-niner, first glimpsed the island from a schooner, you may be certain it was jungle, coconut palms on the sand, mangrove swamp and palmetto thicket ten feet off the beach. But by 1915, they were working the vein. John S. Collins, a New Jersey nurseryman (after whom Collins Avenue is kindly named) brought in bean fields and avocado groves; a gent named Fisher, Carl G., a Hoosier — he invented Prestolite, a million-aire — bought up acres from Collins, brought in a work-load of ma-chinery, men, even two elephants, and jungle was cleared, swamps were filled, small residential islands were made out of baybottom mud, dredged, then relocated, somewhat larger natural islands adjacent to the barrier island found themselves improved, streets were paved, side-walks put in with other amenities — by 1968, one hundred years after Lum first glommed the beach, large areas of the original coastal strip were covered over altogether with macadam, white condominium, white luxury hotel and white stucco flea-bag. Over hundreds, then thousands of acres, white sidewalks, streets and white buildings cov-ered the earth where the jungle had been. Is it so dissimilar from covering your poor pubic hair with adhesive tape for fifty years? The vegetal memories of that excised jungle haunted Miami Beach in a steampot of miasmas. Ghosts of expunged flora, the never-born groaning in vegetative chancery beneath the asphalt came up with a tropical curse, an equatorial leaden wet sweat of air which rose from the earth itself, rose right up through the baked asphalt and into the heated air which entered the lungs like a hand slipping into a rubber glove.

The temperature was not that insane. It hung around 87 day after day, at night it went down to 82, back to the same 87 in the A.M. — the claims of the News Bureau for Miami Beach promised that in 1967 temperature exceeded 90° only four times. (Which the Island of Manhattan could never begin to say.) But of course Miami Beach did not have to go that high, for its humidity was up to 87 as well — it was, on any and every day of the Republican Convention of 1968, one of the hottest cities in the world. The reporter was no expert on tropical heats — he had had, he would admit, the island of Luzon for a summer in World War II; and basic training in the pine woods of Fort Bragg, North Carolina, in August; he had put in a week at Las Vegas during July — temperatures to 110; he had crossed the Mojave Desert once by day; he was familiar with the New York subway in the rush hour on the hottest day of the year. These were awesome immersions — one did not have to hit the Congo to know what it was like in a hothouse in hell — but that 87° in Miami Beach day after day held up in competition against other sulphuric encounters. Traveling for five miles up the broken-down, forever in-a-state-of-alteration and repair of Collins Avenue, crawling through 5 P.M. Miami Beach traffic in the pure miserable fortune of catching an old taxi without air conditioning, dressed in shirt and tie and jacket — formal and implicitly demanded uniform of political journalists — the sensation of breathing, then living, was not unlike being obliged to make love to a 300-pound woman who has decided to get on top. Got it? You could not dominate a thing. That uprooted jungle had to be screaming beneath.

Of course it could have been the air conditioning: natural climate transmogrified by technological climate. They say that in Miami Beach the air conditioning is pushed to that icy point where women may wear fur coats over their diamonds in the tropics. For ten miles, from the Diplomat to the Di Lido, above Hallandale Beach Boulevard down to Lincoln Mall, all the white refrigerators stood, piles of white refrigerators six and eight and twelve stories high, twenty stories high, shaped like sugar cubes and ice-cube trays on edge, like mosques and palaces, shaped like matched white luggage and portable radios, stereos, plastic compacts and plastic rings, Moorish castles shaped like waffle irons, shaped like the baffle plates on white plastic electric heaters, and cylinders like Waring blenders, buildings looking like giant op art and pop art paintings, and sweet wedding cakes, cottons of kitsch and piles of dirty cotton stucco, yes, for ten miles the hotels for the delegates stood on the beach side of Collins Avenue: the Eden Roc and the Fontainebleau (Press Headquarters), the Di Lido and the De Lano, the Ivanhoe, Deauville, Sherry Frontenac and the Monte Carlo, the Cadillac, Caribbean and the Balmoral, the Lucerne, Hilton Plaza, Doral Beach, the Sorrento, Marco Polo, Casablanca, and Atlantis, the Hilyard Manor, Sans Souci, Algiers, Carillon, Seville, the Gaylord, the Shore Club, the Nautilus, Montmartre, and the Promenade, the Bal Harbour on North Bay Causeway, and the Twelve Caesars, the Regency and the Americana, the Diplomat, Versailles, Coronado, Sovereign, the Waldman (dig!), the Beau Rivage, the Crown Hotel, even Holiday Inn, all oases for technological man. Deep air conditioning down to 68°, ice-palaces to chill the fevered brain — when the air conditioning worked. And their furnishings were monumentally materialistic. Not all of them: the cheaper downtown hotels like the Di Lido and the Nautilus were bare and mean with vinyl coverings on the sofas and the glare of plastic off the rugs and tables and tiles, inexpensive hotel colors of pale brown and buff and dingy cream, sodden gray, but the diadems like the Fontainebleau and the Eden Roc, the Doral Beach, the Hilton Plaza (Headquarters for Nixon), the Deauville (Hq for Reagan) or the Americana — Rockefeller and the New York State delegation's own ground — were lavish with interlockings, curves, vaults and runs of furnishings as intertwined as serpents in the roots of a mangrove tree. All the rivers of the very worst taste twisted down to the delta of each lobby in each grand Miami Beach hotel — rare was the central room which did not look like the lobby of a movie palace, imitation of late-Renaissance imitations of Greek and Roman statues, imitations of baroque and rococo and brothel Victorian and Art Nouveau and Bauhaus with gold grapes and cornucopias welded to the modern bronze tubing of the chair, golden moldings which ran like ivy from room to room, chandeliers complex as the armature of dynamos, and curvilinear steps in the shape of amoebas and palettes, cocktail lounge bars in deep rose or maroon with spun-sugar white tubes of plaster décor to twist around the ceiling. There was every color of iridescence, rainbows of vulgarity, aureoles of gorgeous taste, opium den of a middle-class dollar, materialistic as meat, sweat, and the cigar. It is said that people born under Taurus and Capricorn are the most materialistic of us all. Take a sample of the residents in the census of Miami B. — does Taurus predominate more than one-twelfth of its share? It must, or astrology is done, for the Republicans, Grand Old Party with a philosophy rather than a program, had chosen what must certainly be the materialistic capital of the world for their convention. Las Vegas might offer competition, but Las Vegas was materialism in the service of electricity — fortunes could be lost in the spark of the dice. Miami was materialism baking in the sun, then stepping back to air-conditioned caverns where ice could nestle in the fur. It was the first of a hundred curiosities — that in a year when the Republic hovered on the edge of revolution, nihilism, and lines of police on file to the horizon, visions of future Vietnams in our own cities upon us, the party of conservatism and principle, of corporate wealth and personal frugality, the party of cleanliness, hygiene, and balanced budget, should have set itself down on a sultan's strip.

That was the first of a hundred curiosities, but there were mysteries as well. The reporter had moved through the convention quietly, as anonymously as possible, wan, depressed, troubled. Something profoundly unclassifiable was going on among the Republicans and he did not know if it was conceivably good or a concealment of something bad — which was the first time a major social phenomenon like a convention had confused him so. He had covered others. The Democratic Convention in 1960 in Los Angeles which nominated John F. Kennedy, and the Republican in San Francisco in 1964 which installed Barry Goldwater, had encouraged some of his very best writing. He had felt a gift for comprehending those conventions. But the Republican assembly in Miami Beach in 1968 was a different affair — one could not tell if nothing much was going on, or to the contrary, nothing much was going on near the surface but everything was shifting down below. So dialogue with other journalists merely depressed him — the complaints were unanimous that this was the dullest convention anyone could remember. Complaints took his mind away from the slow brooding infusion he desired in the enigmas of conservatism and/or Republicanism, and any hope of perspective on the problem beyond. The country was in a throe, a species of eschatological heave. The novelist

John Updike was not necessarily one of his favorite authors, but after the assassination of Robert F. Kennedy, it was Updike who had made the remark that God might have withdrawn His blessing from America. It was a thought which could not be forgotten for it gave insight to the perspectives of the Devil and his political pincers: Left-wing demons, white and Black, working to inflame the conservative heart of America, while Right-wing devils exacerbated Blacks and drove the mind of the New Left and liberal middle class into prides of hopeless position. And the country roaring like a bull in its wounds, coughing like a sick lung in the smog, turning over in sleep at the sound of motorcycles, shivering at its need for new phalanxes of order. Where were the new phalanxes one could trust? The reporter had seen the faces of too many police to balm his dreams with the sleep they promised. Even the drinks tasted bad in Miami in the fever and the chill.

2

His first afternoon in Miami Beach was spent by the reporter in Convention Hall. He stepped up on the speaker's podium to see how it might feel, nosed into the jerrybuilt back room back of the podium where speakers would wait, and Press be excluded, once the convention was begun. A room unmatched for dreariness. Dull green daybeds and sofas, a nondescript powder-blue rug, open studding and therefore open wall-board color, brown and tan leatherette chairs, a dreary cloth throw on a table. Every quiet color clashed with every other quiet color — it was the sort of room which could have served for the bridge players in an old folks' summer camp in some flat and inland state. In this room, while preparing to orate, would wait some of the more ambitious men in America, and some of the more famous; looking at their manuscripts might be John Wayne, Barry Goldwater, John Lindsay, Thomas E. Dewey, Ronald Reagan, Governor Rockefeller, George Romney, Richard Nixon himself — not to mention Billy Graham — they would pass through the splendors of this profoundly American anteroom. Examination completed, the reporter abruptly decided he would actually go out to the airport to greet the arrival of a baby elephant which was arriving on a Delta cargo plane as a gift to Richard Nixon from the people of Anaheim, California. That seemed an appropriate way to open coverage of the convention.

3

Unless one knows him well, or has done a sizable work of preparation, it is next to useless to interview a politician. He has a mind which is accustomed to political questions. By the time he decides to run for President, he may have answered a million. Or at least this is true if he has been in politics for twenty years and has replied to an average of one hundred-fifty such queries a day, no uncharacteristic amount. To surprise a skillful politician with a question is then approximately equal in difficulty to hitting a professional boxer with a barroom hook. One cannot therefore tell a great deal from interviews with a candidate. His teeth are bound to be white, his manner mild and pleasant, his presence attractive, and his ability to slide off the question and return with an answer is as implicit in the work of his jaws as the ability to bite a piece of meat. Interviewing a candidate is about as intimate as catching him on television. Therefore it is sometimes easier to pick up the truth of his campaign by studying the outriggers of his activity. Therefore the reporter went to cover the elephant.

It was, as expected, a modest story in a quiet corner of International Airport in Miami. Not more than ten reporters and a dozen photographers showed up. And a band, and a quorum of Nixonettes wearing blue dresses and white straw hats with a legend, NIXON'S THE ONE. A publicity puff was handed around which informed the Press that the beast was named Ana (for Anaheim, California) and was 52" high, 2½ years old, weighed 1,266 pounds and had been given to Nixon by the happy citizens of the town — Ana!

Ana came in on a Lockheed 100, a hippo of a four-motor plane with four-bladed propellers. The cargo door was in the rear, and as the musicians, Don Goldie and his Dixieland Band, white musicians from the Hilton-Miami — accordion, tuba, trombone, snares, clarinet, banjo, and trumpet — began to play, and the six Nixonettes began to strut (they looked to be high school juniors) and the plane to unload, so the black cloud on the horizon moved over, and began its drop, black tropical rain so intense even photographers had to take shelter, and a dozen, then another dozen of musicians, Nixonettes, cameramen, photographers, and animal handlers piled into a small 6 x 8 Hertz trailer later to be used for the elephant. In the steam of the interior, the day took on surreal and elegant proportions — two dozen amateurs and professionals on call for one baby elephant (said to be arriving in her tutu) were equal across the board to the logic of one political convention; by the time the rain stopped five minutes later and the elephant crate was unloaded, hoisted on a fork lift off the carrier, brought near the trailer and opened, everyone gave a cheer to Ana who came out nervously from her crate, but with a definite sense of style. She took a quick look at the still photographers surrounding her, and the larger movie cameras to which certain humans were obviously connected, stepped on the still-wet steaming runway, threw a droll red-eye at her handler, dropped a small turd to X the spot of her liberation from the crate (and as a marker in case she wanted later to retrace her steps) then did a good Republican handstand, trunk curved as graciously as a pinkie off a teacup. To which the media corps responded with approval, Nixonettes squealing, Don Goldie Band playing Dixieland, still cameras clicking, movie cameras ticking within the gears of their clockwork, Dade County police grinning as they stood to one side (four men — all armed). Then Ana from Anaheim walked on her hind legs. To much approval. She curtsied, bowed, turned in a circle, obviously pleased with herself, then stretched out her trunk in the general area of everybody's midsection. "Hey, chum, watch your peanuts," a man called out.

It went on for a period, the Nixonettes having their pictures taken, one girl who was not a high school junior but most likely a professional model taking care to see she was in the picture often, and all the girls kept trying to put a straw Nixon hat on Ana, but the hat kept falling off. After ten minutes, the handlers tried to coax Ana into the Hertz trailer, but she was not about to, not yet, so they walked her around a hangar, brought her back, then slipped her 1,200-pound bulk into the box with a bit of elephant handler's legerdemain. The arrival was over.

It had been pleasant; in truth, more pleasant than the reporter had expected. It had not been tense, not even with the four armed cops. The air had been better than one might have thought. So it was a warning to one's perspective and proportion: the Nixon forces and the Nixon people were going to be in command of small subtleties he had not anticipated. It was his first clue to the notion that there was a new Nixon. He could have read a dozen articles which said the same thing and paid no mind, for the men who wrote them were experts and so were wrong in their predictions as often as they were right. Experts he would disregard — so far as he was able — but Ana had been happy doing her handstand: that was an unexpected fact he would have to absorb into the first freshets of his brooding. Of course the reporter had once decided (using similar methods) that Barry Goldwater could win the 1964 election. This, at least, was the method at its extreme. Still, a happy elephant spoke of luck for Nixon, or at the least, agreeable management down the line.

4

Rockefeller came in at Opa Locka Airport next day, and again it rained. The skies over Miami were at their best when rain was near, for cumulus clouds piled high on themselves, making towers, pyramids, turrets, and heavenly Miami Beach hotels two miles up in the air while dark horizontal tides of oncoming tropical storm washed through the sky, crossed the sun, gave gildings of gold and black to the towers of cumulus.

The schedule for arrival was Rockefeller on Saturday, Reagan later that evening, and Nixon on Monday. They were all of course coming in on charter flights, and the Rockefeller plane, an American Airlines 727 jet which had carried the candidate 65,000 miles into forty-five states during the campaign, was landing, for security reasons, at the Coast Guard Airport, Opa Locka, out to the west of Miami, almost in redneck country, the town of Opa Locka still another sad sweet real estate failure of Southern Florida for it had been built to recapitulate a piece of North Africa. Residential streets with names like Ali Baba Avenue, Sesame Street, Sharazad Boulevard, Arabia Avenue, Sultan Avenue, Caliph Street, and Salim Street wound around the center of Opa Locka in complicated ovals and ellipses all planned thirty-plus or forty years ago by a real estate genius, now a town all but deserted in the afternoon sun with the storm coming on, just occasional palmettoes and the crumbling white stucco center where a small old hotel and bar stood like the molderings of a Foreign Legion fort, holding the crossroads before the Coast Guard pushed onto the airport.

Perhaps a hundred or a hundred-fifty newsmen, TV cameras, and still photographers were out at the main hangar with the Press bus, way out in the quiet empty reaches of the all but deserted airdrome, and overhead, light planes and helicopters patrolled the near sky, and four or five police cars were parked in uneasy relation to the crowd. The reporter had to show no identification to enter the gate, and needed none now; a potential assassin, tipped to Rockefeller's entrance at Opa Locka, could have packed a piece to within a yard of him — of course, afterward, he could never have escaped. If he managed to shoot past the twenty-odd cops in the direct vicinity, the helicopters would have followed his car all the way to Miami, maybe nailed him on Arthur Godfrey Causeway from the sky. Like pieces of flesh fragmented from the explosion of a grenade, echoes of the horror of Kennedy's assassination were thus everywhere: helicopters riding overhead like roller coasters, state troopers with magnums on their hip and crash helmets, squad cars, motorcycles, yet no real security, just powers of retaliation. It forced one to cherish major politicians — no matter how colorless, they all had hints of charisma now that they were obviously more vulnerable to sudden death than bullfighters, and so they were surrounded with a suggestion of the awe peasants reserve for the visit of the bishop — some rushed to touch them, others looked ready to drop to their knees. Thus, at least, for Rockefeller and the Press. He was surrounded almost immediately after he came down the landing ramp, and never left alone, surrounded by Press and cameramen five deep, the photographers by long practice holding their cameras and even their movie cameras up over their heads, aiming down by skillful guess, so that from a distance one could always tell exactly where the candidate was situated, for a semicircle of cameras crooned in from above like bulbs of seaweed breaking surface at high tide, or were they more like praying mantises on the heads of tall grass? — a bazaar of metaphor was obviously offered.

Rocky had come off the plane with his entourage and his wife. She was surprisingly attractive, with a marvelous high color which made her vastly better-looking than her photographs, and Rocky looked like much less than his photographs, gray beyond gray in the flesh, gray as New York City pavements, gray as an old con — the sun could not have touched him in a month or else all the fighting blood of the heart was somewhere deep inside the brain, working through the anxiety-ridden calculations with which he must have come to Miami, for Nixon with his six-hundred-plus votes now almost secure was a handful or a score or at best not fifty votes from the first ballot nomination. Anxiety had to be stirred by every omen: the weather, the first unfamiliar face to greet you off the plane, the sudden flight of a bird, the warmth of the policeman's salutation, or the enthusiasm of the Press corps.

But if it were for that, he was elected already. Rockefeller was obviously the near-unanimous choice of the Press, and above all, the television — a mating of high chemical potentials existed between the media and the man as if they had been each conceived for the other. Except for his complexion, Rocky had an all but perfect face for President, virile, friendly, rough-hewn, of the common man, yet uncommon — Spencer Tracy's younger brother gone into politics. He had only one flaw — an odd and unpleasant mouth, a catfish mouth, wide, unnaturally wide with very thin lips. In the center of the mouth there seemed almost another mouth which did the speaking, somewhat thicker lips which pursed, opened, deliberated — all the while the slit-thin corners of the mouth seemed off on their own, not really moving with the center. So he gave the impression of a man to whom expert instruction had disclosed what he might be expected to say — therefore only the middle of the mouth would be on call.

The rain, which had begun to come down and then providentially stopped, was coming on again. So he was able to slip out of the tight ring of interviewers locked about him after answering fifty more of the million political questions he would reply to in his life, and now the Press bus and the private cars were off in a race across Miami to the 72nd Street public beach in Miami Beach maybe ten miles away where a big rally was scheduled. The helicopters rode lead and flank cowhand overhead, the cavalcade sped from Opa Locka; not thirty minutes later, band playing, cymbals smashing, Rocky walked a half-block through a crowd on 72nd Street and Collins Avenue, accepting the mob, walking through them to partial deliriums of excitement, a crazy mob for politicking, dressed in bathing suits, bikinis, bathrobes, surfers' trunks, paper dresses, terry cloth shirts, they jammed the pavement in bare feet, sandals, clod-hoppers, bathers screaming, calling out, falling in line around the free Pepsi-Cola wagon, good-natured but never super-excited — the rally was on the edge of the beach after all, and a leaden milky-green sea was pounding an erratic, nervous foam of surf onto the water's-edge of the beach not fifty yards away.

As Rocky moved forward in his brown-gray business suit, murmurs went up everywhere — "There goes the next President of the United States." But the crowd was somehow not huge enough to amplify this sentiment — they looked more like tourists than Republicans — all those votes he would get some day if ever he would capture the nomination. And as he moved forward through the crowd, shaking hands, saying "Hiya, hiya," big grin on his face at the shouts of "We want Rocky," so also at that instant a tall skinny Negro maybe thirty years old leaped in front to shake hands and with the other hand looking for a souvenir, he flipped Rocky's purple handkerchief out of his breast pocket. But Rockefeller showed true Republican blood. A look of consternation for one stricken gap of an instant — *was this an attempt?* — until seeing the handkerchief in the man's hand, the situation was recovered: Rocky strode forward, pulled the handerchief back, gave an admonishing look, as if to say, "Come on, fellow!" and immediately had some cardboard sunglasses pilfered from the same breast pocket by a heated happy hysterical lady tourist with whom he could not wrestle. Kerchief recovered, sunglasses offered up in tribute, he made the speaker's stand — the flatbed of a truck — and the meeting began. *The New York Times* was to report 3,000 people there, perhaps it was half; they cheered everything he said, those who could hear him. The acoustics varied from punko to atrocious, and the reporter circling the crowd heard one plain buxom girl with long brown hair — hippie hints of trinket and dungarees, girl formed out of the very mold of Rockefeller supporters — turn nonetheless sadly to her friend and say, "I can't hear a thing — bye bye." Next step, a sixty-year-old blonde in a bikini with half of a good figure left (breast and buttocks) the flesh around her navel unhappily equal to the flesh around her neck, wearing orange plastic bracelets, gold charm necklace, rings, rhinestone sunglasses, wedgies, painted toes, red hot momma kisser lips, a transistor radio giving rock, and she — whatever she was hearing — out to yell, "Rocky, we want Rocky," beating out the rhythm on one of her two consorts, the one younger than herself; the older, a husband? had a cigar, a paunch, and that benign cool which speaks of holding property in Flatbush in Brooklyn, and putting up with a live-wire wife.

But indeed it must have been reminiscent to Rocky of campaigning on beaches in Brooklyn and Queens, not Coney Island so much as Brighton or Manhattan Beach or Jacob Riis Park: the crowd had the same propinquity, same raucous cheery wise hard middle-class New York smarts — take the measure of everything and still give your cheer because you are there, Murray. Even the smells were the same — orgiastic onions in red hot dog and knish grease, dirty yellow sand — Rocky had to recognize it all, for when he introduced Claude Kirk, "the young alive Governor of Florida" (sole vote for him in the Florida delegation) a smattering of applause came up, a spattering of comment, and one or two spit-spraying lip blats — it was obvious the crowd didn't know Kirk from a Mafia dance-contest winner. So Rocky shifted

gears. "It's a thrill for us from New York to be here, in Florida," he
said, "and half of you must be here from New York." The laugh told
him he was right. A delicate gloom began to come in equal to the first
tendrils of mist over a full moon; God would know what his advisers
had been telling him about the possible power of this open street rally
on the 72nd Street beach — with luck and a mass turnout massive
enough to break all records in category, he could be on his way — a
people's candidate must ride a tidal wave. This was not even a bona fide
breaker. Half of his audience was from New York. Well, he was no
weak campaigner. He kept it going, hitting the hard spots, "The Republican Party must become again a national party, the voice of the poor
and the oppressed." Great cheers for the size of the crowd. "The Republican Party cannot afford parochialism any longer." Smaller cheer,
slight confusion in his audience. "Parochialism" had vague connotations of Roman Catholic schools. Rocky had a good voice, man-to-man
voice, Tracy, Bogart, hints of Gable. When the very rich desert their
patrician holdings on the larynx (invariably because they have gone
into politics) and would come over as regular grips, mill-hands and
populists, they lean dependably into the imitation of movie stars they
have loved. One could psych a big bet that Spencer Tracy was Rocky's
own Number One and would be on the ticket as Vice-President if the
election were held in heaven. It was an honest voice, sincere, masculine,
vibrant, reedy, slightly hoarse, full of honest range-rider muscle, with
injections from the honest throatiness of New York. It was a near-
perfect voice for a campaigner; it was just a question of whether it was
entirely his own or had gravitated to its function, much as the center of
his mouth had concentrated itself away from the corners of his lips.

"And while we're on it," said Rocky, powers of transition not notably
his true preserve, "Senator McCarthy deserves a vote of commendation
for getting the eighteen-year-olds back into politics again" (was this the
Rockefeller who had once tried to shove fallout shelters into every
suburban back yard?) "and when I'm President, I want to pass a bill
letting the eighteen-year-olds vote." Big cheers for this. The kids were
out — everybody was enjoying Rocky — and those with him on the
flatbed truck. Kirk, Rocky's brother, and several former Republican
National Committee Chairmen, came in on the noise machine. In the
background, Miami Mummers wearing pink and orange and yellow
and white and sky-blue satin outfits with net wings and white feathers,
Miami Beach angels playing triangles and glockenspiels piped up tink-

lings and cracklings of sweet sound. Oompah went the oompah drum. "I offer," said Rocky, "a choice. It is . . . victory in November . . . victory for four years." He held up both hands in V for Victory signs.

"Eight years," shouted someone from the crowd.

"I won't quibble," said Rocky with a grin. But then, defeat licking at the center of this projected huge turnout which was finally not half huge enough, he added drily, "The gentleman who just spoke must be from New York."

The rally ended, and a black sky mopped out the sun for ten minutes, hid the cumulus. Rain came in tropical force, water trying to work through that asphalt, reach the jungle beneath. Everyone scattered, those who were dressed not quite in time. The rain hit with a squall. And the luminaries on the flatbed truck went off with Rocky — Leonard Hall, Bill Miller, and Meade Alcorn. It may be worthwhile to take a look at them.

5

The former Republican National Committee Chairmen who were committed to Rockefeller and had been out at Opa Locka were on display earlier in a press conference in the French Room of the Fontainebleau.

A yellow drape hung behind a long table covered in kelly green. On the walls were wall paintings of pink ribbons and pink trumpets in heraldic hearts ten feet high; dirty blue drapes contested dingy wallpaper. A small piece of plaster was off the ceiling in a corner. It was not a room equal to the talent present.

Meade Alcorn first, his presentation hard, driving, full of Wasp authority — his voice had a ring, "I like to articulate it in terms of the greater electibility of Governor Rockefeller" — he had answered in response to a question whether he thought Richard Nixon, if nominated, might lose the election. By all agreement one of the few superb professionals in the Republican Party, Alcorn had a friendly freckled face and sandy hair, black horn-rims, a jaw which could probably crack a lobster claw in one bite, his voice drilled its authority. He was the kind of man who could look you in the eye while turning down your bid for a mortgage. "We don't name the ballot where Rockefeller is going to take it. Could be the fourth, the fifth. Wendell Willkie took it on the sixth. We expect a convention not unlike the one in 1940." He hadn't been National Committee Chairman for nothing; whatever political stand he might be obliged to support came out with the crackling conviction of personal truth.

Then Senator Hugh Scott of Pennsylvania was on. Scott had modest but impeccable aplomb as he explained that since only 12 percent of the delegates had been in San Francisco in 1964, he did not expect bitterness from old Goldwater followers to hurt Rockefeller's chances now. A fine character actor had been lost when Hugh Scott went to politics — he could have played the spectrum from butler to count.

Leonard Hall, heavy, imperturbable, was there with figures — he counted 535 for Nixon, 350 for Rockefeller. He was a man noted for relative accuracy, but was probably structuring his figures today. He gave the impression of an extraordinarily intelligent man, in appearance not unlike Jack E. Leonard doing a straight turn, as if all of Jack E. Leonard's hyper-acute intelligence had gone into the formidable bastions of Squaresville. "My goodness," said Hall at one point, "Rockefeller means the difference for thirty or forty Republican Congressmen between getting elected . . . and being in trouble." He was not about to say Nixon would certainly make them go down. "These Congressmen are human beings. They want to win." But picture Jack E. Leonard talking like that. Some part of conviction was lacking. When Hall said "My goodness" he looked too much like the director of the most impressive funeral establishment in the nation, the kind of man who certainly couldn't think much of you if, my goodness, you wouldn't spring ten thousand smackeroonies for a casket.

There had also been Bill Miller, the man who had run for Vice-President on Barry Goldwater's ticket in '64. Now he was supporting Rockefeller. When asked if he and Goldwater were still friends, he said, "I've promised to go along with Governor Rockefeller, and he has said that if he is not nominated, he will support the convention's choice. Goldwater has said he will work for anybody the convention nominates. So sooner or later, Barry and I will be together again." Miller had the big head, big nose, and little hunched shoulders which are reminiscent of an ex-jockey. He had become popular with the Press during the last Presidential campaign. Becoming convinced somewhere en route that Barry's cause was hopeless, he had spent his time on the Vice-Presidential campaign plane drinking bourbon and playing cards; when the plane came to a stop, he would get out, give his airport speech to the airport rally — usually a small crowd at a small airport — get back in the plane again, his card hand still warm, and pick up the play. Now he was wending his way through trick questions, emphasizing his long continuing relations with Rockefeller, whom he had supported for election four times while Rockefeller indeed had supported him seven times, so no curiosity that he was back of Rocky now. Miller talked in a barking voice full of snap. Where it had once been disagreeable in a formal speech, it was not unattractive here. Maybe all that bourbon and bridge had mellowed him since '64 — he no longer looked like the nastiest yap in town.

To the contrary, he now had all the political oils. He was for Rockefeller because Rockefeller solved problems through action. "You name a problem, and in New York we've got it." So he went on to cite the Governor's fine record in highways and air pollution and conservation. It was hard to know just what he was talking about. Every year the traffic in New York was worse, and the air less possible to breathe, the Hudson River more polluted. It gave a hint of the extra-terrestrial dimension where Rockefeller and his advisers must live. Plans, large projects, huge campaigns, government fundings, mass participation in government, successful prosecution of air pollution, comprehensive surveys of traffic control, people's candidate, public opinion polls — the feather of doubt would whisper that Rockefeller was better suited for the Democrats than the Republicans. There were nuts and bolts and small tools necessary for unscrewing a Republican delegate from a first attachment to a second, and Rockefeller might have nothing smaller to employ than a bulldozer. But on to the Nixon camp.

6

The Orpheum Room in the Hilton Plaza where Herb Klein, Director of Press Relations for Nixon, held his conferences, looked like a public room for small gatherings which had been converted to a surgical theater. The approach was along a red corridor with red carpet, red ceiling, red velvet flock on the walls, and mirrors in gold frames, but the Orpheum Room had gold flock on a cream base in ivy figured wallpaper with heavy gold molding on the ceiling, and a gold and tan figured rug. Two huge glass chandeliers with about 800 prisms in each completed allegiance to the eighteenth century. The twentieth century was a foot away from the chandeliers in the form of a big square aluminum baffle plate flush in the ceiling for air conditioning. The chairs for Press were the ubiquitous brown leatherette sprinkled with gold dust.

The podium was a structure covered with formica processed to look like walnut grain. Behind it hung a shrine-like photograph of Richard Nixon, exhibiting the kind of colors one saw on Jack Kennedy photographs after his assassination; also on pictures of Manolete, Franklin Delano Roosevelt, Abraham Lincoln.

Klein was a slim neat man with a high forehead, a pleasant demeanor — men in public relations are not noted for disagreeable dispositions — and a smile which would have delivered the simile of a cat licking cream if no previous investor of the simile had yet existed. He was claiming 700 votes for Nixon on the first ballot. Since Leonard Hall had insisted not two hours before that his most careful estimates put Nixon at 535, it was obvious — both men revealing no shiver of incertitude — that one of them was a liar.

Since Nixon would not be arriving until Monday, he had little news to offer before introducing Governor John Volpe of Massachusetts, a Republican of Italian extraction who had come into prosperous political life by way of the construction business. Volpe was a self-made man, and looked not unlike a small version of Rockefeller. He was no great orator as he read his prepared speech which declared him all-out for Nixon, indeed he seemed to hire no great speech writers either. "Americans see in Mr. Nixon a leader who can unite this country in an effort that will preserve and enhance our position in the world, while simultaneously providing the needed inspiration and new thoughts required in the next four years." Sock it to 'em, Volpe! His strength was in other places. In concrete. All the while, standing behind him, Herb Klein smiled his happy tabby-cat smile. They made a good pair standing side by side. When he smiled, Herb Klein's narrow eyes became slits. Just after Volpe smiled, his narrow mouth became a slit. It was a modest conference without much news and nothing was disturbed. Afterward came a fashion show: outfits were shown for the Nixon dancers, and the Nixonaires — airline stewardesses based in Miami who were willing or eager to work for Nixon in their spare time. A bevy of good-looking chicks with sharp noses and tight mouths modeled the stuff. They were carefully balanced between blondes — Women for Nixon — wearing sleeveless blue A-line cotton dresses, and several brunettes —

Nixonaires — in orange leatherette vests, white miniskirts, and black and white leatherette jockey caps.

By the next day, when Nixon's daughters arrived, it was obvious that such notion of balance — blondes to share stage with brunettes — had been calculated for many an aspect of his campaign. There were, for instance, two complete bands in the lobby of the Hilton Plaza to celebrate the arrival of his daughters, and one band was white, the other Black. Yet if not for the mezzanine which was inlaid, it will be recollected, with red velvet flock for the walls and red fleur-de-lis for the rugs, the Hilton Plaza could have been converted to a hospital. Even with entertainment, the lobby was relatively bare and colorless. Compared to the Fontainebleau and the Americana it was ascetic. Hints of some future American empire and some future American sterility were in the seed of the architect's conception.

It was filled now of course with the two bands and the Nixon Dancers and Nixonaires and TV cameras and crowds and Nixon workers and a man dressed like Uncle Sam on ten-foot stilts who bore a curious but undeniable resemblance to Senator Eugene McCarthy. The Nixon daughters had come in to pleasant cheers, cries of pleasure from those who could see them in the crowd, the beating of the two bands, and they had passed through the crowd and into the lobby, both lovely-looking girls. The older (who looked younger) was Tricia, gentle, bemused, a misty look to her face, but incontestably a beauty with very blonde hair. She had an extraordinary complexion — one would be forced to describe it with the terminology of the Victorian novel, alabaster and ivory could vie for prominence with peaches and cream. The other daughter, Julia, brown-haired, apple-cheeked, snub-nosed, was healthy, genial, a perfect soubrette for a family comedy on television. She was as American as Corporate Bakeries apple pie. And now engaged to David Eisenhower, grandson of Old Ike. It was an engagement which had caused much bitter chortling and a predictable tightening of the collective mouth when word came to liberal circles. There seemed at the time no limit to Richard Nixon's iniquity. But in fact daughter Julia was a nice-looking girl, and Ike's grandson who looked to be not yet twenty had a pleasant face, more than a hint of innocence in it, not only small-town but near to yokel, redeemed by the friendliest of simple smiles. An ambitious high school dramatics teacher might have picked him to play Billy Budd.

The arrival of the girls and covert scrutiny of them by the reporter

had produced one incontestable back-slapping turn-of-the-century guf-
faw: a man who could produce daughters like that could not be all bad.
The remote possibility of some reappraisal of Richard Nixon was now
forced to enter the works. It was, of course, remote, but the reporter
was determined to be fair to all, and the notion was incontestably there.
Nothing in his prior view of Nixon had ever prepared him to conceive
of a man with two lovely girls. (Since the reporter had four fine daughters of his own, he was not inclined to look on such matters as accident.)
And indeed later that night, the voice (agreeably well-brought-up but
not remarkable) of one of Nixon's daughters was heard for a fragment
of dialogue on radio. No, she was saying, their father had never
spanked them. It was indicated that Mother had been the dis-
ciplinarian. "But then," the girl's voice went on, simple clarity, even
honest devotion in the tone, "we never wanted to displease him. We
wanted to be good." The reporter had not heard a girl make a remark
like that about her father since his own mother had spoken in such
fashion thirty-odd years ago.

Of course the remote contingency of reappraising Nixon had been
kept comfortably remote by the nature of the entertainment provided
in the lobby of the Hilton Plaza after the daughters had made their
entrance and well-regulated escape to some private suite upstairs. The
Nixon Dancers were now entertaining the crowd. Thirty-six adolescent
girls all seemingly between five feet, four inches and five feet, six inches
came out to dance various sorts of cheerleader-type dances. Impossible
to define the steps more neatly, it was some sort of cross between
television entertainment at half-time and working on a farm team for
the Rockettes. Later the girls made an exit in file, in profile, and a clear
count was there to be made in noses. Six of the thirty-six had aquiline
curves, six were straight-nosed, and the other twenty-four had turned-
up buttons at the tip.

Now heard was the white band. There were sixteen of them, about as
good, and about as simple, as a good high school marching band. The
Black band was something else, Eureka Brass Band by name, right out
of Beale Street sixty years ago, ten Negroes in black pants, white shirts
and white yachting caps with black visors did a Dixieland strut up and
around the floor, led by their master, a tall disdainful wizardly old
warlock, a big Black in a big black tuxedo, black felt Homburg on his
head, medals and green sashes and Nixon buttons all over him. He was
no ad for anybody but the most arcane Black Power, he was an old
prince of a witch doctor — insult him at your peril — but the other ten

musicians with their trumpets and snares and assorted brass would prove no pull for Nixon on TV with any Black votes watching, for they were old and meek, naught but elderly Black Southern musicians, a veritable Ganges of Uncle Toms. They had disappeared with Tom Swift and Little Lord Fauntleroy.

7

That evening at the Fontainebleau, on the night before the convention was to begin, the Republicans had their Grand Gala, no Press admitted, and the reporter by a piece of luck was nearly the first to get in. The affair was well-policed, in fact strict in its security, for some of the most important Republican notables would be there, but strolling through the large crowd in the lobby the reporter discovered himself by accident in the immediate wake of Governor Reagan's passage along a channel of security officers through the mob to the doors of the Gala. It was assumed by the people who gave way to the Governor that the reporter must be one of the plainclothesmen assigned to His Excellency's rear, and with a frown here, judicious tightening of his mouth there, look of concern for the Governor's welfare squeezed onto his map, offering a security officer's look superior to the absence of any ticket, he went right in through the ticket-takers, having found time in that passage to observe Governor Reagan and his Lady, who were formally dressed to the hilt of the occasion, now smiling, now shaking hands, eager, tense, bird-like, genial, not quite habituated to eminence, seeking to make brisk but not rude progress through the crowd, and obviously uneasy in the crowd (like most political figures) since a night in June in Los Angeles. It was an expected observation, but Mr. and Mrs. Reagan looked very much like an actor and actress playing Governor and Wife. Still Reagan held himself sort of uneasily about the middle, as if his solar plexus were fragile, and a clout would leave him like a fish on the floor.

Once inside the ballroom, however, the reporter discovered that the Governor had been among the first guests to enter. His own position was therefore not comfortable. Since there were no other guests among whom to mix (nothing but two hundred and forty empty tables with settings for two thousand people, all still to come in) and no cover to conceal him but small potted trees with oranges attached by green wire, since Security might be furious to the point of cop-mania catching him thus early, there was no choice but to take up a stand twenty feet from the door, his legs at parade rest, his arms clasped behind, while he scrutinized the entrance of everybody who came in. Any security officer studying him might therefore be forced to conclude that he belonged to *other* Security. Suffice it, he was not approached in his position near the entrance, and for the next thirty minutes looked at some thousand Republicans coming through the gate, the other thousand entering out of view by an adjacent door.

It was not a crowd totally representative of the power of the Republican Party. Some poor delegates may have been there as guests, and a few other delegates might have chosen to give their annual contribution of $1,000 for husband and wife here ($500 a plate) rather than to some other evening of fund raising for the party, indeed an air of sobriety and quiet dress was on many of the Republicans who entered. There were women who looked like librarians and schoolteachers, there were middle-aged men who looked like they might be out for their one night of the year. The Eastern Establishment was of course present in degree, and powers from the South, West, Midwest, but it was not a gang one could hold up in comparative glitter to an opening at the Met. No, rather, it was modesty which hung over those well-bred subscribers to the Gala.

Still, exceptions noted, they were obviously in large part composed of a thousand of the wealthiest Republicans in the land, the corporate and social power of America was here in legions of interconnection he could not even begin to trace. Of necessity, a measure of his own ignorance came over him, for among those thousand, except for candidates, politicians and faces in the news, there were not ten people he recognized. Yet here they were, the economic power of America (so far as economic power was still private, not public) the family power (so far as position in society was still a passion to average and ambitious Americans) the military power (to the extent that important sword-rattlers and/or patriots were among the company, as well as cadres of corporations not unmarried to the Pentagon) yes, even the spiritual power of America (just so far as Puritanism, Calvinism, conservatism and golf still gave the Wasp an American faith more intense than the faith of cosmopolitans, one-worlders, trade-unionists, Black militants, New Leftists, acid-heads, tribunes of the gay, families of Mafia, political machinists, fixers, swingers, Democratic lobbyists, members of the

Grange, and government workers, not to include the *Weltanschauung* of every partisan in every minority group). No, so far as there was an American faith, a belief, a mystique that America was more than the sum of its constituencies, its trillions of dollars and billions of acres, its constellation of factories, empyrean of communications, mountain transcendant of finance, and heroic of sport, transports of medicine, hygiene, and church, so long as belief persisted that America, finally more than all this, was the world's ultimate reserve of rectitude, final garden of the Lord, so far as this mystique could survive in every American family of Christian substance, so then were the people entering this Gala willy-nilly the leaders of this faith, never articulated by any of them except in the most absurd and taste-curdling jargons of patriotism mixed with religion, but the faith existed in those crossroads between the psyche and the heart where love, hate, the cognition of grace, the all but lost sense of the root, and adoration of America congregate for some.

Their own value was in this faith, the workings of their seed from one generation into the next, their link to the sense of what might be life-force was in the faith. Yes, primitive life was there, and ancestral life, health concealed in their own flesh from towns occupied and once well-settled, from farms which prospered, and frontiers they had — through ancestors — dared to pass. They believed in America as they believed in God — they could not really ever expect that America might collapse and God yet survive, no, they had even gone so far as to think that America was the savior of the world, food and medicine by one hand, sword in the other, highest of high faith in a nation which would bow the knee before no problem since God's own strength was in the die. It was a faith which had flared so high in San Francisco in 1964 that staid old Republicans had come near to frothing while they danced in the aisle, there to nominate Barry, there to nominate Barry. But their hero had gone down to a catastrophe of defeat, blind in politics, impolite in tactics, a sorehead, a fool, a disaster. And if his policies had prevailed to some degree, to the degree of escalating the war in Vietnam, so had that policy depressed some part of America's optimism to the bottom of the decade, for the country had learned an almost unendurable lesson — its history in Asia was next to done, and there was not any real desire to hold armies on that land; worse, the country had begun to wear away inside, and the specter of Vietnam in every American city would haunt the suburb, the terror of a dollar cut loose from

MIAMI AND THE SIEGE OF CHICAGO

every standard of economic anchor was in the news, and some of the best of the youth were mad demented dogs with teeth in the flesh of the deepest Republican faith.

They were a chastened collocation these days. The high fire of hard Republican faith was more modest now, the vision of America had diminished. The claims on Empire had met limits. But it was none-theless uncommon, yes bizarre, for the reporter to stand like an agent of their security as these leaders of the last American faith came through to the Gala, for, repeat: they were in the main not impressive, no, not by the hard eye of New York. Most of them were ill-propor-tioned in some part of their physique. Half must have been, of course, men and women over fifty and their bodies reflected the pull of their character. The dowager's hump was common, and many a man had a flaccid paunch, but the collective tension was rather in the shoulders, in the girdling of the shoulders against anticipated lashings on the back, in the thrust forward of the neck, in the maintenance of the muscles of the mouth forever locked in readiness to bite the tough meat of resis-tance, in a posture forward from the hip since the small of the back was dependably stiff, loins and mind cut away from each other by some abyss between navel and hip.

More than half of the men wore eyeglasses, young with old — the reporter made his count, close as a professional basketball game, and gave up by the time his score was up to Glasses 87, No Glasses 83. You could not picture a Gala Republican who was not clean-shaven by eight A.M. Coming to power, they could only conceive of trying to clean up every situation in sight. And so many of the women seemed victims of the higher hygiene. Even a large part of the young seemed to have faces whose cheeks had been injected with Novocain.

Yet he felt himself unaccountably filled with a mild sorrow. He did not detest these people, he did not feel so superior as to pity them, it was rather he felt a sad sorrowful respect. In their immaculate cleanli-ness, in the somewhat antiseptic odors of their astringent toilet water and perfume, in the abnegation of their walks, in the heavy sturdy moves so many demonstrated of bodies in life's harness, there was the muted tragedy of the Wasp — they were not on earth to enjoy or even perhaps to love so very much, they were here to serve, and serve they had in public functions and public charities (while recipients of their charity might vomit in rage and laugh in scorn), served on opera com-mittees, and served in long hours of duty at the piano, served as the

128

sentinel in concert halls and the pews on the aisle in church, at the desk in schools, had served for culture, served for finance, served for salvation, served for America — and so much of America did not wish them to serve any longer, and so many of them doubted themselves, doubted that the force of their faith could illumine their path in these new modern horror-head times. On and on, they came through the door, the clean, the well-bred, the extraordinarily prosperous, and for the most astonishing part, the almost entirely proper. Yes, in San Francisco in '64 they had been able to be insane for a little while, but now they were subdued, now they were modest, now they were looking for a leader to bring America back to them, their lost America, Jesusland.

"Nelson Rockefeller is out of his mind if he thinks he can take the nomination away from Richard Nixon," the reporter said suddenly to himself. It was the first certitude the convention had given.

8

Still, Rockefeller was trying. He had been mounting a massive offensive for weeks. In speeches which came most often as prepared announcements for television and in full-page advertisements in newspapers all over the country, he had been saturating America with Rockefeller philosophy, paying for it with Rockefeller money, the rhetoric in the style of that Madison Avenue Eminent, Emmet Hughes.

On Vietnam: The country must never again "find itself with a commitment looking for a justification. . . . The war has been conducted without a coherent strategy or program for peace." Of course he had been until recently a hawk with the hawks — like Nixon, he was now a dove of a hawk, a dove of a hawk like all the Republicans but Reagan.

The ads had come with text in 20-point type, 30-point type, larger. "We must assure to all Americans two basic rights: the right to learn and the right to work." (The right to learn would come in mega-universities with lectures pulled in on television and study halls with plastic bucket seats — the right to work? or was it the right to take pride in one's work?)

On Cities: ". . . the confidence that we can rebuild our great cities — making slums of old despair into centers of new hope. . . ."

Or: "I see . . . the welfare concept . . . as a floor below which nobody will be allowed to fall, but with no ceiling to prevent anyone from rising as high as he wants to rise."

It was the best of potency-rhetoric for the thriving liberal center of America where most of the action was, building contracts, federal money for super-highways, youth programs for the slums, *wars* against poverty, bigotry, violence, and hate. (But how did one go to war with hate? "On your knees, mother-fucker!" said the saint.)

Yes, Rockefeller had only to win the nomination and it might take an act of God to keep him from the Presidency. He was the dream candidate for all Democratic voters — they could repudiate Johnson and Humphrey and still have the New Deal, the Fair Deal, Stevenson, Eleanor Roosevelt, Kennedy, Bobby Kennedy, Gene McCarthy, and Folk Rock with Rocky. He would get three-quarters of the Democrats' votes. Of course he would get only one-fourth of the Republicans' votes (the rest would go to Humphrey or Wallace or stay at home) but he would be in, he could unite the country right down that liberal center which had given birth to a Great Society, a war in Vietnam, and a permanent state of police alert in the cities in the summer.

He was like a general who had mounted the most massive offensive of a massive war but had neglected to observe that the enemy was not on his route, and the line of march led into a swamp. Rockefeller took out ads, pushed television, worked with hip musicians and groovy bands (Cannonball Adderley, Lionel Hampton) got out the young at every rally (the adolescents too young to vote) hobnobbed with governors and senators, made the phone calls, hit the high pressure valve (Bill Miller and Meade Alcorn and Leonard Hall and Thruston Morton called in old debts from old friends) hit the hustings in his plane — "Hiya fellow" — did everything but enter the campaign at the right time, fight it out in the primaries, or design his attack for the mollification of Republican fears. He did everything but exercise choice in serving up the best political greens and liver juice for the rehabilitation of Republican pride. In secret he may have detested the Average Republican — it was no secret that same Republican hated him: they had never forgiven each other for his divorce and his remarriage. A man married for thirty-two years should have known all marital misery by then — to smash such a scene spoke to the average Republican of massive instability, no fear of God, an obvious hankering for the orgiastic fats of the liberal center, and no saving secret gifts of hypocrisy — this latter being indispensable, reasons the conservative mind, to prudence and protection in government.

Besides, the sort of passion for a late-entering candidate which can lead a delegate to make a last-minute switch in his choice must have roots in hysteria, and thereby be near to that incandescent condition of the soul when love and/or physical attraction is felt for three or four people at once. Hysteria is not in high demand among Republicans. Their lives have been geared to keep *ménage-à-trois* at a minimum. If love is then sometimes also at a minimum, well, that's all right. Misers can feel vertiginous titillation if they are worked upon for years to give up their coin, their kiss, their delegate's vote. And Nixon had worked on them for many months and just some of those years, you bet! The miser giving up his gift once is the happiest of men — being asked to switch his choice again is the invitation to hysteria — it can only end by sending him to the nut house, the poorhouse, or a school for the whirling dervish.

What Rockefeller needed was delegate votes, not millions of Americans sending good thoughts. There were dreams of repeating Wendell Willkie's sixth ballot in 1940, but those were scandalous military dreams, for Republicans then hated Roosevelt to such distraction they would have nominated any man who had a chance against him, whereas in 1968 their loyalty was to the philosophy of the party — to Republicanism!

Rocky had spent and would spend, it was said, ten million bucks to get the nomination. (One journalist remarked that he would have done better to buy delegates: at $25,000 a delegate, he could have had four hundred.) On Sunday afternoon, there was an opportunity to see how the money was spent. Some rich men are famous for penury — it was Rocky's own grandfather after all who used to pass out the thin dime. But generosity to a rich man is like hysteria to a miser: once entertain it, and there's no way to stop — the bitch is in the house. Having engaged the habit of spending, where was Rocky to quit? After the television came the rallies and the chartered planes; now in Miami, the rented river boats on Island Creek for delegates who wanted an afternoon of booze on an inland waterway yacht; or the parties. Rocky threw open the Americana for a Sunday reception and supper for the New York delegation. On Monday from 5:00 to 7:00 P.M., after Nixon's arrival, he gave a giant reception for all delegates, alternates and Republican leadership. The party jammed the Continental Room and the Grand Ballroom of the Americana, and the numbers could not be counted; 5,000 could have gone through, 6,000, the *Times* estimated 8,000 guests and a cost of $50,000. Half of Miami Beach may have passed through for the free meal and the drinks. On the tables (eight bars, sixteen buffet tables) thousands of glasses were ready with ice cubes; so, too were ready shrimp and cocktail sauce, potted meat balls, turkeys, hams, goulash, aspic, éclairs, pigs in blankets, chicken liver, *pâté de volailles,* vats of caviar (black), ladyfingers, jelly rings, celebration cakes — where were the crepes suzette? What wonders of the American gut. On the bandstand in each room, a band; in the Continental Room, dark as a night club (indeed a night club on any other night) Lionel Hampton was vibrating a beat right into the rich middle octave of a young Black singer giving up *soul* for Rocky. "We want Rocky," went the chant. *Sock . . . sock . . .* went the beat, driving, lightly hypnotic, something reminiscent in the tempo of shots on the rim of the snare when the drummer backs the stripper's bumps. But Rocky wasn't coming out now, he was somewhere else, so members of his family, his older children and wives of his older children and sister and Helen Hayes and Billy Daniels were out on the stage with Hampton and the happy young Black singer snapping his fingers and the happy Black girl singer full of soul and zap and breasts!

Everybody was eating, drinking — young Rockefeller family up there on happiness beat, arms locked, prancing, natives of Miami Beach on the floor cheering it up, America ready to truck its happiness right out on One World Highway One.

And here and there a delegate, or a delegate's family from Ohio or Colorado or Illinois, delegate's badge on the lapel, mixed look of curiosity, wonder, and pleasure in the eye: "If the man wants to throw his money around like that, well, we're not here to stop him!" And the pleasure in the eye is reserved for the thought of telling the home folks about the swinishness, sottishness, and *waste* expenditure of the occasion. "They were spilling half the drinks they were in such a hurry to serve them up."

And in the corridor between the Caribbean Room and the Ballroom a jam of guests. The line would not move. Trapped in the rush hour again. In the First World War, Marshal Haig used to send a million men over the top in a frontal attack. One hundred yards would be gained, one hundred thousand casualties would be the price. It was possible Nelson Rockefeller was the Marshal Haig of presidential hopefuls. Rich men should not surround themselves with other rich men if they want to win a war.

9

Nixon had come in earlier that day. A modestly large crowd, perhaps six hundred at the entrance to the Miami Hilton, two bands playing "Nixon's the One," and the Nixonettes and the Nixonaires, good clean blonde and brown-haired Christian faces, same two Negresses, a cluster of 2,000 balloons going up in the air, flings of color, thin dots of color, and Nixon himself finally in partial view at the center of the semicircle of cameras held overhead. Just a glimpse: he has a sunburn — his forehead is bright pink. Then he has made it into the hotel, pushed from behind, hands in hand-shakes from the front, hair recognizable — it is curlier than most and combed in roller coaster waves, not unreminiscent of the head of hair on Gore Vidal. (But where was Nixon's Breckinridge?)

The crowd had been enthusiastic without real hurly-burly or hint of pandemonium. More in a state of respectful enthusiasm, and the hot patriotic cupidity to get near the man who is probably going to be the next American President. The office, not the man, is moving them. And Nixon passes through them with the odd stick-like motions which are so much a characteristic of his presence. He is like an actor with good voice and hordes of potential, but the despair of his dramatic coach (again it is High School). "Dick, you just got to learn how to move." There is something almost touching in the way he does it, as if sensitive flesh winces at the way he must expose his lack of heart for being warm and really winning in crowds, and yet he is all heart to perform his task, as if the total unstinting exercise of the will must finally deliver every last grace, yes, he is like a missionary handing out Bibles among the Urdu. Christ, they are filthy fellows, but deserving of the *touch*. No, it is not so much that he is a bad actor (for Nixon in a street crowd is *radiant* with emotion to reach across the prison pen of his own artificial moves and deadly reputation and show that he is sincere) it is rather that he grew up in the worst set of schools for actors in the world — white gloves and church usher, debating team, Young Republicanism, captive of Ike's forensic style — as an actor, Nixon thinks his work is to signify. So if he wants to show someone that he likes them, he must smile; if he wishes to show disapproval of Communism, he frowns; America must be strong, out goes his chest. Prisoner of old habit or unwitting of a new kind of move, he has not come remotely near any modern moves, he would not be ready to see that the young love McCarthy because he plays forever against his line. "If I'm nominated, I can't see how I'd possibly fail to win," says McCarthy in a gloomy modest mild little voice, then his eyes twinkle at the myriad of consequences to follow: raps in the newspaper about his arrogance, the sheer delicious zaniness of any man making any claim about his candidacy — yes, many people love McCarthy because his wan wit is telling them, "We straddle ultimates: spitballs and eternals."

Nixon has never learned this. He is in for the straight sell. No wonder he foundered on "America can't stand pat."

But the reporter is obsessed with him. He has never written anything nice about Nixon. Over the years he has saved some of his sharpest comments for him, he has disliked him intimately ever since his Checkers speech in 1952 — the kind of man who was ready to plough sentimentality in such a bog was the kind of man who would press any button to manipulate the masses — and there was large fear in those days of buttons which might ignite atomic wars. Nixon's presence on television had inspired emotions close to nausea. There had been a gap between the man who spoke and the man who lived behind the speaker which offered every clue of schizophrenia in the American public if they failed to recognize the void within the presentation. Worse. There was unity only in the way the complacency of the voice matched the complacency of the ideas. It was as if Richard Nixon were proving that a man who had never spent an instant inquiring whether family, state, church, and flag were ever wrong could go on in secure steps, denuded of risk, from office to office until he was President.

In 1962 the reporter had given a small celebration for the collapse of Nixon after his defeat in the election for Governor of California. To the Press: "Well, gentlemen," the defeated man had said, "you won't have Nixon to kick any more." It had seemed the absolute end of a career. Self-pity in public was as irreversible as suicide. In 1964, Nixon had stood about in the wings while Barry was nominated. Now, in 1968, he was on the edge of becoming the nominee. It was obvious something was wrong with the reporter's picture. In his previous conception of Richard Nixon's character there had been no room for a comeback. Either the man had changed or one had failed to recognize some part of his character from the beginning. So there was interest, even impatience to hear him speak.

He was not having a press conference, however, on the day of his arrival. That would wait until the next morning at 8:15. Then, he would face the Press.

10

The room filled slowly. By the time Nixon began, it was apparent that 500 seats had been an excessive estimate. Perhaps half of them were filled, certainly no more than two-thirds. It was nonetheless a large press conference. Nixon came in wearing a quiet blue-gray suit, white shirt, black and blue close-figured tie, black shoes, and no handkerchief for the breast pocket. He stepped up on the dais diffidently, not certain whether applause would be coming or not. There was none. He stood there, looked quietly and warily at the audience, and then said that he was ready for questions.

This would be his sole press conference before the nomination. He was of course famous for his lack of sparkling good relation with the Press, he had in fact kept his publicity to a functional minimum these past few months. The work of collecting delegates had been done over the last four years, particularly over the last two. Their allegiance had been confirmed the last six months in his primary victories. He had no longer anything much to gain from good interviews, not at least until his nomination was secured; he had everything to lose from a bad interview. A delegate who was slipping could slide further because of an ill-chosen remark.

To the extent that the Press was not Republican, and certainly more than half, privately, were not, he would have few friends and more than a few determined enemies. Even among the Republicans he could expect a better share of the Press to go to Rockefeller. Even worse, for the mood of this conference, he did not, in comparison with other political candidates, have many reporters who were his personal friends. He was not reputed to smoke or drink so he did not have drinking buddies as Johnson once had, and Goldwater, and Bill Miller, and Humphrey; no brothel legends attached to him, and no outsize admiration to accompany them; no, the Press was a necessary tool to him, a tool he had been obliged to employ for more than twenty years but he could not pretend to be comfortable in his use of the tool, and the tool (since it was composed of men) resented its employment.

Probably Nixon had agreed to this conference only to avoid the excess of bad feeling which no meeting with the Press would be likely to cause. Still, this was an operation where his best hope was to minimize the loss. So he had taken the wise step of scheduling the conference at 8:15 in the morning, a time when his worst enemies, presumably the heavy drinkers, free lovers, and free spenders on the Reagan Right and Far Left of the press corps, would probably be asleep in bed or here asleep on their feet.

Nonetheless his posture on the stage, hands to his side or clasped before him, gave him the attentive guarded look of an old ball player — like Rabbit Maranville, let us say, or even an old con up before Parole Board. There was something in his carefully shaven face — the dark jowls already showing the first overtones of thin gloomy blue at this early hour — some worry which gave promise of never leaving him, some hint of inner debate about his value before eternity which spoke of precisely the sort of improvement that comes upon a man when he shifts in appearance from looking like an under-taker's assistant to looking like an old con seriously determined to go respectable. The Old Nixon, which is to say the young Nixon, used to look, on clasping his hands in front of him, like a church usher (of the variety who would twist a boy's ear after removing him from church). The older Nixon before the Press now — the *new* Nixon — had finally acquired some of the dignity of the old athlete and the old con — he had taken punishment, that was on his face now, he knew the detailed schedule of pain in a real loss, there was an attentiveness in his eyes which gave offer of some knowledge of the abyss, even the kind of gentleness which ex-drunkards attain after years in AA. As he an-swered questions, fielding them with the sure modest moves of an old shortstop who hits few homers but supports the team on his fielding (what sorrow in the faces of such middle-aged shortstops!) so now his modesty was not without real dignity. Where in Eisenhower days his attempts at modesty had been as offensive as a rich boy's arrogance, for he had been so transparently contemptuous of the ability of his au-dience to *witness* him, now the modesty was the product of a man who, at worst, had grown from a bad actor to a surprisingly good actor, or from an unpleasant self-made man — outrageously rewarded with luck — to a man who had risen and fallen and been able to rise again, and so conceivably had learned something about patience and the com-passion of others.

When the reporter was younger, he might have said, "Nixon did not rise again; they raised him; if a new Nixon did not exist, they would have had to invent him." But the reporter was older now — presumably he knew more about the limits of the ruling class for inventing what they needed; he had learned how little talent or patience they had. Yes, at a certain point they might have decided, some of them at any rate, to dress Richard Nixon for the part again, but no one but Nixon had been able to get himself up from the political deathbed to which his failure in California had consigned him. He was here, then, answering questions in a voice which was probably closer to his own than it had ever been.

And some of the answers were not so bad. Much was Old Nixon, extraordinarily adroit at working both sides of a question so that both halves of his audience might be afterward convinced he was one of them. ("While homosexuality is a perversion punishable by law, and an intolerable offense to a law-abiding community, it is life-giving to many of those who are in need of it," he might have said if ever he had addressed a combined meeting of the Policemen's Benevolent Association and the Mattachine Society.) So he worked into the problem of Vietnam by starting at A and also by starting at Z which he called a "two-pronged approach." He was for a negotiated settlement, he was for maintaining military strength because that would be the only way to "reach negotiated settlement of the war on an honorable basis." Later he was to talk of negotiations with "the next superpower, Communist China." He spoke patiently, with clarity, gently, not badly but for an unfortunate half-smile pasted to his face. The question would come, and he would back-hand it with his glove or trap it; like all politicians he had a considered answer for every question, but he gave structure to his answers, even a certain relish for their dialectical complexity. Where once he had pretended to think in sentimentalities and slogans, now he held the question up, worked over it, deployed it, amplified it, corrected its tendency, offered an aside (usually an attempt to be humorous) revealed its contradiction, and then declared a statement. With it all, a sensitivity almost palpable to the reservations of the Press about his character, his motive, and his good intention. He still had no natural touch with them, his half-smile while he listened was unhappy, for it had nowhere to go but into a full smile and his full smile was as false as false teeth, a pure exercise of will. You could all but see the signal pass from his brain to his jaw. SMILE said the signal, and so he flashed teeth in a painful kind of joyous grimace which spoke of some shrinkage in the liver, or the gut, which he would have to repair afterward by other medicine than good-fellowship. (By winning the Presidency, perhaps.) He had always had the ability to violate his own nature absolutely if that happened to be necessary to his will — there had never been anyone in American life so resolutely phony as Richard Nixon, nor anyone so transcendentally successful by such means — small wonder half the electorate had regarded him for years as equal to a disease. But he was less phony now, *that was the miracle,* he had moved from a position of total ambition and total alienation from his own person (at the time of Checkers, the dog speech) to a place now where he was halfway conciliated with his own self. As he spoke, he kept going in and out of focus, true one instant, phony the next, then quietly correcting the false step.

Question from the Press: *You emphasized the change in the country and abroad. Has this led you to change your thinking in any shape or form specifically?*

Answer: *It certainly has.* (But he was too eager. Old Nixon was always ready to please with good straight American boyhood enthusiasm. So he tacked back, his voice throttled down.) *As the facts change, any intelligent man* (firm but self-deprecatory, he is including the Press with himself) *does change his approaches to the problems.* (Now sharp awareness of the next Press attitude.) *It does not mean that he is an opportunist.* (Now modestly, reasonably.) *It means only that he is a pragmatist, a realist, applying principles to the new situations.* (Now he will deploy some of the resources of his answer.) *For example . . . in preparing the acceptance speech I hope to give next Thursday, I was reading over my acceptance speech in 1960, and I thought then it was, frankly, quite a good speech. But I realize how irrelevant much of what I said in 1960 in foreign affairs was to the problems of today.* (The admission was startling. The Old Nixon was never wrong. Now, he exploited the shift in a move to his political left, pure New Nixon.) *Then the Communist world was a monolithic world. Today it is a split world, schizophrenic, with . . . great diversity . . . in Eastern Europe* (a wholesome admission for anyone who had labored in John Foster Dulles' world) . . . *after an era of confrontation . . . we now enter an era of negotiations with the Soviet Union.*

While he was never in trouble with the questions, growing surer and surer of himself as he went on, the tension still persisted between his actual presence as a man not altogether alien to the abyss of a real problem, and the political practitioner of his youth, that snake-oil salesman who was never back of any idea he sold, but always off to the side where he might observe its effect on the sucker. The New Nixon groped and searched for the common touch he had once been able to slip into the old folks with the ease of an incubus on a spinster. Now he tried to use slang, put quotes around it with a touching, almost pathetic, reminder of Nice-Nellyism, the inhibition of the good clean church upbringing of his youth insisting on exhibiting itself, as if he were saying with a YMCA slick snicker, "After we break into slang, there's always the danger of the party getting *rough*." It was that fatal prissiness which must have driven him years ago into all the militaristic muscle-bending witch-hunting foam-rubber virilities of the young Senator and the young Vice-President. So, now he talked self-consciously of how the members of his staff, counting delegates, were "playing what we call 'the strong game.'" SMILE said his brain. FLASH went the teeth. But his voice seemed to give away that, whatever they called it, they probably didn't call it "the strong game," or if they did, *he* didn't. So he framed little phrases. Like "a leg-up." Or "my intuition, my 'gut feelings,' so to speak." Deferential air followed by SMILE — FLASH. Was it possible that one of the secrets of Old Nixon was that his psyche had been trapped in rock-formations, nay, geological strata of Sunday school inhibitions? Was it even possible that he was a good man, not a bad man, a good man who had been trapped by an early milieu whose habits had left him with such innocence about three-quarters of the world's experience that he had become an absolute monster of opportunism about the quarter he comprehended all too well? Listening to Nixon now, studying his new modesty, it was impossible to tell whether he was a serious man on the path of returning to his own true seriousness, out to unite the nation again as he promised with every remark: "Reconciliation of the races is a primary objective of the United States," or whether the young devil had reconstituted himself into a more consummate devil, Old Scratch as a modern Abe Lincoln of modesty.

Question from the Press: *A little less than six years ago, after your defeat for the Governorship of California, you announced at the ensuing press conference that that was going to be your last news conference. Could you recall for us this morning two or three of the most important points in your own thinking which made you reverse that statement and now reach for political office on the highest level?*

Answer: *Had there not been the division of the Republican Party in 1964 and had there not been the vacuum of leadership that was created by that division and by that defeat, I would not be here today. . . . I believe that my travels around the country and the world in this period of contemplation and this period of withdrawal from the political scene* (some dark light of happiness now in his eye, as if withdrawal and contemplation had given him the first deep pleasures, or perhaps the first real religious pleasures of his life) *in which I have had a chance to observe not only the United States but the world, has led me to the conclusion that returning to the arena was something that I should do* (said almost as if he had heard a voice in some visitation of the night) — *not that I consider myself to be an indispensable man.* (Said agreeably in a relaxed tone as if he had thought indeed to the bottom of this and had found the relaxation of knowing he was not indispensable, an absurd vanity if one stares at Nixon from without, but he had been Vice-President before he was forty, and so had had to see himself early, perhaps much too early, as a man of destiny. Now, reservation underlined, he could continue.) *But something that I should do* (go for the Presidency) *because this is the time I think when the man and the moment in history come together.* (An extraordinary admission for a Republican, with their Protestant detestation of philosophical deeps or any personification of history. With one remark, Nixon had walked into the oceans of Marx, Spengler, Heidegger, and Tolstoy; and Dostoevski and Kierkegaard were in the wings. Yes, Richard Nixon's mind had entered the torture chambers of the modern consciousness!)

I have always felt that a man cannot seek the Presidency and get it simply because he wants it. I think that he can seek the Presidency and obtain it only when the Presidency requires what he may have to offer (the Presidency was then a mystical seat, mystical as the choice of a woman's womb) *and I have had the feeling* (comfortably pleasant and modest again — no phony Nixon here) *and it may be a presumptuous feeling, that because of the vacuum of leadership in the Republican Party, because of the need for leadership particularly qualified in foreign affairs, because I have known not only the country, but the world as a result of my travels, that now time* (historical-time — the very beast of the mystic!) *requires that I re-enter the arena.* (Then he brought out some humor. It was not great humor, but for Nixon it was curious and not indelicate.) *And incidentally, I have been very willing to do so.* (Re-enter the arena.) *I am not being drafted. I want to make that very clear. I am very willing to do so. There has never been a draft in Miami in August anyway.* (Nice laughter from the Press — he has won them by a degree. Now he is on to finish the point.) . . . *I believe that if my judgment — and my intuition, my "gut feelings" so to speak, about America and American political tradition — is right, this is the year that I will win.*

The speech had come in the middle of the conference and he kept fielding questions afterward, never wholly at ease, never caught in trouble, mild, firm, reasonable, highly disciplined — it was possible he was one of the most disciplined men in America. After it was over, he walked down the aisle, and interviewers gathered around him, although not in great number. The reporter stood within two feet of Nixon at one point but had not really a question to ask which could be answered abruptly. "What, sir, would you say is the state of your familiarity with the works of Edmund Burke?" No, it was more to get a sense of the candidate's presence, and it was a modest presence, no more formidable before the immediate Press in its physical aura than a floorwalker in a department store, which is what Old Nixon had often been called, or worse — Assistant Mortician. It was probable that bodies did not appeal to him in inordinate measure, and a sense of the shyness of the man also appeared — shy after all these years! — but Nixon must have been habituated to loneliness after all those agonies in the circus skin of Tricky Dick. Had he really improved? The reporter caught himself hoping that Nixon had. If his physical presence inspired here no great joy nor even distrust, it gave the sense of a man still entrenched in toils of isolation, as if only the office of the Presidency could be equal (in the specific density of its importance) to the labyrinthine delivery of the natural man to himself. Then and only then might he know the strength of his own hand and his own moral desire. It might even be a measure of the not-entirely dead promise of America if a man as opportunistic as the early Nixon could grow in reach and comprehension and stature to become a leader. For, if that were possible in these bad years, then all was still possible, and the country not stripped of its blessing. New and marvelously complex improvement of a devil, or angel-in-chrysalis, or both — good and evil now at war in the man, Nixon was at least, beneath the near to hermetic boredom of his old presence, the most interesting figure at the convention, or at least so the reporter had decided by the end of the press conference that Tuesday in the morning. Complexities upon this vision were to follow.

11

The next press conference to be noted was in the French Room of the Fontainebleau for 11:00 A.M. The Reverend Ralph D. Abernathy, former assistant to the Reverend Martin Luther King, Jr., and leader of the Poor People's March after King had been assassinated, was scheduled to read a statement and answer questions. While the assembly was nowhere near so large as Nixon's, close to a hundred reporters must nonetheless have appeared, a considerable number of Negroes among them, and then proceeded to wait. Abernathy had not shown up. About fifteen minutes past the hour, another Negro came to the podium and said that the Reverend was on his way, and could be expected in a few minutes.

The gossip was livelier. "We had to look for him in five hotels," said a Black reporter to some other members of the Press, and there was a mental picture of the leader waking heavily, the woes of race, tension, unfulfilled commitment, skipped promises, and the need for militant effort in the day ahead all staring down into whatever kind of peace had been reached the night before in the stretch before sleep.

Still it was unduly irritating to have to wait at a press conference, and as the minutes went by and annoyance mounted, the reporter became aware after a while of a curious emotion in himself, for he had not ever felt it consciously before — it was a simple emotion and very unpleasant to him — he was getting tired of Negroes and their rights. It was a miserable recognition, and on many a count, for if he felt even a hint this way, then what immeasurable tides of rage must be loose in America itself? Perhaps it was the atmosphere of the Republican convention itself, this congregation of the clean, the brisk, the orderly, the efficient. A reporter who must attempt to do his job, he had perhaps committed himself too completely to the atmosphere as if better to comprehend the subterranean character of what he saw on the surface, but in any event having passed through such curious pilgrimage — able to look at Richard Nixon with eyes free of hatred! — it was almost as if he resented the presence of Abernathy now (or the missing Abernathy) as if the discomfort of his Black absence made him suddenly contemplate the rotting tooth and ulcerated gum of the white patient. What an obsession was the Negro to the average white American by now. Every time that American turned in his thoughts to the sweetest object of contemplation in his mind's small town bower, nothing less than America the Beautiful herself — that angel of security at the end of every alley — then *there* was the face of an accusing rioting Black right in the middle of the dream — smack in the center of the alley — and the obsession was hung on the hook of how to divide the guilt, how much to the white man, how much to the dark? The guiltiest man alive would work around the clock if he could only assign proportions to his guilt; but not to know if one was partially innocent or very guilty had to establish an order of paralysis. Since obsessions dragoon our energy by endless repetitive contemplations of guilt we can neither measure nor forget, political power of the most frightening sort was obviously waiting for the first demagogue who would smash the obsession and free the white man of his guilt. Torrents of energy would be loosed, yes, those same torrents which Hitler had freed in the Germans when he exploded their ten-year obsession with whether they had lost the war through betrayal or through material weakness. Through betrayal, Hitler had told them: Germans were actually strong and good. The consequences would never be counted.

Now if suburban America was not waiting for Georgie Wallace, it might still be waiting for Super-Wallace. The thought persisted, the ugly thought persisted that despite all legitimate claims, all burning claims, all searing claims, despite the fundamental claim that America's wealth, whiteness, and hygiene had been refined out of the most powerful molecules stolen from the sweat of the Black man, still the stew of the Black revolution had brought the worst to surface with the best, and if the Black did not police his own house, he would be destroyed and some of the best of the white men with him, and here — here was the sleeping festering hair of his outrage now that Abernathy was scandalously late in this sweaty room, over-heated by the hot TV camera lights, the waiting bodies, yes, the secret sleeping hair of this anti-Black fury in himself was that he no longer knew what the Black wanted — was the Black man there to save mankind from the cancerous depredations of his own white civilization, or was the Black so steeped in his curse that he looked forward to the destruction of the bread itself? Or worst of all, and like an advance reconnaissance scout of the armies of the most quintessential bigotry, one soldier from that alien army flung himself over the last entrenchment, stood up to die, and posed the question: "How do you know the Black man is not Ham, son of Evil? How do you really know?" and the soldier exploded a defense works in the reporter's brain, and bitterness toward Negroes flowed forth like the blood of the blown-up dead: over the last ten years if he had had fifty friendships with Negroes sufficiently true to engage a part of his heart, then was it ten or even five of those fifty which had turned out well? Aware of his own egocentricity, his ability to justify his own actions through many a strait gate, still it seemed to him that for the most part, putting color to the side — if indeed that were ever permissible — the fault, man to man, had been his less often, that he had looked through the catechism of every liberal excuse, had adopted

143

the blame, been ready to give blessing and forgive, and had succeeded merely in deadening the generosity of his heart. Or was he stingier than he dreamed, more lacking in the true if exorbitant demand for compassion without measure, was the Black liberty to exploit the white man without measure, which he had claimed for the Black so often, "If I were a Negro, I'd exploit everything in sight," was this Black liberty he had so freely offered finally too offensive for him to support? He was weary to the bone of listening to Black cries of Black superiority in sex, Black superiority in beauty, Black superiority in war . . . the claims were all too often uttered by Negroes who were not very black themselves. And yet dread and the woe of some small end came over him at the thought itself — it was possible the reporter had influenced as many Black writers as any other white writer in America, and to turn now . . . But he was so heartily sick of listening to the tyranny of soul music, so bored with Negroes triumphantly late for appointments, so depressed with Black inhumanity to Black in Biafra, so weary of being sounded in the subway by Black eyes, so despairing of the smell of booze and pot and used-up hope in blood-shot eyes of Negroes bombed at noon, so envious finally of that liberty to abdicate from the long year-end decade-drowning yokes of work and responsibility that he must have become in some secret part of his flesh a closet Republican — how else account for his inner, "Yeah man, yeah, go!" when fat and flatulent old Republicans got up in Convention Hall to deliver platitudes on the need to return to individual human effort. Yes, he was furious at Abernathy for making him wait these crucial minutes while the secret stuff of his brain was disclosed to his mind.

Abernathy came in about forty minutes late, several other Negroes with him, his press secretary, Bernard Lee, wearing a tan suede collarless jacket, sullen and composed behind an evil-looking pair of dark sunglasses, possessor of hostility which seemed to say, "I got the right, man, to look at you from behind these shades, but you deserve no chance, man, to look at me."

Abernathy was of different stuff, deep, dreamy, sly, bemused — one could not detect if he were profoundly melancholy, or abominably hung over. He spoke in a measured slow basso, slow almost beyond measure, operatic in his echoes, but everything he said sounded like *recitatif* for he seemed to read his statement with more attention for the music of the language than the significance of the words. "If the Republican Party can afford this lavish convention, and the Administration can spend billions of dollars in a disastrous war, and America can subsidize unproductive farms and prosperous industries, surely we can meet the modest demands of the Poor People's Campaign," he read, and the logic was powerful, the demands well nailed to the mast, but his voice lingered on "lavish" as if he were intrigued with the relation of sounds to palpable luxuries he had known and glimpsed, "disastrous" appealed to him for its sibilants as though he were watching some scythe of wind across a field, so "subsidize" was a run of the voice up and down three steps, and "unproductive" hung like the echo of a stalactite. He was a man from Mars absolutely fascinated with the resonance of earthly sound.

He had begun by apologizing to the Press for being late, and had said this in so deep and gracious a voice that pools of irritability were swabbed up immediately, but then he trod over this first good move immediately by saying, "Of course, I understand much of the convention is running behind schedule." The one indisputable virtue of the convention hitherto had been the promptitude of each event — how casual and complacent, how irresponsibly attracted to massacre! that he must issue the one accusation all courts would find unjustified.

But the reporter was soon caught up in trying to form an opinion of Abernathy. He was no equal, it was unhappily true to see, of Martin Luther King. The reporter had met that eminent just once: King in a living room had a sweet attentive gravity which endeared him to most, for he listened carefully, and was responsive when he spoke. He had the presence of a man who would deal with complexity by absorbing its mood, and so solve its contradiction by living with it, an abstract way of saying that he comprehended issues by the people who embodied them, and so gave off a sense of social comfort with his attendance in a room. Abernathy had no such comfort. A plump, badgered, perhaps bewildered man, full of obvious prides and scars and wounds, one could not tell if he were in part charlatan, mountebank, or merely elevated to monumental responsibility too early. But his presence gave small comfort because he was never in focus. One did not know if he were strong or weak, powerfully vibrant and containing himself, or drenched in basso profundos of gloom. "Poor people," he intoned, with his disembodied presentation, "no longer will be unseen, unheard, and unrepresented. We are here to dramatize the *plight* of poor people ..." — his voice went off on a flight of reverberation along the hard "i" of plight. Later, he asked for "control by all people of their own local communities and their own personal destinies," incontestable as a democratic demand, but no fire in the voice, no power to stir, more an

145

intimation of gloom in the caverns of his enriched tone as if he must push upon a wagon which would never mount his hill, so he went off again on "communities" — the hard "u" concealed certain new mysteries of the larynx — and relations to re*mun*eration. He ended by saying, "Part of our Mule Train will be here on Miami Beach in front of this hotel and Convention Hall to dramatize *poverty*" — he stated the word as if it were the name of a small town — "in this beautiful city of luxury."

In the questioning, he was better. Asked if he considered Ronald Reagan a friend of the Blacks, Abernathy smiled slowly and said with ministerial bonhomie, "Well, he may have *some* friends. . . ." Queried about the failure of the Poor People's March on Washington, he offered a stern defense, spoke of how every campaign of the Southern Christian Leadership Conference had been described as a failure, an obvious cuff at those who had once described King's work as failure, and then for a moment he rose above the dull unhappy scandals of Resurrection City, the mess, the breakdowns of sanitation, the hoodlumism, and the accusations by his own that some had lived in hotels while they had been squalid in tents, and spoke of what had been gained, funds pried loose from the government "to the tune of some many millions," he said in his musical voice, and named the figure, more than 200 million, and the fact of the continuation of the Poor People's Campaign, and the sense came again of the painful drudgery of the day to day, the mulish demands of the operation, the gloom of vast responsibility and tools and aids and lieutenants he could count on even less than himself, and the reporter, as though washed in bowls of his own bile, was contrite a degree and went off to have lunch when the conference was done, a little weary of confronting the mystery of his own good or ill motive.

Of course, having lunch, the reporter, to his professional shame, had not the wit to go looking for it, so here is a quotation from Thomas A. Johnson of *The New York Times* concerning the immediate aftermath of Abernathy's appearance:

> When the news conference ended about 12:30 P.M., 65 members of the Poor People's Campaign, dressed in straw hats and blue work shirts, entered the lobby of the Fontainebleau Hotel.
> With raised fists, they greeted Mr. Abernathy with shouts of "Soul Power! Soul Power!"
> Convention delegates, few of whom are Negroes, crowded around. In the background, two white girls dressed in red and blue

tights, paraded through the hall singing "When Ronnie Reagan comes marching in," to the tune of "When the saints come marching in."

The Negro demonstrators would not be interrupted, however.

Thirteen-year-old James Metcalf of Marks, Miss., wearing an army jungle fatigue jacket that came down to his knees led the group in a chant.

"I may be black," he shouted.

"But I am somebody," the demonstrators responded.

"I may be poor."

"But I am somebody."

"I may be hungry."

"But I am somebody."

It was a confrontation the reporter should not have missed. Were the Reagan girls livid or triumphant? Were the Negro demonstrators dignified or raucous or self-satisfied? It was a good story but the *Times* was not ready to encourage its reporters in the thought that there is no history without nuance.

12

After lunch, in a belated attempt to catch up with the Governor of California and the direction of his campaign, the reporter had gone up to one of the top floors of the Deauville where Mrs. Reagan was scheduled to have a conference at 2:30 P.M., indeed the listing in the National Committee News had stated that the Press was requested to be present by 2:15, but embarrassment prevailed in the high headquarters of the Deauville, for Mrs. Reagan was not there and could not be found: the word given out was that she had not been informed. The inevitable deduction was that no one in his headquarters had read the Schedule for the day, and the Press was disassembled with apologies by an attractive corn-fed blonde young lady possessing a piggie of a turned-up nose and the delicate beginning of a double chin. Her slimness of figure suggested all disciplines of diet. The young lady had been sufficiently attractive for the Press to forgive much, but a few of the more European journalists were forced to wonder if the most proficient of performances had been presented here by representatives of the man who cried out, "What is obviously needed is not *more* government, but better government. . . ."

At any rate it was time to catch up with Nixon again. It was not that

Nixon's activities attracted the reporter's hoarded passion, it was more that there was little else which puzzled him. If he had been more of a reporter (or less of one) he would have known that the Reagan forces were pushing an all-out attack to pry, convert, cozen, and steal Southern delegates from Nixon, and that the Nixon forces were responding with a counter-offensive which would yet implicate their choice of Vice-President, but the reporter worked like a General who was far from the front — if he could not hear the sound of cannon, he assumed the battle was never high. Nothing could have convinced him on this particular intolerably humid afternoon that Nixon's forces were in difficulty, and perhaps he was right, perhaps the lack of any echo of such strife in the lobbies of the Deauville or the Hilton was true sign of the issue, and the long shadows of history would repeat that the verdict was never in doubt.

The reporter was off at any rate to witness the reception for delegates in the same American Scene of the Hilton where Nixon had had his press conference early that morning, and if one was interested in the science of comparative political receptions, the beginning of all such study was here. As many as eight thousand people had ganged through the aisles and banquet rooms and exits of the Americana when Rockefeller had had his party, and that, it may be remembered, was a bash where the glamour was thrown at a man with the cole slaw, and the bottom of every glass the bartender handled was wet, the caviar on the buffet table crawled along the cloth and plopped to the floor. Here in the comparative stateliness of the Hilton — only God could save this mark! — not twenty-two hours later, the Nixon forces were showing how a reception for Republican delegates should be run. If a thousand men and women were waiting outside, jammed in the lobby and the approaches to the stairs, and if the resultant theater-line, six and eight people thick, inched up the stairs at a discouraging slow rate, there was consolation at the top for they were let through a narrow door, two by two, and there advanced behind a cord which ran around a third of the circular curve of the room to move forward at last onto a small dais where Mr. and Mrs. Nixon were receiving, there to be greeted individually by each of them with particular attention, and on from that eminence to the center of the room where a bar was ready to give a drink and food to be picked up from a buffet table, turkey, ham, a conventional buffet, a string orchestra.

Perhaps two thousand people went through in the hours from three to six, probably it was less, for Nixon spent five or ten or fifteen seconds with each delegate or couple who passed by. Perhaps the invitations had been restricted to those delegates who would vote for him or leaned toward his candidacy. No matter how, there were not too many to handle, just the largest number consonant with the problem which was: how to convert a mass of delegates and wives and children back to that sense of importance with which they had left their hometown.

Nixon knew how to do it. Here was Nixon at his very best. He had not spent those eight years in harness, highest flunky in the land, aide-de-camp to a five-star General, now President, who had been given such service in his NATO days that no new servant could ever please him, yes, Nixon had not put in his apprenticeship as spiritual butler to the Number One representative of the High Beloved here on earth without learning how to handle a Republican line of delegates by ones and twos.

This was no line like the wealthy Republicans at the Gala, this was more a pilgrimage of minor delegates, sometimes not even known so well in their own small city, a parade of wives and children and men who owned hardware stores or were druggists, or first teller in the bank, proprietor of a haberdashery or principal of a small-town high school, local lawyer, retired doctor, a widow on tidy income, her minister and fellow-delegate, minor executives from minor corporations, men who owned their farms, an occasional rotund state party hack with a rubbery look, editor of a small-town paper, professor from Baptist teachers' college, high school librarian, young political aspirant, young salesman — the stable and the established, the middle-aged and the old, a sprinkling of the young, the small towns and the quiet respectable cities of the Midwest and the Far West and the border states were out to pay their homage to their own true candidate, the representative of their conservative orderly heart, and it was obvious they adored him in a quiet way too deep for applause, it was obvious the Nixons had their following after all in these middle-class neatly dressed people moving forward in circumscribed steps, constrained, not cognizant of their bodies, decent respectables who also had spent their life in service and now wanted to have a moment near the man who had all of their vote, and so could arouse their happiness, for the happiness of the Wasp was in his moment of veneration, and they had veneration for Nixon, heir of Old Ike — center of happy memory and better days — they venerated Nixon for his service to Eisenhower, and his comeback now — it was his comeback which had made him a hero in their eyes, for America is the land which worships the Great Comeback, and so he was Tricky Dick to them no more, but the finest gentleman in the land; they were proud to say hello.

The Nixons talked to each one in turn. The candidate was first on the receiving line and then his wife, each taking the arm or shaking the hand of the delegate before them and saying a few words, sometimes peering at the name on the delegate's badge, more often recognizing the face from some all-but-forgotten banquet or fund-raiser in Platte, or Akron, or Evansville, Chillicothe, or Iowa City; in Columbia, South Carolina, and Columbia, Mo.; in Boulder or Fort Collins; in Fayette-ville, Arkansas, Fayetteville, North Carolina; in Harrisburg and Keene and Spokane and Fort Lauderdale and Raleigh and Butte — yes, Nixon had traveled the creeping vine of small-town Republicanism, he had won delegates over these last two years by ones and twos, votes pulled in by the expenditure of a half hour here, an hour there, in conversations which must have wandered so far as the burial specifications of Aunt Matty in her will, and the story of the family stock, he had worked among the despised nuts and bolts of the dele-gates' hearts, and it showed up here in the skill and the pleasure with which he greeted each separate delegate, the separate moves of his hands upon them, for some he touched by the elbow, others patted on the back, some he waved on to his wife with a personal word, never repeating the sequence, fresh for each new delegate. He still did not move with any happiness in his body, the gestures still came in such injunctions from the head as: "Grab this old boy by the elbow," but he was obviously happy here, it was one of the things in the world which he could do best, he could be gracious with his own people, and Pat Nixon backed him up, concentrating on the wives and children, also skillful, the tense forbidding face of her youth (where rectitude, ambi-tion, and lack of charity had been etched like the grimace of an addict into every line of the ferocious clenched bite of her jaw) had eased now somewhat; she was almost attractive, as if the rigid muscle of the Amer-ican woman's mind at its worst had relaxed — she looked near to mel-low: as a husband and wife they had taken the long road back together, somewhere in the abyss she must have forgiven him for "America can't stand pat."

And the reporter had an insight that perhaps it was possible the Nixons had grown up last of all. Young ambitious couple, electrified by sudden eminence, and for eight years slave to eminence, false in every move — for how could any young couple so extravagantly advanced ever feel true to themselves (or even perhaps cognizant that there might be a psychic condition one could term *the true*) how was one ever to acquire such a knowledge when one's life was served as a creature of policies, a servant of great men and empty men, a victim of the very power one's ambition had provided. Nixon had entered American life as half a man, but his position had been so high, the power of the half man had been so enormous that he could never begin to recognize until he fell, that he was incomplete. Nor Mrs. Nixon.

As the string orchestra near them played away — five violins (four male musicians and a lady) plus one guitar, one accordion, one bass — as this elderly band continued to pick out the kind of sweet popular string music which is usually background for movie scenes in inexpensive Brighton hotels where elderly retired India colonels brood through dinner, as the afternoon and the orchestra continued and the slow procession of the delegates, so a sense came at last to the reporter of how Nixon must see his mission. There was a modesty among these delegates today, they were the center of the nation, but they were chastened in their pride — these same doctors and small-town lawyers, or men not so unlike them, had had their manic dreams of restoring order to America with the injunction and the lash just four years ago. Then the nation had lived in their mind like the sure strong son of their loins, and they had been ready to take the fight anywhere, to Vietnam, to China, into the Black ghettoes, they had been all for showing the world and some minorities in America where the real grapes of wrath were stored. But the last four years had exploded a few of their secret policies, and they were bewildered now. No matter what excuse was given that there might have been better ways to wage the war, the Wasp had built his nest with statistics, and the figures on the Vietnam war were badly wrong. How could the nation fail to win when its strength was as five to one, unless God had decided that America was not just? — righteousness had taken a cruel crack on the bridge of its marble brow. Much else was wrong, the youth, the Negro, the dollar, the air pollution and river pollution, the pornography, the streets — the Wasps were now a chastened crew. It was probable the Presidency would soon be theirs again, but the nation was profoundly divided, nightmares loomed — for the first time in their existence, the Wasps were modest about power. They were not certain they would know what to do with it.

What a vision must exist then now in Nixon, what a dream to save the land. Yes, the reporter would offer him this charity — the man had become sincere. All evidence spoke for that. How could there be, after all, a greater passion in a man like Nixon, so universally half-depised, than to show the center of history itself that he was not without greatness. What a dream for such a man! To cleanse the gangrenous wounds of a great power, to restore sanity to the psychopathic fevers of the day, to deny the excessive demand, and nourish the real need, to bring a balance to the war of claims, weed the garden of tradition, and show a fine nose for what was splendid in the new, serve as the great educator who might introduce each warring half of the nation to the other, and bring back the faith of other nations to a great nation in adventurous harmony with itself — yes, the dream could be magnificent enough for any world leader; if the reporter did not think that Nixon, poor Nixon, was very likely to flesh such a dream, still he did not know that the attempt should be denied. It was possible, even likely, even necessary, that the Wasp must enter the center of our history again. They had been a damned minority for too long, a huge indigestible boulder in the voluminous ruminating government gut of every cow-like Democratic administration, an insane Republican minority with vast powers of negation and control, a minority who ran the economy, and half the finances of the world, and all too much of the internal affairs of four or five continents, and the Pentagon, and the technology of the land, and most of the secret police, and nearly every policeman in every small town, and yet finally they did not run the land, they did not comprehend it, the country was loose from them, ahead of them, the life style of the country kept denying their effort, the lives of the best Americans kept accelerating out of their reach. They were the most powerful force in America, and yet they were a psychic island. If they did not find a bridge, they could only grow more insane each year, like a rich nobleman in an empty castle chasing elves and ogres with his stick. They had every power but the one they needed — which was to attach their philosophy to history: the druggist and the president of the steel corporation must finally learn if they were both pushing on the same wheel. Denied the center of political power, the corporation and the small town had remained ideologically married for decades; only by wielding the power could they discover which concepts in conservative philosophy were viable, and what parts were mad. One could predict: their budgeting would prove insane, their righteousness would prove insane, their love for order and clear-thinking would be twisted through many a wry neck, the intellectual foundations of their anti-Communism would split into its separate parts. And the small-town faith in small free enterprise would run smash into the corporate juggernauts of technology land; their love of polite culture would collide with the mad aesthetics of the new America; their livid passion for military superiority would smash its nose on the impossibility of having such superiority without more government spending; their love of nature would have to take up arms against the despoiling foe, themselves, their own greed, their own big business. Yes, perhaps the Wasp had to come to power in order that he grow up, in order that he take the old primitive root of his life-giving philosophy — which required every man to go through battles, if the world would live, and every woman to bear a child — yes, take that root off the high attic shelf of some Prudie Parsley of a witch-ancestor, and plant it in the smashed glass and burned brick of the twentieth century's junkyard: see from that what might grow in the arbors of modern anomaly. Of course, Republicans might yet prove frightening, and were much, if not three-quarters, to blame for every ill in sight, they did not deserve the Presidency, never, and yet if democracy was the free and fair play of human forces then perhaps the Wasp must now hold the game in his direction for a time. The Left was not ready, the Left was years away from a vision sufficiently complex to give life to the land, the Left had not yet learned to talk across the rugged individualism of the more rugged in America, the Left was still too full of kicks and pot and the freakings of Sodium Amytal and orgy, the howls of electronics and LSD. The Left could also find room to grow up. If the Left had to live through a species of political exile for four or eight or twelve good years, it might even be right. They might be forced to study what was alive in the conservative dream. For certain the world could not be saved by technology or government or genetics, and much of the Left had that still to learn.

So the reporter stood in the center of the American Scene — how the little dramas of America, like birds, seemed to find themselves always in the right nest — and realized he was going through no more than the rearrangement of some intellectual luggage (which indeed every good citizen might be supposed to perform) during these worthy operations of the democratic soul when getting ready to vote.

13

The force of his proposition, however, was there to taunt him early the following day, so early as two in the morning. He had begun to drink that evening for the first time in several days. He did not like to drink too much when he was working, but the Wednesday session, nominating day, would not begin until five in the afternoon tomorrow, and it would be a long night, seven or nine or ten hours long, and at the end, Nixon all nominated, he did not believe that would be cause sufficient for him to celebrate — besides, it might be too late. Besides, he wanted to drink. Equal to the high contrast a stain can give to a microscope slide, was the clarity his dear booze sometimes offered a revery, and he had the luck to finish downing his drinks at Joe the Bartender's in the Hilton Plaza, a large and this night rollicking cellar bar where the Nixon people came to celebrate. The kids were out, the Young Republicans and the YAF (the Youth for American Freedom), a table or two of Southern delegates, even a table of Rockefeller Republicans he knew, so it was not the political make-up of the audience so much as the mood, a mood he could have found as easily in a dozen bars he knew in New York on almost any night, and a thousand there must have been in America, a thousand at least, maybe ten thousand. It was at first no more than a loud raucousness of the kind one could hear in many a bar with college drinkers, or skiers, or surfers, intricate interlocked songs with nonsense syllables and barnyard howls — "Old Macdonald" is perhaps the first of these songs — but the songs were more sophisticated, variations with fraternity house riffs, and jouncing repetitions, which could twist you off the beat. The band had three singers, girls in electric blue and electric green and electric pink dresses, not miniskirts so much as little girl dresses, girls a cross between cheerleaders, swingers, and Nixonettes — that hard healthy look in the blank and handsome face which spoke of action each night and low tolerance for being bored — they sang with a cornucopia of old-fashioned cutes, hands on hips, dipping at the knees, old-fashioned break into two bars of tap dance, more they could not fake, arms around each other's waist in four bars of can-can, they did solos, made faces, stuck their hips akimbo, and a virtuoso on the trombone played loud gut-bucket backings, cluckings and cryings, trombone imitating unrest in the barnyard, neighings and bleatings in the air-conditioned cool, the trombonist big and fat with a huge black sack of a shirt on which was the legend TUBA 24, and there was a tuba player as well, also virtuoso, top hat in tricolor, Uncle Sam with black coat, black pants. Two banjos in black shirts, red and blue striped pants, were there to whang away, one of the girls played a drum, a red drum, there was a rooty-toot to the barnyard, and rebel yells from the crowd all next to broken eggs and splats, some stew of loutishness, red-eyed beer drinkers pig-faced in the dark, and the hump on the back of their neck begins to grow fat, beef on beef, pig on pig, primeval stirrings, secret glee, fun and games are mounting and vomit washed in blood, it was oom-pah, oom-pah and upsy daisy weight lifters dancing, merry and raw, beer hall, beer hall, bleat of a cow, snort of a pig, oomps went the tuba and yes, the boar of old Europe was not dead, the shade had come to America, America it was.

There was slyness in the air, and patience, confidence of the win — a mood was building which could rise to a wave: if there was nihilism on the Left, there were dreams of extermination on the Right. Technology land had pushed cancer into every pore, so now the cure for cancer was dismemberment of order, all gouging of justice. There would be talk of new order before too long.

Nixon might have his dream to unify the land, but he would yet have to stare, face to face, into the power of his own Right Wing, soon to rise on the wave of these beer-hall bleats, the worst of the Wasp, all bull in his muscles, all murder in his neck — would Nixon have the stance to meet them? Or would he fall captive to the madmen in the pits of his own party, those madmen absent from Miami, those madmen concealed this week? The convention had been peaceful, too peaceful by far.

At large on the ocean, would people yet pray for Nixon and wish him strength as once they had wished strength to old Hindenburg and Dollfuss and Schuschnigg and Von Papen? Oom-pah went the tuba, starts! went the horn. Blood and shit might soon be flying like the red and brown of a *verboten* flag. It had had black in it as well. For death perhaps. Areas of white for purity. They would talk yet of purity. They always did. And shave the shorn. God give strength to Richard Nixon, and a nose for the real news. Oom-pah went the tuba, *farts* went the horn.

14

On Wednesday night Alabama ceded to California, and Reagan was first to be in nomination. Ivy Baker Priest made the speech, Ivy Baker Priest Stevens was her name now, a handsome woman who had been Treasurer of the United States in Eisenhower's cabinet, and then an assistant to Reagan. She had a dual personality. She was a wretched speaker with the parched nasal mean stingy acid driving tones of a typical Republican lady speaker: "A man who will confront the radicals on our campuses and the looters on our streets and say, 'The laws will be obeyed.' " It was a relief when her nasalities began to drive up the hill and one knew the mention of Reagan's name was near. "A man to match our mountains and our plains, a man steeped in the glorious traditions of the past, a man with a vision of the unlimited possibilities of a new era. Yes, Destiny has found the man." A minute later she was done, and a fairly large demonstration went to work. It was to prove milder and less impressive than the Rockefeller and Nixon break-outs, but it was at least notable for a sight of the opposite side of the lady's personality. She now looked confident, enthusiastic, round, sexy, warm, and gloriously vital, the best blonde housemother you could ever see, waving the fraternity boys around the bend as they sang "Dixie" and "California, Here I Come," clapping her hands in absolute delight at signs like "I'm gone on Ron," as if that were absolutely the most attractive thing she'd ever seen, then jazzed it like a cheerleader beating her palms and smiling, smiling at the sight of each new but familiar crew-cut face who had gotten up to whoop and toot it through the aisles for Ronnie. There were five cages of balloons overhead, and Reagan got one of them, the balloons came down in a fast cascade — each one blessed with a drop of water within so as to tend to plummet rather than tend to float — and they came down almost as fast as foam rubber pillows and were detonated with lighted cigarettes and stomping feet thus immediately that a string of firecrackers could have gone off.

When that was done, a monumental sense of tedium overtook the night. Hickel of Alaska and Winthrop Rockefeller of Arkansas were put in as favorite sons, the latter with two seconding speeches and an eight-minute demonstration — he was conceivably giving nothing to his brother — Romney used all of forty minutes, Nelson Rockefeller's band boosting his demonstration as Romney troops were later to boost Rockefeller's. Senator Carlson of Kansas was named as favorite son, then Hiram Fong of Hawaii. It was after nine before Governor Shafer of Pennsylvania stood up to put Nelson Rockefeller on the lists. More than two and a half hours had elapsed between the end of Reagan's presentation and the beginning of Rocky's. Reporters had left the convention hall, and were huddled backstage in places like the Railroad Lounge where free sandwiches and beer were available, and everybody was concerned with the most attractive proposition of the night — that if they were all to go to their hotels, check out, and catch a plane, they could be at their homes before nominations were done and balloting had begun. They could watch it on television, which was the real gloom of the occasion. The convention had demonstrated that no reporter could keep up any longer with the event unless checking in periodically with the tube; the politicians, themselves, rushed forward to TV men, and shouldered note-pads aside. During this lull, therefore, one bitter reporter, a big heavy Southern boy with horn-rimmed glasses, delivered the remark of the evening. Sipping beer and glumly munching his sandwich (which held an inch of paper-dry turkey) he said, "Yessir, the only thing which could liven up this convention is if Ike was to croak tonight." So the respect journalists had been obliged to pay over the years could be tolerated now only by the flensing knives of the club.

Shafer put Rockefeller in ". . . because he is in tune. The people, young and old, rich and poor, Black and white, have responded to him. He has never lost an election. . . . Ladies and gentlemen, we should nominate Nelson Rockefeller because he is the Republican who can most surely win. . . ." It was an inept speech — Rocky's name was mentioned seven times before the signal was given to the delegates, and tension was dissipated. It didn't matter. Everyone knew that Rockefeller would have an enormous demonstration and that it would not matter. The days when demonstrations could turn a convention were gone. The demonstrators knew they would be chided in newspaper editorials the following day, and therefore were sheepish in the very middle of their stomping and their jigging. Soon they would hold conventions in TV studios.

Then came Spiro Agnew for Nixon. If he had not been selected for Vice-President next day, his speech would have gone unnoticed and unremarked — "It is my privilege to place in nomination for the office of President of the United States the one man whom history has so clearly thrust forward, the one whom all America will recognize as a man whose time has come, the man for 1968, the Honorable. . . ."

Nixon's demonstration was about equal to Rockefeller's. Hordes of noise, two cages of balloons, machine-gun drum-fire as they went out — no lift in the audience, no real lift. Nothing this night could begin to recall that sense of barbarians about a campfire and the ecstasy of going to war which Barry Goldwater had aroused in '64.

Still the demonstrations gave another image of the three candidacies: Reagan's men had straight hair cropped short, soldiers and state

157

troopers for Ronnie; so far as Republicans were swingers, so swingers marched with Rocky; and for Nixon — the mood on the floor was like the revel in the main office of a corporation when the Christmas Party is high.

More nominations. Harold Stassen for the seventh time. Senator Case of New Jersey, Governor Rhodes of Ohio, Senator Thurmond who immediately withdrew for Nixon. At 1:07 A.M., eight hours and seven minutes after the convention had opened for nomination, it was closed, and over the floor rested the knowledge that nothing had happened tonight. It had been Nixon on the first ballot from the beginning, and it was Nixon at the end. By the time Alabama, the first state, voted, 14 for Nixon, 12 for Reagan, the next to last doubt was dispelled, for *The New York Times* on Sunday had estimated only 9 solid for Nixon. When Florida came in with 32 out of 34, and Georgia with 21 where only 14 had seemed likely a few days before, there was no need to worry the issue. Wisconsin with 30 votes for Nixon carried it over — the total was 692. The rest had gone: Rockefeller 277, Reagan 182, Rhodes 55, Romney 50, Case 22, Carlson 20, W. Rockefeller 18, Fong 14, Stassen 2, Lindsay 1.

Filing out of the hall, there was the opportunity to see Nixon on television. Where in 1960 he had said, "All I am I owe to my mother and father, my family and my church . . ." he was considerably more of the professional strategist tonight as he spoke of his efforts to win the nomination while unifying the party. "You see," he said to the cameras, "the beauty of our contest this year was that we won the nomination in a way designed to win the election. We didn't make the mistake of breaking up the California delegation or breaking up the Ohio delegation or raiding the Michigan delegation. And in the State of New York also we respected the Rockefeller position, being the candidate for New York. And I think this will pay off in November. We're going to have a united party. Sure we've had a real fight . . . but we have won it in a way that we're going into the final campaign united." He was lucid, he was convincing, he said he felt perfectly "free" to choose his Vice-President. "I won the nomination without having to pay any price, making any deal with any candidate or any individuals representing a candidate. . . . I [will] meet with delegates from all over the country . . . Southern delegates, the Northern delegates, the Midwestern delegates and the Western delegates. But I will make the decision based on my best judgment as to the man that can work best with me, and that will, I think perhaps, if he ever has to do that, serve as President of the United States."

In the old days, he had got his name as Tricky Dick because he gave one impression and acted upon another — later when his language was examined, one could not call him a liar. So he had literally not made any deal with any candidate, but he was stretching the subtle rubber of his own credibility when he claimed he would not have to pay any price. The rest of the night at the Miami Hilton would belong to the South.

15

But let us leave the convention with a look at Reagan. He had come forward immediately after the first ballot was in, and made a move that the nomination be unanimous. Reagan was smiling when he came up for his plea, he looked curiously more happy than he had looked at any point in the convention, as if he were remembering Barry Goldwater's renunciation of the nomination in 1960, and the profitable results which had ensued, or perhaps he was just pleased because the actor in his soul had issued orders that this was the role to play. For years in the movies he had played the good guy and been proud of it. If he didn't get the girl, it was because he was too good a guy to be overwhelmingly attractive. That was all right. He would grit his teeth and get the girl next time out. Since this was conceivably the inner sex drama of half of respectable America, he was wildly popular with Republicans, For a party which prided itself on its common sense, they were curiously, even outrageously, sentimental.

Now as Reagan made his plea for unity, he spoke with a mildness, a lack of charisma, even a simplicity, which was reminiscent of a good middle-aged stock actor's simplicity — well, you know, fellows, the man I'm playing is an intellectual, and of course I have the kind of mind which even gets confused by a finesse in bridge.

They cheered him wildly, and he looked happy, as if something had gone his way. There was much occasion to recollect him on Thursday when Agnew for vice-president was announced; as the story of this selection developed, the reporter was to think of a view of Reagan he had had on Tuesday afternoon after the reception Nixon had given for the delegates in the American Scene.

On Tuesday the reporter had found Reagan at the Di Lido in downtown Miami Beach where the Alabama and Louisiana delegations were
housed. In with Louisiana in a caucus, the Governor came out later to
give a quick press conference, pleading ignorance of his situation. Listening to him, it was hard to believe he was fifty-seven, two years older
than Nixon, for he had a boy's face, no gray in his head — he was
reputed to dye his hair — and his make-up (about which one could
hear many a whisper) was too excellent, if applied, to be detected.

Still, unlike Nixon, Reagan was altogether at ease with the Press.
They had been good to him, they would be good again — he had the
confidence of the elected governor of a big state, precisely what Nixon
had always lacked; besides, Reagan had long ago incorporated the
confidence of an actor who knows he is popular with interviewers. In
fact, he had a public manner which was so natural that his dis-
crepancies appeared only slightly surrealistic: at the age of fifty-seven,
he had the presence of a man of thirty, the deferential enthusiasm, the
bright but dependably unoriginal mind of a sales manager promoted
for his ability over men older than himself. He also had the neatness,
and slim economy of move, of a man not massive enough to be President, in the way one might hesitate, let us say, ever to consider a
gentleman like Mr. Johnny Carson of television — whatever his fine
intelligence — as Chief Executive of a Heavyweight Empire. It was that
way with Reagan. He was somehow too light, a lightweight six feet one
inch tall — whatever could he do but stick-and-move? Well, he could
try to make Generals happy in order to show how heavy he really might
be, which gave no heart to consideration of his politics. Besides, darkening shades of the surreal, he had a second personality which was
younger than the first, very young, boyish, maybe thirteen or fourteen,
freckles, cowlick, I-tripped-on-my-sneaker-lace aw shucks variety of
confusion. For back on Tuesday afternoon they had been firing questions at him on the order of how well he was doing at prying delegates
loose from Nixon, and he could only say over and over, "I don't know. I
just don't know. I've been moving around so quickly talking to so many
delegations in caucus that I haven't had time to read a paper."

"Well, what do the delegations say, Governor?"

"Well, I don't know. They listen to me very pleasantly and politely,
and then I leave and they discuss what I've said. But I can't tell you if
we're gaining. I think we are, but I don't know, I don't know. I honestly
don't know, gentlemen," and he broke out into a grin, "I just don't
know," exactly like a thirteen-year-old, as if indeed gentlemen he *really*

didn't know, and the Press and the delegates listening laughed with him as if there were no harm in Ronald Reagan, not unless the lightning struck.

But in fact the storm was going on all day Tuesday, delegate-stealing flickering back and forth over all the camps, a nomination on the first ballot no longer secure for Richard Nixon, no longer altogether secure, because Reagan's announcement on Saturday of his switch from being a favorite son of California to an open candidate had meant that a great push was on to pull Southern delegates loose from Nixon in numbers sufficient to stop him on first ballot, then get more delegates loose on second ballot to forestall Nixon's strength among the favorite sons. It was a strategy which reasoned as follows: if Nixon could be stopped on the first two ballots, there was little which could keep the overwhelming majority of delegate votes in Alabama, Arizona, California, Florida, Georgia, Idaho, Louisiana, Mississippi, Montana, Nebraska, North Carolina, Oklahoma, South Carolina, South Dakota, Tennessee, Texas and Virginia away from support of Reagan and a possible total of close to 500. Potentially it was a powerful argument, doubly powerful because Reagan was the favorite of the South, and the reporter talking to a leader of the Louisiana caucus heard him say in courtly tones to a delegate, "It breaks my heart that we can't get behind a fine man like Governor Reagan, but Mr. Nixon is deserving of our choice, and he must receive it." Which was a splendid way to talk of a deal.

There were forces out in full panoply to hold Reagan down. Senator Strom Thurmond of South Carolina who ran for President on the Dixiecrat ticket in 1948, now defected from the Democrats and become a Republican, was the first committed to Nixon. The wise money would emphasize he had nowhere to go if Nixon did not make it, because he could not return to the Democrats, was too old to go to the third party, and had to be without his new party if Rockefeller won. Thurmond's point of reasoning with Southern delegates was that Nixon was the best conservative they could get and still win, and he had obtained assurances from Nixon that no Vice-Presidential candidate intolerable to the South would be selected. All that long afternoon while Nixon shook hands with delegates and radiated serenity, the nomination was conceivably in doubt and hung for a few hours on the efforts of Thurmond and Goldwater and Tower and O'Donnell of Texas, and a number of other Southern state chairmen and was probably won on the quiet argument that if the South did not hold firm for Nixon, he might still win with Ohio and Michigan on the second ballot. Then the South

161

would have nothing at all, indeed the South would have driven Nixon to the left.

That the South did hold for Nixon is why perhaps Reagan may have sounded confused. He must have been receiving the double affection of delegates that day who liked him and yet would not be ready to give him their vote, therefore loved him twice. Yet in tangible return, he could not count the gains. Reports conflicted on his team — as indeed they would — he did not know, he *really* did not know.

Nor did the reporter. Tuesday afternoon, watching Nixon with the delegations he had no sense the nomination was in difficulty, or no more sense than the knowledge absorbed from quick conversation with a Louisiana delegate that Lindsay would not be nominated for Vice-President since Nixon had promised as much. It came as no pleasure, but no surprise. The Great Unifier would obviously begin by unifying the South. He could move to the Blacks only when they had been chastened by the absence of any remaining relation to power, which is to say, only after his election. It was a strategy which could work, or fail. If it failed, civil war and a police state were near. But finally he had no choice. The iron demand when one would unify a schism is to strengthen the near side first, since one can always offer less to the far side yet hold them — unless they are indeed ready to revolt — with the consolation they are not being entirely forgotten. Nixon could no more desert the South than would Rockefeller, if he had won, have been able to turn his back on Harlem. The reporter was beginning to recognize for the first time that profound theses to the side, there might be cloud-banks of depression in the way of getting up on election day to cast a vote.

16

For these reasons, the reporter had decided by Thursday morning that Nixon could only nominate a moderate from the South or a conservative from the North. No other arrangement would mollify the South. So he left for home with the confidence that Senator Howard Baker of Tennessee would be the nominee and was only mildly surprised when it went to Agnew. But that night covering the convention before his television set in his own home, he realized he had missed the most exciting night of the convention, at least on the floor, and was able to console himself only with the sad knowledge that he could cover it better on television than if he had been there. Of course he was to find out later that it was an evening which would end in the blackest depression, for many were convinced that Nixon had made a powerful error in picking a man as unknown as Agnew.

No one seemed pleased but Nixon. It occurred to the reporter on reflection that Nixon had not made the worst of moves for himself. The Vice-Presidential nominee was on the surface a man without large appeal and had been the first to say, "I am quite aware that Spiro Agnew is not a household name." Still he was reasonable on television, a big man, soft-spoken and alert. He would not be independent — a necessity to Nixon — he would be loyal, exorbitantly loyal as Nixon had once been exorbitantly loyal to Eisenhower, for there was no choice. So Agnew would give Nixon nourishment, and spare the cankers of considering that the Vice-President was more popular than himself. If Nixon was growing, he was not yet so large as Father Christmas himself. Best of all, he would have no ideological balance to maintain, he could work on his own, scrambling broken-field from Right to Left and back again, no ideologue running with him to halt and complain.

The liberal press was quick to declare that Nixon had lost the election with that one move, and indeed he could not hide the fact that Thurmond and other Southerners had eliminated Lindsay, Percy and Hatfield. Yet Nixon had fulfilled his Southern debts with a minimum of — from his point of view — damage to himself, and Nixon would never have to sleep with the particular terror that some conceivable Left-wing maniac, finding the Vice-President more tolerable than himself would hunt for a silver bullet . . . Nixon, on television, seemed cheerful with his choice. Of course, others were not.

Seen from the Americana on television, Rockefeller looked like he had had a few life-giving drinks in the middle of the afternoon. Sounding more than ever congruent to Spencer Tracy in the middle of new-found wounds, Rockefeller said huskily, "I have no comment on Mr. Agnew. I'm going for a swim. I need some sun, and I'm going for a swim."

"They say," said the interviewer, "that Mr. Nixon saw a hundred leading Republicans before making his choice."

"I guess," said Rocky, "that makes me, fella, the hundred and first."

But Nixon would seek to ride it out. As he came to Convention Hall for his acceptance speech, he was high with success and happy, cautious with reporters about Agnew, but benign about the attempt of the rebel moderates to run Romney in protest. Romney had gone down 186 votes to 1,128, the bitterness of being passed over for a man so inconsequential as Agnew all visible in the red of his face, the gray-green glow of his eyes, but Nixon had made a point of calling up Romney on his entrance so that he approached the podium with the Governor of Michigan on his arm. "It was good to have a floor fight," he told the reporters, "a healthy thing for the party, it helped to clear the air. We'll be more united afterward." Nixon was obviously tense with waiting to begin his speech, he was obviously going to make every effort to deliver the greatest speech of his life.

His ovation on introduction was large but in no way frantic, it was the formal massing of a large sound which the convention would give to its nominee, but for him up on the podium, it had to sound very good because it lasted for minutes, time for him to call up his wife and children, and Spiro Agnew and his wife and two of his girls (the third girl was a child, and his son was in Vietnam) there was time for Nixon to stand there alone and wave his hands on high and grin like a winner, time for him to canter over to the side of the speaker's platform and receive a kiss from the starchy old lady who had read the roll call of the states in the balloting last night and tonight, time for him to grin and grin again, time for him to reveal the austere moves of his decorum and the little mincing gestures distantly reminiscent of a certain dictator long gone. The enigma of the night in Joe the Bartender's returned — was Nixon a man who would prove strong enough, or was one to fear his weaknesses would make him prove too strong?

He began at last by waving the audience to silence, begging them for silence with smiles and laughter. Then he began the speech he had worked on for weeks, his major effort, written in large part it could be assumed by himself, for the flavor of the man, old and new, old tricks and new dreams, stale sentiment and hints of bright new thought were all in it, he was to touch every base and he played a game which had twenty bases. He began by talking of sixteen years ago when he stood "before this convention to accept your nomination as the running mate of one of the greatest Americans of our time or anytime — Dwight D. Eisenhower. . . ." Tonight, Ike was critically ill in Walter Reed Hospital. "There is nothing that would lift him more than for us to win in November. And I say, let us win this one for Ike."

He had probably expected a roar which would shiver the Secret Service men on the catwalks high above the hall, but the cheer was empty. Ike had been used and re-used and used again, Ike was the retread on the bandwagon, and echoes sour as the smell of a broken mood came in at the thought of Pat O'Brien saying, "Let's win this one for the Gipper," yes, Old Nixon had popped up first, copping his plea. Unhappy as old Scratch was New Nixon with Old Nixon, for the line surprisingly had not been delivered well. Where Old Nixon would have dropped the fly right on the yawping hollering mouths of a cheering multitude of Republicans conditioned like fish, New Nixon blew the cast, some unconscious embarrassment jerking the line. He had gotten smarter than his habits.

The speech went on. He talked of sending the power of government back from Washington to the states and the cities, he congratulated Rockefeller and Reagan and Romney for their hard fight, and knew they would fight even harder for the win in November. "A party that can unite itself will unite America," he said, and it was possible the remark was not without its truth, but he was still squeezed into the hard sell; one could all but hear the mother of that remark, "A family which prays together, stays together."

If he had been wooing old Republicans up to now with sure-fire vulcanized one-line zingers, he could hardly be unaware that millions of Independents, some of them young, were also watching. Therefore, he shifted over to the electorate at large. "As we look at America we see cities enveloped in smoke and flame. We hear sirens in the night. We see Americans dying on distant battlefields abroad. We see Americans hating each other, fighting each other, killing each other at home. . . . Did we come all this way for this? . . . die in Normandy and Korea and Valley Forge for this? Listen to the answers. . . ." And his voice had converted to the high dramatic-operatic of a radio actor's voice circa 1939 in a Norman Corwin play; we hear: ". . . the quiet voice in the tumult and the shouting . . . voice of the great majority of Americans, the forgotten Americans — the non-shouters; the non-demonstrators. They are not racists or sick; they're not guilty of the crime that plagues the land; they are Black, they are white" — and he pushed on with the forgotten Americans who worked in factories, ran businesses, served in government, were soldiers who died. "They give drive to the spirit of America . . . life to the American dream . . . steel to the backbone of America . . . good people . . . decent people . . . work and save . . ." (and watch their television sets) "pay their taxes and they care . . . they know this country will not be a good place for any of us to live in unless it's a good place for all of us to live in."

He proceeded to attack the leaders who had wasted the substance and the pride of America, mismanaged the wars, and the economy and the city ". . . the time has come for . . . complete reappraisal of America's policies in every section of the world." That was incontestable. "I pledge to you tonight . . . to bring an honorable end to the war in Vietnam."

Now, whether he would underline it so, or not, Nixon was calling for an end to Henry Luce's American Century. "There are 200 million Americans and there are two billion people that live in the free world, and I say the time has come for other nations . . . to bear their fair share." Cheers. The old parched throats of Republican isolationism gave an atrophied cheer. "To the leaders of the Communist world, we say . . . the time has come for an era of negotiations" — now protecting his flank — "we shall always negotiate from strength and never from weakness." More cheers. Perfunctory cheers. But later: "We extend the hand of friendship to all people. To the Russian people. To the Chinese people . . . the goal of an open world, open sky, open cities, open hearts, open minds." Yes, he would move to the Right on civil rights and he would move to the Left of the Democrats on foreign affairs, but he was careful to invoke the heats of the patriotic heart: "My friends, we live in an age of revolution in America and in the world . . . let us turn to a revolution . . . that will never grow old, the world's greatest continuing revolution, the American Revolution." And he went on to call for progress, and reminded everyone that progress depended on order. He was of course in these matters shameless, he had no final passion for the incorruptible integrity of an idea; no, ideas were rather like keys to him on which he might play a teletype to program the American mind. And yet the American mind was scandalously bad — the best educational system in the world had produced the most pervasive conditioning of mind in the history of culture just as the greatest medical civilization in history might yet produce the worst plagues. It opened the thought that if the Lord Himself wished to save America, who else could he possibly use for instrument by now but Richard Nixon? Of course if the Devil wished to push America over the edge — well, for that, Humphrey would serve as well.

Another key on the teletype: "The first civil right of every American is to be free from domestic violence." A feint to the Right, a feint to the Left. "To those who say law and order is the code word for racism, here is a reply: Our goal is justice — justice for every American. . . . America is a great nation today not because of what government did for people, but because of what people did for themselves over 190 years in this country . . . what we need are not more millions on welfare rolls but more millions on payrolls. . . . The greatest engine of progress ever developed in the history of man — American private enterprise." Or did he mean American corporate enterprise. It had been locked in common-law marriage with government for thirty-five years.

But Nixon was off on the power of positive thinking, "Black Americans [want to have] an equal chance to own their own homes, to own their own businesses, to be managers and executives as well as workers, to have a piece" — and he looked like a YMCA secretary: here came the little quotes — "a piece of the 'action' in the exciting ventures of private enterprise." But of course he was not necessarily all wrong. Private enterprise, *small* private enterprise, was an entrance to existential life for the mediocre and the courageous.

He went into the peroration. The year 2000 was coming. A great period of celebration and joy at being alive in America was ahead. "I see a day," he began to say, as Martin Luther King had once said, "I have a dream." Every orator's art which had lately worked would become Nixon's craft. So he said "I see a day" nine times. He saw a day when the President would be respected and "a day when every child in this land, regardless of his background has a chance for the best education . . . chance to go just as high as his talents will take him." Nixon, the Socialist! "I see a day when life in rural America attracts people to the country rather than driving them away. . . ." Then came a day he could see of breakthrough on problems of slums and pollution and traffic, he could see a day when the value of the dollar would be preserved, a day of freedom from fear in America and in the world . . . this was the cause he asked them all to vote for. His speech was almost done, but he took it around the track again. "Tonight I see the face of a child . . . Mexican, Italian, Polish . . . none of that matters . . . he's an American child." But stripped of opportunity. What pain in that face when the child awakes to poverty, neglect and despair. The ghost of J. M. Barrie stirred in Nixon's voice, stirred in the wings and on the catwalks and in the television sets. "Let's all save Peter Pan," whispered the ghost. Then Nixon saw another child tonight, "He hears a train go by. At night he dreams of faraway places where he'd like to go . . . he is helped on his journey through life . . . a father who had to go to work before he finished the sixth grade . . . a gentle Quaker mother with a passionate concern for peace . . . a great teacher . . . a remarkable football coach . . . courageous wife . . . loyal children . . . in his chosen profession of politics, first there were scores, then hundreds, then thousands, and

167

finally millions who worked for his success. And tonight he stands before you, nominated for President of the United States. You can see why I believe so deeply in the American dream . . . help me make that dream come true for millions to whom it's an impossible dream today."

Yes, Nixon was still the spirit of television. Mass communication was still his disease — he thought he could use it to communicate with masses. "Today I leave you. I go to assume a greater task than devolved on General Washington. The Great God which helped him must help me. Without that great assistance I will surely fail. With it, I cannot fail." Somberly Nixon said, "Abraham Lincoln lost his life, but he did not fail. The next President of the United States will face challenges which in some ways will be greater than those of Washington or Lincoln . . . not only the problem of restoring peace abroad, but of restoring peace at home . . . with God's help and your help, we shall surely succeed. . . . My fellow Americans, the dark long night for America is about to end. . . . The time has come for us to leave the valley of despair and climb the mountain. . . ." (And now one could hear Martin Luther King crying out in his last passionate church utterance, "I have gone to the top of the mountain — I have seen the top.") Nixon was certainly without shame and certainly without fear; what demons to invoke! — "To the top of the mountain so that we may see the glory of the dawn of a new day for America, a new dawn for peace and freedom to the world." And he was done, and who would measure the good and bad, the strength and weakness, sincerity and hypocrisy of what he had said, and the cage of balloons emptied — a union had charged 33 cents to blow up each single balloon — and the cheers and applause came, and the band, and Nixon and his family looked happy, and Agnew and his family looked bewildered and happy, and the cheers came down, not large, not small, cheers for Richard Nixon's greatest effort in oratory, and a better speech could not have been written by any computer in existence, not even Hal the super-computer in *2001,* and out in Miami, six miles from Convention Hall, in the area from 54th to 79th streets, and Seventh Avenue to Twenty-Seventh Avenue, the Negroes were rioting, and three had been killed and five in critical condition as Miami policemen exchanged gunfire with snipers: "Firefights like in Vietnam," said a police lieutenant and five hundred armed National Guard were occupying one hundred square blocks, and one hundred and fifty Blacks had been arrested since Wednesday night when it had all begun, Governor Kirk had gone with the Reverend Abernathy who said, "I will lead you by the hand," to plead with the rioters. Tonight the

Governor said, "Whatever force is needed," in answer to how the uprising would be quelled. It was the first major riot in the history of Miami.

The reporter was 1,500 miles away by then and could hardly have covered it, but indeed he did not know if he saw the need. There would be more of the same in Chicago. Maybe Chicago would help him to see which horse might be most deserving of backing into the greatest office on earth. It occurred to him that the intelligent American voter was now in the situation of the poor Southern Black forced these last fifty years to choose his ballot between the bad racist and the racist who might conceivably be not all bad. Humphrey versus Nixon.

But this was poor species of wit by which to look into the glazed eye of the problem — for in truth he was left by the television set with the knowledge that for the first time he had not been able to come away with an intimation of what was in a politician's heart, indeed did not know if he was ready to like Nixon, or detested him for his resolutely non-poetic binary system, his computer's brain, did not know if the candidate were real as a man, or whole as a machine, lonely in his sad eminence or megalomaniacal, humble enough to feel the real wounds of the country or sufficiently narcissistic to dream the tyrant's dream — the reporter did not know if the candidate was some last wry hope of unity or the square root of minus one, a rudder to steer the ship of state or an empty captain above a directionless void, there to loose the fearful nauseas of the century. He had no idea at all if God was in the land or the Devil played the tune. And if Miami had masked its answers, then in what state of mind could one now proceed to Chicago? He felt like an observer deprived of the privilege to witness or hold a chair.

TWO

THE SIEGE OF CHICAGO

Chicago, August 24–29

CHICAGO is the great American city. New York is one of the capitals of the world and Los Angeles is a constellation of plastic, San Francisco is a lady, Boston has become Urban Renewal, Philadelphia and Baltimore and Washington wink like dull diamonds in the smog of Eastern Megalopolis, and New Orleans is unremarkable past the French Quarter. Detroit is a one-trade town, Pittsburgh has lost its golden triangle, St. Louis has become the golden arch of the corporation, and nights in Kansas City close early. The oil depletion allowance makes Houston and Dallas naught but checkerboards for this sort of game. But Chicago is a great American city. Perhaps it is the last of the great American cities.

The reporter was sentimental about the town. Since he had grown up in Brooklyn, it took him no time to recognize, whenever he was in Chicago again, that the urbanites here were like the good people of Brooklyn — they were simple, strong, warm-spirited, sly, rough, compassionate, jostling, tricky and extraordinarily good-natured because they had sex in their pockets, muscles on their back, hot eats around the corner, neighborhoods which dripped with the sauce of local legend, and real city architecture, brownstones with different windows on every floor, vistas for miles of red-brick and two-family wood-frame houses with balconies and porches, runty stunted trees rich as farmland in their promise of tenderness the first city evenings of spring, streets where kids played stick-ball and roller-hockey, lots of smoke and iron twilight. The clangor of the late Nineteenth Century, the very hope of greed, was in these streets. London one hundred years ago could not have looked much better.

Brooklyn, however, beautiful Brooklyn, grew beneath the sky-scrapers of Manhattan, so it never became a great city, merely an as-phalt herbarium for talent destined to cross the river. Chicago did not have Manhattan to preempt top branches, so it grew up from the savory of its neighborhoods to some of the best high-rise architecture in the world, and because its people were Poles and Ukrainians and Czechs as well as Irish and the rest, the city had Byzantine corners worthy of Prague or Moscow, odd tortured attractive drawbridges over the Chicago River, huge Gothic spires like the skyscraper which held the *Chicago Tribune,* curves and abutments and balconies in cylindrical structures thirty stories high twisting in and out of the curves of the river, and fine balustrades in its parks. Chicago had a North Side on Lake Shore Drive where the most elegant apartment buildings in the world could be found — Sutton Place in New York betrayed the cost analyst in the eye of the architect next to these palaces of glass and charcoal colored steel. In superb back streets behind the towers on the lake were brownstones which spoke of ironies, cupidities and intricate ambition in the fists of the robber barons who commissioned them — substantiality, hard work, heavy drinking, carnal meats of pleasure, and a Midwestern sense of how to arrive at upper-class decorum were also in the American grandeur of these few streets. If there was a fine American aristocracy of deportment, it was probably in the clean tough keen-eyed ladies of Chicago one saw on the streets off Lake Shore Drive on the near North Side of Chicago.

Not here for a travelogue — no need then to detail the Loop, in death like the center of every other American city, but what a dying! Old department stores, old burlesque houses, avenues, dirty avenues, the El with its nineteenth-century dialogue of iron screeching against iron about a turn, and caverns of shadow on the pavement beneath, the grand hotels with their massive lobbies, baroque ceilings, resplendent as Roman bordellos, names like Sheraton-Blackstone, Palmer House, red fields of carpet, a golden cage for elevator, the unheard crash of giant mills stamping new shapes on large and obdurate materials is always pounding in one's inner ear — Dreiser had not written about Chicago for nothing.

To the West of the Lake were factories and Ciceros, Mafia-lands and immigrant lands; to the North, the suburbs, the Evanstons; to the South were Negro ghettoes of the South Side — belts of Black men amplifying each the resonance of the other's cause — the Black belt had the Blackstone Rangers, the largest gang of juvenile delinquents on earth, 2,000 by some count — one could be certain the gang had leaders as large in potential as Hannibal or Attila the Hun — how else account for the strength and wit of a stud who would try to rise so high in the Blackstone Rangers?

Further South and West were enclaves for the University of Chicago, more factories, more neighborhoods for Poles, some measure of more good hotels on the lake, and endless neighborhoods — white neighborhoods which went for miles of ubiquitous dingy wood houses with back yards, neighborhoods to hint of Eastern Europe, Ireland, Tennessee, a gathering of all the clans of the Midwest, the Indians and Scotch-Irish, Swedes, some Germans, Italians, Hungarians, Rumanians, Finns, Slovaks, Slovenes — it was only the French who did not travel. In the Midwest, land spread out; not five miles from the Loop were areas as empty, deserted, enormous and mournful by night as the outer freight yards of Omaha. Some industrial desert or marsh would lie low on the horizon, an area squalling by day, deserted by night, except for the hulking Midwestern names of the boxcars and the low sheds, the warehouse buildings, the wire fences which went along the side of unpaved roads for thousands of yards.

The stockyards were like this, the famous stockyards of Chicago were at night as empty as the railroad sidings of the moon. Long before the Democratic Convention of 1968 came to the Chicago Amphitheatre, indeed eighteen years ago when the reporter had paid his only previous visit, the area was even then deserted at night, empty as the mudholes on a battlefield after a war has passed. West of the Amphitheatre, railroad sidings seemed to continue on for miles, accompanied by those same massive low sheds larger than armories, with pens for tens of thousands of frantic beasts, cattle, sheep, and pigs, animals in an orgy of gorging and dropping and waiting and smelling blood. In the slaughterhouses, during the day, a carnage worthy of the Disasters of War took place each morning and afternoon. Endless files of animals were led through pens to be stunned on the head by hammers, and then hind legs trussed, be hoisted up on hooks to hang head down, and ride along head down on an overhead trolley which brought them to Negroes or whites, usually huge, the whites most often Polish or Hunkies (hence the etymology of Honkie — a Chicago word) the Negroes up from the South, huge men built for the shock of the work, slash of a knife on the neck of the beast and gouts of blood to bathe their torso (stripped of necessity to the waist) and blood to splash their legs. The animals passed a psychic current back along the overhead trolley — each cut throat released its scream of death into the throat not yet cut and just behind, and that penultimate throat would push the voltage up, drive the current back and further back into the screams of every animal upside down and hanging from that clanking overhead trolley, bare electric bulbs screaming into the animal eye and brain, gurglings and awesome hollows of sound coming back from the open plumbing ahead of the cut jugular as if death were indeed a rapids along some undergound river, and the fear and absolute anguish of beasts dying upside down further ahead passed back along the line, back all the way to the corrals and the pens, back even to the siding with the animals still in boxcars, back, who knew — so high might be the psychic voltage of the beast — back to the farm where first they were pushed into the truck which would take them into the train. What an awful odor the fear of absolute and unavoidable death gave to the stool and stuffing and pure vomitous shit of the beasts waiting in the pens in the stock-yard, what a sweat of hell-leather, and yet the odor, no, the titanic stench, which rose from the yards was not so simple as the collective diarrhetics of an hysterical army of beasts, no, for after the throats were cut and the blood ran in rich gutters, red light on the sweating back of the red throat-cutters, the dying and some just-dead animals clanked along the overhead, arterial blood spurting like the nip-ups of a little boy urinating in public, the red-hot carcass quickly encountered another Black or Hunkie with a long knife on a long stick who would cut the belly from chest to groin and a stew and a stink of two hundred pounds of stomach, lungs, intestines, mucosities, spleen, exploded cowflop and pigshit, blood, silver lining, liver, mother-of-pearl tissue, and general gag-all would flop and slither over the floor, the man with the knife getting a good blood-splatting as he dug and twisted with his blade to liberate the roots of the organ, intestine and impedimenta still integrated into the meat and bone of the excavated existence he was working on.

Well, the smell of the entrails and that agonized blood electrified by all the outer neons of ultimate fear got right into the grit of the stock-yard stench. Let us pass over into the carving and the slicing, the boiling and scraping, annealing and curing of the flesh in sugars and

honeys and smoke, the cooking of the cow carcass, stamp of the inspec-
tor, singeing of the hair, boiling of hooves, grinding of gristle, the wax-
papering and the packaging, the foiling and the canning, the burning
of the residue, and the last slobber of the last unusable guts as it went
into the stockyard furnace, and up as stockyard smoke, burnt blood and
burnt bone and burnt hair to add their properties of specific stench to
fresh blood, fresh entrails, fresh fecalities already all over the air. It is
the smell of the stockyards, all of it taken together, a smell so bad one
must go down to visit the killing of the animals or never eat meat again.
Watching the animals be slaughtered, one knows the human case — no
matter how close to angel we may come, the butcher is equally there. So
be it. Chicago makes for hard minds. On any given night, the smell may
go anywhere — down to Gary to fight with the smog and the coke, out
to Cicero to quiet the gangs with their dreams of gung ho and mop-up,
North to Evanston to remind the polite that *inter faeces et urinam* are we
born, and East on out to Lake Michigan where the super felicities in the
stench of such earth-bound miseries and corruptions might cheer the
fish with the clean spermy deep waters of their fate.

Yes, Chicago was a town where nobody could ever forget how the
money was made. It was picked up from floors still slippery with blood,
and if one did not protest and take a vow of vegetables, one knew at
least that life was hard, life was in the flesh and in the massacre of the
flesh — one breathed the last agonies of beasts. So something of the
entrails and the secrets of the gut got into the faces of native Chica-
goans. A great city, a strong city with faces tough as leather hide and
pavement, it was also a city where the faces took on the broad beastiness
of ears which were dull enough to ignore the bleatings of the doomed,
noses battered enough to smell no more the stench of every unhappy
end, mouths — fat mouths or slit mouths — ready to taste the gravies
which were the reward of every massacre, and eyes, simple pig eyes,
which could look the pig truth in the face. In any other city, they would
have found technologies to silence the beasts with needles, quarter
them with machines, lull them with Muzak, and have stainless steel for
floors, aluminum beds to take over the old overhead trolley — animals
would be given a shot of vitamin-enrichment before they took the last
ride. But in Chicago, they did it straight, they cut the animals right out
of their hearts — which is why it was the last of the great American
cities, and people had great faces, carnal as blood, greedy, direct, too
impatient for hypocrisy, in love with honest plunder. They were big
and human and their brother in heaven was the slaughtered pig —

THE SIEGE OF CHICAGO

they did not ignore him. If the yowls and moans of his extinction was the broth of their strength, still they had honest guts to smell him to the end — they did not flush the city with Odorono or Pinex or No-Scent, they swilled the beer and assigned the hits and gave America its last chance at straight-out drama. Only a great city provides honest spectacle, for that is the salvation of the schizophrenic soul. Chicago may have beasts on the street, it may have a giant of fortitude for Mayor who grew into a beast — a man with the very face of Chicago — but it is an honest town, it does not look to incubate psychotics along an air-conditioned corridor with a vinyl floor.

2

If the face of Chicago might be reduced to a broad fleshy nose with nostrils open wide to stench, stink, power, a pretty day, a well-stacked broad, and the beauties of a dirty buck, the faces in the crowd of some 5,000 Eugene McCarthy supporters out at Midway Airport to greet the Senator's arrival on Sunday, August 25th, could have found their archetype in any one of a number of fairly tall slim young men in seersucker suits with horn-rimmed glasses, pale complexions, thin noses, and thin — this was the center of the common denominator — thin nostrils. People who are greedy have extraordinary capacities for waste disposal — they must, they take in too much. Whereas, the parsimonious end up geared to take in too little — viz., Chicago nostrils versus McCarthy nostrils. Of course, the parsimony of the McCarthyites was of a special sort — they had hardly been mean with funds in supporting their candidate, nor small in the boldness of their attempt, and no one could claim that the loyalty of their effort had been equaled in many a year — certainly not since Adlai Stevenson, perhaps not since Henry Wallace. No, like all crusaders, their stinginess could be found in a ferocious lack of tolerance or liaison to their left or right — the search for Grail seems invariably to proceed in a straight line. It was no accident that an extraordinary number of McCarthyites seemed to drive Volkswagens (or was it that an extraordinary number of Volkswagens bore the white and blue psychedelic flower? — if psychedelic it could truly be called, since the blue was too wan and the white too milky for the real sports of psychedelia land). Support of Eugene McCarthy was, of course, a movement whose strength was in the suburbs and the academy — two bastions of that faith which would state that a man must be allowed to lead a modest and reasonable life without interference by large forces. If corruption in politics, opportunism, and undue ambition excited their contempt, and injustice in race relations their disapproval (because injustice was inflammatory to reason) the war in Vietnam encouraged their most honorable suppressed fury for it spoke of a large and outrageous outside force which would sweep their lives away. In the suburbs and the academy, parents and children came together in detestation of that war.

The moral powers of the vegetarian, the pacifist, and the internationalist have been so refined away from the source of much power — infantile violence — that their moral powers exhibit a leanness, a keenness, and total ferocity which can only hint at worlds given up: precisely those sensuous worlds of corruption, promiscuity, fingers in the take, political alliances forged by the fires of booze, and that sense of property which is the fundamental of all political relations.

Talk of that later — for now, at the airport, enough to observe that the crowd of 5,000 at Midway waiting for Gene McCarthy were remarkably homogeneous, young for the most part, too young to vote, a disproportionate number of babies in mother's arms — sly hint of middle-class Left mentality here at work! (The middle-class Left would never learn that workingmen in greasy dungarees make a point of voting against the mother who carries the babe — the righteous face of any such mother reminds them of schoolteachers they used to hate!) Yes, the rally taking place in a special reserved area of the parking lot at Midway gave glimpses of faces remarkably homogeneous for a political rally. One could pass from heavy-set young men with a full chop of beard and a fifty-pound pack on their back to young adolescent poetesses, pale as Ophelia, prim as Florence Nightingale, from college boys in sweaters with hints of hippie allegiance, to Madison Avenue types in sideburns, straw hats, and a species of pill-taking panache; through decent, mildly fanatic ranks of middle-class professionals — suggestion of vitiated blood in their complexion — to that part of theater and show biz which dependably would take up cause with the cleaner cadres of the Left. One of their ranks, a pretty brunette in a red dress, was leading a set of foot-tapping songs while the crowd waited for the Senator's plane, the style of the lyrics out on that soft shoulder between liberalism and wit, and so reminiscent of the sort of songs Adolph Green and Betty Comden had been composing and Tom Lehrer singing for years. "The special fascination of . . . we think he's just sensa-

tional . . . *Gene! ! !*" two notes sounding on "Gee-yene," so humorous in
its vein, for the lyrics implied one was team with a limited gang of
humans who derived from Noel Coward, Ogden Nash, and juke hill-
billy — "Gee-yene! Gee-yene!"

Song went on: "The GOP will cry in its beer, for here is a man who
will change the scene. Gee-yene! Gee-yene!" Depression came over the
reporter. Try as he would, he could not make himself happy with
McCarthy supporters. Their common denominator seemed to be
found in some blank area of the soul, a species of disinfected idealism
which gave one the impression when among them of living in a loboto-
mized ward of Upper Utopia. George Wallace, pay heed!

Of course, the reporter had been partisan to Bobby Kennedy, excited by precisely his admixture of idealism plus willingness to traffic
with demons, ogres, and overloads of corruption. This had character-
ized the political style of the Kennedys more than once. The Kennedys
had seemed magical because they were a little better than they should
have been, and so gave promise of making America a little better than
it ought to be. The reporter respected McCarthy, he respected him
enormously for trying the vengeance of Lyndon Johnson, his heart had
been given a bit of life by the success of the New Hampshire primary
campaign. If there had then been little to make him glad in the abrupt
and unhappy timing of Bobby Kennedy's immediate entrance into the
race for nomination, he had, nonetheless, remained Kennedy's man —
he saw the battle between the two as tragic; he had hardly enjoyed the
Kennedy-McCarthy debate on television before the California primary; he had not taken pleasure in rooting for Kennedy and being
thereby forced to condemn McCarthy's deadness of manner, blankness
of affect, and suggestion of weakness in each deep pouch beneath each
eye. The pouches spoke of clichés — eyes sitting in sagging brassieres
of flesh, such stuff. He knew that McCarthy partisans would find equal
fault somewhere in Kennedy.

A few nights after this debate, the reporter was awakened from a
particularly oppressive nightmare by the ringing of a bell. He heard
the voice of an old drinking friend he had not seen in two years. "Cox,"
he shouted into the phone, "are you out of your skull? What do you
mean calling at three A.M.?"

"Look," said the friend, "get the television on. I think you ought to
see it. Bobby Kennedy has just been shot."

"No," he bellowed. "No! No! No!" his voice railing with an ugliness
and pain reminiscent to his ear of the wild grunts of a wounded pig.

(Where he had heard that cry he did not at the moment remember.) He felt as if he were being despoiled of a vital part of himself, and in the middle of this horror noted that he screamed like a pig, not a lion, nor a bear. The reporter had gone for years on the premise that one must balance every moment between the angel in oneself and the swine — the sound of his own voice shocked him therefore profoundly. The balance was not what he thought it to be. He watched television for the next hours in a state which drifted rudderless between two horrors. Then, knowing no good answer could come for days, if at all, on the possible recovery of Bobby Kennedy, he went back to bed and lay in a sweat of complicity, as if his own lack of moral *witness* (to the subtle heroism of Bobby Kennedy's attempt to run for President) could be found in the dance of evasions his taste for a merry life and a married one had become, as if this precise lack had contributed (in the vast architectonics of the cathedral of history) to one less piton of mooring for Senator Kennedy in his lonely ascent of those vaulted walls, as if finally the efforts of brave men depended in part on the protection of other men who saw themselves as at least provisionally brave, or sometimes brave, or at the least — if not brave — balanced at least on a stability between selflessness and appetite and therefore — by practical purposes — decent. But he was close to having become too much of appetite — he had spent the afternoon preceding this night of assassination in enjoying a dalliance — let us leave it at that — a not uncharacteristic way to have spent his time, and lying next to his wife now, TV news pictures of the assassination rocketing all over the bruised stone of his skull, he hated his wife for having ever allowed such a condition to come to be, hated her subtle complicity in driving him out, and then apart, and knew from the other side of his love that he must confess this afternoon now, as if that would be a warrant of magic to aid Senator Kennedy on the long voyage through the depth of the exploded excavations in his brain, and did not have the simple courage to confess, stopped in his mental steps as if confronting a bully in an alley and altogether unable to go on — the bully in the alley no less than his wife's illimitable funds of untempered redneck wrath. So he did what all men who are overweight must do — he prayed the Lord to take the price on his own poor mortal self (since he had flesh in surfeit to offer) he begged that God spare Senator Kennedy's life, and he would give up something, give up what? — give up some of the magic he could bring to bear on some one or another of the women, yes, give that up if the life would be saved, and fell back into the horror of trying to rest with the sense that his offer might have been given too late and by the wrong vein — confession to his wife was what the moral pressure had first demanded — and so fell asleep with some gnawing sense of the Devil there to snatch his offering after the angel had moved on in disgust.

Kennedy dead, he was doubly in gloom, passionate gloom for the loss of that fine valuable light — like everyone else he loved Bobby Kennedy by five times more in death than life — a few lives have the value to illumine themselves in their death. But he was also dull in dejection at what he might have given away that other night. For he believed a universe in which at stricken moments one could speak quietly to whichever manifest of God or Devil was near, had to be as reasonable a philosophical proposition as any assumption that such dialogues were deluded. So it was possible he had given something away, and for nothing: the massive irreversible damage to the Senator's brain had occurred before the spring of his own generosity had even been wet. Indeed! Who knew what in reality might have been granted if he had worked for the first impulse and dared offer confession on a connubial bed. A good could have come to another man and by another route.

He never knew for certain if something had been given up — he was working too hard in too many ways to notice subtle change. (Although it seemed to him that a piece of magic had probably been relinquished.) Who cared but the reporter? He was, in general, depressed; then he met Senator McCarthy at a cocktail party in Cambridge not a week after the assassination. McCarthy was in depression as well.

3

At this party, McCarthy looked weary beyond belief, his skin a used-up yellow, his tall body serving for no more than to keep his head up above the crowd at the cocktail party. Like feeder fish, smaller people were nibbling on his reluctant hulk with questions, idiotic questions, petulant inquiries he had heard a thousand times. "Why?" asked a young woman, college instructor, horn-rimmed glasses, "Why don't we get out of Vietnam?" her voice near hysterical, ringing with the harsh electronics of cancer gulch, and McCarthy looked near to flinching with the question and the liverish demand on him to answer. "Well," he said in his determinedly mild and quiet voice, last drop of humor never voided — for if on occasion he might be surrounded by dolts, volts, and empty circuits, then nothing to do but send remarks up to the angel of laughter. "Well," said Senator McCarthy, "there seem to be a few obstacles in the way."

But his pale green eyes had that look somewhere between humor and misery which the Creation might offer when faced with the bull-dozers of boredom.

Years ago, in 1960, the reporter had had two glimpses of Eugene McCarthy. At the Democratic Convention in Los Angeles which nominated John F. Kennedy, McCarthy had made a speech for another candidate. It was the best nominating speech the reporter had ever heard. He had written about it with the metaphor of a bullfight:

> . . . he held the crowd like a matador . . . gathering their emotion, discharging it, creating new emotion on the wave of the last, driving his passes tighter and tighter as he readied for the kill. "Do not reject this man who made us all proud to be called Democrats, do not leave this prophet without honor in his own party." McCarthy went on, his muleta furled for the *naturales*. "There was only one man who said let's talk sense to the American people. He said, the promise of America is the promise of greatness. This was his call to greatness . . . Do not forget this man . . . Ladies and gentlemen, I present to you not the favorite son of one state, but the favorite son of the fifty states, the favorite son of every country he has visited, the favorite son of every country which has not seen him but is secretly thrilled by his name." Bedlam. The kill. "Ladies and gentlemen, I present to you Adlai Stevenson of Illinois." Ears and tail. Hooves and bull. A roar went up like the roar one heard the day Bobby Thompson hit his home run at the Polo Grounds and the Giants won the pennant from the Dodgers in the third playoff game of the 1951 season. The demonstration cascaded onto the floor, the gallery came to its feet, the sports arena sounded like the inside of a marching drum.

Perhaps three months later, just after his piece on that convention had appeared, and election time was near, he had met Senator McCarthy at another cocktail party on Central Park West to raise money for the campaign of Mark Lane, then running for State Assemblyman in New York. The reporter had made a speech himself that day. Having decided, on the excitements of the Kennedy candidacy and other excitements (much marijuana for one) to run for Mayor of New York the following year, he gave his maiden address at that party, a curious, certainly a unique political speech, private, personal, tortured in metaphor, sublimely indifferent to issues, platform, or any recognizable paraphernalia of the political process, and delivered in much too rapid a voice to the assembled bewilderment of his audience, a collective (and by the end very numb) stiff clavicle of Jewish Central Park West matrons. The featured speaker, Senator McCarthy, was to follow, and climbing up on the makeshift dais as he stepped down, the Senator gave him a big genial wide-as-the-open-plains Midwestern grin.

"Better learn how to breathe, boy," he whispered out of the corner of his mouth, and proceeded to entertain the audience for the next few minutes with a mixture of urbanity, professional elegance, and political savvy. That was eight years ago.

But now, near to eight years later, the hour was different, the audience at this cocktail party in Cambridge with their interminable questions and advice, their over-familiarity yet excessive reverence, their desire to touch McCarthy, prod him, *galvanize* him, seemed to do no more than drive him deeper into the insulations of his fatigue, his very disenchantment — so his pores seemed to speak — with the democratic process. He was not a mixer. Or if he had ever been a mixer, as he must have been years ago, he had had too much of it since, certainly too much since primaries in New Hampshire, Wisconsin, Indiana, Oregon, and California — he had become, or he had always been, too private a man for the damnable political mechanics of mixing, fixing, shaking the hands, answering the same questions which had already answered themselves by being asked. And now the threat of assassination over all, that too, that his death might come like the turn of a card, and could a man be ready? The gloomy, empty tomb-like reverberations of the last shot shaking rough waves doubtless through his own dreams, for his eyes, sensitive, friendly, and remote as the yellow eyes of an upper primate in a cage, spoke out of the weary, sagging face, up above the sagging pouches, seeming to say, "Yes, try to rescue me — but as you see, it's not quite possible." And the reporter, looking to perform the errand of rescue, went in to talk about the speech of 1960 in Los Angeles, and how it was the second best political speech he had ever heard.

"Oh," said McCarthy, "tell me, what was the best?"

And another questioner jostled the circle about McCarthy to ask another question, the Secret Service man in the gray suit at McCarthy's elbow stiffening at the impact. But McCarthy held the questioner at a distance by saying, "No, I'd like to listen for a while." It had obviously become his pleasure to listen to others. So the reporter told a story about Vito Marcantonio making a speech in Yankee Stadium in 1948, and the Senator listened carefully, almost sadly, as if remembering other hours of oratory.

On the way out the door, in the press of guests and local party workers up to shake his hand before he was gone, a tall bearded fellow, massive chin, broad brow for broad horn-rimmed glasses, spoke out in a resonant voice marred only by the complacency of certain nasal in-trigues. "Senator, I'm a graduate student in English, and I like your politics very much, but I must tell you, I think your poetry stinks."

McCarthy took it like a fighter being slapped by the referee across the forearms. "You see what it is, running for President," said the laughter in his eyes. If he worshiped at a shrine, it was near the saint of good humor.

"Give my regards to Robert Lowell," said the reporter. "Say to him that I read 'The Drunken Fisherman' just the other day."

McCarthy looked like the victim in the snow when the St. Bernard comes up with the rum. His eyes came alight at the name of the poem ... "I will catch Christ with a greased worm" might have been the line he remembered. He gave a little wave, was out the door.

Yet the reporter was depressed after the meeting. McCarthy did not look nor feel like a President, not that tall tired man with his bright subtle eyes which could sharpen the razor's edge of a nuance, no, he seemed more like the dean of the finest English department in the land. There wasn't that sense of a man with vast ambition and sufficient character to make it luminous, so there was not that charisma which leaves no argument about the nature of the attempt.

4

If that meeting had been in the beginning of June, there were differences now by the end of August. McCarthy, at Midway Airport to greet his followers, looked big in his Presidential candidate's suit this sunny afternoon, no longer tired, happy apparently with the crowd and the air of his reception. He went down the aisle of friends and reporters who had managed to get ahead of the restraining rope for the crowd and shook hands, giving a confident wink or good twinkle, "Whatever are you doing *here*, Norman?" he said with a grin, quick as a jab, and made his way up to the platform where a clump of microphones on spikes garnished the podium. But the microphones were dead. Which set McCarthy to laughing. Meanwhile posters waved out in the crowd: AMERICA'S PRIMARY HOPE; LUCIDITY, NOT LUNACY; MAKE MINE MCCARTHY. He scanned the home-made posters, as if his sense of such language, after a decade and more, had become sufficiently encyclopedic to treasure every rare departure, and he laughed from time to time as he saw something he liked.

Finally, he called out to the crowd, "*They* cut the power line. *We're* trying to fix it." Great college moans at the depravity of the opposition — wise laughter at the good cheer of the situation. "Let's sing," said Gene McCarthy; a shout from the crowd. His standard was theirs: good wit could always support small horror. So they sang, "This land is your land, this land is my land," and McCarthy moved along to another mike, with much shifting of position in his entourage to be near him, then he gave up and came back to the first mike. Things were now fixed. He introduced Senator Yarborough from Texas who would in turn introduce him. Yarborough looked like a florid genial iron-ribbed barrel of a British Conservative MP, and spoke with a modest Texas accent; he told the audience that McCarthy had "won this campaign in the hearts of the American people." While he spoke, McCarthy sat next to his wife Abigail, a warm-colored woman with a pleasant face full of the arch curves of a most critical lady of the gentry. Something in her expression spoke of uncharitable wit, but she was elegant — one could see her as First Lady. Indeed! One could almost see him now as President. He had size, he had humor. He looked strong. When he got up to speak, he was in easy form. Having laughed at a poster which said, WELCOME TO FORT DALEY, he began by paying his respects to the Mayor of Chicago who is "watching over all of us."

"Big Brother," shouted a powerhouse in the crowd.

McCarthy talked for six or seven minutes. The audience was looking for a bust-out-of-the-corrals speech but the Senator was not giving it. He talked mildly, with his throwaway wit, his almost diffident assertion — "We can build a new society and a new world," said he at one point in the mildest tones of his mild register, and then added as if to take the curse off such intellectual presumption, "We're not asking for too much — just a modest use of intelligence."

"Too much," murmured a news-service man admiringly.

A good yell came up. Even a modest use of intelligence would forbid Vietnam.

McCarthy drew one more big cheer by declaring he was not interested in being Vice-President. "I'm not here to compromise what we've all worked for," he said to cheers, and shortly after, to the crowd's disappointment, was done. The band played — Warren King's Brass Impact, four trombones, two guitars, drums, six trumpets, one tenor sax, two Negroes not very black among the musicians.

Yes, he had compromised nothing, not even the musicians. If he was at heart a conservative, and no great man for the Blacks, then damned if he would encourage harmoniums and avalanches of soul music. No, he had done it his way up to now, cutting out everyone from his councils who was interested in politicking at the old trough, no, his campaign had begun by being educational, and educational had he left it — he had not compromised an inch, nor played the demagogue for a moment, and it had given him strength, not strength enough perhaps to win, certainly not enough to win, but rectitude had laid the keel, and in that air of a campaign run at last for intelligent men, and give no alms to whores, he left.

It was no great meeting, but excitement was there, some thin weal of hope that victory, impossible to spring aloft, might still find wings. Take a good look, for it is the last of such pleasant occasions. Later that day, Hubert Humphrey came into O'Hare, but there was no crowd to receive him, just a few of the Humphrey workers. Hubert Humphrey had two kinds of workers. Some, with crew-cut or straight combed hair, could have gone with Ronald Reagan. Others were out of that restaurant where Mafia shakes hands with the union. Let no one say that Hubert was unfriendly to the real people. But there is more to see of all these men.

5

Here, my friends, on the prairies of Illinois and the Middle West, we can see a long way in all directions . . . here there are no barriers, no defenses to ideas and to aspirations. We want none. We want no shackles on the mind or the spirit, no rigid patterns of thought and no iron conformity. We want only the faith and the convictions of triumph and free and fair contest.

(From an address by Adlai Stevenson, Governor of Illinois, to the Democratic Convention in Chicago in 1952.)

It may be time to attempt a summary of the forces at work upon the convention of 1968.

A similar consideration of the Republican convention never seemed necessary. The preliminaries to Miami Beach were simple: Nixon, by dint of an historical vacuum whose presence he was the first to discern, and by the profit of much hard work, early occupied the Republican center — the rest of the history resides in Rockefeller's attempts to clarify his own position to himself. Was he to respond only to a draft of Republicans desperate not to lose to Johnson, then to Kennedy, or was he to enter primaries, and divide the party? Since he was perfectly capable of winning the election with a divided Republican Party, because his presence as a nominee would divide the Democratic Party even further, the question was academic. But Rockefeller's history can not be written, for it is to be found in the timing of his advisers and the advice of his intimates, and they are not ready, one would assume, to hang themselves yet.

Where it is not to remain hidden, the Republican history was relatively simple and may be passed over. It is the Democratic which insists on presenting itself, for no convention ever had such events for prelude.

On March 31, on a night when the latest Gallup Poll showed LBJ to be in favor with only 36% of the American public (while only 23% approved his handling of the war) Johnson announced on national television that he would not seek nor "accept the nomination of my party as your President." On April 2, there was talk that Humphrey would run — McCarthy had taken the Wisconsin primary with 57% of the vote to Johnson's 35% (and it was estimated that if Johnson had not resigned, the vote would have been more like 64% to 28%).

On April 4, Martin Luther King, Jr., was assassinated by a white man, and violence, fire and looting broke out in Memphis, Harlem, Brooklyn, Washington, D.C., Chicago, Detroit, Boston and Newark over the next week. Mayor Daley gave his famous "shoot to kill" instruction to the Chicago police, and National Guard and U.S. troops were sent to some of these cities.

On April 23 Columbia students barricaded the office of a Dean. By another day the campus was disrupted, then closed, and was never to be comfortably open again for the rest of the semester. On May 10, as if indicative of a spontaneous world-wide movement, the students of the Sorbonne battled the Paris police on barricades and in the streets.

185

On the same day, Maryland was quietly pledging its delegates to Humphrey.

On June 3, Andy Warhol was shot. On June 4, after winning the California primary 45% to 42% for McCarthy, and 12% for Humphrey, RFK was shot in the head and died next day. The cannibalistic war of the McCarthy and Kennedy peace forces was at an end. McCarthy had been all but finished in Indiana, Nebraska, Iowa, and South Dakota; Kennedy had been badly mauled by his defeat in Oregon. Meanwhile Humphrey had been picking up delegates in states like Missouri, which did not have primaries, and the delegates in states which did, like Pennsylvania, after it had given 90% of its vote to McCarthy.

So went the month. Cleveland with its first Negro Mayor still had a riot. Spock, Goodman, Ferber and Coffin were sentenced to two years in jail. Kentucky with 46 delegates gave 41 to HH , and the McCarthy supporters walked out. There were stories every other day of Humphrey's desire to have Teddy Kennedy for Vice-President, and much comment in columns on the eagerness of the Democrats to move the convention from Chicago. Chicago had a telephone strike and the likelihood of a taxi strike and a bus strike. Chicago was to be unwilling host to a Yippie (Youth International Party) convention the week the Democrats would be there. Chicago had the massive bull temper of Mayor Daley for the Democratic Party to contend with — much work went on behind the scenes to move the convention to Miami where the telephone and television lines were in, and Daley would be out. But Daley was not about to let the convention leave his city. Daley promised he would enforce the peace and allow no outrageous demonstrations, Daley hinted that his wrath — if the convention were moved — might burn away whole corners of certain people's support. Since Hubert Humphrey was the one who could most qualify for certain people, he was in no hurry to offend the Mayor. Lyndon Johnson, when beseeched by interested parties to encourage Daley to agree to the move, was rumored to have said, "Miami Beach is not an American city."

The TV networks applied massive pressure to shift the convention. In Chicago, because of the strictures of the strike, their cameras would be limited to the hotels and to the Amphitheatre — they would not be able to take their portable generators out to the street and run lines to their color cameras. That would not be permitted. They were restricted to movie cameras, which would make them half a day late in reporting action or interviews in the streets (half a day late for television is equal to being a week late). How they must have focused their pressure on Daley and Johnson. It is to the Mayor's curious credit that he was strong enough to withstand them. It should have been proof interior that Daley was no other-directed Twentieth-Century politician. Any such man would have known the powers of retaliation which resided in the mass media. One did not make an enemy of a television network for nothing; they could repay injury with no more than a chronic slur in the announcer's voice every time your deadly name was mentioned over the next twelve months, or next twelve years. Daley, however, was not a national politician, but a clansman — he could get 73% of the vote in any constituency made up of people whose ancestors were at home with rude instruments in Polish forests, Ukrainian marshes, Irish bogs — they knew how to defend the home: so did he. No interlopers for any network of Jew-Wasp media men were going to dominate the streets of his parochial city, nor none of their crypto-accomplices with long hair, sexual liberty, drug license and unbridled mouths. It was as if the primitive powers of the Mayor's lungs, long accustomed to breathing all variety of blessings and curses (from the wind of ancestors, constituents, and screaming beasts in the stockyards where he had once labored for a decade and more) could take everything into his chest, mighty barrel of a chest in Richard J. Daley, 200 pounds, 5 feet 8 inches tall. These blessings and curses, once prominently and in public breathed in, could be processed, pulverized, and washed into the choleric blood, defiance in the very pap and hemoglobin of it — "I'll swallow up their spit and shove it through," the Mayor could always bellow to his electorate. So Daley was ready to take on the electronic wrath of the semi-conductors of the world, his voter-nourished blood full of beef and curses against the transistorized communicatory cabals of the media. And back of him — no evidence will ever be produced to prove such a thought — must have been Lyndon Johnson, great wounded secret shaman of the Democratic Party. If Teddy Roosevelt had once wrecked William Howard Taft and the Republican Party by running as a Bull Moose, so Lyndon Johnson was now a warlock of a Bull Moose, conceiving through all the months of June, July, and August how he would proceed to create a cursed convention, a platform, a candidate, and a party which would be his own as much as the nightmarish vision of a phantom ship is the soul of a fever; he would seek to rend his party, crack it in two — that party to which his own allegiance in near to forty years could hardly be questioned —

because that party had been willing to let him go. In revenge he would create a candidate who need never run, for his campaign would be completed by the nomination. Conceive what he would have thought of a candidate who could attract more votes than himself.

6

"Politics is property," said Murray Kempton, delegate from New York, over the epiphanies of a drink, and never was a new science comprehended better by a young delegate. Lyndon Johnson was first preceptor of the key that politics-is-property so you never give something away for nothing. Convention politics is therefore not the art of the possible so much as the art of what is possible when you are dealing with property holders. A delegate's vote is his holding — he will give it up without return no more than a man will sign over his house entire to a worthy cause.

The true property-holder is never ambivalent about his land, he does not mock it, or see adjacent estates as more deserving than his own — so a professional in politics without pride in his holding is a defector. The meanest ward-heeler in the cheapest block of Chicago has his piece — he cannot be dislodged without leaving his curse nor the knotty untangling of his relations with a hundred job-holders in the area; he gives up tithes in the umbilical act of loyalty to his boss, he receives protection for his holding in return.

Such property relations are to be witnessed for every political sinecure in the land — judgeships, jobs, contracts, promises — it comes down to chairs in offices, and words negotiable like bonds: all of that is politics as simple property. Everybody in the game has a piece, and that piece is workable, it is equivalent to capital, it can be used to accrue interest by being invested in such sound conservative enterprises as decades of loyalty to the same Machine. So long as the system progresses, so will one's property be blessed with dividends. But such property can also be used as outright risk capital — one can support an insurgent movement in one's party, even risk the loss of one's primary holding in return for the possibility of acquiring much more.

This, of course, is still politics at city hall, county or state house, this is the politics of the party regular, politics as simple property, which is to say politics as concrete negotiable power — the value of their engagement in politics is at any moment just about directly convertible to cash.

Politics at the national level can still be comprehended by politics-as-property provided one remembers that moral integrity (or the public impression of such) in a high politician is also property, since it brings power and/or emoluments to him. Indeed a very high politician — which is to say a statesman or leader — has no political substance unless he is the servant of ideological institutions or interests and the available moral passions of the electorate, so serving, he is the agent of the political power they bestow on him, which power is certainly a property. Being a leading anti-Communist used to be an invaluable property for which there was much competition — Richard Nixon had once gotten in early on the equivalent of an Oklahoma landgrab by staking out whole territories of that property. "End the war in Vietnam" is a property to some, "Let no American blood be shed in vain" is obviously another. A politician picks and chooses among moral properties. If he is quick-witted, unscrupulous, and does not mind a life of constant anxiety, he will hasten — there is a great competition for things valuable in politics — to pick up properties wherever he can, even if they are rival holdings. To the extent a politician is his own man, attached to his own search for his own spiritual truth — which is to say willing to end in any unpalatable position to which the character of his truth could lead him — then he is ill-equipped for the game of politics. Politics is property. You pick up as much as you can, pay the minimum for the holding, extract the maximum, and combine where you may — small geniuses like Humphrey saw, for example, that devout trade-unionism and devout anti-Communism might once have faced each other across No Man's Land but right after the Second World War were ready to enrich each other into the tenfold of national respectability.

There is no need to underline Lyndon Johnson's ability to compre-hend these matters. (For the higher game of international politics-is-property he was about as well-equipped as William F. Buckley, Eleanor Roosevelt, Barry Goldwater, George Patton, J. Edgar Hoover, Ronald Reagan, and Averell Harriman, but that is another matter.) Johnson understood that so far as a man was a political animal (and therefore not searching for some private truth which might be independent of politics) he was then, if deprived of his properties, close to being a dead man. So the true politicial animal is cautious — he never, except in the most revolutionary times, permits himself to get into a position where he will have to dare his political stake on one issue, one bet, no, to avoid

189

that, he will even give up small pieces of his stuff for nothing, he will pay tribute, which is how raids are sometimes made, and how Barry Goldwater won his nomination. (For his followers promised political extermination with all dispatch to those marginal delegates not quite ready to come along.)

The pearl in the oyster of this proposition is that there is only one political job in America which has no real property attached to it, except for the fantastical property of promotion by tragedy, and that, of course, is the Vice-Presidency. It is the only high office to which all the secondary characteristics of political property may adhere — comprehensive public awareness of the name, attention in the press to one's speeches, honorary emoluments in the Senate, intimacy (of varying degree) with the President, junkets abroad. If you are very active as Vice-President, everyone in America knows your name. But that is your only property. It is not the same thing as real power — more like being a movie star. Taken in proportion to the size of the office, the Vice-President has less real holding than the ward-heeler in his anteroom chair. The Vice-President can promise many things, but can be certain of delivering on nothing. So he can never be certain of getting anything back. It is not a job for a politician but a philosopher.

It is the thesis of this argument that Lyndon Johnson, having recognized that he could not win the election in 1968 (and could win the nomination for a candidate of his choice only by exploding his own party into two or more fragments) nonetheless set out to make the party vindicate him. The last property of political property is ego, ego intact, ego burnished by institutional and reverential flame. Not all men wish statues of themselves on their tomb, but it is hard to think of LBJ with a plain stone — "Here lies a simple fellow with many victories and one catastrophic mistake" — Lyndon would carry his emoluments into the debating chambers of Hell. He had had to live after all through March and April and May with the possibility of Bobby Kennedy winning the nomination, winning the election, the laughter of the Kennedys playing echoes off the walls of his own bad dreams; Lyndon had learned during the propertyless period of his own Vice-Presidential days how rapid could be the slide of your holdings, how soluble the proud salts of your ego. How quickly might come his deterioration if a Kennedy were again in office — his own bleak death in such a case may have spoken to him already. Men whose lives are built on ego can die of any painful disease but one — they cannot endure the dissolution of their own ego, for then nothing is left with which to face emotion, nothing but the urge to grovel at the enemy's feet. It is the primitive price one pays for holding onto property which possesses no moral value. How much Johnson must have been ready to offer in March and April and May in order that Bobby Kennedy be stopped. Perhaps even his own vindication might have been sacrificed.

After the Senator's assassination, however, nomination for Humphrey was empty for Johnson. If Humphrey wished to win the election, his interest was to separate himself from the President. Since this was counter to Johnson's interest, the torture of Hubert Humphrey began.

Mark it: politics is the hard dealing of hard men over properties; their strength is in dealing and their virility. Back of each negotiator is the magic of his collected properties — the real contention of the negotiation is: whose properties possess the more potent magic? A good politician then can deal with every kind of property-holder but a fanatic, because the fanatic is disembodied from his property. He conceives of his property — his noble ideal! — as existing just as well without him. His magic partakes of the surreal. That is why Lyndon Johnson could never deal with Ho Chi Minh, and why he could manipulate Hubert Humphrey with absolute confidence. Humphrey had had to live for four years with no basic property, and nobody knew better than the President what that could do to an animal as drenched in politics as Hubert. Humphrey could never make his move. Deprived for four years of his seat as Senator, deprived of constituency, and the power to trade votes, the small intricate nourishing marrow of being able to measure the profit or loss of concrete favors traded for concrete favors, the exchange of political affections based on solid property-giving, property-acquiring negotiations, forced to offer influence he now might or might not possess, Humphrey never knew where to locate himself in negotiations spoken or unspoken with Lyndon Johnson. So his feet kept slipping. Against the crusades of law and order building on the Right, his hope was to build a crusade on the Left, not to divide the Left. But to do that, he would have had to dare the enmity of Lyndon Johnson, have had to dare the real chance that he might lose the nomination, and that was the one chance he could not take for that would be the hollowest death of them all. He would be lost in retirement, his idle flesh would witness with horror the decomposition of his ego. A politician in such trouble can give away the last of his soul in order not to be forced to witness how much he has given away already.

Hubert Humphrey was the small genius of American politics — his horror was that he was wed to Lyndon Johnson, the domestic genius of us all. Humphrey could not find sufficient pride in his liver to ask for divorce. His liver turned to dread. He came to Chicago with nobody to greet him at the airport except a handful of the faithful — the Vice-President's own poor property — those men whose salary he paid, and they were not many. Later, a group of a few hundred met him at the Sherman House, the boys and the Humphrey girls were out. In 1964 some of the Goldwater girls had looked like hookers on horses, now in '68, some of the women for Humphrey looked like hookers. The Mafia loved Humphrey; they always loved a political leader who kept a well-oiled pair of peanuts in his pants, and there was big money behind Humphrey, $800,000 had been raised for him in one night in New York; he would be the perfect President — for a time — for every speculator who liked a government contract to anchor his line while he got off that touchdown pass. So Humphrey money was there in Chicago for convention frolics, and a special nightclub or cabaret in the Hilton called the Hubaret where you needed a scorecard to separate the trade-union leaders from the Maf, and the women — let us not insult women. Suffice it that the beehives were out, and every girl named Marie had a coif like Marie Antoinette. Every Negro on the take was there as well — some of the slickest, roundest, blackest swingers ever to have contacts in with everyone from Mayor Daley to the Black-stone Rangers. There was action at the Hubaret, and cheer for every late-night drinker. If Hubie got in, the after-hours joints would prosper; the politics of joy would never demand that all the bars be dead by four —who could argue with that?

Negroes in general had never been charmed with McCarthy. If he was the epitome of Whitey at his best, that meant Whitey at ten removes, dry wit, stiff back, two and a half centuries of Augustan culture and their distillate — the ironic manners of the tightest country gentry; the Blacks did not want Whitey at his best and boniest in a year when they were out to find every justification (they were not hard to find) to hate the Honkie. But if the Black militant and the Black workingman would find no comfort or attraction in McCarthy, think then of how the Black mixer-dixer was going to look on Clean Gene. He wasn't about to make a pilgrimage up to some Catholic rectory in the Minnesota North Woods where they passed one bean through the hot water for bean soup, no, he wanted some fatback in his hand. You couldn't take the kind of hard and sanctified little goat turds McCarthy was passing out for political marbles back to the Black homefolk when they were looking for you to spread the gravy around. So Hubie Humphrey came into Chicago with nine-tenths of the organized Democratic Party — Black support, labor support, Mafia support, Southern delegates support, and you could find it all at the Hubaret if you were looking, as well as a wet wash of delegates with buttons for Humphrey, the big bold HH with its unwitting — though who knew these days what was unwitting? — reference to barbed-wire fences, concentration camps, gas chambers. The letter H went marching to the horizon.

There were 1,400–1,500 delegates secured for Hubert Humphrey on the day he came to town — such was the hard estimate of the hardest hands on his staff, Larry O'Brien, Norman Sherman, Bill Connell; the figure was low, they were not counting on the favorite sons of the South, nor on the small reserve of uncommitted delegates. Still there were rumors up of gale warnings, and much anxiety — Mayor Daley had led the Illinois delegation into caucus on Sunday, and led them out again without committing a single one of the state's 118 votes to a single delegate and there were stories Daley wanted Teddy Kennedy. John Connally of Texas, furious that the unit rule was about to be abolished in this convention, gave threats on Sunday of nominating Lyndon Johnson.

Either the convention was sewed up for Humphrey or the convention was soft. No one really knew. Usually it was enough to come to conventions with less than a first ballot victory, even two hundred votes less, and you were certain of winning. The panic among delegates to get on the winning side at the last minute is always a stampede. It is as though your land will double in value. Humphrey came in with one hundred to two hundred votes more than he needed, yet he was not without his own panic; he took care to announce on "Meet the Press" before taking the plane to Chicago that he supported President Johnson's Vietnam policies because they were "basically sound." For two months he had been vacillating, giving hints one day that he was not far from the doves, rushing back the next to be close in tone to the Administration. It could be said, of course, that it was part of his political skill to keep the McCarthyites uncertain of his position; once convinced that he would take a line close to Lyndon Johnson on the war in Vietnam, they might look — McCarthy included — to induce Teddy Kennedy to run. So Humphrey played at being a dove as a way of holding the youngest Kennedy in Hyannis. But what was he to gain besides the approval of Lyndon Johnson? A liaison with McCarthy could even give him a chance for victory in November. Yet Humphrey engaged in massive safe play after massive safe play, paying court to the South, paying court to LBJ, to Daley, to Meany, to Connally; even then, he came to Chicago with his nomination insecure. He had 1,500 votes, but if something went wrong he did not know if he could count on a single one of them — they could all wash away in the night. Humphrey was staying at the Conrad Hilton, but his first act after landing at O'Hare was to proceed to the Sherman House to visit the Illinois delegation. Daley was working to induce Teddy Kennedy to run — once Teddy Kennedy ran and lost, he might have to accept a draft as Vice-President. At the same time, once running, he might show huge strength — Daley would then be able to claim he stole the nomination from Humphrey and got it over to Kennedy. Daley could not lose. All the while he was encouraging Kennedy to run, Humphrey was promising Daley more and more treasures, obliged — since he had no political property of his own just yet — to mortgage future property. He was assigning future and double substance to Daley, to the unions, to the South, to business interests. His holding operations, his safe plays to guarantee the nomination once the nomination was already secure, became exorbitantly expensive. A joke made the rounds of the convention:

"What was Hubert able to keep?"

"Well, he was able to keep Muriel."

His dangers were absurdly small. McCarthy, three times unpopular with the delegates, for being right, for being proud that he was right, and for dealing only in moral property, had no chance whatsoever. Moreover, he was disliked intensely by the Kennedyites. If Bobby Kennedy and Gene McCarthy had been in the Sinn Fein together they would have carried their guns in holsters under opposite shoulders — they embodied the ultimate war of the Irish. McCarthy was reputed to carry volumes of Augustine and Aquinas in his suitcase; it is possible Bobby Kennedy thought one of the penalties of being Irish is that you could get lost in the *Summa Theologica*.

But Hubert Humphrey carried no gun and no tome. Finally he was a hawk not a dove for the most visceral of reasons — his viscera were not firm enough to face the collective wrath of that military-industrial establishment he knew so well in Washington, that rifleman's schizophrenia one could see in the eyes of the clerks at the Pentagon, yes, his fear went beyond political common sense and a real chance to win, it went even beyond slavery to LBJ (because LBJ finally had also been afraid of the Pentagon) it came down to the simple fear that he was not ready to tell the generals that they were wrong. Peace they might yet accept, but not the recognition that they were somewhat insane — as quickly tell dragons to shift their nest.

7

It was a curious convention, all but settled before it began, except for the bile-bubbling fear of the nominee that he would lose; it was locked, yet extraordinarily unsettled, even if totally dominated by Lyndon Johnson. He had his men everywhere — Hale Boggs, Majority Whip of the House on the Platform Committee; Carl Albert, Majority Leader of the House as Chairman of the convention; John B. Connally, Governor of Texas, and Mayor Daley, Governor of Chicago, in front of the rostrum with their Texas and Illinois delegations, the rostrum indeed so layered about with Humphrey delegations that if one took a swing in semicircle through the states nearest to the podium, Minnesota, Utah, Kentucky, Tennessee, Texas, Rhode Island, the Virgin Islands, Illinois, Pennsylvania, West Virginia, Hawaii, Connecticut, New Jersey, Delaware and Florida, the final returns for Johnson's candidate were 730 votes out of a possible 834, and in none of those states did he have less than two-thirds of the delegates. To the rear of the Amphitheatre, in a semicircle through the seats farthest removed from the podium, Vermont, Puerto Rico, New York, California, Colorado, Virginia, Wisconsin, Arkansas, Oregon, Missouri, Mississippi, and New Hampshire, the vote for Humphrey was only 297 out of 720.

It could be asked to what end go such picayune preparations, and the answer is politics is property. A good seat at a convention, strong, central and down front, is as important as a good seat at a show. Politicians do not have egos which sleep far from their property; since they are all a hint psychopathic (their sense of the present being vastly more intense than their sense of the past) a poor seat depresses their view of themselves. This might have an effect of no more than one percent on the stout-hearted, but Lyndon Johnson, like the Mafia, worked on point spread and picked up nickels and dimes in every percentage.

The man who made the arrangements was John Criswell, Treasurer of the Democratic National Convention, an unknown until installed by the President; such a Johnson man, he even gave the Humphrey people a difficult time on small matters, which was precisely the way to remind a man like the Vice-President that he was yet politically land-less. Nonetheless, Humphrey contingents had front seats — they could boo the speaker or cheer him, threaten his delivery with the imminence of their presence, not insignificant when one had to look at Illinois goons humphing in concert with Daley. Some of them had eyes like drills; others, noses like plows; jaws like amputated knees; they combed their hair straight with a part to the side in imitation of the Mayor who from up close had a red skin with many veins and hair which looked like dirty gray silk combed out straight — at his worst, Daley looked in fact like a vastly robust old peasant woman with a dirty gray silk wig. (At his best, he looked respectable enough to be coach of the Chicago Bears.) At any rate, no small matter to have the Illinois delegation under your nose at the podium, all those hecklers, fixers, flunkies, and musclemen scanning the audience as if to freeze certain obstreperous faces, make them candidates for a contract and a hit. The guys with eyes like drills always acted this way, it was their purchase on stagecraft, but the difference in this convention were the riots outside, and the roughing of the delegates in the hall, the generator trucks on the perimeter of the stockyards ready to send voltage down the line of barbed wire, the police and Canine Corps in the marshes west of the Amphitheatre. Politics is property. Rush forward with your standard. Push and push. When you get near the podium, there is nothing to see but Daley and Connally. Take a look at Connally, Governor of Texas, who once sat across from John F. Kennedy in the Presidential limou-sine passing the Elm Street Book Depository. Connally is a handsome man, mean, mean right to the gum, he has wavy silver hair, is cocky as a dude, sports a sharp nose, a thin-lipped Texas grin, a confident grin — it spoke of teeth which knew how far they could bite into every bone, pie, nipple or tit. Connally belonged to the Texas pure-property school of politics: there were the Ins and the Outs, and the Outs had one philosophy. Get where the Ins are. The Ins had one philosophy. Keep the Outs out. That was politics. Your seat was very important.

It was also important because the microphones for the delegates were varied in their volume. The Illinois, Texas, Michigan, Ohio, and other Humphrey microphones were very clear. The New York, Wiscon-sin, and California microphones were weak in volume. In an emer-gency, in any attempt to gain the attention of the Chair, how much more difficult to yell from the rear, how much more futile to wave the standard. In any total emergency when all the mikes were dead — one hand on one switch could accomplish that — who would ever be heard in the rear if the front was demanding the floor? Yes, it was Lyndon's convention, and he controlled it with Criswell and Daley and the Andy Frain ushers, controlled it with plastic passes to enter the Amphitheatre — so specially magnetized, it was advertised in advance, that you had not only to insert them in a box when you went in, but were obliged to insert them again when you went out so that they might be demagnetized. What fury and ushers' fists fell on a delegate from New Hampshire who used a credit card to go in and out, and was detected the second time when he had a reporter to accompany him. But checks by every member of the Press who held a card in the Diners' Club revealed that they were precisely, micrometrically equal in size to the admission passes — what a preparation had obviously been made to load the galleries or floor if the need came. What an absence of real security! And in the interim, how difficult to get to the floor. Television, press, radio and periodicals were drastically restricted in the number of their passes. Whenever the convention came alive, it was next to impossible to reach the floor, so the amount of damage which could be done by keen press coverage was limited. It was not a practical objective, so much as the air of oppression of the convention itself. LBJ hated the Press by now, hated them for the freedom they took to criticize his heart, his good intentions, and his purchase on the truth. He hated them for showing the scar of his gall bladder operation on every front page, hated them for revealing the emptiness of his war in Vietnam, must have blamed them secretly for losing the war — it was no mystery that the Pentagon detested the Press by now, they were some curious fourth dimension in the solid three dimensions of old-fashioned politics-is-property, they opened the door to mockery of high office, gave eminence to hippies, broadcast criticism of the war, and purveyed some indefinable nihilism. They sped the wrong things up. So Lyndon closed the convention down for them so far as he could; Daley was his arm.

Yet for all the power of his command on that convention floor, Johnson never appeared in person to speak, was rarely mentioned, and the convention sat without a photograph of him anywhere in sight. In Atlantic City in '64 there had been two photos four stories high from floor to upmost balcony. Whereas Lyndon's presence at this convention was felt more as a brain the size of a dirigible floating above the delegates in the smoke-filled air.

Yet for all that he controlled it, the convention was the wildest Democratic Convention in decades, perhaps in more than forty years, and the bitterest, the most violent, the most disorderly, most painful, and in certain ways the most uncontrolled — so it was like his Administration: utterly controlled down to the last echo of his voice, and beyond was absolute chaos. At one end was Carl Albert, Chairman, taking his cue on what to do next by nods, fingers, and other signs from Daley's henchmen, transparent in their signification — "Let the boss speak" or "Shut that guy up" — to thirty million TV viewers. At the other end was the chaos of Michigan Avenue when the police fulfilled their Yippie christening and flailed at the forage like wild pigs. With it all was the comedy, sad, dim and sorrowful as a tender laugh, when Senator Daniel K. Inouye of Hawaii, a Johnson man, the keynoter, spent ten pages of his thirteen-page speech in describing the ills of the country. He was not supposed to do that. The keynote speech extols the glories of the party and the iniquities of the opposition. The keynote speech is pure and automatic dividend from collective holdings. It is like passing Go in Monopoly, 200 bucks, but the country was in straits so poor that even with a Johnson man on the podium, the keynoter was obliged to dwell on America's crisis and deliver a troubled and most literate speech.

There was the unit rule fight which had Connally sufficiently furious to be ready to nominate Johnson. There were the credentials fights which reached such a peak of fury at two-thirty of Tuesday morning with the first Monday night session not yet done, that the Chair was booed for many minutes. Tuesday evening when the Georgia delegation by voice acclamation was seated in a great hurry to establish a split, half to Maddox, half to Julian Bond, broader comedy was played. "I had my seat taken away from me," complained a thin boyish white delegate from Georgia, "without their even asking me, notifying me, or the Chair even deigning or condescending to have a vote. That was the way they took my seat away from me. Very high-handed, I call it," said the Georgia delegate in a whining voice like a car singing through the gears. "That was my seat, and they never had no right to it. I feel kind of funny now not having my seat." Yes, politics went right back through the multiplicities of its negotiation and barter to the primal seat in the family ring around the kitchen table and if Older Brother or Sis has taken your seat, then cause for complaint. But when Mom is gone, or any authority to whom you can appeal, well, politics has ceased to exist, Southern politics at any rate.

"Yes sir," said the delegate from Georgia, "I'm going back home to think for a while, and then I might just decide to work for Mr. Wallace."

"Then, sir," said the interviewer, "you do not plan to work for the Democratic nominee?"

"How can I, sir? They took my seat."

8

Tuesday morning, the California delegation met in the Grand Ballroom of the LaSalle to hear an impromptu debate between Senator McCarthy, Hubert Humphrey, and Senator McGovern. There had been another debate planned for television between Humphrey and McCarthy, but it had never taken place. When McGovern and Lester Maddox announced their candidacies, they insisted at the same time on joining the debate. In the confusion, Humphrey had withdrawn.

Now he was back, however. The onus of refusing to debate McCarthy would no longer be his — besides it was too late to gain or lose more than a few votes by this kind of activity, and indeed, McGovern who was to do very well this particular morning probably did not gain a total of twenty extra delegates from his efforts. Politics is property, and to fall in love with a man's voice sufficiently to vote for him next day is not to get much return for your holding — besides, the votes McGovern stole were in the main from McCarthy, who was not going to give much return either.

The Grand Ballroom of the LaSalle was on the nineteenth floor, and a noble room, perhaps fifty feet wide, three times as long, with an arched ceiling thirty feet high. Nearly a thousand delegates, guests and newspapermen were to crowd into its space, a hunger for confrontation feeding not only the crowds of students and Yippies in the streets below, but the delegates and Press themselves, as if the frustration of listening to Johnson and Humphrey defend the war for more than four years had begun unconscious dialogues in many a man and woman not accustomed to muttering to themselves on the street — indeed with proper warning twenty thousand tickets could have been sold in a day for this meeting of the three men.

Yet it proved curiously anti-climactic. If the atmosphere of the Ball-room was tense, theatrical, even *historical,* no great debate ensued. The technologies of television and convention politics were often curious, they seemed calculated to work to the deterrence of dramatic possibility, and nowhere was this more evident than in the format arrived at (perhaps hammered out by Humphreyites, for it benefited no one else) since it left each man to make a ten-minute opening state-ment, then threw the meeting open to questions from the delegates. Each candidate who was asked a question could reply for three min-utes, his opponents could comment for two minutes. At the end a short summation was in order for each. It was a decorous format, designed precisely to inhibit the likelihood of a continuing confrontation be-tween the principals, since any quarrel which started could hardly con-tinue beyond the time allotted to each question. Politics is property, and Humphrey's property here was twenty years of service in the Sen-ate and the Administration — he wasn't about to limit debate to a slug-fest on Vietnam, no, he would sit on his seat and let the format cover other subjects as well, legislative service, the Supreme Court, willing-ness to support Democratic candidates; they got to talk about Vietnam for a few minutes. That was later, however. The beginnings were not altogether congenial. Scheduled to begin at 10:00 A.M., McGovern came in at 10:05, McCarthy at 10:13. Humphrey, following the logic of championship fights which keeps the contender waiting in the ring, did not appear in any hurry. At 10:26, McCarthy left the platform and moved slowly toward the door, shaking hands with friends and talking. He looked about ready to leave.

But a winner cannot have bad timing. Humphrey came into the room at 10:30, and the debate, half an hour late, was on. McCarthy was the first to speak, and something of the testiness of defeat had gotten into his presentation. He spoke in his cool, offhand style, now famous for its lack of emphasis, lack of power, lack of dramatic concentration, as if the first desire of all men must be not the Presidency, but the necessity to avoid any forcing of one's own person (as if the first desire of the Devil might be to make you the instrument of your own will). He had insisted over all these months of campaigning that he must remain himself, and never rise to meet any occasion, never put force into his presentation because external events seemed to demand that a show of force or oratorical power would here be most useful. No, McCarthy was proceeding on the logic of the saint, which is not to say that he necessarily saw himself as a saint (although there must have been moments!) but that his psychology was kin: God would judge the importance of the event, not man, and God would give the tongue to speak, if tongue was the organ to be manifested. He would be good when the Lord chose him to be good, powerful when the Lord needed power, dominating when that was God's decision. To attempt to carry the day by the energy of his own means would be vanity, an exercise for the devil in oneself, perhaps an offering to the Devil. Everything in McCarthy's manner, his quiet voice, his resolute refusal to etch his wit with any hint of emphasis, his offhand delivery which would insist that remarks about the future of the world were best delivered in the tone you might employ for buying a bottle of aspirin, gave hint of his profound conservatism. He was probably, left to his own inclinations, the most serious conservative to run for nomination since Robert Taft — yes, everything in McCarthy's manner spoke out in profound detestation of the Romantic impulse. Man was not his own project, not his own creation to be flung across the void in the hope that a thread of gray matter he might be carrying would end as a bridge right over the abyss, no, man was probably damned and where not damned, a damn fool, and so must always distrust the boldest and most adventurous of his own impulses. That McCarthy was also a Romantic could hardly be denied — only a Romantic would have dared the incalculable wrath aroused in Lyndon Johnson by the disruption of his volcanic properties, but McCarthy reaching out with his left hand for the taboo would restrain himself by the right. It was one thing to run, another to betray one's principles by running. The central requirement was to remember that all the filth and all the mess of all the world had come from men extending themselves further than their means, marshaling emotions they did not quite feel, pushing the stuff of the heart into theatrical patterns which sought to manipulate others — *there* was the very TNT of spiritual damnation. So McCarthy was damned if he would move a phony finger for any occasion.

The occasion today in the Grand Ballroom called for an heroic historic set of speeches which would demolish Humphrey, smelt him down to the suet at the center of his seat, but there were no false moves for the Senator. The fire to kill, the fire to condemn, the fury to wield the saint's own sword was nowhere in him today. Defeat hung over his cause. Teddy Kennedy would not be nominated, nor any favorite sons from the South. The months of campaigning were all but over. The Romantic in his own heart, which must have hoped against all gray irons of restraint in his intelligence that somehow, somewhere, the politics of the party would prove not property but spirit, was as dead as the taste of death today — he spoke with the quiet controlled bitterness of a man whose greatest vice was bitterness. If there was a grave flaw in McCarthy, it came out of some penury of his own spirit: too bitter even to express his bitterness, it leaked out of the edges of his wit, turned as punishment upon his own people in the determined bland tone of his presentation in a dramatic hour, and leaking, seemed to get into the very yellow of his skin, his single most unattractive feature.

He was not furious so much at losing as at the lack of recognition given by his party for the isolation and stamina of his performance; he was furious at the indifference, even antipathy, of the bulk of the Kennedy cadres; he was hurt probably more than he could admit even to himself at the entrance of Senator George McGovern, now running on a set of issues almost identical to his own, but softer, more compromising. He had to be icy with wrath at McGovern's comments in the Nebraska caucus yesterday. McGovern had said of McCarthy that he "has taken the view that a passive and inactive Presidency is in order, and that disturbs me. Solving our domestic problems will be much more difficult and that will require an active and compassionate President."

So McCarthy now in his opening remarks to the California delegation spent but a word on Vietnam, even emphasizing that he did not wish to restate his case, and then — no man a match for the glide and slash of McCarthy's wit, the shark in the man could best show here — he said in speaking of criticism of him, ". . . Most recently the suggestion that I would be a passive President. Well, I think a little passivity in that office is all right, a kind of balance, I think. I have never quite known what active compassion is. Actually, compassion, in my mind, is to suffer with someone, not in advance of him." He paused, "Or not in public necessarily." He paused again. Here came the teeth. The voice never altered. "But I have been, whether I have been passive or not, the most active candidate in the party this year."

He had been a baseball pitcher once for a minor league team — he had learned presumably to throw two or three kinds of pitch off the same delivery; some of his pitches could take a man's head off. He went on to talk of New Hampshire in the cold and snow, Wisconsin in the ice, "raising issues all the way" — there was ice enough in his soul now — "They say I was impersonal, I want you to know I am the only candidate who said he would get rid of J. Edgar Hoover and that is a person."

McGovern was next. McGovern was friendly. McGovern was the friendliest man in Chicago. He was a reasonably tall, neatly built man, with an honest Midwestern face, a sobriety of manner, a sincerity of presentation, a youthfulness of intent, no matter his age, which was reminiscent of Henry Fonda. Now, he was making his amends to McCarthy. "I will say to my friend and colleague, Gene McCarthy, that I appreciate what he has done in moving out first in this Presidential race to help turn the course of American policy in Southeast Asia." But he was friends with everyone, "and I don't have a short memory. I remember Vice-President Humphrey as one who for twenty years has carried the standard of civil and human justice in our own country." McGovern gave his sweet smile. "What I am trying to say here this morning is that I am no fan of Richard Nixon." He was to win the audience over both hours in just such a way. Now he ended his opening remarks by suggesting that we "tame the savageness of man and make gentle the life of the world." A Christian sweetness came off him like a psychic aroma — he was a fine and pleasant candidate but for that sweetness. It was excessive. Not artificial, but excessive, as the smell of honeysuckle can be excessive.

He had spoken one and a half times as long as McCarthy. Humphrey spoke three times as long, trudging through an imprecision of language, a formal slovenliness of syntax which enabled him to shunt phrases back and forth like a switchman who locates a freight car by moving everything in the yard.

"I happen to believe that one of the unique qualities of the Democratic Party is its leadership over the years — recognizing its fallibility, recognizing its inadequacies, because it is a human instrument — is the capacity of this country to come to this party and its leadership, to come to grips with change, and to be responsive to the future." Where Lyndon Johnson spoke and wrote in phrases which could be hyphenated like Mayor Daley's temporary fences on the way to the Amphitheatre, making you keep your eye off the weeds in the vacant lot, and on the dual highway ahead, so Hubert Humphrey's phrases were like building plots in sub-developments, each little phrase was sub-property — the only trouble was that the plots were all in different towns, little clichés from separate speeches made on unrelated topics in distinctly different years were now plumped down next to each other in the rag-bag map of his mind. He went on for many minutes planting shrubs in each separate little plot, saying sweet things about his opponents, talking of the difficulties of the twentieth century, and the honor of his own record, the unflagging fight he had made, the need for unity. His voice had a piping cheerfulness which seemed to come from the very act of exercising the faculty of speech; once the current of air started to move out from his lungs, he was as vibrant as a set of organ pipes — the thing for him to do was keep striking notes off those pipes, it did not matter which precise music came out. So he went on and on, and by the time he was done, close to half the debate was gone.

Finally the question of Vietnam came up. A delegate got the floor — doubtless he had it arranged with Jesse Unruh in advance, why not?

Delegate: "Mr. Vice-President, specifically, in what ways, if at all, do you disagree with President Johnson's position with reference to Vietnam?"

Humphrey took his time going to the podium. It was a question he had obviously been ready to expect, and yet he seemed agitated. It is one thing to know that some day we will die, it is another to wake in the middle of the night and hear your heart. Humphrey tried to be grand in his reply; but the organ pipes had a mote — he was a crack squeaky. "Would you mind," he asked, "if I just stated my position on Vietnam?"

"No," the crowd shouted. "No! No!"

"Because," he went on in his little determined voice, "the President of the United States is not a candidate and I did not come here to repudiate the President of the United States. I want that made quite clear."

They shouted no, there were hints of boos, cries of muted disgust. A professional round of applause from his supporters in the audience came to back him up, a sort of peremptory we-run-the-meeting-and-we-salute-the-flag was in the sound. Actually, his supporters did not run this meeting. It was the California delegation, led by Jesse Unruh, pledged once to Bobby Kennedy, now more or less split between McCarthy and McGovern, which held the power here, but there was enough authority in the heavy medicine-ball palms of the Humphrey hand-beaters to remind the crowd of other meetings the hand-beaters had run, and meetings they would yet run again. The sound of the Machine was in the percussion-effects of their skin.

So Humphrey was delivered of any need to delineate separation of Lyndon Johnson's position on Vietnam from his own. And proceeded to give his characteristic little talk — the one which had been losing him the love of the liberal Left for the last three years. They had, of course, never had much taste, or they would never have admired him so much in the first place, but then they had never had an opportunity before to recognize in intimate continuing detail that Hubert Humphrey simply could not attach the language of his rhetoric to any reality; on the contrary, he was perfectly capable of using the same word, "Freedom" let us say, to describe a ward fix in Minneapolis and a gathering of Quakers. So he still spoke of our presence in Vietnam as "there to prevent the success of an aggression." It would do no good to tell him that one million American and South Vietnamese troops were fighting the aggression of 200,000 or 250,000 Vietcong and North Vietnamese. If he said there was aggression, then aggression became his reality — the figures had nothing to do with it. So "Democracy in South Vietnam" was established because the use of the word by Lyndon Johnson and himself had established it. The radiance of the sensation of democracy came from the word itself, "Democracy!" Halos in his eyes. "When you look over the world scene, those elections [in South Vietnam] stand up pretty well and the basis of the Government today is a broader-based Government." Earlier he had actually said, "We have not sought to impose a military solution. Regrettably, wars have their built-in escalation." One would have to be a great novelist to dare to put this last remark in the mouth of a character so valuable as Humphrey. "The roadblock to peace, my dear friends, is not in Washington, D.C. It is in Hanoi, and we ought to recognize it as such."

The medicine-balls gave him a good hand, and he was pleased with himself when he stepped down. He had given a warm sincere little speech which he obviously believed, or rather, had actually experienced. While he spoke, the sensation of truth quivered about him like a nimbus. He must have felt bathed in light. He had the same kind of truth that an actor has while playing Napoleon — with the lights on him, he *is* Napoleon. So with the lights on Hubert, democracy did exist in South Vietnam, and our inability to end the war was indeed Hanoi's fault (even though we had never declared war on North Vietnam and were still bombing half of everything which moved). Hubert Humphrey loved America. So the madness of America had become his own madness. He was a lover after all.

It was McCarthy's turn to speak. Everyone leaned forward. The confrontation was at hand. But McCarthy, receiving no inner voice, drinking some bitter cup of rejection or despair, a simple distaste for the whole human race backing up in him, contented himself with remarking in his most penurious tones, "The people know my position."

Perhaps his silence was meant to convey some absolute contempt for Humphrey's remarks, or some absolute statement of his political belief that one must not move without an inner sanction no matter what the occasion; it was still an extraordinary abstention.

Dull anger passed through the audience — but, of course! This was exactly why McCarthy had not been able to win the candidacy. Indeed had he ever wanted to win it, or had he moved like some sinister stalking-horse over the paths of new possibility? Or was he just in a thoroughgoing Irish miff because McGovern was obviously everyone's pet? Once again, the gulf between the answer on one side of the question and the other was greater than the question itself. If Nixon had been an enigma, McCarthy was a larger one.

McGovern picked up all the chips. "Coming in as late as I did," he said in reference to his candidacy, "I can't afford to give up any free time." And he gave an angelic grin. The crowd roared. They were his. They were waiting for an answer to Humphrey.

If a casting director in Hollywood had to find a Boy Scout leader who could play Romantic lead in a ten-million-dollar movie, McGovern would be his find. There was nobody nicer or cleaner than George McGovern in the city of Chicago. And he made all the points in his sweet troubled vibrant honest good guy Good Christian missionary voice. "I think we Democrats bear a special burden before the American people in 1968 in that four years ago we sought their votes, we sought their confidence on a rallying cry of 'No wider war.'" The house broke down. Wild cheers. Hints of an impromptu demonstration. "It is all very well and good," said McGovern, riding the energy of this enthusiasm, "to talk about the recent election in Vietnam, but let's remember that one of the most honorable candidates in that election, Presidential candidate Chu, was recently sent to jail for five years at hard labor for the single crime of advocating what Senator McCarthy and George McGovern and others have advocated, and that is a 'negotiated end of this war.' Thank you very much."

They gave him a standing ovation. They were delighted. They loved him. He was not really a big enough man to think of him seriously as President, he had more than a hint of that same ubiquitous sweetness which had finally melted away Humphrey's connection between the simplest fact and his own dear brain, but McGovern had years to go before he would sing *castrat'*. He would even — if he had entered earlier, but of course he had not, no accident he had not — have done modestly well in taking delegates from McCarthy, he offered every-thing McCarthy did not, including the pleasure of watching Hubert Humphrey smile like a roasted cherub at the standing ovation given the speaker who had just demolished his speech. What a passion was in the air to tell Humphrey of the fury of the doves.

They had been squeezed, squashed, gunned down, outmaneuvered, driven in rout from the summits of power at this convention, had seen their party escape from them and race to the abyss with the Fool for their unwanted candidate — so it was their one opportunity to shout into his face, and they took it. Fool!

When this ovation was done, the debate went on, anti-climactic but for a later speech by McCarthy, a speech in which he as much as said farewell to those who had hopes for him in this room, and in that land of suburbs and television sets where his crusade had first been cheered. Asked if he would throw his support "to another person who has sim-ilar views," he began quietly, proceeded quietly, but his metaphor on this occasion was equal to his bitterness, his pride, and his high sense of the standards. He brought the curtain down with that dignity which was his most unique political possession. ". . . Many stood on the side-lines, as I said earlier, on the hilltops, dancing around the bonfires. Few came down into the valley where the action was. And I said then that if one challenged the President he had to be prepared to be President. It is like striking at the King — it is a dangerous thing." How dangerous only he could know. Only he could know how far a pressure could push a terror, and how many mutations might a nightmare produce, yes, he had had to face Lyndon Johnson at eight in the morning and three in the morning, in the fatigue of five o'clock on a hard-working afternoon and after midnight in the effulgence of a full moon — only he had had to face Lyndon Johnson with such thoughts after Bobby Kennedy was dead. Perhaps there was bitterness so justifiable a man's mouth could pucker at the invitation to speak. "I said early in New Hampshire, during the New Hampshire primary — I was asked whether I could support Senator Robert Kennedy if he should become the nominee and his views were the same as my views. I said I could. . . . I have been waiting for them to say the same thing about me." He turned, started to go away, then came back. "One other thing. I said that I could not support a Democratic candidate whose views did not come close to what mine are."

Now he was gone, now back in his seat, the hand of applause started

MIAMI AND THE SIEGE OF CHICAGO

slowly, continued, built in volume. It grew for a suprising time, never wild in its force nor released in its enthusiasm, but it went on. The force of respect was also source for a modest ovation.

9

Later that day, early in the evening, McCarthy went into a meeting with Steve Smith, Teddy Kennedy's brother-in-law, and told him that he was willing to withdraw from the race if Kennedy would enter, and that he would instruct his delegates that they were free; further, he would suggest that they give their support to Kennedy.

Would there be anything he desired in return?

No, he was not asking for anything in victory or defeat. (McCarthy was obviously a fanatic — he was seeking to destroy politics-is-property.)

Smith thanked him, told him he would relay his message to Teddy Kennedy, made some comment on the munificence of the offer, perhaps thinking to himself that it came a little late, and left.

Perhaps two hours after this, the reporter encountered McCarthy by chance in a Chicago restaurant on the North Side.

The Senator, sitting at a long table in the corner of the main dining room, a modest room (for the restaurant was situated in a brownstone) had his back comfortably to the wall, and was chatting over the coffee with his guests. The atmosphere was sufficiently relaxed for the reporter and his friend, another reporter who had been doing a story on McCarthy for *Look,* to come up past the Secret Service without great strain and greet the Senator. Neither of the reporters was to know anything about the meeting with Steve Smith until some days later, but it was likely McCarthy had come to some decision — at the least, he was more relaxed than at any time the reporter had seen him in Chicago. Perhaps it was the friends he was with, big Irishmen like himself for the most part, a couple of them present with their wives, or at least such was the reporter's impression, for he was introduced to more than a half-dozen people in the aftermath of meeting the Senator and some were big genial Irishmen with horn-rimmed glasses and some were lean Irishmen with craggy faces, and one was an Irishman from Limerick with a Dublin face, one-third poet, one-third warrior, one-third clerk. Perhaps it was the company, but the reporter had never seen McCarthy in such a mood. The benign personality of the public meetings, agreeable but never compelling, was gone — the personality which suggested that serious activity had something absurd about it — gone. The manner which declared, "I'm a nice guy, and look what I got into" — gone!

Speaking with the license a man has when his dinner is interrupted, McCarthy struck back to the conversation twelve weeks earlier in a living room in Cambridge, "Still waiting for me to repeat that 1960 speech?"

"Well, Senator," said the reporter — he was trying to become sufficiently presumptuous to say, "if you could make a speech like that on the war in Vietnam tonight when the peace plank is debated . . ."

But McCarthy cut him off. "That was then. We don't retain all our abilities necessarily. Once the ability leaves you, how do you regain it?" It was impossible to tell if he was mocking the reporter or mocking himself. "I used to be angry then," he said across the table with an evil look of amusement, as if recording these remarks for posterity as well, his yellow eyes gleaming in the light, "but I can't seem to get angry again. It's a gift to get angry when you wish to get angry, Mailer."

"A grace I would say, sir."

If the table had been laughing at McCarthy's sallies, they chuckled now with his. The Senator's friends looked tough and were tough-minded, but they were obviously open to wit from any corner.

"Then you also want to ask yourself if you should get people angry." McCarthy went on in a voice of the hardest-tempered irony. "Once you get them angry, you've got to get them quieted down. That's not so easy. Lyndon, for instance, has never understood the problem. He thinks politicians are cattle, whereas in fact most politicians are pigs. Now, Norman, there's a little difference between cattle and pigs which most people don't know. Lyndon doesn't know it. You see, to get cattle started, you make just a little noise, and then when they begin to run, you have to make more noise, and then you keep driving them with more and more noise. But pigs are different. You have to start pigs running with a great deal of noise, in fact the best way to start them is by reciting Latin, very loudly, that'll get them running — then you have to quiet your voice bit by bit and they'll keep moving. Lyndon has never understood this."

These gnomic remarks now concluded, the reporter had no idea precisely what the Senator was talking about. He had been expanding a metaphor, and images of the stockyards, the convention, the war on the streets, the expression on the face of Humphrey delegates and McCarthy delegates, and some tidal wave of contempt at the filthy polluted plumbing of things was in the remark. In the laughter which followed, the reporter was silent.

"It's a funny thing about pigs," McCarthy went on. "They have an odd way of keeping warm in winter if they find themselves outside. You see, pigs don't know if they're cold, provided their nose is warm. So they stand around in a circle with their nose between the hind legs of the pig in front of them. Wouldn't you call that a curious relationship?"

"Oh, Senator, I would call that a Satanic relationship."

McCarthy joined in the laughter. Hard was his face, hard as the bones and scourged flesh of incorruptibility, hard as the cold stone floor of a monastery in the North Woods at five in the morning. The reporter leaned forward to talk into his ear.

"You see, sir," he said, "the tragedy of the whole business is that you should never have had to run for President. You would have been perfect for the Cabinet." A keen look back from McCarthy's eye gave the sanction to continue. "Yessir," said the reporter, "you'd have made a perfect chief for the FBI!" and they looked at each other and McCarthy smiled and said, "Of course, you're absolutely right."

The reporter looked across the table into one of the hardest, cleanest expressions he had ever seen, all the subtle hints of puffiness and doubt sometimes visible in the Senator's expression now gone, no, the face that looked back belonged to a tough man, tough as the harder alloys of steel, a merciless face and very just, the sort of black Irish face which could have belonged to one of the hanging judges in a true court of Heaven, or to the proper commissioner of a police force too honest ever to have existed.

The reporter left. But the memory of McCarthy at this table persisted. And the memory of his presence, harder than the hardest alloys of steel. But not unjust. What iron it must have taken to be annealed in Lyndon's volcanic breath. Yes, the reporter had met many candidates, but McCarthy was the first who felt like a President, or at least felt like a President in that hard hour after he had relinquished the very last of his hopes, and so was enjoying his dinner.

10

We have been present until now at an account of the Democratic Convention of 1968. It has not, however, been a description of the event. The event was a convention which took place during a continuing five-day battle in the streets and parks of Chicago between some of the minions of the high established, and some of the nihilistic of the young. But if we had begun with a description of this superb battle, it might not have been automatic to transfer interest to the convention, since the greatest excitement in the Amphitheatre was often a reflection of the war without.

Yet, let us hesitate for one last patriot's cry before slogging to the front. It is from the speech of Governor Lester G. Maddox of Georgia which announced his candidacy for the Democratic nomination on August 17, 1968. Since we will see the Governor but once again, and he is a fellow of pithy comment, let us describe him pithily: Governor Maddox has the face of a three-month-old infant who is mean and bald and wears eyeglasses.

From our Governor's speech:

> I am proud to be an American. Aren't you?
> I love my country and its flag and I regard defending them as a privilege as well as a duty. Don't you?
> I . . . when I sing God Bless America, I mean it with all of my heart.
> . . . the problems which confront us are the direct result of our failure to insist that our leaders put first things first . . . the safety of law-abiding citizens ahead of the safety of law-defying citizens. . . .

Politics is property; property relations are law-abiding. Even seizure of property can be accomplished legally. So the history of a convention must concern itself with law-abiding citizens; conversely, a study of law-defying citizens who protested the deliberations of this convention in the street ought to find them propertyless, therefore not in politics. In fact, it does not. Not quite. There were two groups to the army of young people who assembled in Chicago; one could divide them conveniently as socialists and existentialists. The socialists, you can be certain, believed in every variety of social and revolutionary idea but membership in the Socialist Party, which of course, being young people, they detested; for the most part they were students of the New Left who belonged to SDS, the Resistance (a movement of confirmed draft resisters) and a dozen or more peace organizations. While their holdings were almost entirely in moral property, it would take a strong country mind to claim that socialists have no property relations in their own politics, since indeed there are ideologies among these sissies, Governor Maddox, which have passed down like a family trust through the generations, and the war for control of a radical committee will often revolve around the established seat of the Chairman.

Emphasis, however, on the New Left is directed away from power struggles; the old Marxist splinter groups reduced all too many old radical admirals to command of leaking rowboats, or, to maintain our corporate metaphor of property, squires in command of chicken coops. The New Left was interested for the most part in altering society (and being conceivably altered themselves — they were nothing if not Romantic) by the activity of working for a new kind of life out in the ghettoes, the campuses, and the anti-war movement. If one would still refer to them generically as socialists, it is because the product of their labor was finally, one must fear, ideological: their experience would shape their ideas, and ideally these ideas would serve to clarify the experience of others and so bring them closer to the radical movement. While they detested almost to a man the repressive, obsessive and finally — they were modern minds — the anally compulsive oppressions of Russian Communism (as much as they detested the anally retentive ideologies of the corporation) there were many among them who were all for the Czechoslovakian Communists, for Che Guevara, for Castro, for Tito up to a point, for Rumania, and for the North Vietnamese. Some of them even made a point of carrying the flags of the NLF in meetings and marches. A number, devoted to the memory of Che, were elevated as well to militant ideals of revolution. A few had come to Chicago ready to fight the police. (We can be certain that their counterparts in Eastern Europe and the Soviet were being attacked and imprisoned by all the Russian bureaucrats who look like Spiro Agnew, Dick Nixon, and Hubert Humphrey.)

First organized for this action in Chicago back on March 23 in a YMCA camp in Lake Villa, Illinois, in a conference of about one hundred anti-war groups, the project had then seemed a direct action capable of attracting large numbers, for Johnson was still in office, and the war in Vietnam showed no sign of ending. Plans, more or less under the aegis of the National Mobilization to End the War in Vietnam (the same clearing house organization which had led the march on the Pentagon) were made for mass demonstrations to protest the nomination of Lyndon Johnson. Since the President was to announce a week later that he would not run again, and the start of the Paris peace talks soon followed, many of the members of the anti-war groups were distracted, and efforts for this huge mobilization under the leadership of David Dellinger, editor of *Liberation* and chief architect of the march on the Pentagon, Rennie Davis, who headed the Center for Radical Research, and Vernon Grizzard, a Boston draft-resistance leader, were lost in the move of many of the younger workers to the Kennedy and McCarthy campaigns. The dream of a broad front of radical groups to meet in Chicago seemed no longer practical. So more modest plans were consolidated between Rennie Davis and Tom Hayden, perhaps the outstanding young leader of the New Left now that Jerry Rubin was a Yippie and Mario Savio was relatively quiescent. Between Hayden, Davis, and Dellinger, the Mobilization would function. Where aims were similar to the Yippies, led by Abbie Hoffman, Paul Krassner — editor of *The Realist* — and Jerry Rubin there would even be cooperation. Rubin, a former associate of Dellinger on the march to the Pentagon, had been working since December 1967 with a vision of bringing one hundred thousand kids to Chicago to hold a Youth Festival which by a sheer mixture of music, witchcraft, and happy spontaneous disruption would so exacerbate the anxiety of the Establishment that Johnson would have to be nominated under armed guard and real Texas guns. Needless to say, plans of the Yippies had also suffered from Johnson's withdrawal.

Nonetheless, by mid-summer, the wings of the MOB and Yippie army were more or less ready. On one flank was the New Left, still generically socialist, believing in a politics of confrontation, intelligent programmatic warriors, Positivists in philosophy, educational in method, ideological in their focus — which is to say a man's personality was less significant than his ideas; on the other flank, Yippies, devoted to a politics of ecstasy (we will avoid comparisons with Hubert Humphrey's politics of joy) programmatic about drug-taking, Dionysiacs, propagandists by example, mystical in focus. (Rubin had once burned some money in a debate with a Trotskyist.) By the summer of 1968 each group had however so influenced the other on campus, via street activity and in demonstrations, that their differences were no longer significant. Indeed under the impact of Rubin's ideas, the emphasis was

213

much on a politics of confrontation which searched to dramatize the revolution as theater.

But let them speak for themselves. Here is a quotation from Tom Hayden of the New Left:

> . . . The overdevelopment of bureaucracy and technology can lead to a breakdown. A clock can be wound too tight. The super-carrier *Forrestal* was destroyed by one of its own rockets. In Chicago this week, the military and security machinery . . . might devour its mother the Democratic Party. . . .
>
> Consider the dilemmas facing those administering the . . . apparatus. They are centralized, suited to confront (or negotiate with) a centralized opposition, but poorly prepared for spontaneous waves of action. . . . They cannot distinguish "straight" radicals from newspapermen or observers from delegates. . . . They cannot distinguish rumors about demonstrations from the real thing. They cannot be certain whether bomb threats are serious no matter how much they have "sanitized" the hotels and Amphitheatre. . . .
>
> We always knew that storming or physically disrupting the convention, or conducting guerrilla war in strange territory, was insane. The perspective has been to show the unrepresentative character of the political system by exposing its essentially repressive response to human need and protest. . . .
>
> . . . Twenty-five thousand troops are being brought here not to stop "disrupters" — no amount of security can stop an assassin or bomber — but because the rulers . . . are relying on coercion. . . . We are forced into a military style not because we are "destructive" and "nihilistic" but because our normal rights are insecure. . . .

Here is a quotation from Ed Sanders, characteristic of the visionary aspects of hippie prose:

> Gentlemen, joy, nooky, circle groups, laughing, dancing, sharing, grass, magic, meditation, music, theatre, and weirdo mutant-jissomed chromosome-damaged ape-chortles have always been my concern for Lincoln Park.
>
> Yours for the power of the lob-throb.

The more practical — by Abbie Hoffman in *The Realist:*

> A Constitutional Convention is being planned . . . visionary mind-benders who will for five long days and nights address themselves to the task of formulating the goals and means of the New Society.
>
> It will be a blend of technologists and poets, of artists and community organizers, of anyone who has a vision. We will try to develop a Community of Consciousness.

214

There will be a huge rock-folk festival for free . . . theater groups from all over the country are pledged to come. They are an integral part of the activities. . . .

Workshops in a variety of subjects such as draft resistance, drugs, commune development, guerrilla theater and underground media will be set up. . . .

There will probably be a huge march across town to haunt the Democrats.

People coming to Chicago should begin preparations for five days of energy-exchange. Do not come prepared to sit down and watch and be fed and cared for. . . . If you don't have a thing to do, stay home, you'll only get in the way.

All of these plans are contingent on our getting a permit, and it is toward that goal that we have been working. A permit is a definite contradiction in philosophy since we do not recognize the authority of the old order, but tactically it is a necessity.

We are negotiating, with the Chicago city government, a six-day treaty. All of the Chicago newspapers as well as various pressure groups have urged the city of Chicago to grant the permit. They recognize full well the huge social problem they face if we are forced to use the streets of Chicago for our action. . . . We have had several meetings, principally with David Stahl, Deputy Mayor of Chicago, and it remains but to iron out the terms of the treaty — suspension of curfew laws, regulations pertaining to sleeping on the beach, etc. — for us to have a bona fide permit on our hands.

The possibility of violence will be greatly reduced. There is no guarantee that it will be entirely eliminated. This is the United States, 1968, remember. If you are afraid of violence you shouldn't have crossed the border.

This matter of a permit is a cat-and-mouse game. The Chicago authorities do not wish to grant it too early, knowing this would increase the number of people that descend on the city. They can ill afford to wait too late, for that will inhibit planning on our part and create more chaos.

It is not our wish to take on superior armed troops who outnumber us on unfamiliar enemy territory. It is not their wish to have a Democrat nominated amidst a major bloodbath. The treaty will work for both sides.

The Yippies like the hippies were famous for their optimism. The permit was not granted by Stahl or Daley. In turn, an offer by Daley on August 21 to allow a march from 1 P.M. to 4 P.M. in a part of Chicago miles away from the convention was rejected by the Mobilization. Hayden said that marchers coming to Chicago "by the tens of thousands" preferred to be at the Amphitheatre. So the city got ready for a week of disorders its newspapers had advised it to avoid. One can only divine the expression on Daley's face when he read literature like the follow-

215

ing — it comes from a throwaway in Lincoln Park, given out on Sunday afternoon August 25:

YIPPIE!

LINCOLN PARK

VOTE PIG IN 68

Free Motel
"come sleep with us"

REVOLUTION TOWARDS A FREE
SOCIETY: YIPPIE!
By A. Yippie

1. An immediate end to the War in Vietnam. . . .

2. Immediate freedom for Huey Newton of the Black Panthers and all other black people. Adoption of the community control concept in our ghetto areas. . . .

3. The legalization of marihuana and all other psychedelic drugs. . . .

4. A prison system based on the concept of rehabilitation rather than punishment.

5. . . . abolition of all laws related to crimes without victims. That is, retention only of laws relating to crimes in which there is an unwilling injured party, i.e. murder, rape, assault.

6. The total disarmament of all the people beginning with the police. This includes not only guns, but such brutal devices as tear gas, MACE, electric prods, blackjacks, billy clubs, and the like.

7. The Abolition of Money. The abolition of pay housing, pay media, pay transportation, pay food, pay education, pay clothing, pay medical help, and pay toilets.

8. A society which works toward and actively promotes the concept of "full unemployment." A society in which people are free from the drudgery of work. Adoption of the concept "Let the Machines do it."

9. . . . elimination of pollution from our air and water.

10. . . . incentives for the decentralization of our crowded cities . . . encourage rural living.

11. . . . free birth control information . . . abortions when desired.

12. A restructured educational system which provides the student power to determine his course of study and allows for student participation in over-all policy planning. . . .

13. Open and free use of media . . . cable television as a method of increasing the selection of channels available to the viewer.

14. An end to all censorship. We are sick of a society which has no hesitation about showing people committing violence and refuses to show a couple fucking.

15. We believe that people should fuck all the time, anytime, whomever they wish. This is not a program to demand but a simple recognition of the reality around us.

16. ... a national referendum system conducted via television or a telephone voting system . . . a decentralization of power and authority with many varied tribal groups. Groups in which people exist in a state of basic trust and are free to choose their tribe.

17. A program that encourages and promotes the arts. However, we feel that if the Free Society we envision were to be fought for and achieved, all of us would actualize the creativity within us. In a very real sense we would have a society in which every man would be an artist.

... Political Pigs, your days are numbered. We are the Second American Revolution. We shall win. Yippie!

But let us go to Lincoln Park on this Sunday afternoon.

1 1

A moment:
The following is a remark by Dino Valente, an electric guitarist. It ran as the headline in an advertisement in the *East Village Other* for an album of his records.

> You take this electrical power out of the wall and you send it through the guitar and you bend it and shape it and make it into something, like songs for people and that power is a wonderful thing.

Yes, the Yippies were the militant wing of the hippies, Youth International Party, and the movement was built on juice, not alcoholic juice which comes out of the mystery of fermentation — why, dear God, as fruits and grains begin to rot, does some distillate of this art of the earth now in decomposition have the power to inflame consciousness and give us purchase on visions of Heaven and Hell? — no, rather, we are speaking of the juice which comes from another mystery, the passage of a metallic wire across a field of magnetism. That serves to birth the beast of all modern technology, electricity itself. The hippies founded their temple in that junction where LSD crosses the throb of an electric guitar at full volume in the ear, solar plexus, belly, and loins. A tribal unity had passed through the youth of America (and half the nations of the world) a far-out vision of orgiastic revels stripped of violence or even the differentiation of sex. In the oceanic stew of a nonviolent, tribal ball on drugs, nipples, arms, phalluses, mouths, wombs, armpits, short-hairs, navels, breasts and cheeks, incense of odor, flower and funk went humping into Breakthrough Freak-out Road together, and children on acid saw Valhalla, Nepenthe, and the Taj Mahal. Some went out forever, some went screaming down the alleys of the mad where cockroaches drive like Volkswagens on the oilcloth of the moon, gluttons found vertigo in centrifuges of consciousness, vomitoriums of ingestion; others found love, some manifest of love in light, in shards of Nirvana, sparks of satori — they came back to the world a Twentieth-Century tribe wearing celebration bells and filthy garments. Used-up livers gave their complexions a sickly pale, and hair grew on their faces like weeds. Yet they had seen some incontestable vision of the good — the universe was not absurd to them; like pilgrims they looked at society with the eyes of children: society was absurd. Every emperor who went down the path was naked, and they handed flowers to policemen.

It could hardly last. The slum in which they chose to live — for they were refugees in the main from the suburbs of the middle class — fretted against them, fretted against their filth, their easy casual cohabiting, their selflessness (which is always the greatest insult to the ghetto, for selflessness is a luxury to the poor, it beckons to the spineless, the undifferentiated, the inept, the derelict, the drowning — a poor man is nothing without the fierce thorns of his ego). So the hippies collided with the slums, and were beaten and robbed, fleeced and lashed and buried and imprisoned, and here and there murdered, and here and there successful, for there was scattered liaison with bikers and Panthers and Puerto Ricans on the East Coast and Mexicans on the West. There came a point when, like most tribes, they divided. Some of the weakest and some of the least attached went back to the suburbs or moved up into commerce or communications; others sought gentler homes where the sun was kind and the flowers plentiful; others hardened, and like all pilgrims with their own vision of a promised land, began to learn how to work for it, and finally, how to fight for it. So the Yippies came out of the hippies, ex-hippies, diggers, bikers, drop-outs from college, hipsters up from the South. They made a community of sorts, for their principles were simple — everybody, obviously, must be allowed to do (no way around the next three words) his own thing, provided he hurt no one doing it — they were yet to learn that society is built on many people hurting many people, it is just who does the hurting which is forever in dispute. They did not necessarily understand how much their simple presence hurt many good citizens in the secret velvet of the heart — the hippies and probably the Yippies did not quite recognize the depth of that schizophrenia on which society is built. We call it hypocrisy, but it is schizophrenia, a modest ranch-house life with Draconian military adventures; a land of equal opportunity where a white culture sits upon a Black; a horizontal community of Christian love and a vertical hier- archy of churches — the cross was well-designed! a land of family, a land of illicit heat; a politics of principle, a politics of property; nation of mental hygiene with movies and TV reminiscent of a mental pigpen; patriots with a detestation of obscenity who pollute their rivers; citizens with a detestation of government control who cannot bear any situation not controlled. The list must be endless, the comic profits are finally small — the society was able to stagger on like a 400-pound policeman walking uphill because living in such an unappreciated and obese state it did not at least have to explode in schizophrenia — life went on. Boys could go patiently to church at home and wait their turn to burn villages in Vietnam. What the Yippies did not recognize is that their demand for all-accelerated entrance into Twentieth-Century Utopia (where modern mass man would have all opportunities before him at once and could thus create and despoil with equal conscience — up against the wall mother-fucker, let me kiss your feet) whether a vision to be desired or abhorred, was nonetheless equal to straight madness for the Average Good American, since his liberated expression might not be an outpouring of love, but the burning of his neighbor's barn. Or, since we are in Chicago, smashing good neighbor's skull with a brick from his own back yard. Yippies, even McCarthyites, represented nothing less by their presence than the destruction of every saving hypocrisy with consequent collision for oneself — it is not so easy to live every day of your life holding up the wall of your own sanity. Small wonder the neighborhood whites of Chicago, like many small-town whites in other places, loved Georgie Wallace — he came in like cavalry, a restorer of every last breach in the fort.

Somber thoughts for a stroll through Lincoln Park on a Sunday afternoon in summer, but the traffic of the tourists and the curious was great; one had to leave the car six blocks away. Curiosity was contained, however, in the family automobile: the burghers did not come to the park. Young tourists and cruisers were there in number, tough kids, Polish and Irish (not all plainclothesmen) circulating around the edges of the crowd, and in the center of the southern part of Lincoln Park where the Yippies had chosen to assemble on an innocuous greensward undistinguished from similar meadows in many another park, a folk-rock group was playing. It was an orderly crowd. Somewhere between one and two thousand kids and young adults sat on the grass and listened, and another thousand or two thousand, just arrived, or too restless to sit, milled through an outer ring, or worked forward to get a better look. There was no stage — the entrance of a flatbed truck from which the entertainers could have played had not been permitted, so the musicians were half hidden, the public address system — could it work off batteries? — was not particularly clear. For one of the next acts it hardly mattered — a young white singer with a cherubic face, perhaps eighteen, maybe twenty-eight, his hair in one huge puff ball teased out six to nine inches from his head, was taking off on an interplanetary, then galactic, flight of song, halfway between the space music of Sun Ra and "The Flight of the Bumblebee," the singer's head shaking at the climb like the blur of a buzzing fly, his sound an electric caterwauling of power come out of the wall (or the line in the grass, or the wet plates in the batteries) and the singer not bending it, but whirling it, burning it, flashing it down some arc of consciousness, the sound screaming up to a climax of vibrations like one rocket blasting out of itself, the force of the noise a vertigo in the cauldrons of inner space — it was the roar of the beast in all nihilism, electric bass and drum driving behind out of their own non-stop to the end of mind. And the reporter, caught in the din — had the horns of the Huns ever had noise to compare? — knew this was some variety of true song for the hippies and adolescents in the house, in this enclave of grass and open air (luxury apartments of Lake Shore Drive not five football fields away) crescendos of sound as harsh on his ear, ear of a generation which had danced to "Star Dust," as to drive him completely out of the sound, these painted dirty under-twenties were monsters, and yet, still clinging to recognition in the experience, he knew they were a generation which lived in the sound of destruction of all order as he had known it, and worlds of other decomposition as well; there was the sound of mountains crashing in this holocaust of the decibels, hearts bursting, literally bursting, as if this were the sound of death by explosion within, the drums of physiological climax when the mind was blown, and forces of the future, powerful, characterless, as insane and scalding as waves of lava, came flushing through the urn of all acquired culture and sent the brain like a foundered carcass smashing down a rapids, revolving through a whirl of demons, pool of uproar, discords vibrating, electric crescendo screaming as if at the electro-mechanical climax of the age, and these children like filthy Christians sitting quietly in the grass, applauding politely, whistles and cries of mild approval when the song was done, and the reporter as affected by the sound (as affected by the recognition of what nihilisms were calmly encountered in such musical storm) as if he had heard it in a room at midnight with painted bodies and kaleidoscopic sights, had a certainty which went through gangs and groups and rabble, tourists and consecrated saints, vestal virgins with finger bells, through the sight of Negroes calmly digging Honkie soul, sullen Negroes showing not impressed, but digging, cool on their fringe (reports to the South Side might later be made) through even the hint of menace in the bikers, some beaks alien to this music, come to scoff, now watching, half turned on by noise so near to the transcendencies of some of their own noise when the whine of the gears cohabited with the pot to hang them out there on the highway singing with steel and gasoline, yeah, steel and gasoline exactly equal to flesh plus hate, and blood plus hate; equations were pure while riding the balance of a machine, yes, even the tourists and the college boys who would not necessarily be back contributed nonetheless to the certainty of his mood. There was a mock charade going on, a continuation of that celebration of the Yippie Convention yet to come, when Pigasus, a literal pig, would be put in nomination. VOTE PIG IN '68, said the Yippie placards, and now up at the stage, music done, they announced another candidate to a ripple of mild gone laughter across the grass, Humphrey Dumpty was the name, and a Yippie clown marched through the crowd, a painted egg with legs, "the next President of the United States," and in suite came a march of the delegates through an impromptu aisle from the stage to the rear of the crowd. A clown dressed like a Colorado miner in a fun house came first; followed Miss America with hideous lipsticked plastic tits, stars of rouge on her cheeks; Mayor Daley's political machine — a clown with a big box horizontal to his torso, big infant's spoon at the trough on top of the box, and a green light which went on and off was next; then the featured delegate, the Green Beret, a clown with a toy machine gun, soot, and red grease on his face, an Australian bush hat on his head. Some sort of wax vomit pop-art work crowned the crown. Yes, the certainty was doubled. Just as he had known for one instant at the Republican Gala in Miami Beach that Nelson Rockefeller had no chance of getting the nomination, so he knew now on this cool gray Sunday afternoon in August, chill in the air like the chill of the pale and the bird of fear beginning to nest in the throat, that trouble was coming, serious trouble. The air of Lincoln Park came into the nose with that tender concern which air seemed always ready to offer when danger announced its presence. The reporter took an unhappy look around. Were these odd unkempt children the sort of troops with whom one wished to enter battle?

12

The justifications of the March on the Pentagon were not here. The reporter was a literary man — symbol had the power to push him into actions more heroic than himself. The fact that he had been marching to demonstrate against a building which was the living symbol of everything he most despised — the military-industrial complex of the land — had worked to fortify his steps. The symbol of the Pentagon had been a chalice to hold his fear; in such circumstances his fear had even flavored his courage with the sweetest emotions of battle.

But in Chicago, there was no symbol for him. Not the Amphitheatre in the stockyards, for he had a press pass to enter, and had entered indeed — it did not seem as much of a protest to march to a building he had entered already. Besides, the city would not allow a march: one was offered then the choice to be tear-gassed or abstain. Of course, there was the Conrad Hilton for a convenient symbol, but it was Democratic Party Headquarters and Press Headquarters, and he had a room in the Hilton, in fact it was the only Hilton Hotel he did not dislike, for it was old, not new, and had thousands of little rooms, or so it seemed, like the St. George in Brooklyn, plus a dingy rear twenty-five stories high with the sad legend, "World's Largest and Friendliest Hotel" painted in black and white on the weary color-dead elephantine brick. There was

THE SIEGE OF CHICAGO

Lincoln Park, and anyone who wished to protest the horrors of the continuing war in Vietnam, or the horrors of this Democratic Convention which would choose the candidate least popular and least qualified by strength, dignity, or imagination to lead, could bed down in Lincoln Park. The city, we may remember, had refused to issue a permit to the Yippies. So they could not sleep in the park. They had been ordered to vacate it by eleven. Their leaders had even told them to vacate it.

Paul Krassner:

"Sleeping in Lincoln Park after 11 P.M. isn't as important as living our revolution there the rest of the day (the park opens at 6 A.M.)."

Jerry Rubin:

". . . Chicago is a police state, and we must protect ourselves. The cops want to turn our parks into graveyards. But we, not them, will decide when the battle begins."

In fact, as everyone knew, many were not going to vacate the park, they were going to force the police to drive them out; so one could protest with one's body, one could be tear-gassed — with what unspoken later damage to the eyes had never necessarily been decided — and one could take a crack on the head with a policeman's stick, or a going-over by plainclothesmen. The reporter had an aversion to this. Besides, he was afraid of his *own* violence. It was not that he was such a good fighter, but he was not altogether courteous either — he had broken a man's jaw in a fight not so long before, and was not certain the end of that was yet heard; it had left him nervous and edgy about fights. He was not afraid of his own violence because he necessarily thought it would be so heinous to break a policeman's jaw, good law-abiding citizen that he was! It was more that he was a little concerned with what the policeman's friends and associates might do to him immediately afterward. He had taken a hint of a bad beating once or twice in his life; he was, conceivably, ready to take much more, but he could not pretend that he welcomed it.

So he went that night — after the visit to the park on Sunday afternoon — to a party, and from there to the Hilton and a quick visit on impulse to Humphrey's private headquarters, where, late at night, there was nobody to receive him but six or eight young Secret Servicemen or FBI with bullet-faces, crew cuts, and an absurd tension at the recognition of his name.

The mission to see Humphrey fruitless as he had known it would be, he had merely wanted to look at the style of Humphrey's cops, he then went down a few floors and to bed, and did not know until the morning

223

that there had been a battle already in Lincoln Park, and the Yippies driven out long after the 11 P.M. curfew with tear gas, and what was more sensational, some reporters and photographers showing press cards had been beaten with the rest.

Monday night, the city was washed with the air of battle. Out at the stockyards, some hours after the convention had begun, the streets were empty but for patrol cars and police barricades at every approach. The stench of the yards was heavy tonight, and in a district nearby where the Mayor lived like the rest of his neighbors in a small wooden frame house, the sense of Chicago as a city on the plains (like small railroad cities in North Dakota and Nebraska) was clear in image, and in the wan streetlights, the hushed sidewalks, for almost no one was out in this area, the houses looked ubiquitously brown, the fear within almost palpable outside. The average burgher of Chicago, cursed with the middling unspiked culture of that flat American midcult which lay like a wet rag on the American mind, was without those boulevards and mansions and monuments of the mind which a thoroughgoing culture can give to paranoia for enrichment; no, the Chicagoan hiding this Monday night (as he was to hide Tuesday night, Wednesday night, Thursday night) inside his home was waiting perhaps for an eruption of the Blacks or an avalanche of Yippies to storm the chastity of his family redoubts. So fear was in these empty streets, and the anger of the city at its own fear, an anger which gave promise not soon to be satisfied by measures less than tyranny.

Seven miles to the northeast, just so far as from Greenwich Village to the middle of Harlem, the air of men ready for combat was up in Lincoln Park. It was after eleven, even close to midnight, and police cars were everywhere, and platoons of policemen every few hundred feet, enough for a parade. In the meadow in the angle between North Clark Street and LaSalle Drive, where the reporter had heard the music the afternoon before, there were now a few hundred people milling about. In the dark, there was no way to count, perhaps a few thousand in all of the park, youths up for an event with every muted mix of emotion, fear as clean as skiers before a steep downhill run, and vigorous crazy gaiety in the air like college pranksters before a panty raid; with it, the night nonetheless not without horror, very much not without horror, as if a fearful auto accident had taken place but ten minutes before and people wandered about now in the dark with awareness that bodies wrapped in bloodstained blankets might be some-where off a shoulder of the road. In the near distance, the blue light of a police car was revolving through the dark, the menacing blue light turning 360 degrees around and around again, and a white-silver light pierced the retina in alternation, lighting up the face of boys not twenty-two, not twenty, some of them in Indian blankets or ponchos, others in white shirts and khaki pants, sleeves rolled up, some with jackets, some with bikers' helmets, others with football helmets, a fencing jacket or two, and the hint of a few with private weapons, spade cats drifting in and out, emitting that high smoke of action carried from night to night in the electrified cool of the blood.

Twenty or thirty of the kids were building a barricade. They brought in park benches and picnic tables, and ran it a distance of fifty feet, then a hundred feet. A barricade perhaps six feet high. It made no sense. It stood in the middle of a field and there were no knolls nor defiles at the flanks to keep the barricade from being turned — the police cars would merely drive around it, or tear-gas trucks would push through it.

It was then the reporter decided to leave. The park was cool, it was after midnight, and if the police had not come yet, they might not come for hours, or perhaps not at all — perhaps there were new orders to let the kids sleep here — he simply did not know. He only knew he did not wish to spend hours in this park. For what was one to do when the attack came? Would one leave when asked — small honor there — why wait to offer that modest obedience. And to stay — to what end? — to protest being ejected from the park, to take tear gas in the face, have one's head cracked? He could not make the essential connection between that and Vietnam. If the war were on already, if this piece of ground were essential to the support of other pieces of ground . . . but this ridiculous barricade, this symbolic contest with real bloody heads — he simply did not know what he thought. And he had a legitimate excuse for leaving. One of his best friends was with him, a professional boxer, once a champion. If the police ever touched him, the boxer would probably be unable to keep himself from taking out six or eight men. The police would then come near to killing the boxer in return. It was a real possibility. He had the responsibility to his friend to get him out of there, and did, even encountering Allen Ginsberg, William Burroughs, Jean Genêt, Richard Seaver and Terry Southern on the way in. They had the determined miserable look of infantrymen trudging to the front; and Ginsberg, who had no taste for the violence ahead, and no conception whatsoever of looking for a way to avoid it, gave him a friendly salute, free of prejudice, and shuffled on forward to the meadow while Genêt, large as Mickey Rooney, angelic in appearance, glanced at him with that hauteur it takes French intellectuals at least two decades to acquire. Burroughs merely nodded. Nothing surprised him favorably or unfavorably.

There was, of course, now every pressure to return but he would not — there was the real (if most fortuitous) danger of exposing the boxer; there was his own decision. He was either being sensible, militarily sensible, revolutionary in the hard way of facing into twenty years of a future like this, and the need for patience till the real battles came; or he was yellow. And he did not know. Fear was in him, but he had acted boldly in the past with much more fear than this. He could not decide whether he was in danger of deteriorating, or becoming sufficiently tough to be able to take a backward step.

And enjoyed the party he went to after this, enjoyed himself until the morning when he discovered the attack by the police had been ferocious, and Ginsberg had been tear-gassed, his throat so injured he could hardly speak — and since the chanting of his Hindu hymns was a spiritual manna for Ginsberg, how the injury to his voice would hurt. And worse. Seventeen newsmen had been attacked by police, a photographer for the *Washington Post,* two reporters for the *Chicago American,* one for the *Chicago Daily News,* two photographers and a reporter for the *Chicago Sun-Times,* a reporter and a photographer for *Life,* cameramen for three television networks, and three reporters and a photographer for *Newsweek* magazine. But since the reporter was not there, let us quote from the *Washington Post* in a story by Nicholas von Hoffman:

> The attack began with a police car smashing the barricade. The kids threw whatever they had had the foresight to arm themselves with, rocks and bottles mostly. Then there was a period of police action before the full charge.
> Shrieks and screams all over the wooded encampment area while the experienced militants kept calling out, "Walk! Walk! For Chrissakes don't run." There is an adage among veteran kids that "panicky people incite cops to riot."
> Rivulets of running people came out of the woods across the lawn area, the parking lots toward Clark Street. Next, the cops burst out of the woods in selective pursuit of news photographers. Pictures are unanswerable evidence in court. They'd taken off their badges, their name plates, even the unit patches on their shoulders to become a mob of identical, unidentifiable club swingers.
> . . . There is the scene at Henrotin Hospital with editors coming

in to claim their wounded. Roy Fischer of the Chicago Daily News, Hal Bruno of Newsweek. Television guys who took a special clobbering waiting in the anteroom describing what happened and looking angry-eyed at the cops hanging around with the air of guys putting in a routine night.

The counterrevolution had begun. It was as if the police had declared that the newspapers no longer represented the true feelings of the people. The true feelings of the people, said the policemen's clubs, were with the police.

13

Next day was Johnson's birthday, which the President celebrated on the ranch. Three thousand youths went to the Chicago Coliseum, an old and crumbling convention hall, to attend an anti-birthday party sponsored by the Mobilization to End the War in Vietnam, and the Holocaust No-Dance Band played at total volume; speeches were made; a song called "Master of Hate" was dedicated to LBJ. It went:

> Suicide is an evil thing
> But at times it is good
> If you've been where the master lives
> I think you surely should.

Phil Ochs sang: "It's always the old who lead us to war; it's always the young who fall," and the crowd rose, held their hands high in a V for Victory sign, and chanted, "No, no, we won't go."

Burroughs and Genêt spoke of the police as mad dogs, statements were read for Terry Southern and Allen Ginsberg, and Dick Gregory gave the last speech. "I've just heard that Premier Kosygin has sent a telegram to Mayor Daley asking him to send 2,000 Chicago cops immediately."

The reporter was not present at the Coliseum. He had been covering the convention in the stockyards, expecting the debate to take place that night on the majority versus the minority plank on Vietnam, but the convention adjourned after midnight with the debate postponed for the next afternoon. Little had happened that night worth reporting. So he drove up to Lincoln Park about one-thirty in the morning, and everything seemed calm. A few police were still about, and one or two boys walked along holding wet handkerchiefs to their mouths. The streets were acrid with old tear gas. The reporter did not know that the worst battle of the week had taken place not an hour ago. Let us read a long account but an excellent one by Steve Lerner in *The Village Voice:*

> . . . Around midnight on Tuesday some four hundred clergy, concerned local citizens, and other respectable gentry joined the Yippies, members of Students for a Democratic Society, and the National Mobilization Committee to fight for the privilege of remaining in the park. Sporting armbands decorated with a black cross and chanting pacifist hymns, the men of God exhorted their radical congregation to lay down their bricks and join in a nonviolent vigil.
>
> Having foreseen that they could only wage a symbolic war with "little caesar Daley," several enterprising clergymen brought with them an enormous wooden cross which they erected in the midst of the demonstrators under a street lamp. Three of them assumed heroic poses around the cross, more reminiscent of the Marines raising the flag over Iwo Jima than any Christ-like tableau they may have had in mind.
>
> During the half-hour interlude between the arrival of the clergy and the police attack, a fascinating debate over the relative merits of strict non-violence versus armed self-defense raged between the clergy and the militants. While the clergy was reminded that their members were "over thirty, the opiate of the people, and totally irrelevant," the younger generation was warned that "by calling the police pigs and fighting with them you become as bad as they are." Although the conflict was never resolved, everyone more or less decided to do his own thing. By then the demonstrators, some eight hundred strong, began to feel the phalanx of police which encircled the park moving in; even the most militant forgot his quibbles with "the liberal-religious sellout" and began to huddle together around the cross.
>
> When the police announced that the demonstrators had five minutes to move out before the park was cleared, everyone went into his individual kind of panic. One boy sitting near me unwrapped a cheese sandwich and began to stuff it into his face without bothering to chew. A girl standing at the periphery of the circle who had been alone all evening walked up to a helmeted boy with a mustache and ground herself into him. People all over the park were shyly introducing themselves to each other as if they didn't want to die alone. "My name is Mike Stevenson from Detroit; what got you into this?" I heard someone asking behind me. Others became increasingly involved in the details of survival: rubbing Vaseline on their face to keep the Mace from burning their skin, buttoning their jackets, wetting their handkerchief and tying it over their nose and mouth. "If it's gas, remember, breathe through your mouth, don't run, don't pant, and for Christsake don't rub

228

your eyes," someone thoughtfully announced over the speaker. A boy in the center of the circle got up, stepped over his seated friends, and made his way toward the woods. "Don't leave now," several voices called in panic. The boy explained that he was just going to take a leak.

Sitting in a cluster near the main circle, Allen Ginsberg, Jean Genet, William Burroughs, and Terry Southern were taking in the scene. Ginsberg was in his element. As during all moments of tension during the week, he was chanting OM in a hoarse whisper, occasionally punctuating the ritual with a tinkle from his finger cymbals. Burroughs, wearing a felt hat, stared vacantly at the cross, his thin lips twitching in a half smile. Genet, small, stocky, bald-headed, with the mug of a saintly convict rubbed his nose on the sleeve of his leather jacket. I asked him if he was afraid. "No, I know what this is," he replied. "But doesn't knowing make you more afraid?" I asked. He shook his head and started to speak when the sky fell on us.

It happened all in an instant. The night which had been filled with darkness and whispers exploded in a fiery scream. Huge tear-gas canisters came crashing through the branches, snapping them, and bursting in the center of the gathering. From where I lay, groveling in the grass, I could see ministers retreating with the cross, carrying it like a fallen comrade. Another volley shook me to my feet. Gas was everywhere. People were running, screaming, tearing through the trees. Something hit the tree next to me, I was on the ground again, someone was pulling me to my feet, two boys were lifting a big branch off a girl who lay squirming hysterically. I couldn't see. Someone grabbed onto me and asked me to lead them out of the park. We walked along, hands outstretched, bumping into people and trees, tears streaming from our eyes and mucus smeared across our faces. I flashed First World War doughboys caught in No Man's Land during a mustard gas attack. I felt sure I was going to die. I heard others choking around me. And then everything cleared.

Standing on the sidewalk at the edge of the park I looked back at a dozen little fires which lit up the woods, still fogged with gas. The police were advancing in a picket line, swatting at the stragglers and crumpled figures; huge trucks, usually used for cleaning the streets, swept toward us spraying more gas. Kids began ripping up the pavement and hurling snowball-size chunks at the truck windows. Then they flooded out into the streets, blocking traffic, fighting with plainclothesmen who awaited our exodus from the park, and bombarding hapless patrol cars which sped through the crowds.

The ragged army split up into a series of mobs which roamed through the streets breaking windows, setting trash cans on fire, and demolishing at least a dozen patrol cars which happened to cruise down the wrong street at the wrong time. Smoke billowed from a house several blocks from me and the fire engines began arriving. A policeman ran from an angry brick-throwing mob, lost his cap, hesitated, and ran away without it. At the intersection of Clark and Division, four cop cars arrived simultaneously and policemen leapt out shooting in the air. From all four sides the demonstrators let them have it; most of the missiles were overthrown and hit their comrades or store windows on the other side of the street. Diving down into the subway, I found a large group of refugees who had escaped the same way. The tunnel looked like a busy bomb shelter; upstairs the shooting continued.

14

They were young men who were not going to Vietnam. So they would show every lover of war in Vietnam that the reason they did not go was not for lack of the courage to fight; no, they would carry the fight over every street in Old Town and the Loop where the opportunity presented itself. If they had been gassed and beaten, their leaders arrested on fake charges (Hayden, picked up while sitting under a tree in daylight in Lincoln Park, naturally protested; the resulting charge was "resisting arrest") they were going to demonstrate that they would not give up, that they were the stuff out of which the very best soldiers were made. Sunday, they had been driven out of the park, Monday as well, now Tuesday. The centers where they slept in bedrolls on the floor near Lincoln Park had been broken into by the police, informers and provocateurs were everywhere; tonight tear-gas trucks had been used. They were still not ready to give up. Indeed their militancy may have increased. They took care of the worst of their injured and headed for the Loop, picking up fellow demonstrators as they went. Perhaps the tear gas was a kind of catharsis for some of them, a letting of tears, a purging of old middle-class weakness. Some were turning from college boys to revolutionaries. It seemed as if the more they were beaten and tear-gassed, the more they rallied back. Now, with the facility for underground communication which seemed so instinctive a tool in their generation's equipment, they were on their way to Grant Park, en masse, a thousand of them, two thousand of them, there were conceivably as many as five thousand boys and girls massed in Grant Park at three in the morning, listening to speakers, cheering, chanting, calling across Michigan Avenue to the huge brooding façade of the Hilton, a block wide, over twenty-five stories high, with huge wings and deep courts (the better to multiply the number of windows with a view of the street and a view of Grant Park). The lights were on in hundreds of bedrooms in the Hilton, indeed people were sleeping and dreaming all over the hotel with the sound of young orators declaiming in the night below, voices rising twenty-five stories high, the voices clear in the spell of sound which hung over the Hilton. The Humphrey headquarters were here, and the McCarthy headquarters. Half the Press was quartered here, and Marvin Watson as well. Postmaster General and Presidential trouble-shooter, he had come to bring some of Johnson's messages to Humphrey. His suite had a view of the park. Indeed two-thirds of the principals at the convention must have had a view early this morning, two and three and four A.M. of this Tuesday night, no, this Wednesday morning, of Grant Park filled across the street with a revolutionary army of dissenters and demonstrators and college children and McCarthy workers and tourists ready to take a crack on the head, all night they could hear the demonstrators chanting, "Join us, join us," and the college bellow of utter contempt, "Dump the Hump! Dump the Hump!" all the fury of the beatings and the tear-gassings, all the bitter disappointments of that recently elapsed bright spring when the only critical problem was who would make a better President, Kennedy or McCarthy (now all the dread of a future with Humphrey or Nixon). There was also the sense that police had now entered their lives, become an element pervasive as drugs and books and sex and music and family. So they shouted up to the windows of the Hilton, to the delegates and the campaign workers who were sleeping, or shuddering by the side of their bed, or cheering by their open window; they called up through the night on a stage as vast and towering as one of Wagner's visions and the screams of police cars joined them, pulling up, gliding away, blue lights revolving, lines of police hundreds long in their sky-blue shirts and sky-blue crash helmets, penning the demonstrators back of barriers across Michigan Avenue from the Hilton, and other lines of police and police fences on the Hilton's side of the street. The police had obviously been given orders not to attack the demonstrators here, not in front of the Hilton with half the Democratic Party watching them, not now at three in the morning — would anyone ever discover for certain what was to change their mind in sixteen hours?

Now, a great cheer went up. The police were being relieved by the National Guard. The Guard was being brought in! It was like a certificate of merit for the demonstrators to see the police march off and new hundreds of Guardsmen in khaki uniforms, helmets, and rifles take up post in place, army trucks coughing and barking and filing back and forth on Michigan Avenue, and on the side streets now surrounding the Hilton, evil-looking jeeps with barbed-wire gratings in front of their bumpers drove forward in echelons, and parked behind the crowd. Portable barbed-wire fences were now riding on Jeeps.

Earlier in the week, it had been relatively simple to get into the Hilton. Mobs of McCarthy workers and excited adolescents had jammed the stairs and the main entrance room of the lobby chanting all day, singing campaign songs, mocking every Humphrey worker they could recognize, holding station for hours in the hope, or on the rumor, that McCarthy would be passing through, and the cheers had the good nature and concerted rhythmic steam of a football rally. That had been Saturday and Sunday and Monday, but the police finally had barricaded the kids out of the lobby, and now at night covered the entrances to the Hilton, and demanded press passes, and room keys, as warrants of entry. The Hilton heaved and staggered through a variety of attacks and breakdowns. Like an old fort, like the old fort of the old Democratic Party, about to fall forever beneath the ministrations of its high shaman, its excruciated warlock, derided by the young, held in contempt by its own soldiers — the very delegates who would be loyal to Humphrey in the nomination and loyal to nothing in their heart — this spiritual fort of the Democratic Party was now housed in the literal fort of the Hilton staggering in place, all boilers working, all motors vibrating, yet seeming to come apart from the pressures on the street outside, as if the old Hilton had become artifact of the party and the nation.

Nothing worked well in the hotel, and much didn't work at all. There was no laundry because of the bus strike, and the house phones usually did not function; the room phones were tapped so completely, and the devices so over-adjacent, that separate conversations lapped upon one another in the same earpiece, or went jolting by in all directions like three handballs at play at once in a four-wall handball court. Sometimes the phone was dead, sometimes it emitted hideous squawks, or squeals, or the harsh electronic displeasure of a steady well-pulsed static. Sometimes one got long distance by taking it through the operator, sometimes one got an outside line only by ringing the desk and demanding it, sometimes one could get the hotel operator only by dialing the outside line. All the while, a photograph of Mayor Daley the size of a postage stamp was pasted on the cradle of the phone. "Welcome to the 1968 National Democratic Convention," it said. Often, one could not even extract a whimper from the room phone. It had succumbed. Sometimes the phone stayed dead for hours. Success in a convention is reduced to success in communications, as the reporter was yet to learn; communications in the headquarters of the largest party in the nation most renowned for the technology of its communications was breaking apart under strikes, pressure, sabotage, security, security over-check, overdevelopment and insufficient testing of advanced technical devices: at the base of the pyramid, sheer human inefficiencies before the combined onslaught of pressure and street war.

The elevators worked abominably. On certain floors the signal did not seem to ring. One could wait a half hour for an elevator to stop on the way down. After a time everybody went up to the top in order to be able to go down. Yet one could not use the stairs, for Secret Servicemen were guarding them. It could, at worst, demand an hour to go to one's room and go down again. So it might have been better to live in a hotel across the Loop; but then there were traffic jams and police lines and demonstrators every night, demonstrators marching along with handkerchiefs to their noses.

This night with the demonstrators up and aroused in Grant Park, tear gas was blowing right into the hotel. The police had tried to gas the kids out of the park when they first arrived in numbers from Lincoln Park, but the wind blew the wrong way, blew the tears across the street into the air conditioning of the Hilton lobby, and delegates and Press and officials walked about with smarting eyes, burning throats, and the presentiment that they were going to catch a cold. The lobby stunk. Not from the tear gas, but from stink bombs, or some advanced variety of them, for the source of the odor was either mysterious, or unremovable, or had gotten into the very entrails of the air conditioning since it got worse from day to day and drenched the coffee shop and the bars and the lobby with a stench not easily forgettable. Standing near someone, the odor of vomit always prevailed from the bombs — no, it was worse than vomit, rather like a truly atrocious body odor which spoke of the potential for sour vomit in every joint of a bad piece of psychic work. So personal relations were curious. One met attractive men or women, shook hands with them, chatted for a time, said goodbye. One's memory of the occasion was how awful it had smelled.

Delegates, powerful political figures, old friends, and strangers all smelled awful.

So nothing worked well in the hotel, and everything stank, and crowds — those who could get in — milled about, and police guarded the entrance, and across the street as the reporter moved through the tight press of children sitting packed together on the grass, cheering the speakers, chanting "Join us! Join us!" and "Dump the Hump" the smell of the stink bombs was still present, but different now, equally evil and vomitous but from a faded odor of Mace. The nation divided was going to war with stinks; each side would inflict a stink upon the other. The years of sabotage were ahead — a fearful perspective: they would be giving engineering students tests in loyalty before they were done; the FBI would come to question whoever took a mail order course in radio. It was possible that one was at the edge of that watershed year from which the country might never function well again, and service in American hotels would yet be reminiscent of service in Mexican motels. Whatever! the children were alive with revolutionary fire on this fine Tuesday night, this early Wednesday morning, and the National Guard policing them was wide-awake as well. Incidents occurred. Flare-ups. A small Negro soldier started pushing a demonstrator with his rifle, pushing him in sudden fury as at the wild kickoff of a wild street fight; the demonstrator — who looked to be a kindly divinity student — aghast at what he had set off; he had not comprehended the Negro wished no special conversation from him. And a National Guard officer came running up to pull the Negro back. (On the next night, there would be no Negroes in the line of National Guards.)

The kids were singing. There were two old standards which were sung all the time. An hour could not go by without both songs. So they sang "We Shall Overcome" and they sang "This Land Is Your Land," and a speaker cried up to the twenty-five stories of the Hilton, "We have the votes, you have the guns," a reference to the polls which had shown McCarthy to be more popular than Hubert Humphrey (yes, if only Rockefeller had run for the Democrats and McCarthy for the Republicans this would have been an ideal contest between a spender and a conservative) and then another speaker, referring to the projected march on the Amphitheatre next day, shouted, "We're going to march without a permit — the Russians demand a permit to have a meeting in Prague," and the crowd cheered this. They cheered with wild enthusiasm when one speaker, a delegate, had the inspiration to call out to the delegates and workers listening in the hundreds of rooms at the Hilton with a view of the park, "Turn on your lights, and blink them if you are with us. If you are with us, if you are sympathetic to us, blink your lights, blink your lights." And to the delight of the crowd, lights began to blink in the Hilton, ten, then twenty, perhaps so many as fifty lights were blinking at once, and a whole bank of lights on the fifteenth floor and the twenty-third floor went off and on at once, off and on at once. The McCarthy headquarters on the fifteenth and the twenty-third were blinking, and the crowd cheered. Now they had become an audience to watch the actors in the hotel. So two audiences regarded each other, like ships signaling across a gulf of water in the night, and delegates came down from the hotel; a mood of new beauty was in the air, there present through all the dirty bandaged kids, the sour vomit odor of the Mace, the sighing and whining of the army trucks moving in and out all the time, the adenoids, larynxes, wheezes and growls of the speakers, the blinking of lights in the Hilton, yes, there was the breath of this incredible crusade where fear was in every breath you took and so breath was tender, it came into the lungs as a manifest of value, as a gift, and the children's faces were shining in the glow of the headlights of the National Guard trucks and the searchlights of the police in front of the Hilton across Michigan Avenue. And the Hilton, sinking in its foundations, twinkled like a birthday cake. Horrors were coming tomorrow. No, it is today. It is Wednesday already.

15

If Wednesday was nominating day, it was also the afternoon when the debate on the Vietnam peace plank took place. Indeed, it was also the evening when the Massacre of Michigan Avenue occurred, an extraordinary event: a massacre, equal on balance to some of the old Indian raids, yet no one was killed. Of course, a great many people were hurt. And several hundred delegates started to march back from the stockyards, early Thursday morning after the nomination, carrying lit candles in protest. It was obviously one of the more active days in the history of any convention.

Worn out by his portentous Southern sense of things to come, Lester

Maddox, the fourth candidate, Governor of Georgia, even resigned his candidacy Wednesday morning. We quote from Walter Rugaber of *The New York Times:*

> His wife, Virginia, sat beside him weeping softly as Mr. Maddox ended his 11-day fling with a last news conference in the brightly lit Grand Ballroom of the Conrad Hilton Hotel.
> He talked about misinformed socialist and power-mad politicians. He assailed the Democrats as the party of "looting, burning, killing and draft-card burning. What's more," he said, "I denounce them all."

Then he caught a plane back to Atlanta. Who would declare that the chanting in Grant Park through the long hours of Tuesday night and the semi-obscene shouts — Dump the Hump! — had done nothing to accelerate his decision?

Originally, the debate on the Vietnam plank had been scheduled for Tuesday night, but the convention went on past midnight, so the hawks attempted to have it early in the morning. It was their hope to begin at 1 A.M. New York time, and thus obtain the pleasure of denying the doves a large television audience. But the doves raised a post-midnight demonstration on the floor which became progressively more obstreperous until Mayor Daley made the mistake of rising to remonstrate with the gallery, warning that they would be cleared out of their seats if they did not quiet down. "Let's act like ladies and gentlemen, and let people be heard," said Daley to the convention and to millions on television, looking for all the world like the best b.o. ever to come out of *Guys and Dolls.* But it was obvious the greater share of the noise came from behind Daley on the floor, from the rear where McCarthy and McGovern delegates from New York, California, South Dakota, Massachusetts, Wisconsin and Oregon were placed far from the podium. At any rate, the Administration forces lost their play. It was one thing for them to cut off a discussion — that was simply accomplished. One had only to give a signal, then make a quick motion which could as quickly be recognized by the Chairman who would whip in a lightning move for a voice-vote. "The ayes . . . the nays . . . The ayes have it," he would say, and rap his gavel, walk off the podium, close the session. But here, after midnight, the hawks were not trying to cut off a discussion, rather they wished to begin one; the doves had nothing to lose by a noisy non-stop protest. Moves for silence, whacks of the gavel by Carl Albert looking poisonous for being ignored, loud music of the band to drown out the rear delegation. Nothing worked. The television cameras were focused on the doves who were protesting the lateness of the hour. The hawks could insist on their move, but they would look like the worst of the cattle gang on television. So a signal was passed to Daley by an Administration spokesman who drew his finger across his throat, an unmistakable sign to cut off conversation for the night. Daley, looking like he had just been stuffed with a catfish, stood up, got the floor, made a move to adjourn. Immediately recognized by Carl Albert. The little Chairman was now sufficiently excited to start to say Mayor Daley of the Great State of Chicago. He recovered quickly, however, quick enough to rap his gavel, and declare that the Chair accepted the motion, snapping it through with a slick haste, as if it had been his idea all along! The debate was postponed until Wednesday afternoon.

The debate, however, proved anti-climactic. There had been hopes that McCarthy would speak, idle dreams he might make a great speech; but it was rumored that the Senator, weighing the inponderable proto-col of these profoundly established convention manners, had decided he would not enter debate unless Lyndon Johnson came to the Amphi-theatre for his birthday party. Johnson, however, was not in the hall; he was still in Texas where he would remain (on the advice of his best wise men since they could not guarantee the character of his reception in the Amphitheatre, nor the nature of the stimulation it might give the streets). Therefore, McCarthy, respecting the balance, was not present either.

The hawks had first proposed fifteen minutes for the debate, then thirty. An hour was the maximum obtainable by the doves. On the greatest national issue any convention had faced since the Second World War, debate would provide an hour of speech for each side. Moreover, the sides would make alternate speeches. Thus, no massive presentation of argument nor avalanche of emotion would ever result.

These restrictions having limited the outcome before they began, Rep. Philip Burton of California spoke first for the minority, then Senator Muskie of Maine for the majority. Burton asked that we "heed the voices of men and women of good will who across the land call for peace," Muskie went through the differences in the majority and minority planks, and the similarities, and then concluded that the majority protected our soldiers, whereas the minority was too quick to desire peace at any price.

The speakers came on. They seemed careful to abstain from rich, extravagant, or passionate language. No one got up to say that one

237

million men on our side could not dominate a quarter million men on the other, for that would have been unpatriotic (which for a politician is sacrilege equal to burning money or flooding property) no, the best of the majority roamed mean and keen over the legalities, the technicalities of commitment, the safety of American soldiers, the tempo for establishing representative government; they spoke in styles sometimes reminiscent of the eminent sanity of Dean Rusk; he was always a model of sanity on every detail but one: he had a delusion that the war was not bottomless in its lunacy. Of course, words like lunacy were not for the floor of the convention. Muskie; Sen. McGee of Wyoming; Governor Hearnes of Missouri; Mrs. Geri Joseph of Minnesota; David Pryor of Arkansas; Rep. Ed Edmondson of Oklahoma; Mayor Wilson Wyatt of Louisville; Rep. Zablocki of Wisconsin, and Rep. Hale Boggs of Louisiana, Chairman of the Platform Committee, spoke for the majority long enough to put in nitpicking points and intone against Communism. The whine in one American's nasal passages obviously stimulated something in the inner canal of other American ears when Communism was given its licks. The hawks then extolled the dove-like nature of the majority plank. The doves, however, came back by way of Senator Morse to reply that the "majority report stripped of its semantics is nothing but a naked proposal to continue the failures of our policy in Vietnam." Also speaking for the doves: Paul O'Dwyer of New York; Ken O'Donnell of Massachusetts; John Gilligan of Ohio; Senator Gore of Tennessee; Ted Sorensen of New York, and Pierre Salinger of California.

For those who are curious let us give excerpts of a few speeches.

> *Senator Edmund Muskie:* "The choice is this: A negotiated settlement with, or a negotiated settlement without safeguards to protect free elections. . . . A bombing halt with, or a bombing halt without consideration of the air protection for our troops against military risks arising north of the demilitarized zone. . . . Mr. Chairman, I urge the adoption of the majority plank." (Muskie was obviously a contented rooster.)

> *Theodore Sorensen:* "We call for an end to the bombing now — they call for an end if and when and maybe.
> "Second, we call for a mutual withdrawal of all U.S. and North Vietnamese troops now. . . . The majority plank says maybe, sometime, if all Vietcong hostilities can somehow cease first.
> "Third, we call, as Ted Kennedy called, for letting the South Vietnamese decide for themselves the shape of their own future. They call for the United States to stay and conform the Vietnamese to our political and economic standards.

"Fourth, we call for a reduction of American troops now. . . . They call for a reduction in troops only when the South Vietnamese Army can take over. . . ."

Governor Warren Hearnes: ". . . many of the decisions that are being made here in this convention hall by we politicians have been dictated by the prospects of victory or defeat. Victory or defeat in November.

". . . For God's sake, if you adopt the minority report, you are going to jeopardize the lives of the servicemen in Vietnam."

Kenneth O'Donnell: ". . . we were forced to watch a Congress of the United States . . . cut the budget $6 billion in the last Congress, and they cut it out of all the programs affecting the lives of every single American, out of the programs of health, in education and the problems that face our children . . . we will not have the money unless we are able in some fashion to disengage ourselves from the expeditures not only of our best treasure, the young men, but the fact that we are spending $30 billion a year in a foreign adventure in South Vietnam. It must end."

Representative Hale Boggs: "Can General Abrams supply an answer to me on this question, and I pose the question:

"Is there any possibility of your providing even an approximate estimate of the additional casualties we would take if we stopped the bombing of North Vietnam unilaterally and unconditionally?

"And the answer came back and here I read it to you — these are not my words, these are the words of General Abrams: 'If the bombing in North Vietnam now authorized were to be suspended unilaterally, the enemy in ten days to two weeks could develop a capability in the DMZ area in terms of scale, intensity, and duration of combat on the order of five times what he now has.'

"I cannot agree. I cannot agree to place our forces at the risk which the enemy's capability would then pose. That, my friends, concludes our debate." (Hale Boggs was the hawk's own tern.)

The Administration was taking no chances on birds. A confidential White House briefing had been thrown into the shot-load for this debate, and by the time the last speaker had his word, the military were concluding the debate, that same military which had been giving expert guesses for years on just how many troops and just how many bombs would be necessary to guarantee victory in exactly so many weeks or exactly so many months; the party was still buying just such expert advice. "Scale, intensity, and duration of combat on the order of five times." The Texas delegation up front cheered. Put a big man in a big uniform, let him recite big figures, and they would take the word of no priest or pope. In America the uniform always finished first, the production expert second, and Christ was welcome to come in third. So the vote came out as 1,567¾ to 1,041½ — the majority plank was passed. Lyndon Johnson was vindicated by the same poor arguments which had originally implicated him. Politics was property, and the gravitational power of massive holdings was sufficient to pull you out of your own soup.

But the floor would not rest. The New York and California delegations began to sing "We Shall Overcome." Quickly, the Platform was passed; still the New York delegation sang. Now Wisconsin stood on its seats. The rear of the floor booed the front of the floor. A few hundred posters, STOP THE WAR, quickly printed a couple of hours earlier for this occasion, were held up. Defeated delegates yelled, "Stop the war," in the fierce frustration of knowing that the plank was Lyndon Johnson's and the party was still his. The convention recessed. Still the New York delegation sang, "We Shall Overcome," standing on their seats. The convention band across the way tried to drown them out. It played in ever-increasing volume "We Got a Lot of Living to Do."

The managers of the convention turned the New York microphones down, and amplified the public address system for the band. So on the floor of the convention, the doves were drowned in hostile sound, but on the television sets, the reception was opposite, for the networks had put their own microphones under the voices of the delegates, and they sang in force across the continent. Thus a few thousand people on the floor and the gallery heard little of the doves — all the rest of America heard them well. Politics-is-property had come to the point of fission. He who controlled the floor no longer controlled the power of public opinion. Small wonder the old party hands hated the networks — it was agitating to have mastered the locks and keys in the house of politics and discover that there was a new door they could not quite shut. In disgust the hawk delegations left the floor. The doves continued to sing "We Shall Overcome." Now, the orchestra played "Happy Days Are Here Again."

The demonstrators chanted, "We want peace! We want peace!" "I'm Looking Over a Four-Leaf Clover" the orchestra offered, then rejected, then switched over to "If You Knew Suzy," then they gave up. The demonstrators began to sing "The Battle Hymn of the Republic." New York, California, Oregon, Wisconsin, South Dakota and other delegations marched around the empty floor. It was half an hour after the convention had recessed. Still they sang. It had been a long war to lose.

16

Meanwhile, a mass meeting was taking place about the bandshell in Grant Park, perhaps a quarter of a mile east of Michigan Avenue and the Conrad Hilton. The meeting was under the auspices of the Mobilization, and a crowd of ten or fifteen thousand appeared. The Mayor had granted a permit to assemble, but had refused to allow a march. Since the Mobilization had announced that it would attempt, no matter how, the march to the Amphitheatre that was the first purpose of their visit to Chicago, the police were out in force to surround the meeting.

An episode occurred during the speeches. Three demonstrators climbed a flag pole to cut down the American flag and put up a rebel flag. A squad of police charged to beat them up, but got into trouble themselves, for when they threw tear gas, the demonstrators lobbed the canisters back, and the police, choking on their own gas, had to fight their way clear through a barrage of rocks. Then came a much larger force of police charging the area, overturning benches, busting up members of the audience, then heading for Rennie Davis at the bullhorn. He was one of the coordinators of the Mobilization, his face was known, he had been fingered and fingered again by plainclothesmen. Now urging the crowd to sit down and be calm, he was attacked from behind by the police, his head laid open in a three-inch cut, and he was unconscious for a period. Furious at the attack, Tom Hayden, who had been in disguise these last two days to avoid any more arrests for himself, spoke to the crowd, said he was leaving to perform certain special tasks, and suggested that others break up into small groups and go out into the streets of the Loop "to do what they have to do." A few left with him; the majority remained. While it was a People's Army and therefore utterly unorganized by uniform or unity, it had a variety of special troops and regular troops; everything from a few qualified Kamikaze who were ready to charge police lines in a Japanese snake dance and dare on the consequence, some vicious beatings, to various kinds of small saboteurs, rock-throwers, gauntlet-runners — some of the speediest of the kids were adept at taunting cops while keeping barely out of range of their clubs — not altogether alien to running the bulls at Pamplona. Many of those who remained, however, were still nominally pacifists, protesters, Gandhians — they believed in non-violence, in the mystical interposition of their body to the attack, as if the violence of the enemy might be drained by the spiritual act of passive resistance over the years, over the thousands, tens of thousands, hundreds of thousands of beatings over the years. So Allen Ginsberg was speaking now to them.

The police looking through the Plexiglas face shields they had flipped down from their helmets were then obliged to watch the poet with his bald head, soft eyes magnified by horn-rimmed eyeglasses, and massive dark beard, utter his words in a croaking speech. He had been gassed Monday night and Tuesday night, and had gone to the beach at dawn to read Hindu Tantras to some of the Yippies, the combination of the chants and the gassings had all but burned out his voice, his beautiful speaking voice, one of the most powerful and hypnotic instruments of the Western world, was down to the scrapings of the throat now, raw as flesh after a curettage.

"The best strategy for you," said Ginsberg, "in cases of hysteria, overexcitement or fear, is still to chant 'OM' together. It helps to quell flutterings of butterflies in the belly. Join me now as I try to lead you."

The crowd chanted with Ginsberg. They were of a generation which would try every idea, every drug, every action — it was even possible a few of them had made out with freaky kicks on tear gas these last few days — so they would chant OM. There were Hindu fanatics in the crowd, children who loved India and scorned everything in the West; there were cynics who thought the best thing to be said for a country which allowed its excess population to die by the millions in famine-ridden fields was that it would not be ready soon to try to dominate the rest of the world. There were also militants who were ready to march. And the police there to prevent them, busy now in communication with other detachments of police, by way of radios whose aerials were attached to their helmets, thereby giving them the look of giant insects.

A confused hour began. Lincoln Park was irregular in shape with curving foot walks; but Grant Park was indeed not so much a park as a set of belts of greenery cut into files by major parallel avenues between Michigan Avenue and Lake Michigan half a mile away. Since there were also cross streets cutting the belts of green perpendicularly, a variety of bridges and pedestrian overpasses gave egress to the city. The park was in this sense an alternation of lawn with superhighways. So the police were able to pen the crowd. But not completely. There were too many bridges, too many choices, in effect, for the police to anticipate. To this confusion was added the fact that every confrontation of demonstrators with police, now buttressed by the National

Guard, attracted hundreds of newsmen, and hence began a set of attempted negotiations between spokesmen for the demonstrators and troops. The demonstrators finally tried to force a bridge and get back to the city. Repelled by tear gas, they went to other bridges, still other bridges, finally found a bridge lightly guarded, broke through a passage and were loose in the city at six-thirty in the evening. They milled about in the Loop for a few minutes, only to encounter the mules and three wagons of the Poor People's Campaign. City officials, afraid of provoking the Negroes on the South Side, had given a permit to the Reverend Abernathy, and he was going to march the mules and wagons down Michigan Avenue and over to the convention. An impromptu march of the demonstrators formed behind the wagons immediately on encountering them and ranks of marchers, sixty, eighty, a hundred in line across the width of Michigan Avenue began to move forward in the gray early twilight of 7 P.M.; Michigan Avenue was now suddenly jammed with people in the march, perhaps so many as four or five thousand people, including onlookers on the sidewalk who jumped in. The streets of the Loop were also reeking with tear gas — the wind had blown some of the gas west over Michigan Avenue from the drops on the bridges, some gas still was penetrated into the clothing of the marchers. In broken ranks, half a march, half a happy mob, eyes red from gas, faces excited by the tension of the afternoon, and the excitement of the escape from Grant Park, now pushing down Michigan Avenue toward the Hilton Hotel with dreams of a march on to the Amphitheatre four miles beyond, and in the full pleasure of being led by the wagons of the Poor People's March, the demonstrators shouted to everyone on the sidewalk, "Join us, join us, join us," and the sidewalk kept disgorging more people ready to march.

But at Balbo Avenue, just before Michigan Avenue reached the Hilton, the marchers were halted by the police. It was a long halt. Perhaps thirty minutes. Time for people who had been walking on the sidewalk to join the march, proceed for a few steps, halt with the others, wait, get bored, and leave. It was time for someone in command of the hundreds of police in the neighborhood to communicate with his headquarters, explain the problem, time for the dilemma to be relayed, alternatives examined, and orders conceivably sent back to attack and disperse the crowd. If so, a trap was first set. The mules were allowed to cross Balbo Avenue, then were separated by a line of police from the marchers, who now, several thousand compressed in this one place, filled the intersection of Michigan Avenue and Balbo. There, dammed

243

by police on three sides, and cut off from the wagons of the Poor People's March, there, right beneath the windows of the Hilton which looked down on Grant Park and Michigan Avenue, the stationary march was abruptly attacked. The police attacked with tear gas, with Mace, and with clubs, they attacked like a chain saw cutting into wood, the teeth of the saw the edge of their clubs, they attacked like a scythe through grass, lines of twenty and thirty policemen striking out in an arc, their clubs beating, demonstrators fleeing. Seen from overhead, from the nineteenth floor, it was like a wind blowing dust, or the edge of waves riding foam on the shore.

The police cut through the crowd one way, then cut through them another. They chased people into the park, ran them down, beat them up; they cut through the intersection at Michigan and Balbo like a razor cutting a channel through a head of hair, and then drove columns of new police into the channel who in turn pushed out, clubs flailing, on each side, to cut new channels, and new ones again. As demonstrators ran, they reformed in new groups only to be chased by the police again. The action went on for ten minutes, fifteen minutes, with the absolute ferocity of a tropical storm, and watching it from a window on the nineteenth floor, there was something of the detachment of studying a storm at evening through a glass, the light was a lovely gray-blue, the police had uniforms of sky-blue, even the ferocity had an abstract elemental play of forces of nature at battle with other forces, as if sheets of tropical rain were driving across the street in patterns, in curving patterns which curved upon each other again. Police cars rolled up, prisoners were beaten, shoved into wagons, driven away. The rain of police, maddened by the uncoiling of their own storm, pushed against their own barricades of tourists pressed on the street against the Hilton Hotel, then pressed them so hard — but here is a quotation from J. Anthony Lukas in *The New York Times:*

> Even elderly bystanders were caught in the police onslaught. At one point, the police turned on several dozen persons standing quietly behind police barriers in front of the Conrad Hilton Hotel watching the demonstrators across the street.
> For no reason that could be immediately determined, the blue-helmeted policemen charged the barriers, crushing the spectators against the windows of the Haymarket Inn, a restaurant in the hotel. Finally the window gave way, sending screaming middle-aged women and children backward through the broken shards of glass.
> The police than ran into the restaurant and beat some of the victims who had fallen through the windows and arrested them.

Now another quote from Steve Lerner in *The Village Voice:*

> When the charge came, there was a stampede toward the sidelines. People piled into each other, humped over each other's bodies like coupling dogs. To fall down in the crush was just as terrifying as facing the police. Suddenly I realized my feet weren't touching the ground as the crowd pushed up onto the sidewalk. I was grabbing at the army jacket of the boy in front of me; the girl behind me had a stranglehold on my neck and was screaming incoherently in my ear.

Now, a longer quotation from Jack Newfield in *The Village Voice.* (The accounts in *The Voice* of September 5 were superior to any others encountered that week.)

> At the southwest entrance to the Hilton, a skinny, long-haired kid of about seventeen skidded down on the sidewalk, and four overweight cops leaped on him, chopping strokes on his head. His hair flew from the force of the blows. A dozen small rivulets of blood began to cascade down the kid's temple and onto the sidewalk. He was not crying or screaming, but crawling in a stupor toward the gutter. When he saw a photographer take a picture, he made a V sign with his fingers.
>
> A doctor in a white uniform and Red Cross arm band began to run toward the kid, but two other cops caught him from behind and knocked him down. One of them jammed his knee into the doctor's throat and began clubbing his rib cage. The doctor squirmed away, but the cops followed him, swinging hard, sometimes missing.
>
> A few feet away a phalanx of police charged into a group of women, reporters, and young McCarthy activists standing idly against the window of the Hilton Hotel's Haymarket Inn. The terrified people began to go down under the unexpected police charge when the plate glass window shattered, and the people tumbled backward through the glass. The police then climbed through the broken window and began to beat people, some of whom had been drinking quietly in the hotel bar.
>
> At the side entrance of the Hilton Hotel four cops were chasing one frightened kid of about seventeen. Suddenly, Fred Dutton, a former aide to Robert Kennedy, moved out from under the marquee and interposed his body between the kid and the police.
>
> "He's my guest in this hotel," Dutton told the cops.
>
> The police started to club the kid.
>
> Dutton screamed for the first cop's name and badge number. The cop grabbed Dutton and began to arrest him, until a *Washington Post* reporter identified Dutton as a former RFK aide.
>
> Demonstrators, reporters, McCarthy workers, doctors, all began to stagger into the Hilton lobby, blood streaming from face and head wounds. The lobby smelled from tear gas, and stink bombs dropped by the Yippies. A few people began to direct the wounded to a makeshift hospital on the fifteenth floor, the McCarthy staff headquarters.

Fred Dutton was screaming at the police, and at the journalists to report all the "sadism and brutality." Richard Goodwin, the ashen nub of a cigar sticking out of his fatigued face, mumbled, "This is just the beginning. There'll be four years of this."

The defiant kids began a slow, orderly retreat back up Michigan Avenue. They did not run. They did not panic. They did not fight back. As they fell back they helped pick up fallen comrades who were beaten or gassed. Suddenly, a plainclothesman dressed as a soldier moved out of the shadows and knocked one kid down with an overhand punch. The kid squatted on the pavement of Michigan Avenue, trying to cover his face, while the Chicago plainclothesman punched him with savage accuracy. Thud, thud, thud. Blotches of blood spread over the kid's face. Two photographers moved in. Several police formed a closed circle around the beating to prevent pictures. One of the policemen squirted chemical Mace at the photographers, who dispersed. The plainclothesman melted into the line of police.

Let us escape to the street. The reporter, watching in safety from the nineteenth floor, could understand now how Mussolini's son-in-law had once been able to find the bombs he dropped from his airplane beautiful as they burst, yes, children, and youths, and middle-aged men and women were being pounded and clubbed and gassed and beaten, hunted and driven, sent scattering in all directions by teams of policemen who had exploded out of their restraints like the bursting of a boil, and nonetheless he felt a sense of calm and beauty, void even of the desire to be down there, as if in years to come there would be beatings enough, some chosen, some from nowhere, but it was as if the war had finally begun, and this was therefore a great and solemn moment, as if indeed even the gods of history had come together from each side to choose the very front of the Hilton Hotel before the television cameras of the world and the eyes of the campaign workers and the delegates' wives, yes, there before the eyes of half the principals at the convention was this drama played, as if the military spine of a great liberal party had finally separated itself from the skin, as if, no metaphor large enough to suffice, the Democratic Party had here broken in two before the eyes of a nation like Melville's whale charging right out of the sea.

A great stillness rose up from the street through all the small noise of clubbing and cries, small sirens, sigh of loaded arrest vans as off they pulled, shouts of police as they wheeled in larger circles, the intersection clearing further, then further, a stillness rose through the steel and stone of the hotel, congregating in the shocked centers of every room where delegates and wives and Press and campaign workers innocent until now of the intimate working of social force, looked down now into the murderous paradigm of Vietnam there beneath them at this huge intersection of this great city. Look — a boy was running through the park, and a cop was chasing. There he caught him on the back of the neck with his club! There! The cop is returning to his own! And the boy stumbling to his feet is helped off the ground by a girl who has come running up.

Yes, it could only have happened in a meeting of the Gods, that history for once should take place not on some back street, or some inaccessible grand room, not in some laboratory indistinguishable from others, or in the sly undiscoverable hypocrisies of a committee of experts, but rather on the center of the stage, as if each side had said, "Here we will have our battle. Here we will win."

The demonstrators were afterward delighted to have been manhandled before the public eye, delighted to have pushed and prodded, antagonized and provoked the cops over these days with rocks and bottles and cries of "Pig" to the point where police had charged in a blind rage and made a stage at the one place in the city (besides the Amphitheatre) where audience, actors, and cameras could all convene, yes, the rebels thought they had had a great victory, and perhaps they did; but the reporter wondered, even as he saw it, if the police in that half hour of waiting had not had time to receive instructions from the power of the city, perhaps the power of the land, and the power had decided, "No, do not let them march another ten blocks and there disperse them on some quiet street, no, let it happen before all the land, let everybody see that their dissent will soon be equal to their own blood; let them realize that the power is implacable, and will beat and crush and imprison and yet kill before it will ever relinquish the power. So let them see before their own eyes what it will cost to continue to mock us, defy us, and resist. There are more millions behind us than behind them, more millions who wish to weed out, poison, gas, and obliterate every flower whose power they do not comprehend than heroes for their side who will view our brute determination and still be ready to resist. There are more cowards alive than the brave. Otherwise we would not be where we are," said the Prince of Greed.

Who knew. One could thank the city of Chicago where drama was still a property to the open stage. It was quiet now, there was nothing to stare down on but the mules, and the police guarding them. The mules had not moved through the entire fray. Isolated from the battle, they had stood there in the harness waiting to be told to go on. Only once in a while did they turn their heads. Their role as actors in the Poor People's March was to wait and to serve. Finally they moved on. The night had come. It was dark. The intersection was now empty. Shoes, ladies' handbags, and pieces of clothing lay on the street outside the hotel.

17

There have been few studies on the psychological differences between police and criminals, and the reason is not difficult to discover. The studies based on the usual psychological tests fail to detect a significant difference. Perhaps they are not sufficiently sensitive.

If civilization has made modern man a natural schizophrenic (since he does not know at the very center of his deliberations whether to trust his machines or the imperfect impressions still afforded him by his distorted senses and the more or less tortured messages passed along by polluted water, overfertilized ground, and poisonously irritating air) the average man is a suicide in relation to his schizophrenia. He will suppress his impulses and die eventually of cancer, overt madness, nicotine poisoning, heart attack, or the complications of a chest cold. It is that minority — cop and crook — which seeks issue for violence who now attract our attention. The criminal attempts to reduce the tension within himself by expressing in the direct language of action whatever is most violent and outraged in his depths; to the extent he is not a powerful man, his violence is merely antisocial, like self-exposure, embezzlement, or passing bad checks. The cop tries to solve his violence by blanketing it with a uniform. That is virtually a commonplace, but it explains why cops will put up with poor salary, public dislike, uncomfortable working conditions and a general sense of bad conscience. They know they are lucky; they know they are getting away with a successful solution to the criminality they can taste in their blood. This taste is practically in the forefront of a cop's brain; he is in a stink of perspiration whenever he goes into action; he can tolerate little in the way of insult, and virtually no contradiction; he lies with a simplicity and quick confidence which will stifle the breath of any upright citizen who encounters it innocently for the first time. The difference between a good cop and a bad cop is that the good cop will at least do no more than give his own salted version of events — the bad cop will make up his version. That is why the police arrested the pedestrians they pushed through the window of the Haymarket Inn at the Conrad Hilton: the guiltier the situation in which a policeman finds himself, the more will he attack the victim of his guilt.

There are — it is another commonplace — decent policeman. A few are works of art. And some police, violent when they are young, mellow into modestly corrupt, humorous and decently efficient officials. Every public figure with power, every city official, high politician, or prominent government worker knows in his unspoken sentiments that the police are an essentially criminal force restrained by their guilt, their covert awareness that they are imposters, and by a sprinkling of career men whose education, rectitude, athletic ability, and religious dedication make them work for a balance between justice and authority. These men, who frighten the average corrupt cop as much as a priest frightens a choirboy, are the thin restraining edge of civilization for a police force. That, and the average corrupt cop's sense that he is not wanted that much by anyone.

What staggered the delegates who witnessed the attack — more accurate to call it the massacre, since it was sudden, unprovoked and total — on Michigan Avenue, was that it opened the specter of what it might mean for the police to take over society. They might comport themselves in such a case not as a force of law and order, not even as a force of repression upon civil disorder, but as a true criminal force, chaotic, improvisational, undisciplined, and finally — sufficiently aroused — uncontrollable.

Society was held together by bonds no more powerful proportionately than spider's silk; no one knew this better than the men who administered a society. So images of the massacre opened a nightmare. The more there was disorder in the future, the more there would be need for larger numbers of police and more the need to indulge them. Once indulged, however, it might not take long for their own criminality to dominate their relation to society. Which spoke then of martial law to replace them. But if the Army became the punitive force of society, then the Pentagon would become the only meaningful authority in the land.

249

So an air of outrage, hysteria, panic, wild rumor, unruly outburst, fury, madness, gallows humor, and gloom hung over nominating night at the convention.

18

The Amphitheatre was the best place in the world for a convention. Relatively small, it had the packed intimacy of a neighborhood fight club. The entrances to the gallery were narrow as hallway tunnels, and the balcony seemed to hang over each speaker. The colors were black and gray and red and white and blue, bright powerful colors in support of a ruddy beef-eating Democratic sea of faces. The standards in these cramped quarters were numerous enough to look like lances. The aisles were jammed. The carpets were red. The crowd had a blood in their vote which had traveled in unbroken line from the throng who cheered the blood of brave Christians and ferocious lions. It could have been a great convention, stench and all — politics in an abattoir was as appropriate as license in a boudoir. There was *bottom* to this convention: some of the finest and some of the most corrupt faces in America were on the floor. Cancer jostled elbows with acromegaly, obesity with edema, arthritis with alcoholism, bad livers sent curses to bronchiacs, and quivering jowls beamed bad cess to puffed-out paunches. Cigars curved mouths which talked out of the other corner to cauliflower ears. The leprotic took care of the blind. And the deaf attached their hearing aid to the voice-box of the dumb. The tennis players communicated with the estate holders, the Mob talked bowling with the Union, the principals winked to the principals, the honest and the passionate went hoarse shouting through dead mikes.

Yet the night was in trouble and there was dread in the blood, the air of circus was also the air of the slaughterhouse. Word ripped through delegations of monstrosities unknown. Before the roll call was even begun, Peterson of Wisconsin, Donald Peterson, McCarthy man from the winning primary in Wisconsin, was on his feet, successful in obtaining the floor. (Since he was surrounded by TV, radio, and complements of the Press, the Chair knew it would be easier to accede than to ignore his demand for a voice.) Peterson wanted . . . Peterson wanted to have the convention postponed for two weeks and moved to another hall in some city far away, because of the "surrounding violence" and the "pandemonium in the hall." Before a mighty roar could even get off the ground, the Chair had passed to other business, and nominations were in order and so declared to a round of boos heavy as a swell of filthy oil. The sense of riot would not calm. Delegates kept leaving the floor to watch films on TV of the violence, McCarthy was reported to have witnessed the scene from his window and called it "very bad." McGovern described the fighting he saw as a "blood bath" which "made me sick to my stomach." He had "seen nothing like it since the films of Nazi Germany."

But that was the mood which hung over the hall, a revel of banquetry, huzzah and horror, a breath of gluttony, a smell of blood. The party had always been established in the mansions and slaughterhouses of society; Hyde Park and the take from policy, social legislation and the lubricating jelly of whores had been at the respective ends of its Democratic consensus, the dreams and the nose for power of aristocrat and gentry were mixed with beatings in the alley, burials at sea in concrete boots, and the poll tax with the old poll-tax rhetoric. The most honorable and the most debauched had sat down at table for Democratic luncheons. Now, the party was losing its better half, and the gang in the gashouse couldn't care less. They were about to roll up their sleeves and divide the pie, the local pie — who cared that the big election was dead? They had been pallbearers to moral idealism for too many years. Now they would shove it in the ground. The country was off its moorings and that was all right with them — let the ship of state drift into its own true berth: let patriotism and the fix cohabit in the comfort for which they were designed and stop these impossible collaborations.

So episodes popped up all over the place. The police dragged a delegate from the floor when a sergeant-at-arms told him to return to his seat and the delegate refused and exchanged words. Paul O'Dwyer, candidate for the Senate from New York, was pulled from the hall as he hung onto him. Mike Wallace of CBS was punched on the jaw when he asked some questions — they went out in a flurry of cops quickly summoned, and rumors raced into every corner. Clear confidence in the location of the seat of power was gone. A delegate had now to face the chimera of arrest by the police, then incarceration. Who would get him out? Did Daley have the power or Johnson? Would Humphrey ever be of use? Should one look for the U.S. Marines? A discomfiture of the fundamental cardinal points of all location was in the rumblings of the gut. A political man could get killed in this town by a cop, was the

Presidential candidate Hubert Humphrey and his wife Muriel at the
Democratic National Convention.

George Wallace.

Robert F. Kennedy announces his candidacy for the Democratic Presidential nomination at a press conference in the Senate Caucus Room.

Robert and Ethel Kennedy after victory in Nebraska's Democratic Presidential primary.

Robert Kennedy campaigning in Harrisburg, Oregon.

Rockefeller speaks to supporters.

Dr. Billy Graham, Tricia Nixon, Julie Nixon, and David Eisenhower
at the Republican National Convention.

Presidential candidate Richard M. Nixon.

Vice-Presidential candidate Spiro Agnew and Presidential candidate
Richard Nixon with their families.

Nixon and Agnew board helicopter to attend briefing sessions
at the LBJ ranch.

Senator Eugene McCarthy, Vice-President Hubert Humphrey and Senator George McGovern meet at the LaSalle Hotel in Chicago.

Democratic Presidential candidate Hubert Humphrey and Vice-Presidential candidate Edmund Muskie with their wives.

Police skirmish with demonstrators at Democratic National Convention in Chicago.

Chicago Mayor Richard Daley, Illinois Governor Sam Shapiro, and Vice-President Hubert Humphrey at Chicago Stadium.

Shirley Chisholm.

Eldridge Cleaver.

President Johnson greets President-elect Nixon.

Richard Nixon, John Mitchell, Robert H. Finch, Robert Haldeman.

Three of the Chicago Seven (from left to right): Jerry Rubin,
Abbie Hoffman and Rennie Davis.

general sentiment, and who would dare to look the Mayor in the eye? If politics was property, somebody had tipped the plot: West was now up in the North! To the most liberal of the legislators and delegates on the floor must have come the real panic of wondering: was this how it felt with the Nazis when first they came in, the fat grin on the face of that cigar who had hitherto been odious but loyal? Hard suppressed guffaws of revelry rumbled among the delegates with the deepest greed and the most steaming bile. There was the sense of all centers relocated, of authority on a ride.

The nominations took place in muted form. The Democrats had declared there would be no demonstrations at their convention. The Democrats! Famous for their demonstrations. But they were afraid of maniacal outbursts for McCarthy, fist fights on the floor, whole platoons of political warriors grappling rivals by the neck. So each candidate would merely be put in nomination, his name then cheered, seconding speeches would follow, the roll would be called, the next nominated.

McCarthy was put in by Governor Harold Hughes of Iowa, Humphrey by Mayor Alioto of San Francisco. Let us listen to a little of each — they are not uncharacteristic of their men. Hughes said:

> We are in the midst of what can only be called a revolution in our domestic affairs and in our foreign policy as well.
> And as the late President Kennedy once said: "Those who would make peaceful revolution impossible make violent revolution inevitable."
> . . . We must seek a leader who can arrest the polarization in our society, the alienation of the blacks from the whites, the haves from the have-nots and the old from the young.
> We must choose a man with the wisdom and the courage to change the direction of our foreign policy before it commits us for an eternity to a maze of foreign involvements without clear purpose or moral justification.
> But most of all the man we nominate must embody the aspirations of all those who seek to lift mankind to its highest potential. He must have that rare intangible quality that can lift up our hearts and cleanse the soul of this troubled country.
> Gene McCarthy is such a man.

Mayor Alioto said:

> I came here to talk to you about the man who has been for twenty years, right up to the present time, the articulate exponent of the aspirations of the human heart — for the young, for the old, and for those of us in between.

I'm not going to read to you, but I am going to ask you to project yourselves to January 20, 1969, to project yourselves to the steps of the great Capitol of Washington, and in your mind's eyes to picture a man standing on those steps with his hands raised pledging that he will execute the office of the President of the United States and that he will in accordance with his ability preserve, protect and defend the Constitution of the United States, so help him God.

That man will look down on a country that is gripped in an earnest desire to find its way out of the confusion and the frustration that now infect this country. And the people at that moment will be looking for a decisive leader.

Let me put it directly to you — that man on January 20 of 1969 is going to have to be an extraordinary man. And if he isn't an extraordinary man, the burdens of that office will crack him and the turbulence of the times will overwhelm us.

McGovern was nominated by Ribicoff, Senator Abraham Ribicoff of Connecticut, formerly Governor, a Kennedy man for many years — his career had prospered with the Kennedys. He was not a powerful looking man. He had wings of silver gray hair, dark eyebrows, a weak mouth which spoke of the kind of calculation which does not take large chances. He had a slim frame with a hint of paunch. He was no heavyweight. He had gotten along by getting along, making the right friends. He was never famous as a speaker, but he began by saying, "Mr. Chairman . . . as I look at the confusion in this hall and watch on television the turmoil and violence that is competing with this great convention for the attention of the American people, there is something else in my heart tonight, and not the speech that I am prepared to give."

It was a curious beginning, but as he went on, the speech became boring despite the force of a few of the phrases: "500,000 Americans in the swamps of Vietnam." Ribicoff droned, he had no flair, he was indeed about as boring as a Republican speaker. There were yawns as he said:

George McGovern is not satisfied that in this nation of ours, in this great nation of ours, our infant mortality rate is so high that we rank twenty-first in all the nations of the world.

We need unity and we can only have unity with a new faith, new ideas, new ideals. The youth of America rally to the standards of men like George McGovern like they did to the standards of John F. Kennedy and Robert Kennedy.

And with George McGovern as President of the United States we wouldn't have those Gestapo tactics in the streets of Chicago.

With George McGovern we wouldn't have a National Guard.

Seconds had elapsed. People turned to each other. Did he say, "Gestapo tactics in the streets of Chicago"? But he had. His voice had quavered a hint with indignation and with fear, but he had said it, and Daley was on his feet, Daley was shaking his fist at the podium, Daley was mouthing words. One could not hear the words, but his lips were clear. Daley seemed to be telling Ribicoff to go have carnal relations with himself.

There was a roundhouse of roars from the floor, a buzz from the gallery. Daley glowered at Ribicoff and Ribicoff stared back, his ordinary face now handsome, dignified with some possession above itself. Ribicoff leaned down from the podium, and said in a good patrician voice, "How hard it is to accept the truth."

Perhaps it was Ribicoff's finest moment. Later, backstage, in McGovern Headquarters, he looked less happy, and considerably less in possession of himself as people came up to congratulate him for his speech. Indeed, Ribicoff had the winded worried heart-fatigued expression of a lightweight fighter who had just dared five minutes ago in the gym to break off a jab which broke the nose of a middleweight champ who had been working out with him. Now the lightweight would wake up in the middle of the night, wondering how they were going to pay him in return. Let us think of the man rather in his glory.

The balloting was finally begun. There were no surprises expected and none arrived. North Dakota actually said, "North Dakota, which modestly admits to being cleaner and greener in the summer and brighter and whiter in the winter, casts 25 votes, 18 for Hubert Humphrey, 7 for Gene McCarthy." Then Ohio gave 94, Oklahoma was 37½, the floor began to shout. Pennsylvania offered up 103¾ of 130 and Humphrey was in. It was the state where McCarthy had gotten 90% of the primary vote. The deed was completed. The future storefront of the Mafia was now nominated to run against the probable prince of the corporation. In his hotel suite at the Hilton, Humphrey kissed Mrs. Fred R. Harris, wife of the Oklahoma Senator and co-chairman of his campaign; then as if to forestall all rumors, and reimpose propriety in its place, he rushed to the television screen and kissed the image of his own wife, which was then appearing on the tube. He was a politician; he could kiss babies, rouge, rubber, velvet, blubber and glass. God had not given him oral excellence for nothing.

Then the phone calls came. President Johnson, to whom Humphrey said with Southern grace, "Bless your heart," Mrs. Johnson, Lynda Bird and Luci; then Dick Nixon who congratulated him for winning the nomination earlier on the roll call than himself. Nixon was reported to have said that he enjoyed watching Mrs. Humphrey and the Humphrey family on television.

The vote when tabulated went like this: Humphrey, 1,761¾; McCarthy 601; McGovern 146½; Channing Philips (first Negro to be nominated for the Presidency) 67½; Dan Moore 17½; Edward Kennedy (without nomination) 12¾; James H. Gray ½; Paul W. "Bear" Bryant, coach of Alabama, 1½; and George C. Wallace ½. George C. Wallace would do a lot better in November.

19

The disease was beneath the skin, the century was malignant with an illness so intricate that the Yippies, the Muslims, and the rednecks of George Wallace were all in attack upon it. They might eat each other first, but that was merely another facet of the plague — cannibalism was still the best cure for cancer.

If these were the medical reveries of the reporter after the nomination, the counterpart was to be seen in the faces of the delegates who exhibited the depression people show on leaving a bad fight: basic emotion has been aroused for too little.

A company of delegates, several hundred in number from New York, California, Wisconsin, Oregon, and a few of the other delegations, were going to meet in one of the caucus rooms to discuss immediate strategy. They were obviously not a happy gang, but since the characteristic tone of McCarthy supporters predominated — academics with horn-rimmed glasses in seersucker suits or pale generally lean politicians with hard bitten integrity on their lips, and the women for the most part too wholesome, some looked as if they had not worn lipstick in years — the cynical wonder intruded itself how they would celebrate a victory. Defeat was built into the integrity of their characters. Vinegar was the aphrodisiac of their diet.

Paul O'Dwyer was talking to them now. Candidate for the Senate against Jacob Javits in the coming election, he would make a fine opponent for that most worthy Senator — O'Dwyer was a small man with white hair, black eyebrows, an honest well-cut Irish look, an accent still clear with the tone of County Mayo, and a working-class sense of humor. He was also a gentleman. He had a natural elegance. So he would make a fine candidate. He was talking to the caucus now about the bitterness of the defeat, working to take the sting out of it. A man who had obviously been in many political battles, some of which he had won and many lost, he had learned how to discover the balanced mixture between indignation and hope so necessary to getting up off the defeat and looking for a new contest. So he fed their losers' fury first by commenting on the convention — "an unbelievable stifling of the democratic process," he said, and then proceeded to laud the group for their devotion, their hard work, their confidence, and the fact they could know that the voters out there were really with them, and that was a power which time would prove. He grinned. "If we keep working and do this for a few years, I think in the next convention it's the other side that will have its caucus here in Room 2." They cheered him happily for this, almost a little hysterically, as if close to the recognition that their best happiness often came when they felt hope in the midst of defeat. It is an emotion shared by the noblest of meat-eaters and the most confirmed vegetarians.

O'Dwyer was the spirit of this caucus, and when he did not speak, gloom came in again. Congressman Bill Ryan of New York talked for five minutes about his meeting with Daley. He spun it out properly, telling how he went down the aisle to speak to the Mayor of Chicago, expecting an appropriate show of courtesy since they were both, after all, of the same party, and he was a Congressman (and they were both Irish — which Ryan didn't quite get to say, although he phumphered on the edge) and finally after five minutes of dramatic preparation for this incisive private piece of information about to be delivered of some new and intimate villainy by Richard J., Mayor Daley, the end of the story could be delayed no longer and Ryan confessed: Daley had looked at him and said, "Get back to your delegation." An unbelievable stifling of the democratic process.

The reporter discovered an impulse in himself to get drunk. This caucus was composed of naught but honorable people, anxious now, even dedicated to the desire to find some way of protesting the nomination, the brutality of the police, the sheer disjointedness of the time — they were in politics because the philosophical anguish of brooding upon a problem which might not be soluble — exactly what gave unique dignity to McCarthy — was not near to them. They needed an action to fit every ill, they were the dearest descendants of Eleanor, the last of Roosevelt hygiene; now out of their passion to act, act even this night, act especially this night, they came up with a proposal to march in vigil from the Amphitheatre to the Conrad Hilton. It would be a way of expressing their concern for the victims of the police. They even had candles. Richard Goodwin, assistant to McCarthy, prepared for everything on this nominating night, had brought in a thousand tapers in case they wished to protest on the floor and the lights would be cut off. Now they could be used for the march through the dark lonely streets of Chicago.

O'Dwyer laughed unhappily. "How far is it?" he asked. "Some of us may not be so young as some of you. Isn't it eight miles?"

"No, four," people cried out.

He asked for a vote. They were overwhelmingly in favor. "So be it," he said, and sighed, and grinned.

Then they began to discuss singing all the way with Theo Bikel, one of the N.Y. delegates. But Bikel pointed out that he had sung sufficiently these few days, that his voice was not up to it — besides, they would be marching through streets where people were sleeping — that could only cause needless trouble. "Besides," said Bikel, "a silent vigil of men and women marching with lit candles is most impressive. Let us sing our way out of here, and through the blocks immediately about the stockyards, but once we pass the barrier, let us be silent." They agreed. He struck up a song immediately on his guitar, and they moved out.

The reporter did not join them. He had felt an unmistakable pang of fear at the thought of marching with these people through the Black Belt of Chicago or even the Polish neighborhoods in the immediate surroundings. He could see them attacked by gangs, and the thought of taking a terrible beating in this company of non-violent McCarthyites and McGovernites, shoulder to shoulder with Arthur Miller, Jules Feiffer, Theo Bikel and Jeremy Larner, no, if he was going to take a beating, it was best to take it alone or with people he felt close to, people who were not so comparatively innocent of how to fight.

In consequence, as they left the Amphitheatre, he went off by a different route to his car, agitated, ashamed, overcome with the curiosity that these liberals whom he had always scorned had the simple dedication tonight to walk through strange streets, unarmed, and with candles. Was it remotely possible that they possessed more courage than himself?

He drove from the stockyards in a hurry, went up to Lincoln Park to look it over, but the area was dead. Here the war had ended. So he drove back to the Hilton, found a bar in a little hotel called the Essex on Michigan Avenue and had a couple of drinks. He did not know that the march was already finished. The leaders accompanied by a most respectful group of police — he should have anticipated that! — had decided it was too long a walk after all, so they had been driven in buses to a rallying point not far from the Hilton, and then had walked up Michigan Avenue with their lighted candles, joined soon by the hippies and the young McCarthy workers in Grant Park, and were now almost directly across the street in the park listening to speeches. He did not know that. He was drinking and contemplating his fear. It seemed to him that he had been afraid all his life, but in recent years, or so it seemed, he had learned how to take a step into his fear, how to take the action which frightened him most (and so could free him the most). He did not do it always, who could? but he had come to think that the secret to growth was to be brave a little more than one was cowardly, simple as that, indeed why should life not be just so simple that the unlettered and untrained might also have their natural chance? It was a working philosophy and he had tried to follow it, but it seemed to him that he was deserting his own knowledge in these hours. Had his courage eroded more than his knowledge of fear the last few days? He continued to drink.

20

The focus of his fear had begun for him on Tuesday, no, put it back to Monday night in Lincoln Park when he had left as Ginsberg and Burroughs and Genêt and Terry Southern were going in — up to the front. Of course, he could even put the fear back to Sunday afternoon, when he had heard the music, seen the children on the grass and the police on the walks and felt a sensation in his stomach not different from the dread in the bottom of the lungs one knows after hours of driving on ice. But then he had been afraid of Chicago ever since he had word in December of a Youth Festival which might attempt to make the Democrats nominate Lyndon Johnson under armed guard. So, in fact, this had been a fear he had been living with for a long time — like many another. It was as if different fears found different abodes in the body and dwelled in their place for years.

But yesterday, Tuesday, the fear had grown dimensions, forced consciousness to surface. Usually he did whatever he would do — be it courageous or evasive — without living too intimately with his anxiety. But, this time, it revealed itself. He had a particular reluctance to go to the meeting at the bandshell in Grant Park on Wednesday afternoon, then on the march to the Amphitheatre which would follow. This march would never be allowed to approach the Amphitheatre — one had not felt Mayor Daley's presence in Chicago these days for nothing!

There was much structure to the fear, much reasoned argument in its support. He had an enormous amount of work before him if he was going to describe this convention, and only two weeks in which to do it if his article were to appear before the election. A bad beating might lose him days, or a week; each day of writing would be irreplaceable to him. Besides, a variety of militant choices would now be present for years. One simply could not accept the dangerous alternative every time; he would never do any other work. And then with another fear, conservative was this fear, he looked into his reluctance to lose even the America he had had, that insane warmongering technology land with its smog, its superhighways, its experts and its profound dishonesty. Yet, it had allowed him to write — it had even not deprived him entirely of honors, certainly not of an income. He had lived well enough to have six children, a house on the water, a good apartment, good meals, good booze, he had even come to enjoy wine. A revolutionary with taste in wine has come already half the distance from Marx to Burke; he belonged in England where one's radicalism might never be tested; no, truth, he was still enough of a novelist to have the roots of future work in every vein and stratum he had encountered, and a profound part of him (exactly that enormous literary bottom of the mature novelist's property!) detested the thought of seeing his American society — evil, absurd, touching, pathetic, sickening, comic, full of novelistic marrow — disappear now in the nihilistic maw of a national disorder. The Yippies might yet disrupt the land — or worse, since they would not really have the power to do that, might serve as a pretext to bring in totalitarian phalanxes of law and order. Of course that was why he was getting tired of hearing of Negro rights and Black Power — every Black riot was washing him loose with the rest, pushing him to that point where he would have to throw his vote in with revolution — what a tedious perspective of prisons and law courts and worse; or stand by and watch as the best Americans white and Black would be picked off, expended, busted, burned and finally lost. No, exile would be better. Yet he loathed the thought of living anywhere but in America — he was too American by now: he did not wish to walk down foreign streets and think with imperfect nostalgia of dirty grease on groovy hamburgers, not when he didn't even eat them here. And then there might not be any foreign lands, not for long. The plague he had written about for years seemed to be coming in — he would understand its social phenomena more quickly than the rest. Or would, if he did not lose his detachment and have to purchase cheap hope. Drinking across the street from Grant Park, the possibility of succumbing to fears larger than himself appeared, if no more than a spot on the horizon, still possible to him. No more than a spot on the horizon had seemed Humphrey's candidacy when first it was bruited. Was that why delegates were marching now with candles? So that they would not succumb to fears larger than themselves?

It was as if the historical temperature in America went up every month. At different heats, the oils of separate psyches were loosened — different good Americans began to fry. Of course their first impulse was to hope the temperature would be quickly reduced. Perhaps they could go back to the larder again. But if it continued, then the particular solution which had provided him with a modicum at least of worldly happiness — the fine balance he might have achieved between the satisfaction of idealism and the satisfaction of need (call it greed) would be disrupted altogether, and then his life would not go on as it had. In the size of his fear, he was discovering how large a loss that would be. He liked his life. He wanted it to go on, which meant that he wanted America to go on — not as it was going, not Vietnam — but what price was he really willing to pay? Was he ready to give up the pleasures of making his movies, writing his books? They were pleasures finally he did not want to lose.

Yet if he indulged his fear, found all the ways to avoid the oncoming ugly encounters, then his life was equally spoiled, and on the poorer side. He was simply not accustomed to living with a conscience as impure as the one with which he had watched from the nineteenth floor. Or had it really been impure? Where was his true engagement? To be forty-five years old, and have lost a sense of where his loyalties belonged — to the revolution or to the stability of the country (at some painful personal price it could be suggested) was to bring upon himself the anguish of the European intellectual in the Thirties. And the most powerful irony for himself is that he had lived for a dozen empty hopeless years after the Second World War with the bitterness, rage, and potential militancy of a real revolutionary, he had had some influence perhaps upon this generation of Yippies now in the street, but no revolution had arisen in the years when he was ready — the timing of his soul was apocalyptically maladroit.

These are large thoughts for a reporter to have. Reporters live happily removed from themselves. They have eyes to see, ears to hear, and fingers for the note in their report. It was as if the drink he took in now moved him millimeter by millimeter out from one hat into another. He would be driven yet to participate or keep the shame in his liver — the last place to store such emotion! Liver disease is the warehousing of daily shame — they will trace the chemistry yet!

He had spoken this afternoon at the meeting. He had not wanted to; he had told David Dellinger on Tuesday afternoon that he would not speak — he did not wish to expose prematurely the ideas being stored for his piece. Dellinger nodded. He would not argue. He was a man of sturdy appearance with a simplicity and solidity of manner that was comfortable. He gave the impression of a man who told the truth, but as decently as possible. The reporter had called him to say he wished to visit Mobilization Headquarters to talk to him but since Dellinger was going to be in the Hilton, he came up in fact to the reporter's room on Tuesday afternoon with his son and Rennie Davis. The reporter told him he would not go on the march because he did not wish to get arrested — he could not afford even a few days in jail at this point if they chose to make him an example. So he would not appear at the bandshell either. He simply did not wish to stand there and watch others march off. Dellinger did not argue, nor did he object. He was a man of obvious patience and seemed of the conclusion that everybody brought his own schedule of militancy to each occasion. So he merely sipped his drink and watched the convention on television for a few minutes. It had been his first opportunity to watch it, his first opportunity doubtless to relax in a week. As he got up to go he grinned at the set, and said, "You know, this is kind of interesting."

Wednesday afternoon, the reporter had been at the same set in the same room, watching the debate on the peace plank. After a while, he knew that he would not be able to stay away from the meeting. Yet when he got there, past the police, the marshals, and stood in the crowd, he knew nothing of what had happened already, he did not know Rennie Davis had been beaten unconscious, nor of Tom Hayden's angry speech and others — there was just Allen Ginsberg giving his address on the calming value of OM. Then Burroughs spoke and Genêt. He had to go up himself — it was now impossible not to. So he highstepped his way forward in the crowd, awkwardly, over people seated in the grass, came to the shell, climbed up — there were a dozen people sitting on various chairs back of the podium — then went up to

Dellinger and asked if he could speak. Dellinger gave a smile. He was welcome.

So he had spoken at the bandshell. Standing there, seeing the crowd before him, feeling the predictable warmth of this power, all his courage was back, or so it felt — he was finally enough of an actor to face perils on a stage he would not meet as quickly other ways. And felt a surprising respect, even admiration, for the people on the benches and in the grass who had been tear-gassed day after day and were here now ready to march. He had even begun by saying to them, "You're beautiful," a show-biz vulgarity he detested to the root of his nerve, but he said it, and then made jokes about the smell of Mace on the microphone — the odor of stink bombs or Mace pervaded the charcoal-colored sponge over the microphone. Next, he went on to say that they were all at the beginning of war which would continue for twenty years and this march today would be one battle in it. Then he explained that he would not be on this march because he had a deadline and could not take the chance, "but you will all know what I am full of, if you don't see me on other marches," he had added, and they cheered him, cheered him enthusiastically even before he said that he had come there merely to pay his respects and salute them. It affected him that they cheered him for even this relatively quietistic speech, and when he was done, they cried out, "Write good, baby," and some young Negro from the Panthers or the Rangers or from where he did not know, serving as some kind of pro tem master of ceremonies, now held his arm up high with his own, Black and white arms together in the air, he had been given a blessing by this Black, and felt rueful at unkind thoughts of late. And kept his word, and left soon after, and had a good early dinner with friends in order not to get to the convention too late. And had happened to be in his room washing up when the massacre on the march, three hours later, had come. Now, he was drinking in this bar across the street from Grant Park with a pleasant Californian who worked for McGovern. The reporter enjoyed his drinks. The bar was closing and he would go to bed. But the memory of his speech that afternoon was bothering him. It had been too easy. He knew it would have been better if he had been on the march, been in the massacre, even been on the vigil marching up from the Amphitheatre. Through the drinks, shame was warehousing in his liver.

So it was that when he got up to go, and said good night to his new-found friend, he did not then enter and cross the lobby but stepped outside the hotel and went across Michigan Avenue.

2 1

The National Guard was out in force. On the side streets of the hotel, two-and-a-half-ton Army trucks were parked, jamming every space. Traffic was cut off. The Daley-dozers, named yesterday by a newspaper man, those Jeeps with barbed-wire grids in front of their bumpers, were lined in file across Michigan Avenue just south of the Hilton, and he crossed over to Grant Park with the sound of Army vehicles revving up, the low coughing urgency of carburetors flooded and goosed and jabbed and choked by nervous drivers, feet riding the accelerator and clutch while their truck waited in place. The huge searchlights near the Hilton were shining from a height of ten or fifteen feet, from a balcony or a truck, he could not see in the glare, but they lit up the debris and clangor of Michigan avenue, the line of soldiers on the sidewalk of Michigan Avenue just off the edge of Grant Park, the huge pent crowd, thousands here, facing the line of troops. For some reason or other, a hydrant had been opened on Michigan Avenue in the hollow square formed by lines of National Guard and police barriers before the Hilton, and the lights of the searchlight reflecting from the wet street gave that dazzle of light and urgency and *glamour* unique to a movie company shooting in a city late at night, crowds dazzled themselves by their own good luck in being present.

At that moment, he had a sign of what to do, which is to say, he had an impulse. His impulses, perhaps in compensation for his general regime of caution, were usually sufficiently sensational to need four drinks for gasoline before they could even be felt. Now without questioning the impulse, he strode down the line of troops walking under their raised guns, not a foot away from their faces, looking (he supposed — perhaps he even did) like an inspecting officer, for he stared severely or thoughtfully or condescendingly into each separate soldier's face with that official scrutiny of character which inspecting officers had once drilled into him. He was in fact fulfilling an old military dream. Since some of the soldiers did not like what he was doing, not altogether! and shifted their rifles abruptly with loud claps of their hand like stallions now nervous and therefore kicking the boards of their stall with abrupt and warning displeasure, he had the obverse pleasure of finding his nerve was firm again, he was sublimely indifferent to the possibility that any of these soldiers might give him a crack on the head with their rifle.

In the middle of examining this line — it must have been two hundred soldiers long, some weary, some bored, some nervous, some curious or friendly, some charged with animosity; nearly all sloppy in their uniforms which he noticed with displeasure — he was indeed an inspecting officer — he passed by the speaker's stand, a park table, or something of the sort, on which a dozen men were standing, one with a microphone attached by a wire to a big portable bullhorn held by another demonstrator. The speeches were going on, and a couple of guitarists appeared ready to perform next.

A woman he knew, who worked on the McCarthy staff, approached him. "Will you speak?" she asked.

He nodded. He felt more or less ready to speak and would have answered, "Yes, just as soon as I conclude this inspection," if some saving wit in a corner of his brain had not recognized how absurd this would seem to her.

So he concluded his inspection, taking the time to regard each soldier in that long line, and felt as if he had joined some private victory between one part of himself and another — just what, would have been tedious to consider at the moment, for he felt charged, ready, full of orator's muscle.

A Yippie wearing a dirty torn sweater, his hair long, curly, knotted, knuckled with coils and thrusting vertically into the air, hair quite the match of Bob Dylan's, was running the program and whispered hello cordially, worked him to the center of this ridiculously small platform, perhaps the area of two large bathtubs put side by side, and told him he would speak as soon as the electric guitarists were done.

He stood then in the center between two guitars who were singing a loud wild banging folk rock, somewhat corny, a patriotic song of the Left whose title eluded him. He did not like the song usually, but up on the platform, flanked by the singers, the bullhorn being held just back of his head turned out to the crowd, he felt insulated by the sound, blasted with it completely and so somehow safe with it, womb-safe with it, womb-cushioned — did the embryo live in such a waterfall of uproar each time the mother's digestion turned over? His mind was agreeably empty as he waited, good sign generally that he was ready to deliver a real speech.

When the song ended and he was given the mike after a generous introduction and a sweet surge of applause beefed up to its good point precisely by the introduction of the youth in the dirty sweater and the hair like Bob Dylan, he spoke out to the crowd just long enough to tell them he wanted to speak first to the soldiers. Then he turned his back, and the loudspeaker turned with him, and he talked to the line of troops he had not long ago passed, introducing himself as a novelist whose war novel some of them might possibly have read since it was famous in many barracks for its filthy passages and four-letter words, although not nearly so famous as another work, *From Here to Eternity,* with whose author he was often confused. He did not wish to disappoint the soldiers, he said, but he was not that fine author, Mr. James Jones, but the other, the one who had written the other book.

These remarks given and enjoyed by him, he then talked to the soldiers as a man who had been a soldier once. "As I walked down your line, inspecting you, I realized that you are all about the kind of soldier I was nearly twenty-five years ago, that is to say, not a very good soldier, somewhat unhappy with the army I found myself in." But, he went on, the war in which he himself had fought had not bothered his sense of what might be right the way this war in Vietnam must bother them. And he went on to talk about how American soldiers could take little pride in a war where they had the superiority and yet could not win, and he thought that was because they were ashamed of the war. Americans were conceivably the best fighting soldiers in the world if they could ever find a war which was the most honorable war in the world for them, but the war in Vietnam was the worst war for them, and so they could not fight with enthusiasm. At their best, Americans were honest; so they needed an honest war.

It would have been a first rate talk to give to fighting troops. In the general excitement of this occasion he did not necessarily arrive at the central point — the soldiers before him had no wish to serve in Vietnam. That was why they were in the National Guard. Still, his speech to the troops pleased him, it warmed him for his next address which he was able to begin by turning around in place 180 degrees, the loudspeaker doing the same, and now addressing his remarks to the crowd in the park. They were seated in a semicircle perhaps two hundred feet in diameter, a crowd of several thousand at least, with an attention he knew immediately was superb, for it was tender as the fatigue of shared experience and electric as the ringing of pain from a new bruise.

He began once again by paying his respects, explaining how he had missed one fray and then another, not certain if for the best or worst of motives. They were polite even to this, as if a manifest of honesty in a speaker was all they had come to hear. But he had seen them, he explained, over these few days, taking beatings and going back, taking beatings, going back; so he now found himself in this park talking to them (although he had had no such intention earlier). They were fine troops, he declared, they were the sort of troops any general would be proud to have. They had had the courage to live at war for four days in a city which was run by a beast.

A roar of delight came back from them. He felt the heights of the Hilton behind him, the searchlights, and the soldiers. Before him, these revolutionary youth — they were no longer the same young people who had gone to the Pentagon at all. They were soldiers.

"Yes, this is a city run by a beast, and yet we may take no pleasure in it," he said, "because the man is a giant who ended as a beast. And that is another part of the horror. For we have a President who was a giant and ended also as a beast. All over the world are leaders who have ended as beasts; there is a beastliness in the marrow of the century," he said, or words like that, and went on, "Let us even have a moment of sorrow for Mayor Daley for he is a fallen giant and that is tragic," and they cheered Daley out of good spirit and some crazy good temper as if Mayor Daley was beautiful, he had given them all this — what a great king of the pigs! and somebody yelled, "Give us some of that good grass, Norman," and he bellowed back, "I haven't had pot in a month." They all roared. "Four good bourbons is all you need," said the demagogue, and the troops were in heaven.

The exchange fired him into his next thought. He repeated again that he had not been ready to march, repeated his desire to avoid arrest or a blow on the head, and "Write! Write!" they yelled back, "You're right, baby, do the writing!" But now, he went on, the time had come for Democratic delegates to march. He had not gone, he said, on the vigil and march from the stockyards to the hotel, because "that was in the wrong direction." Demagogue's metaphor, demagogue's profit. They cheered him richly. No, tomorrow, he told them (the idea coming to his mind at just this instant) he was going to try to get three hundred delegates to march with them to the Amphitheatre. He would march along then! But he would not if there were less than three hundred delegates! Because if little more than a tenth of the Democratic Party was not ready to go out with their bodies as a warrant of safekeeping for all of them, then there was no sense in walking into still one more mauling. They had taken enough. If there was not real outrage in the Democratic Party, then it was time they knew that as well; they could then prepare to go underground. A roar came back again from the new soldiers seated on the grass.

Were there delegates here, he asked? Candles waved in the dark —
he was aware of them for the first time. "Spread the word," he called
out, "I'll be here tomorrow."

Then he went on to speak of that underground. He would try to
explain it. The other side had all the force, all the guns, all the power.
They had everything but creative wit. So the underground would have
to function on its wit, its creative sense of each new step. They must
never repeat a tactic they had used before, no matter how successful.
"Once a philosopher, twice a pervert," he bawled out. And in the
middle of the happy laughter which came back, he said, "Voltaire!" and
they were happy again. It was as good a speech as he had ever made.

For example, he continued, the march tomorrow with three hundred delegates would be a new tactic, and might offer a real chance of
reaching the police barriers outside the Amphitheatre, where they
could have a rally and quietly disband. That could make the point, for
the Mayor had refused to let them even get near until now. Of course if
the police chose to attack again tomorrow, well, three hundred Democratic delegates would also be in the crowd — so the nation would
know that the authority was even determined to mop up its own. So he
would march, he repeated, if the delegates would go, but he was
damned, he told the crowd, if he was about to give cops the chance to
maul him for nothing after he had made a point of here insulting the
Mayor; no, he would not take that chance unless a tenth of the Democratic delegates were also willing to take a chance. On that note, he
stepped down, and took a walk forward through the crowd, stopping to
shake hands every step with the young men and women on the grass.
Some were well-dressed, some were near to wearing rags, some looked
as dusty and war-like as Roger's Rangers, others were small and angelic. Everything from ghosts of Robin Hood's band to the worst of the
descendants of the worst Bolshevik clerks were here in the Grant Park
grass at five in the morning and McCarthyites and McGovernites, and
attractive girls, and college boys, and a number of Negroes, more now
than any day or night before, and they were shaking hands with him,
Black Power was revolving a hint in its profound emplacements. There
were kooks and plainclothesmen and security and petty thieves and
provocateurs with calculating faces and mouths just out of balance,
eyes that glinted with a tell-tale flick; but there were also more attractive adolescents and under-twenties in this crowd than in any like crowd
of New Left and Yippies he had seen before, as if the war had indeed
been good for them. And he was modest in the warmth of their greet-

ing, and not honored with himself, for they were giving him credit he did not possess — they were ready to forgive all manner of defection on the pleasure of a good speech.

So he circulated, talking, came back to the platform to make one quick amendment. Delegates in the crowd had told him three hundred was too great a number to seek in so short a time. It would not be possible to reach them all. Two hundred was a better expectation. So he relayed that information to the crowd, and added that he would be back in this Park at noon.

He returned to the hotel, pleased with his project, and aware of one whole new notion of himself. All courage was his and all determination, provided he could lead. There seemed no rank in any Army suitable for him below the level of General — extraordinary events deliver exceptional intuitions of oneself. No wonder he had spent so many years being General of an army of one. It was something to discover the secret source of the river of one's own good guts or lack of them. And booze was no bad canoe. He went to bed prepared for heroic events on the morrow.

22

He was to receive instead a lesson in the alphabet of all good politick: which is, that a passion is nothing without a good horse to carry you in visit over your neighbor's lands. He went to sleep at six A.M. prepared to visit different leaders as soon as he had finished his next speech at noon; by six in the evening he hoped they would be ready for the march, all delegates assembled.

Be prepared for total failure.

If this were essentially an account of the reporter's actions, it would be interesting to follow him through the chutes on Thursday, but we are concerned with his actions only as they illumine the event of the Republican Convention in Miami, the Democratic Convention in Chicago, and the war of the near streets. So his speech to the Yippies and children assembled was of value, since he learned for the record of his report that they were a generation with an appetite for the heroic, and an air not without beauty had arisen from their presence; they had been better than he thought, young, devoted, and actually ready to die — they were not like their counterparts ten years ago. Something had happened in America, some forging of the steel. He had known while speaking that if it came to civil war, there was a side he could join. At what a cost! At what a cost!

But such discoveries are unsettling. He lay in bed not able to sleep; he lay in fact on the edge of a twilight slumber rich as Oriental harems in the happiness of their color, but he was thus celebrating too soon, because by nine o'clock in the morning, the last of his liquor now beautifully metabolized, he was in that kind of unhappy shape on which comedy is built. Quick calisthenics, a shower, a shave, and the urgency of his mission did not quite give him a brain the equal of three hours in slumber. He would begin to think well for a minute, then lapse into himself like a mind become too weak for the concentration of consecutive thoughts.

We can spare the day, and report the lesson. He made his speech in Grant Park at noon, talked then to reporters, then to delegates (who had been in the Park) at the Hilton, discussed problems, arranged to meet them again, and never was able to keep the meetings. He could never get to see McCarthy quite alone, nor McGovern, lost hours on the hope he might talk to the New York delegation, did not know how to reach Peterson of Wisconsin, could have wept at the absence of a secretary, or a walkie-talkie, since phones refused to function, or beginning to work, could reach no soul. He ran back and forth over Chicago, sent messages — by whomever he could find, to the Park; he would be back at three, he would be back at four, he saw Murray Kempton who was ready to march all alone if only to interpose himself between the police and the body of one demonstrator (Kempton was indeed to be arrested later in the day) he saw others, lost connection with delegates who had volunteered to help, was helpless himself in his lack of sleep, was too early or too late for each political figure he wished to find, he was always rushing or waiting in hallways — he learned the first lesson of a convention: nothing could be accomplished without the ability to communicate faster than your opponent. If politics was property, a convention was a massive action, and your bid had to reach the floor in time.

So he was defeated. He could put nothing together at all. Hung-over, drained, ashen within, and doubtless looking as awful as Rockefeller at Opa Locka or McCarthy in Cambridge, he went back to Grant Park in the late afternoon to make a speech in which he would declare his failure, and discovered the Park instead was near empty. Whoever had wanted to march had gone off already with Peterson of Wisconsin, or later with Dick Gregory. (Perhaps a total of fifty Democratic delegates were in those walks.) Now the Park was all but deserted except for the National Guard. Perhaps a hundred or two hundred onlookers, malcontents, hoodlums, and odd petty thieves sauntered about. A mean-looking mulatto passed by the line of National Guard with his penknife out, blade up, and whispered, "Here's my bayonet." Yes, Grant Park was now near to Times Square in Manhattan or Main Street in L.A. The Yippies were gone; another kind of presence was in. And the grass looked littered and yellow, a holocaust of newspapers upon it. Now, a dry wind, dusty and cold, gave every sentiment of the end of summer. The reporter went back to his room. He had political lessons to absorb for a year from all the details of his absolute failure to deliver the vote.

23

Let us look at the convention on the last night. Two hours before the final evening session the Progress Printing Company near the stockyards finished a rush order of small posters perhaps two feet high which said: CHICAGO LOVES MAYOR DALEY. They were ready to be handed out when the crowds arrived tonight; thousands of workers for the city administration were packed into the spectators' gallery, then the sections reserved for radio, TV and periodicals. The crowd fortified with plastic tickets cut to the size of Diner's Club cards, and therefore cut to the size of the admission pass one had to insert in the signal box to enter, had flooded all available seats with their posters and their good Chicago lungs-for-Daley. The radio, television and periodical men wandered about the outer environs of the Amphitheatre and were forced to watch most of the convention this night from the halls, the ends of the tunnels, the television studios.

Daley had known how to do it. If he had been booed and jeered the first two nights and openly insulted from the podium on Wednesday, despite a gallery already packed in his favor, he was not going to tolerate anything less than a built-in majesty for tonight. Power is addicted to more power. So troughs of pigs were sweet to him as honey to a mouse, and he made certain of the seats.

Shortly after convening, the convention showed a movie thirty-two minutes long, entitled *Robert Kennedy Remembered,* and while it went on, through the hall, over the floor, and out across the country on television, a kind of unity came over everyone who was watching, at least

283

for a little while. Idealism rarely moved politicians — it had too little to do with property. But emotion did. It was closer to the land. Somewhere between sorrow and the blind sword of patriotism was the fulcrum of reasonable politics, and as the film progressed, and one saw scene after scene of Bobby Kennedy growing older, a kind of happiness came back from the image, for something in his face grew young over the years — he looked more like a boy on the day of his death, a nice boy, nicer than the kid with the sharp rocky glint in his eye who had gone to work for Joe McCarthy in his early twenties, and had then known everything there was to know about getting ahead in politics. He had grown modest as he grew older, and his wit had grown with him — he had become a funny man as the picture took care to show, wry, simple for one instant, shy and off to the side on the next, but with a sort of marvelous boy's wisdom, as if he knew the world was very bad and knew the intimate style of how it was bad, as only boys can sometimes know (for they feel it in their parents and their schoolteachers and their friends). Yet he had confidence he was going to fix it — the picture had this sweet simple view of him which no one could resent for somehow it was not untrue. Since his brother's death, a subtle sadness had come to live in his tone of confidence, as though he were confident he would win — if he did not lose. That could also happen, and that could happen quickly. He had come into that world where people live with the recognition of tragedy, and so are often afraid of happiness, for they know that one is never in so much danger as when victorious and/or happy — that is when the devils seem to have their hour, and hawks seize something living from the gambol on the field.

The reporter met Bobby Kennedy just once. It was on an afternoon in May in New York just after his victory in the Indiana primary and it had not been a famous meeting, even if it began well. The Senator came in from a conference (for the reporter was being granted an audience) and said quickly with a grin, "Mr. Mailer, you're a mean man with a word." He had answered, "On the contrary, Senator, I like to think of myself as a gracious writer."

"Oh," said Senator Kennedy, with a wave of his hand, "that too, that too!"

So it had begun well enough, and the reporter had been taken with Kennedy's appearance. He was slimmer even than one would have thought, not strong, not weak, somewhere between a blade of grass and a blade of steel, fine, finely drawn, finely honed, a fine flush of color in his cheeks, two very white front teeth, prominent as the two upper teeth of a rabbit, so his mouth had no hint of the cruelty or calculation of a politician who weighs counties, cities, and states, but was rather a mouth ready to nip at anything which attracted its contempt or endangered its ideas. Then there were his eyes. They were most unusual. His brother Teddy Kennedy spoke of those who "followed him, honored him, lived his mild and magnificent eye," and that was fair description for he had very large blue eyes, the iris wide in diameter, near to twice the width of the average eye, and the blue was a milky blue like a marble so that his eyes, while prominent, did not show the separate steps and slopes of light some bright eyes show, but rather were gentle, indeed beautiful — one was tempted to speak of velvety eyes — their surface seemed made of velvet as if one could touch them, and the surface would not be repelled.

He was as attractive as a movie star. Not attractive like his brother had been, for Jack Kennedy had looked like the sort of vital leading man who would steal the girl from Ronald Reagan every time, no, Bobby Kennedy had looked more like a phenomenon of a movie star — he could have filled some magical empty space between Mickey Rooney and James Dean, they would have cast him sooner or later in some remake of *Mr. Smith Goes to Washington,* and everyone would have said, "Impossible casting! He's too young." And he was too young. Too young for Senator, too young for President, it felt strange in his presence thinking of him as President, as if the country would be giddy, like the whirl of one's stomach in the drop of an elevator or jokes about an adolescent falling in love, it was incredible to think of him as President, and yet marvelous, as if only a marvelous country would finally dare to have him.

That was the best of the meeting — meeting him! The reporter spent the rest of his valuable thirty minutes arguing with the Senator about Senator McCarthy. He begged him to arrange some sort of truce or liaison, but made a large mistake from the outset. He went on in a fatuous voice, sensing error too late to pull back, about how effective two Irish Catholics would be on the same ticket for if there were conservative Irishmen who could vote against one of them, where was the Irish Catholic in America who could vote against two? and Kennedy had looked at him with disgust, as if offended by the presumption in this calculation, his upper lip had come down severely over his two front white teeth, and he had snapped, "I don't want those votes." How indeed did the reporter presume to tell him stories about the benightedness of such people when he knew them only too well. So the joke had been a lame joke and worse, and they got into a dull argument about McCarthy, Kennedy having little which was good to say, and the reporter arguing doggedly in the face of such remarks as: "He doesn't even begin to campaign until twelve."

They got nowhere. Kennedy's mind was altogether political on this afternoon. It did not deal with ideas except insofar as ideas were attached to the name of bills, or speeches, or platforms, or specific debates in specific places, and the reporter, always hard put to remember such details, was forced therefore to hammer harder and harder on the virtues of McCarthy's gamble in entering the New Hampshire primary until Kennedy said, "I wonder why you don't support Senator McCarthy. He seems more like your sort of guy, Mr. Mailer," and in answer, oddly moved, he had said in a husky voice, "No, I'm supporting you. I know it wasn't easy for you to go in." And even began to mutter a few remarks about how he understood that powerful politicians would not have trusted Kennedy if he had moved too quickly, for his holding was large, and men with large holdings were not supportable if they leaped too soon. "I know that," he said looking into the Senator's mild and magnificent eye, and Kennedy nodded, and in return a little later Kennedy sighed, and exhaled his breath, looked sad for an instant, and said, "Who knows? Who knows? Perhaps I should have gone in earlier." A few minutes later they said goodbye, not unpleasantly. That was the last he saw of him.

The closest he was to come again was to stand in vigil for fifteen minutes as a member of the honor guard about his coffin in St. Patrick's. Lines filed by. People had waited in line for hours, five hours, six hours, more, inching forward through the day and through the police lines on the street in order to take one last look at the closed coffin.

The poorest part of the working-class of New York had turned out, poor Negro men and women, Puerto Ricans, Irish washerwomen, old Jewish ladies who looked like they ran grubby little newsstands, children, adolescents, families, men with hands thick and lined and horny as oyster shells, calluses like barnacles, came filing by to bob a look at that coffin covered by a flag. Some women walked by praying, and knelt and touched the coffin with their fingertips as they passed, and after a time the flag would slip from the pressure of their fingers and an usher detailed for the purpose would readjust it. The straightest line between two points is the truth of an event, no matter how long it takes or far it winds, and if it had taken these poor people six hours of waiting in line to reach that coffin, then the truth was in the hours. A river of working-class people came down to march past Kennedy's coffin, and this endless line of people had really loved him, loved Bobby Kennedy like no political figure in years had been loved.

The organ played somewhere in the nave and the line moved forward under the vast — this day — tragic vaults of the cathedral so high overhead and he felt love for the figure in the coffin and tragedy for the nation in the years ahead, the future of the nation seemed as dark and tortured, as wrenched out of shape, as the contorted blood-spattered painted sculpture of that garish Christ one could find in every dark little Mexican church. The horror of dried blood was now part of the air, and became part of the air of the funeral next day. That funeral was not nearly so beautiful; the poor people who had waited on line on Friday were now gone, and the mighty were in their place, the President and members of the Congress, and the Establishment, and the Secret Service, and the power of Wall Street; the inside of St. Patrick's for the length of the service was dank with the breath of the over-ambitious offering reverence — there is no gloom so deep unless it is the scent of the upholstery in a mortician's limousine, or the smell of morning in a closed Pullman after executives have talked through the night.

24

The movie came to an end. Even dead, and on film, he was better and more moving than anything which had happened in their convention, and people were crying. An ovation began. Delegates came to their feet, and applauded an empty screen — it was as if the center of American life was now passing the age where it could still look forward; now people looked back into memory, into the past of the nation — was that possible? They applauded the presence of a memory. Bobby Kennedy had now become a beloved property of the party.

Minutes went by and the ovation continued. People stood on their chairs and clapped their hands. Cries broke out. Signs were lifted. Small hand-lettered signs which said, BOBBY, BE WITH US, and one enormous sign eight feet high, sorrowful as rue in the throat — BOBBY, WE MISS YOU, it said.

Now the ovation had gone on long enough — for certain people. So signals went back and forth between floor and podium and phone, and Carl Albert stepped forward and banged the gavel for the ovation to end, and asked for order. The party which had come together for five minutes, after five days and five months and five years of festering discord, was now immediately divided again. The New York and California delegations began to sing "The Battle Hymn of the Republic," and the floor heard, and delegations everywhere began to sing, Humphrey delegations as quick as the rest. In every convention there is a steamroller, and a moment when the flattened exhale their steam, and "Mine eyes have seen the glory of the coming of the Lord!" was the cry of the oppressed at this convention, even those unwittingly oppressed in their mind, and not even knowing it in their heart until this instant, now they were defying the Chair, clapping their hands, singing, stamping their feet to mock the chairman's gavel.

Carl Albert brought up Dorothy Bush to read an appreciation the convention would offer for the work of certain delegates. The convention did not wish to hear. Mrs. Bush began to read in a thin mean voice, quivering with the hatreds of an occasion like this, and the crowd sang on, "Glory, Glory, Hallelujah, his truth goes marching on," and they stamped their feet and clapped their hands, and were loose finally and having their day as they sang the song which once, originally, had commemorated a man who preached civil disorder, then mutiny, and attacked a fort in his madness and was executed, John Brown was also being celebrated here, and the Texas and Illinois delegations were now silent, clapping no longer, sitting on their seats, looking bored. Every delegate on the floor who had hated the Kennedys was now looking bored, and the ones who had loved them were now noisier than ever. Once again the party was polarized. Signs waved all over the floor, BOBBY, WE'LL REMEMBER YOU, BOBBY, WE'LL SEEK YOUR NEWER WORLD, and the ever-present BOBBY, WE MISS YOU. Yes they did, missed him as the loving spirit, the tender *germ* in the living plasma of the party. Nothing was going to make them stop: this offering of applause was more valuable to them than any nutrients to be found in the oratorical vitamin pills Hubert would yet be there to offer. The demonstration went on for twenty minutes and gave no sign of stopping at all. Dorothy Bush had long ago given up. Carl Albert, even smaller than Georgie Wallace, was now as furious as only a tiny man can be when his hard-earned authority has turned to wax — he glared across the floor at the New York delegation like a little boy who smells something bad.

However did they stop the demonstration? Well, convention mechanics can be as perfect as the muscle in a good play when professionals have worked their football for a season. Mayor Daley, old lover of the Kennedys, and politically enough of an enigma six months ago for Bobby to have said in his bloodwise political wisdom, "Daley is the ballgame," Mayor Daley, still flirting with the Kennedys these last three days in his desire for Teddy as Vice-President, now had come to the end of this political string, and like a good politician he pulled it. He gave the signal. The gallery began to chant, "We love Daley." All his goons and clerks and beef-eaters and healthy parochial school students began to yell and scream and clap, "We love Daley," and the power of their lungs, the power of the freshest and the largest force in this Amphitheatre soon drowned out the Kennedy demonstrators, stuffed their larynxes with larger sound. The Daley demonstration was bona fide too — his people had suffered with their Mayor, so they screamed for him now and clapped their hands, and Mayor Daley clapped his hands too for he also loved Mayor Daley. Simple narcissism gives the power of beasts to politicians, professional wrestlers and female movie stars.

At the height of the Daley demonstration, it was abruptly cut off. By a signal. "Shut your yaps" was an old button, no matter how the signal came. In the momentary silence, Carl Albert got his tongue in, and put Ralph Metcalfe (Daley's Black Man) who was up on the podium already, in voice on the mike, and Metcalfe announced a minute of silence for the memory of Martin Luther King. So New York and California were naturally obliged to be silent with the rest, the floor was silent, the gallery was silent, and before the minute was up, Carl Albert had slipped Dorothy Bush in again, and she was reading the appreciation of the convention for certain delegates. Business had been resumed. The last night proceeded.

25

Senator Edmund S. Muskie of Maine was nominated for Vice-President. He was a pleasant fellow with a craggy face, a craggy smile on top of a big and modest jaw, and he had a gift for putting together phrases which would have stood him well if he had been stacking boxes of breakfast food on a grocery shelf. "Freedom does not work unless we work at it," he said, "and that I believe to be part of the reason for the spirit and determination of so many of the young people." Of course, it took a brave man to mention the young on the floor of this convention — Dump the Hump! — but Muskie's rhetoric owed more to supermarket than any Maine country store. Washington, D.C., is a national town!

The balloting for Muskie's candidacy had been void of incident but for the nomination of Julian Bond who was also put up for Vice-President as a symbolic gesture to protest police brutality in Chicago. Bond was extraordinarily — no other adverb — popular in this convention, his name alone possessed an instant charisma for the rear of the floor — people cheered hysterically whenever it was mentioned on the podium, and the sound, "Julian Bond," became a chant. He was, of course, at twenty-eight, already an oncoming legend for his skill in gaining and then regaining a seat in the Georgia legislature, for his courage on discovering himself the only man in that legislature to speak out openly against the war in Vietnam, a Negro! and he was adored for his magically good looks. He was handsome not like a movie star, but like a highly touted juvenile, good looking as actors like John Derek, even Freddie Bartholomew, had been when they came along. Bond stood up when his state delegation was called, and gracefully withdrew himself from the nomination because — his direct legal explanation — he was too young (the required age was thirty-five) but he had done this, as he did everything else at the convention, with the sort of fine-humored presence which speaks of future victories of no mean stature. Talking to a few people about his race for Congress, he assured them it was secure. "I don't have any opposition," he said, "just like Daley," and he winked, looked wicked, and was off.

At length, the moment came for Humphrey's acceptance speech. Tonight, he looked good — which is to say he looked good for Humphrey. Indeed if a man could not look good on the night he accepted the nomination of his party for President, then his prospects of longevity must certainly be odd. Humphrey, of course, had been looking terrible for years. His defeat in West Virginia in 1960 by Jack Kennedy seemed to have done something of a permanent nature, perhaps had dissolved some last core of idealism — it was a cruel campaign: if one would dislike the Kennedys, West Virginia was the place to look. Since then, Humphrey had had a face which was as dependent upon cosmetics as the protagonist of a coffin. The results were about as dynamic. Make-up on Hubert's face somehow suggested that the flesh beneath was the color of putty — it gave him the shaky put-together look of a sales manager in a small corporation who takes a drink to get up in the morning, and another drink after he has made his intercom calls: the sort of man who is not proud of drinking; and so in the coffee break, he goes to the john and throws a sen-sen down his throat. All day he exudes odors all over; sen-sen, limewater, pomade, bay rum, deodor-ant, talcum, garlic, a whiff of the medicinal, the odor of Scotch on a nervous tum, rubbing alcohol! This resemblance Hubert had to a sales manager probably appeared most on those average days when he was making political commercials to be run as spots all over the land — in such hours he must have felt like a pure case of the hollows, a disease reserved usually for semi-retired leading men. They have been actors so long they must be filled with something — lines of a script, a surprise bouquet of attention, a recitation of Shakespeare, a bottle of booze, an interview. Something! Don't leave them alone. They're hollow. That was how Humphrey must have looked on average days, if his commer-cials were evidence.

Tonight, however, he was not hollow but full. He had a large au-dience, and his actor's gifts for believing a role. Tonight he was the bachelor uncle who would take over a family (left him by Great-Uncle Baines) and through kindness, simple courtesy, funds of true emo-tional compassion, and stimulating sternness upon occasion of the sort only a bachelor uncle could comprehend — ". . . rioting, burning, snip-ing, mugging, traffic in narcotics, and disregard for law are the ad-vance guard of anarchy, and they must and they will be stopped . . ." he would bring back that old-fashioned harmony to his ravaged folks. Since he was now up on the podium, the crowd was cheering, and the gallery on signal from Daley roared like a touchdown just scored. Hu-bert Humphrey was warm; he could believe in victory in the fall. He smiled and waved his hands and beamed, and the delegates, loosened by the film on Bobby Kennedy (their treachery spent in revolt against the Chair) demonstrated for Humphrey. The twenty years in Wash-ington had become this night property to harvest; politicians who didn't even like him could think fondly of Hubert at this instant, he was part of their memory of genteel glamour at Washington parties, part of the dividend of having done their exercise in politics with him for twenty years, for having talked to him ten times, shaken his hand forty, corresponded personally twice, got drunk with him once — small property glows in memory, our burning glass! These Humphrey politicans and delegates, two-thirds of all this convention, had lived their lives in the shadow of Washington's Establishment, that eminence of Perle Mesta parties and Democratic high science, they had lived with nibbles of society, and gossip about it, clumps of grass from Hubert's own grounds; but it was their life, or a big part of it, and it was leaving now — they all sensed that. The grand Establishment of the Democratic Party and its society life in Washington would soon be shattered — the world was shattering it. So they rose to cheer Humphrey. He was the end of the line, a sweet guy in personal relations so far as he was able — and besides the acceptance speech at a convention was pure rite. In such ceremonies you were required to feel love even if you didn't like him. Politicians, being property-holders, could feel requisite emotions at proper ceremonies. Now they gave proper love to Humphrey, two-thirds of them did. They would only have to give it for an hour. Everybody knew he would lose. The poor abstract bugger.

He gave his speech out of that bolt of cloth he had been weaving for all his life, that springless rhetoric so suited to the organ pipes of his sweet voice, for it enabled him to hold any note on any word, and he could cut from the sorrows of a sigh to the injunctions of a wheeze. He was a holy Harry Truman. Let us not quote him except where we must, for the ideas in his speech have already entered the boundless deep of yesterday's Fourth of July, and ". . . once again we give our testament to America . . . each and every one of us in our own way should once again reaffirm to ourselves and our posterity that we love this nation, we love America!" If sentiment made the voter vote, and it did! and sentiment was a button one could still prick by a word, then Humphrey was still in property business because he had pushed "Testament" for button, "America" for button, "each and every one of us in our own way" — *in our own way* — what a sweet button is that! and "reaffirm" — pure compost for any man's rhetoric, "our posterity," speaks to old emotion from the land of the covered loins, "we love this nation" pure constipation is now relieved — "we love America." The last was not exactly property but rather a reminder to pay the dues. Not every last bit of politics was property — some portion consisted of dunning the ghost-haunted property of others. Nobody had to tell HH. One could deduce the emotional holdings and debts of the most mediocre Americans by studying HH in the art of political speaking — he showed you how to catalogue your possessions: Franklin Roosevelt, Harry Truman, winner! John F. Kennedy, Lyndon Johnson — there were sudden boos. Lyndon Johnson, he repeated, and got the cheers from the medicine balls and gallery ding-dongs for Daley. "And tonight to you, Mr. President, I say thank you. Thank you, Mr. President." His presumption was that Lyndon Johnson was necessarily listening.

Humphrey went on to speak of the new day. That would be his real-estate development for the campaign — New Day Homes. The doors would stick, the dishwashers would break down, the vinyl floor would crack with the extra sand in the concrete foundation, but the signs might be all right.

Then he called for Peace in Vietnam, and the crowd roared and the band played *Dianas* as if he had made a glorious pass. Peace in Vietnam was now the property of all politicians; Peace in Vietnam was the girl who had gone to bed with a thousand different guys, but always took a bath, and so was virgin. Hubert felt like a virgin every time he talked of Peace in Vietnam. He spoke with the innocent satisfaction of a drop of oil sliding down a scallion.

Of course, Hubert was no vegetable. He was the drugstore liberal. You had better believe it. He knew who had asthma and who had crabs. It is important to locate him in the pharmacopoeia. Back of that drop of oil, he was an emollifacient, a fifty-gallon drum of lanolin — "We are and we must be one nation, united by liberty and justice for all, one nation, under God, indivisible, with liberty and justice for all. This is our America." He was like honey from which the sugar had been removed and the saccharine added, he was a bar of margarine the color of makeup. He had the voice of a weeper, a sob in every arch corner and cavern of his sweet, his oversweet heart; he was pious with a crooning invocation of all the property of sentiment, he was all the bad faith of twenty years of the Democratic Party's promises and gravy and evasion and empty hollers. He was the hog caller of the mountain and the pigs had put him in — he would promise pig pie in the sky. ". . . With the help of that vast, unfrightened, dedicated, faithful majority of Americans, I say to this great convention tonight, and to this great nation of ours, I am ready to lead our country!" And he ended, and the rite of love went up to its conclusion, and the band played, and the simple common people, and the villainous faces, and the whores with beehive headdresses in on passes, and the boys and the Southern pols stomped around and were happy, because their man was in, which meant they had won this game, this game, anyway, and happiness consisted of thinking of no future. And Hubert looked shining up on the stage, and made jokes with photographers, and jumped in the air to be tall as Edmund Muskie for one still shot — Humphrey would be a

293

sport at a party — and McGovern came up to the podium and Hubert took him in, and his eyes were bright with light and love and tears. It is not every man who can run for President after four long years as towel boy in Unca Baines' old haw-house with Madame Rusk. He turned to greet others, and from the back had the look of a squat little Mafioso of middle rank, a guy who might run a bookie shop and be scared of many things, but big with his barber, and the manicurist would have Miami hots for him. Let us give the day to Hubert. He had always seen himself as such a long shot and out.

26

Have a Whopping Double Burger,
Fingerlicking good!

This sign had been glimpsed on a hash-house past the stockyards along the road to Midway for the McCarthy rally back so long ago as Sunday. The sign spoke of a millennium when every hash-house owner would be poet to his own promotion, and the stardust of this thought made the reporter sad enough to smile. He was drinking again in the bar where he had had four bourbons last night; but tonight was different. At 3 A.M. the cocktail lounge was full; some of the boys were on the town to celebrate that HH oratory!

Our reporter was not a bigot about the Mafia; or maybe he was — some of his best friends were in the Mafia. (Mafia stands for Mothers-and-Friends-in-America.) A nice joke for a quiet drink; in fact, if one had to choose between the Maf running America and the military-industrial complex, where was one to choose? The corporation might build the airports, but they could never conceive of Las Vegas. On the other hand, a reasonably intelligent President working for the corporation was not to be altogether despised, not at least when the Mafia was receiving its blessing from the little bishop now installed — our reporter's thoughts were flavorless to him this night.

Punches did not often hurt in a fight, but there came a point in following hours when you descended into your punishment. Pain would begin; a slow exploration of the damage done. His ineffective effort to get two hundred delegates had left him with no good view of his own size; as news had come of two marches on the Amphitheatre turned back, and one group tear-gassed, he knew he was buried once again in those endless ledgers he kept of the balance between honor and shame, yes, on the way to the Amphitheatre tonight, driving south on a street parallel to Michigan Avenue, he had passed a gas station where many National Guard were standing about, and the odor of tear gas was prevalent. There had been a suggestion to stop and investigate, but he had refused. Perhaps it had been his fatigue, but he had been feeling undeniably timorous. He spent time reassuring himself that he had made an honest effort, and by an honest effort had he lost. There had been no need to go out on these last marches. By the terms of his speech, it made no sense to scuffle along with a token number of delegates who could be easily arrested and as easily look foolish — of that, he was still convinced he was correct. No sense therefore to poke one's nose into a scene of tear-gassing a block away. These arguments were no good: all the while he drank he knew he was floundering in bad conscience. He had an early plane in the morning, he was done, the job was done but for the writing. The reporter knew he had much to write about, but could he now enjoy writing it?

Sometimes he thought that the rate of one's ability to do good writing day after day was a function of good conscience. A professional could always push a work by an exercise of will, yet was writing himself right out of his liver if the work was obliged to protect the man. Sipping a drink he consulted his liver, and drank some more. The night was spiritless. Depression hung over his friends.

They tried to talk of the future, of how the party system might finally be dead. For by brute fact there were six or seven parties in America now; the Right, or the party of Wallace and Reagan — they were essentially the same, but for class, the lower and upper classes of the Wild Wasp — and then there was the party of hard-core Republicans — Nixon, we know, was doubtless perfect; next some huge government trough of the Caesarian center where the liberal spenders ought to have a home — Rockefeller and Humphrey might run with Teddy Kennedy here. (They could even use the same speeches.) That made a total of three parties, and Gene McCarthy ought to compose a fourth, a very pure party since his followers would be virtually a sect, although numerous as Volkswagens with their understated sell. Then on the

Left was another party, or two or three. The Peace and Freedom Party with Eldridge Cleaver, the talented Black writer and convicted rapist, was one; the Yippies might yet be another. It did not seem so bad an idea for America to have many parties. Everyone would at least be present, and politics could function through coalitions; they would shift from issue to issue. One would learn the shape of the time by the shift. And the parties would be obliged to stay alert. It was an interesting future to discuss. It was actually the sort of thing reporters could talk about late at night. Of course, the reporters also gossiped; they considered the fact Eugene McCarthy had gone over to Grant Park on Thursday at three in the afternoon to speak to the demonstrators — Get-Clean-with-Gene had gone over to talk to America's dirtiest — the Yippies. And the reporters argued mildly whether McCarthy indeed was hitherto not too clean — how much better it might have been if the peace candidate had been willing to get his hands dirty just a little. "It isn't getting your hands dirty that hurts," said one of the journalists, "It's the asses you have to kiss." They laughed. They were unwinding. The job was done.

From time to time, the reporter thought again of matters which did not balance him. He thought of the fear Bobby Kennedy must have known. This was a thought he had been trying to avoid all night — it gave eyes to the darkness of his own fear — that fear which came from knowing some of *them* were implacable, *Them!* All the bad cops, U.S. marshals, generals, corporation executives, high government bureaucrats, rednecks, insane Black militants, half-crazy provocateurs, Right-wing faggots, Right-wing high-strung geniuses, J. Edgar Hoover, and the worst of the rich surrounding every seat of Establishment in America.

Yet his own side — his own side as of last night — made jokes about putting LSD in drinking water. They believed in drugs and he did not. They talked of burning money — he thought money was the last sanity for a Romantic (and part of the game). They believed in taking the pill and going bare-ass in the park — he had decided by now that the best things in life were most difficult to reach, for they protected themselves, so beware of finding your true love in a night. (For it could be true love, or the disaster of your life.) Or perhaps he was too old for orgies on the green. Still, these white children were his troops. (And all the Left-wing Blacks would be his polemical associates — the Lord protect him!) The children were crazy, but they developed honor every year, they had a vision not void of beauty; the other side had no vision, only a nightmare of smashing a brain with a brick. The fear came back again. His own brain would not be reserved necessarily for the last brick. Of course, a lot of people were going to be living with some such fear over the next few years.

Now it was after four, and the last drinks were on the table, were being consumed. The waitresses were closing up. So they talked of going to the Playboy mansion. A party had been going on there all week. While they debated, the reporter was having psychic artillery battles with the Mafia at the next table. (One might take a look at *An American Dream,* Chap. IV.)

Mafia, of course, was a generic word to him. A crooked politician with a tell-tale jowl was Mafia; so was a guy with a bad cigar, so a crooked judge. They were not real Mafia — real Mafia was subtle and had its own kind of class. (The reporter was sentimental about real Mafia, he gave dispensation the way Lenin in secret preferred Hapsburgs to Romanoffs.) The conservative in his nature admired the wisdom of real Maf! But *petty* Mafia (which is what he generally meant when he used the word) were half of what was wrong with America. (The other half was obviously The Corporation.) Petty Mafia would not know how to get into a fight if the odds for them were less than two to one. So he entered a psychic artillery battle with a nearby foe — a short fat evil-looking type who had a confidence about the blank space he carried between his eyes, a glistening confidence sufficient to suggest he carried a gun. Petty Mafia gun sent curses their way. The reporter received them, sent them back. If the thoughts you sent back were sadistic enough, you could see the other man move. Now the other man moved, looked up, uneasily gathered his curse and took a drink. Here came the return. The reporter felt something unpleasant enter his system — a bona fide and very tricky curse. But he was careful to look unconcerned. That was part of this game: to keep the other from knowing he had had any perceptible effect. Done well, the opponent would worry he had gone into the brink. Now his opponent was leaving. It had been a successful war.

Now they were paid up and on the street — ready to go to Hefner's.

There was an excess of good feeling in him, however, when they reached the street. (The artillery battle had been his first premium victory of the week.) Outside, the Jeeps and trucks were still gunning to be parked, the police barricades were up, the line of National Guard still stood on the far side of Michigan Boulevard. The crowd was small in Grant Park at this hour, the battle was coming to an end. But speakers were still talking, rock groups still played, sound still rose to Humphrey Headquarters on the twenty-fifth floor, and the search-lights from the Hilton still put high illumination on the scene.

He had to take one last look. So the reporter and his two friends took a walk down the line of National Guard. "Once a philosopher, twice a pervert." Still, he was conducting an inspection again. Perhaps it was due to the reduction in the crowd, but the Guard looked meaner tonight.

That was all right. He was now feeling mean himself. He came to a stop before a Jeep with a rectangle of barbed wire on its front. In the exhibition-hall glamour of the searchlight, it glistened like a hard-shell insect eight feet long with an unforgettable radar-like conception of a mouth. He thought it was the most degrading instrument of war he had ever seen; it spoke of a gulf between the people who would admin-ister the law and the people who would be on the wrong side at the wrong minute. They would not necessarily have the rights accorded to cattle behind a fence. The reporter took out his notebook and stood in front of one of these Jeeps and took notes of the dimensions. On a grid by his estimate sixty inches wide and forty-eight inches high, there were thirty-two vertical strands of barbed wire. He made a point of counting each strand with his extended finger before the eyes of the soldiers by each side of the Jeep; he was careful however not to touch this altered Jeep, just to count with his finger a clear inch or two away. After the count, he took out his pencil, made an entry, put his pencil back, made a new estimate of specification. (The reporter had, after all, studied engineering at Harvard.) All the while, the Jeep's motor was running, and the driver, now nervous, gunned it once or twice.

A National Guard officer said, "You'll have to step back."

"Why?"

"Just step back."

"I'm a reporter for *Harper's Magazine,* and I wish to be able to de-scribe the barbed wire on this Jeep."

"I'm asking you to step back." The officer had his name stenciled on a piece of one-inch tape across the breast pocket of his fatigues. HORWITZ, it said. If a Horwitz was an officer in the National Guard, as quickly ask for a Rasmussen! But the Jeep was — *force majeure!* — too offensive. "On days when you take it out," the reporter asked, "what do you do to get the old flesh off?"

"Don't be wise-apple around me," said the officer. "Step back."

"I'm doing a story."

"Step back."

Well, he could not step back. He really had no desire to be taken in, but the officer — he could hardly blame him — had forced the issue. Now one of them would have to lose face; or else Horwitz would have to arrest him.

"It's not quite possible to step back yet," he said in his best Harvard voice.

"All right, take him in!"

"For what? Describing your Jeep?"

He was seized. Three or four soldiers seized him. A complicated little scuffle on the arrest. No one wanted to get marked for life, or even for tomorrow.

Then, victim secure, they all walked across Michigan Avenue in a stiff-armed body-locked routine, the soldiers on each arm trying to bend his arm, and his arms now turned as catatonic as he could make them — in this general grab and rush across the road, their collective limbs must have looked like some odd peripatetic unit of twelve or sixteen compressed sticks of absolute catatonic dynamite. If they had ever struck him, he was ready to go amok; if he struck them! they were equally ready. Stiff and tense and jostling like jockstrap mystics on a collective web of isometric exercises, they went in separate springing steps and yaws across the street, where he was promptly turned over to the cops, and as promptly felt the violence in the cops' arms, more personal, less green, it was like a barroom brawl for maniacs but for the suspended fact that nobody was swinging — everybody holding every-body — and forthwith into the downstairs entrance of the Hilton where the cops delivered him to an officer, while all the while in his ear, he could hear his drinking companions following behind, loyal enough to stay near. He could hear them saying to the soldiers, then the cops, "Have you guys gone crazy? He's a journalist."

At the terminus, in the low lobby of the Hilton, his police officer looked to be a man in his middle fifties, doubtless Irish, with a freckled face, light eyes, and a head of orange-red hair now turning yellow and gray. By the emoluments of his braid, he was obviously a high officer, and as obviously by his smile, he had a sense of humor! A sense of humor!

"Well, what have you been doing?" he asked with a grin.

The reporter had an inkling of how to talk to this officer; this was one officer who knew how to handle gentry — an old-fashioned cop with a wink — so the reporter looked for tag-ends of gentry in himself.

"That's an excellent question," he said, "just ask what I was doing. I was making a report" — into his voice went a hint of genteel Irish "r" — "I'm a reporter for *Harper's Magazine* and I was trying to describe . . ."

"He wouldn't move back," said Horwitz who had just come in.

"I was not touching the equipment. I have a right to describe what I see. It's generally considered the right of a journalist, whether Lieutenant Horwitz is aware of that or not."

"Well, there's been so much trouble in the air," said the police officer. He smiled at the disputants, then cooled them with a sigh. "He was just taking notes," the friends of the reporter made a point of getting in rapidly.

"He wouldn't move back," said Horwitz.

"Are you ready to prefer charges?" the police officer asked the National Guard officer with deliberate sadness.

"It's up to you," Horwitz answered stiffly.

"You see you'll have to bring in charges . . ."

Horwitz nodded. In the pause, he deliberated, gave a look, went off.

"What is your rank, Officer Lyons?" the reporter asked, for he had now had time to notice the nameplate.

"Oh, I'm a Commander. Commander Tom Lyons."

"Commander, you ought to get more of your family on the force," said one of his friends, also an Irishman.

Lyons winked. "You fellows have given us a hell of a time. You don't know what we been through." But he was interested in the hero he had freed. "You write for *Harper's*. Ohh! What sort of material do you write . . .?"

"Officer," said his friend, "this man wrote *The Naked and the Dead*."

"Brother, does *that* have bad language in it," stated Commander Lyons with a happy face. In the pause, he inquired deftly, "Gentlemen, there won't be any more trouble, will there?"

"Remember that the trouble came because I was taking notes for a factual description of the Jeep!"

"Say, we don't have to go around and get into that again," said Lyons with a hint of woe in his look: God save us from honest men, was the expression in his eye.

So they left the lobby the way they had come in, through the front entrance.

"Let's go to Grant Park again," said the reporter. The speaker in Grant Park had just made a telling point, and the crowd had cheered.

"Norman, let's get out of here," said one of his friends.

"I want to go over there for just a minute," and then as if to make his point, he took a few quick steps, and was stopped by a man about his own height, an Italian with pop-eyes. He was wearing a delegate's badge, and looked to be Petty Mafia. But there was something wrong about him. His credentials were false, or he was a police provocateur, or both — who knew what? Maybe he was even a delegate. The man said, "I'd like to kill those cocksuckers across the street."

"Don't call them cocksuckers," the reporter said. "They're my troops, and they're great." It was precisely that kind of conversation.

"They're no good," said the man with pop-eyes. "They're cock-suckers."

"What are you? A musician?" He meant by that: what are you: the kind of guy who plays saxophone at a cheap wedding? and the delegate, bona fide or false, immediately socked him in the eye. It was not much of a punch, but the reporter was just as immediately grabbed from behind by one or two cops — he never knew, because the guy with the pop-eyes hit him again fast enough for him to think the man had once worked in the ring, although not for long because the punches while fast had little enough back of them.

His good friends — in lieu of the cops — now pulled the other guy off, more cops came running up, then the same gripping and grabbing, stiff-armed lurching, isometric dance of the limbs, it all started up once more, but the cops were bad, this time there was murder in their arms, murder with clubs and bats, he felt, as he was forced along between them like a traveler in the center of that universe the screech of a subway car will make in sounding around a rail — that electric senti-ment of electric hatred, virile in its rage, it was madness, what in hell was going on? They went flying down some stairs in the hotel, past the men's room in the basement lobby, now through strange doors into a large room, a squad room where a dozen police were standing about. His friends were now barred, he could hear them protesting outside — here there was nobody but cops, the man who had hit him, and Com-mander Lyons who looked significantly less friendly now.

The delegate, real or false, surrounded by cops, was telling his story. He had to be a cop himself — his story was a point-by-point lie: "Then after the guy finishes using his foul language, he stands off, and for no reason at all, hits me," he heard the pop-eyed saxophone say with passion.

Meanwhile, they had left the reporter standing all alone. There were five cops eyeing him. He felt a complete program of violence in their cat walk, these athletic cops, with crew-cuts like Marines. He had the idea that in about a minute they were going to come over and beat him up. He had been without sleep for almost two nights, he had half a bottle in him now, he had been hit and arrested, and the hatred of the cops' hands on his arms had been a quiver of murderous starts, he had seen everything he had seen in this city, thought everything he had thought, and now it seemed probable to him the police had finally gone privately as well as publicly amok, and soon were going to gang him on this floor right out of the violent creativity of their paranoia — there was so much television for them to absorb in the long winters. And as he thought this, he realized suddenly that he was not really afraid, he did not feel weak — scared, he felt, and very awake, but he was ready, he was going to try to do his best when they started to work. He did not feel in a jelly or a bath — he felt as electric and crazy as the cops. The fact that he had this sentiment now, that he was ready to fight, made him feel close to some presence with a beatific grace (for he felt it, he felt with this readiness to fight as if the air were beautiful where it was near to him) and that left him happy, happier than he had been at any moment since he had heard the awful cry of the wounded pig in his throat at the news Bobby Kennedy was shot: so he stood there and glared at the policemen who were glaring at him and knew he could wait like this for an hour and not feel weak.

And now Commander Lyons was talking to him. The Commander's face was taking a wicked delight in the powers of his own cynicism, for the Commander's face had succeeded in repressing the twinkle and was now moderately severe and composed. "It's a serious matter, Mr. Mailer, for you to be hitting people for no reason at all, especially after I just let you go."

He liked Commander Lyons, liked him for the relish this officer took in the absolute wickedness of his occupation — a born actor enjoys his life in any station — and so he replied with a wild if internal merriment, for he liked himself again. Dirty he might be, but they were so much filthier. "You wouldn't care to hear my side of it, would you, Commander?"

"I don't know. Look what happened to me the last time I listened to you."

The delegate was repeating his tale, word for word, and the cops on the prance, ten feet away, were pacing again up and back the floor of the room.

"Everything he's saying is a lie," the reporter said huskily, "and you know it even better than me."

But the Commander's eyes had lost their light. The bouncing little light in his look, like the white ball which used to bounce over the printed words of songs on a movie screen, was not bouncing now. "Why do you always get into trouble?" the Commander asked.

Then the phone rang. Lyons went to answer it. He waited, looking at the cops, the cops looking at him.

Some word must just have come down. When Lyons came back, he was smiling. "Tell me your story again," he said. He was one of the few people in the world who could wink while looking at you with honest Irish orbs. Now it was obvious they were going to let him go.

"Why," asked the Commander, "do you always want to get arrested?"

The reporter thought of his children, and for an instant tears nearly came. Not real tears so much as — the Victorians used to say — his eyes were wet with dew.

"Commander, I don't want to get arrested," he said.

"I'm glad to hear that, Mr. Mailer. But it's your reputation that you like to get arrested."

"Newspapers lie all the time. Look what they say about you fellows."

Happiness came again into Lyons' face. "I got," he said, "to read one of your books."

In the next two minutes before they let him out to join his friends, even escorted him to a cab — for the trip was still on to Hefner's — he talked with Lyons and a city official (who had suddenly appeared) about the beauties of architecture in Chicago. It was a great city, he made a point of telling them. They did not know from which direction he was putting them on.

And yes, he thought, Chicago was a great city. Finally, it brought everyone into the sort of ratiocinated confrontation which could end a novel about a week in this big city. You could not say that of Miami.

Of course, he never did find out if shortly before or shortly after his own curious double-bust, the police had charged the McCarthy Head-quarters, arrested every kid in sight, beat up on a few, and generally created such consternation that the Senator himself remained in town until Friday afternoon for fear his children would be wasted.

No, Norman Mailer went with his good drinking friends, Pete Ham-ill and Doug Kiker, to Hugh Hefner's Playboy mansion where they had a few last drinks and talked to friends and cheered the end of the week.

On the last trip back to the Hilton, Mailer took a pass through Grant Park. It was all but empty. Fifty communicants sat on the grass, mountaineers, varlets, knaves, Hindu saints, musketeers, tank men, and wanly beautiful Yippie girls, while a priest in a violet satin chasuble recited the Mass over their bloody heads and an acolyte held the cross. The sight, by now, after all the sights, seemed perfectly conventional. Then he crossed the line of National Guard for the last time — Horwitz was not there on this sunny Friday morning — and went into the Hilton. On the steps he met Senator McCarthy's daughter, a lovely and formidable young dark-haired lady, now in a quiet horror over the fury of the bust, and she asked him what he would do about it.

"I'm going to catch a plane and see my family," he told her, smiling into the proud disapproval of her eyes. "Dear Miss," he could have told her, "we will be fighting for forty years."

27

And had no second thoughts about anything all the while he was writing the piece — except for Spiro Agnew. The Greek was conducting himself like a Turk. There was a day when he accused Hubert Humphrey of being soft on Communism. Everyone knew that Communism was the only belief Hubert Humphrey had ever been hard on. Nixon had obviously gotten himself an ignoramus or a liar.

So while the writer thought that the Republic might survive a little longer with old Tricky Dick and New Nixon than Triple Hips, Norman Mailer would probably not vote — not unless it was for Eldridge Cleaver.

Eldridge at least was there to know that the barricades were building across the street from the camps of barbed wire where the conscience of the world might yet be canned. Poor all of us. The fat is in the fire, and the corn is being popped. Mayor Daley, looking suspiciously like a fat and aged version of tough Truman Capote on ugly pills, decried the shame outsiders visited on Chicago. He was a strong and protective mother of a man, but for his jowl which hung now beneath his neck in that lament of the bull frog which goes:

> *I was born to run the world*
> *And here I am;*

KNEE-DEEP
KNEE-DEEP

Perhaps good Mayor Daley's jowl was the soft underbelly of the New American axis. Put your fingers in V for victory and give a wink. We yet may win, the others are so stupid. Heaven help us when we do.

St. George and the Godfather

ONE

PORTRAITS AND POWERS

1

GREETINGS TO Charles Dickens across vales of karma: it was the best and worst of conventions. The hope that democracy would yet be virtuous lived in the broth and marrow of the mood. Nonetheless, our convention was so dismaying in its absence of theater that the sourest law of the police reporter was also confirmed — deaths are more interesting than births. The Democratic gathering of 1968 had been martial, dramatic, bloody, vainglorious, riotous, noble, tragic, corrupt, vicious, vomitous, appalling, cataclysmic; the old Democratic Party foundered with a stroke, even if the patient got up from bed, staggered around America through September and October and only gave out on Election Day to that somber undertaker's assistant Richard Milhous Nixon. In contrast, history might yet decide that the Convention of '72, no matter how tedious, boring, protean, and near to formless, came out a rare and blithe watershed in the civil affairs of men. (Plus the expanding affairs of Ms.) So Norman Mailer, who looked to rule himself by Voltaire's catch-all precept, "Once a philosopher, twice a pervert," and preferred therefore never to repeat a technique, was still obliged to call himself Aquarius again for he had not been in Miami two days before he knew he would not write objectively about the Convention of '72. There were too many questions, and (given the probability of a McGovern steamroller) not enough drama to supply answers. He would be obliged to drift through events, and use the reactions of his brain for evidence. A slow brain, a muddy river, and therefore no name better suited to himself again than the modest and half-invisible Aquarius. Enough of Ego Liberation.

2

There were ghosts at the convention. And the sense of having grown old enough to be passing through life a second time. Flying to San Francisco in 1964 to write up the convention which nominated Barry Goldwater, he had met an Australian journalist who asked why Americans made the interior of their airplanes look like nurseries, and he had answered, in effect, that dread was loose in American life. Was it still loose, that sense of oncoming catastrophe going to fall on the nation like the first bolt from God? Such dread had taken many a turn — from fear of Communism to fear of walking the streets at night, which was a greater fear if one thought about it (since the streets were nearer). It was a fear when all was said which suggested that the nation, in whatever collection of its consciousness, was like a person who wakes up often in the middle of the night with the intolerable conviction that something is loose in the system, and the body is on a long slide from which there will be no remission unless a solution is found: the body does not even know where the disease is at. Nor will the doctors, is what the body also knows in the dark.

Now, eight years later, on a plane to Miami, comfortable middle-aged Aquarius finds himself in another conversation about the convention to come, and the old dread is still loose. Only now it is buzzing about McGovern and the thousand dollars a year George would give to every living American. The man in the Whisperjet seat next to him is a distinguished Senior Citizen, one vigorous and far from elderly Jewish gentleman named Bernhard whose son it soon develops is Berl Bernhard, main gear of the campaign staff for Ed Muskie. The father, a retired banker, has the sun-tanned freckled hands and face and white hair of a man who not only has retired to live in the sun, but still plays respectable sports in the sun, golf one would guess, and some tennis. Mr. Bernhard talks with all the force and authority, the barking opinionated good manners, of a Jewish banker who has spent his life living with other men of boldness and restraint. He is cockaloo with wrath about McGovern. Bernhard hates Nixon, but he is still not going to vote in November just so deep is his rage at McGovern.

They get into a discussion of McGovern's economics, and it is quickly evident that the numbers cannot be calculated — McGovern's friends and enemies have been putting the problem into computers whose answers sink deeper into the bottoms of the bottomless. It is possible that the unsounded mysteries of economics will burble up and alter everything if you give a thousand dollars a year to every living American. But there is not even a chance to talk to Bernhard about the feasibility of paying for the idea through taxes. Bernhard is an intelligent tough-minded man and must certainly be cynical enough by now to know that even if McGovern were wholly sincere in his scheme, he would never find a Congress to match him, but it is as if something else is loose, something formerly nailed down in the banker's scheme of things, for Bernhard's wrath shifts next to McGovern on questions concerning Israel. Much discussion of many bills and how McGovern voted quickly ensues.

Aquarius let the argument go. He was not certain himself how he felt about McGovern, and by now he had an absolute disbelief in political argument. Just as there used to be mating customs in Southern colleges which required boys and girls to talk about fraternities and sororities for a couple of hours in the back seat of cars before they explored their first kiss, so he had been bemused many a time by the peculiar protocol of political argument over issues and records. It was as if each side in such a debate was trying to lay down bricks fast enough to build a wall which would be higher than the other's even if the wall when built would obscure the view. Politics was a game in which points were scored and one tried to obscure the depth and gravity of the process. Yet the ways in which people governed one another were ultimately as intimate as carnal relations. One had only to think of the death penalty to recognize this. One had only to think of a solution to the death penalty he had once offered — which is that all States not ready to banish capital punishment ought then to provide a professional executioner who would be obliged to kill each condemned man with his bare hands by open gladiatorial combat in a stadium (like the Astrodome?) before the citizenry. This idea naturally met with much success.

No, at the least, it seemed to him that the concern people took with their vote was certainly much out of proportion to its effect — even the average hour or two-hour wait on line Election Day was a sizable demand upon the collective selfishness of the citizenry — or was, unless people voted out of deeper motives than they recognized. Was it altogether impossible that the average man might be engaged in some inarticulate transaction with eternity? — a cosmic whale of a thought for a man like Mailer who usually did not get around to vote. Of course, Mailer was nowhere near so good at answers as he was at posing questions, but he had the instinct to know when his question was good. This question was swell. It was, on consideration, incredible how people could keep studying the minutiae of a convention on a television set for hours when the greatest part of those details had to be incomprehensible to them, or at best next to void of connotation, low in entertainment value, and usually boring — the TV men were first to yawn. What mysterious human ceremony was in process?

Nor did the sense of having passed through similar events diminish once he was in Miami Beach. Collins Avenue, however, hot as ever in July, seemed tolerable, as if he had grown forgiving to heat. Having written with more detestation about Miami Beach than any author he knew — "the sensation of breathing, then living [in that city], was not unlike being obliged to make love to a 300-pound woman who has decided to get on top," it was as if he had written out his hatred, and the good citizens of this incredible city were cordial to him. They did not seem to mind what he wrote. It was, he concluded, the only place left on earth which still looked on bad publicity as good publicity. But he was irritated. He could not grasp why his own mood was so different until he recognized that Miami Beach was the true surrealist froth on the wave of Populism, not a 300-pound woman, but a deep red-orange female Senior Citizen, sexy as hell, her age balanced by her baubles, her infirmities as goofy and vulgar and overloaded as Wolfe's and Pumpernik's, or her Moulin Rouge Motel with a sign outside: HAVE YOUR NEXT AFFAIR HERE! and so if the Republican convention of '68 had been as much of a mismatch as bluegrass sown in the swamps of the Everglades, this convention was perfect. Miami Beach was as crazy as any group of Democrats, and the pride of the city was to show that life would still be good even if you were getting along on one leg and one breast — there was sunlight, makeup, plastic and prosthetics, mutual interest at all ages, and tolerance for every kookery of the middle class. If the older residents had been fearful at first of the arrival of the Yippies, their meeting would yet provide a ceremony — the "marriage of the generations" — and indeed the first news Aquarius picked up on his arrival was the description of a march the week before from Convention Hall to a golf course named Par Three. It was the first street action for the Yippies, but what a long throw from the darkening shadows of every police-congested block in Chicago. Here the Yippies came out with flags painted on their faces, and a blonde girl dressed as Martha Mitchell was led by Jerry Rubin up to the Press where it was announced that the Republicans should free her by convention time. A very fat girl was gotten up as Rocky Pomerance, the police chief, and another girl dressed as a Vietnamese. Every few blocks she would fall to the street and scream and the surrounding Yippies would make guerrilla theater of kicking and beating her. In front of Convention Center the march was joined by Mayor Hall who led the Yippies until they began a chant to end the fornicating war. So the Mayor turned around and put a finger to his lips. When they chanted louder, he left. It was cool. The Yippies were welcome to be obscene, but not even a Miami Beach politician could afford to hang around. Still, there was no sweat on either side, and people watching applauded from time to time. Some even joined the march for a block or two. There was probably more spectators' applause than one would get marching through any other city in America. That night the Yippies gathered at the tube and glued themselves in to watch TV news they had made.

What a town! A police chief who permits himself to be parodied by a fat girl, and a mayor who can put a set of permissions together.

3

But good Mayor Hall — if the reader can take the shock of this truly American shift-transmission — is out at Miami International Airport, Blast Site One, to give his city's greetings when George C. Wallace comes in. Tall, with silver-white hair, and the look of a man who has lived agreeably in the tropics, he has the quiet almost too agreeable confidence of a movie star of medium rank who has begun to enjoy his white hair and his retirement. Actually, Hall is a millionaire, and by repute could play lead hound of the Baskervilles if the spoor was publicity.

He was obviously too intelligent to expect any himself this day — there was something self-effacing in the way he bent over to whisper a few words to Wallace, but indeed who in America would dispute the throne of publicity when Wallace was near? The Governor's arrival in

Miami was a form of Instant Déjà Vu, spooky to the recurring sense of a dream, for the Press had watched him on TV just two hours before when he landed at Montgomery long enough to give a speech and shake the hand of Acting Governor Jere Beasley in order to reassume (by the laws of Alabama) his power to be governor. Aquarius and others of the Press had studied the TV set like primitives looking at reflections in a pond of water — what omens for the tribe were here to be gathered? Indeed attention was high enough to read significance into every rollover of the color from red to green to gray, or from any flipover of image or burst of dots. Yet, it was just TV, and all the television colors were keyed to the baby-blue sky above the Governor's gray-silver suit, with peaches and pinks and creamy tans in the background: perhaps a new genre was being created — Soap Opera Sublime — and they played "The Star-Spangled Banner" after his plane came in, huge Air Force Military Airlift of a plane Richard Nixon had been careful to turn over to Wallace for the Governor's private use, complete with a ramp which flew out in sections like an animated giant pterodactyl's tongue in a King Kong film, and lo! the strains of the music came up as they wheeled the Governor down the ramp with an awe which pushed through every electronic valve in every TV transmitter and actually socked into the room where they were watching — it was obvious that the thin body in the wheelchair being rolled down one ramp and up another to give his speech had become an object of veneration (in Montgomery, Alabama, at least) which was equal to any relic of any major saint's bone that could be certified as a thousand years dead. And the band played "The Star-Spangled Banner" as slowly as a hymn to the martyred spirits beyond. When the speech was over, and the Governor in his new voice, the measured dignified voice (almost beautiful in its modulation away from the old gut-bucket banjo-string twang of the mean folksy natural voice), had come to his conclusion by saying, "And my campaign should make it clear that the average citizens are now the kings and queens of American politics. And we are going to be responsible for your desires," the process was reversed, and the wheelchair drawn back up the ramp, the long tongue pulled into the plane again. With the banshee scream of the jet's motors shrilling over the set, there was discussion in the watching Miami Press over how *he* had looked, as if the set would *reveal*, when they all knew that a little too much green and the Governor would look like fare for the scavenger fish, a little too much red and he would impress as ready to run again, yet they would all insist on interpreting every clue, Aquarius as much as the others, perhaps as part of an obsession with some force or desire he could not name, not yet, but it was the political mystery to him, and as close to disclosure as the filling of a tooth which promises it will soon fall out. He felt that with this convention he might finally discover something about politics which had eluded him until now, some mystery, yes, would be at last discovered, and had the opportunity to brood upon this near to pleasant sensation after the rush from the TV set to the Miami Airport, Blast Site One, where the Press, after being inched up and testified to, vouched on and sworn for by man or credential and sometimes both, were squeezed through a Secret Service gate one by one and disgorged into the Democratic National Convention area, a small enclosure of white gravel on one of the fringes of the airport where, surrounded by high wire fence, they could stand to the side of a space extending thirty feet across from one camera stand with a red-and-white-striped peppermint awning over to an identical stand with a podium for the speaker. Banks and batteries of light glared in the bright sunlight high up on light trees made of pipe and painted silver, and in the near distance like a military unit on the march which had stopped to bivouac for an afternoon there were ambulances and white trailers parked about, olive-drab trucks and orange TV trucks, wires, cables, tools, even the Miami populace, a couple hundred of them, stuck out on one side of the wire fence to yell hello to Wallace.

It had been a rush to get there and then a long wait. While they waited, reporters entertained themselves by talking to Endicott Peabody, campaigning for an open convention to pick the Vice-President, ideally himself, Chub Peabody, last Harvard man to make All-American, and he looked and talked like George Plimpton might have if George had made the Detroit Lions and stayed in pro ball long enough to get his face broken a couple of times through the face mask. Peabody kept telling the reporters that he was pleased Senator Mike Gravel had also announced for Vice-President. "We're happy to have some opposition," said Peabody. "Makes it more reportable."

There was a bead of ketchup on the corner of his mouth. He was finishing a hamburger one of his daughters had handed him, and the wrapper showed where it had been bought.

"Governor Peabody, a tough political question — what do you think of McDonald's hamburgers?" (Were 11,000,000 votes shivering on his reply?)

"Well," said Peabody, listening to the mills of his digestion, "they keep you going."

To tell the truth and lose nothing — there was a little applause from the Press.

Now Wilbur Mills' plane came in, a private jet with seats perhaps for a dozen corporation executives, and the Press tried to ask him questions, but helicopters overhead were patrolling the asphalt fields around Blast Site One and the noise of their motors scourged the mood. The Press could not hear Mills and the candidate could not hear the Press — Wilbur Mills, Chairman of what was invariably called the *prestigious* Ways and Means Committee. He was probably the most powerful representative in Congress, but it was unsettling to wonder which defect in his judgment had permitted all the compliments he was forever receiving to blow lesions into the stretched balloon of his judgment. For Mills was a man whose face and build said clearly, "Stop in the House of Representatives!" His head was pear-shaped. It was as if there had been a yeast set loose in his flesh, and most of it had settled around his jaw rather than his brow. So even his ears were big on the bottom and pointed on top. The lower part of his face was full, even bulbous, a beanbag — his features got skinnier as your eyes went up, his forehead was narrow and his straight hair plastered on top of his flat little head must have been half a millimeter thick. If he had ever run for President, *Mad* magazine would have flown themselves to the moon on the whoomph of such unexpected gas.

Mills was gruff. He had nowhere near enough delegates to interest anybody, and besides he was not a man to divulge information — he had gotten where he was by keeping his counsel. So in response to the question "Who will win the nomination?" Mills replied, "We'll know next week." The Press groaned. He was the living embodiment of investiture, of muscle, money, and all the constipations of power. That thin head and those broad jaws! How many bulldogs from the corporations, unions, Mafia and Pentagon had given dead news conferences over all the years of the old politics. Now, it was as if Media didn't have to listen to him anymore. Since no political purpose would be served, Mills didn't have to talk to them either. The conference ended as it began, with one's ears in the shredder of the helicopter noise — it gave intimation of what the blade of grass might hear when the lawn mower goes over.

Wallace came in at last. Off the airplane, all motions repeated, like the film run again, he was promenaded past the Press in his wheelchair and up the ramp to the podium. As he progressed he moved his left hand (the limb most visible to the Media) through a set of small and artful movements. His hand was cupped as if in salute, the gesture was military — he could have been an honored general, as honored indeed as MacArthur, returning in that salute all recognition of the legitimate homage due him, and yet the gesture was not without pathos, for he was also reminiscent of a boy who has military dreams, and practices saluting the trees as he walks on a road. Wallace was so small in the chair! And so dignified! It was the quality he had never possessed. Aquarius had heard him speak once at a private dinner in New York and expected to like him more than he cared to. Instead, he had liked him less. There had been a dull bullying streak in his remarks, and one did not have to know a great deal about New York politics to understand how unpleasant was the majority of his audience — they had monomaniacal faces, mean, pinched and recidivist to the root of that worst of Christian essences which is Christian venom, faces to suggest that their only problem with sanity was to keep in line all remarks about wiping out certain unnamed hordes of the Asiatic, the Near Eastern and the African. But they were Wallace's people in New York. If not typical of *folks* in the South and Midwest, still Wallace was their leader that night, and worked them up on a set of verbal combinations which went through the problems of New York from innuendo to snarl, and was reminiscent of some of the worst of the Southern mess sergeants Aquarius had worked under in the Army, the kind who lost patience watching Filipino kids salvage edibles to take home from the garbage cans. Sooner or later such mess sergeants would always mutter, "Them gooks better get out of my way."

Wallace in Miami Beach today was another man, however. If, by more than one account, he had moved from Left to Right over the early years of his career, every evidence in recent months spoke of how he was now moving back to the center. For a time at least. The mail-order hate-you-fancy-pants clothes which once he wore had been replaced by tailored weeds. The influence of a new and beautiful wife, niece of Big Jim Folsom, was evidence no one could ignore, never ignore a deep brunette with eyes like black diamonds who had gone to Rollins College to become a movie star, had worked as a professional water skier, and in the Florida primaries drove the pace car to start the Daytona 500 (invitation delivered by the president of the race track, who was chairman of the pro-Wallace Florida delegation). No, Wallace was no longer the small-town demagogue with the gas to go as far as that could get him. He seemed interested in inching away from political positions too hopelessly penned off to the side of a national consensus — he had even in Florida suggested to audiences that if they didn't agree with his stand, they should vote for Shirley Chisholm for she at least "tells the truth unlike all those pointy-headed liberals." Shrewd politics which would draw votes from his nearest competitors Jackson and Humphrey, but it was certainly not a speech to issue from the Curtis LeMay Wallace of 1968.

Then in the wake of the assassination attempt had come pilgrimages: the Kennedys, McGovern, Muskie, Humphrey, Larry O'Brien, visits and gifts from Nixon, recognition from the Pope. If never respectable before, now respectable: grand opening of the tightest psychic sphincter of them all — small-town Southern pride. He was indisputably a national figure. With all "the grabs" of an abdominal pain. The tree falling in the forest knocks down another tree and one thinks of the Ronald Reagan part in *King's Row*. "Where's the rest of me?" was his scream in the middle of the night at the maniacal injustice of infirmity. Even as they wheel him up to the podium at Blast Site One, his hands and arms betray involuntary fear, and indeed as the wheelchair stops, he starts to topple forward — his body ends at his navel and he is like a top-heavy toy. So he grabs the podium like a boy learning to swim will grab the dock. Yet his face is handsome now in the instant of fear. The hint of hog-jowl complacency is gone, all gone, smelted out by pain and by meditations conceivably of retribution for acts of the past, perhaps he looks now the way he was meant to look, an ex-bantamweight boxer with all the lean dignity little boxers have when they retire and keep from gaining weight. And a band supplied by the Democratic National Committee, with straw boaters, black pants, bow ties and red-and-white-striped shirts, a bit of political brass with electric guitar, drums, two trumpets, a trombone with a hank of Confederate flag attached to the end of its slide and a whistling eel of a clarinet all finish saluting him. Hello Dolly alias Hello Lyndon alias Hello George is done and played and Wallace speaks in the new voice of the national hero, legions of the dead from every American war in the shadowy Taps of his voice, telling the crowd that he is "a national Democrat in a national Democratic convention" and the ear hears him again on TV, "I'm going to insist that they adopt a platform that tells the average citizen we are responsive to his needs and conscious of his desires." A fine sentence.

If every politician is an actor, only a few are consummately talented. Wallace is talented. The new modest measured voice creates another

318

man. If one did not know of his history, he could be a slim and small Southern general of impeccable dignity with a warming touch left of the common folk, all this as he speaks at the airport now, but the stories which follow the flight of the plane and will soon see print speak of the uncontrollability of his internal plumbing and his fears before speaking which are so terrifying that his wife must assure him she will, if necessary, go on in his place. He is the first note of the real that Aquarius has encountered at this convention, and his presence, a work of art, remains in the back of the mind, for Wallace brings with him the clank of chains down in the dungeons of the moon-reaching blood-pumped crazy American desire. Now he finishes by thanking "Gawd for having spared my life" and is given a rich and lingering farewell by Wilbur Mills, who, trademark face, never makes a move without significance to those who can read the blockbuster body language of the old politics. And all the sadness of the South, and the rage of Southerners that they know about a life which others don't, and it is going to perish (it has been perishing for a hundred and ten years and more), is in the muggy air of Blast Site One.

4

Hubert Horatio Humphrey, having arrived in the hollow hour after the Governor from Alabama was gone from the airport scene, stated when asked whether he expected to win, "You bet I do. I didn't come down for a vacation. I came for the nomination." His flair in the campaign had been to talk to Black audiences. With Jewish Senior Citizens he was as always super-sensational — when the moment came, he would lean in toward his wife and say, "Muriel and I can hardly wait until we pay a visit to Israel again and charge up our batteries in that lovely land," but such talk was analogous to strip-mining the emotions of the aged. Coming on with Blacks had been his unique ability among all these white candidates — for years! — he had a rhythm when he spoke. He laid down every favor he had ever done for Blacks, did it in cadence, you could hear the repetitive roll of the soul drummer harkening to a Black *duende* at these rhythmic calls on history, and when Hubert was done with his deeds, he would bark up in a little electronic voice-box of a voice — his larynx grown rough enough to scrub floors — "Yes, now, and now my friends, I need a favor from you," and his audience, Black respectables and Black Mafia, would go roaring down the oratorical river with him.

But this morning, day after his arrival, giving a press conference in the Carillon Hotel, he had nothing like the same happiness. The room had a very low ceiling and was overlit; the effect was to crush the Press in upon him, exaggerate all scrutiny and he had the old wounded bitter-mule look of a nag whose teeth had been counted too often — the Press, part of his first love affair with politics (for they had adored him once), now were next to openly contemptuous. And he was wary with them. He knew their need for a villain. A story flies best when it has a hero for one wing and a villain for the other. And Hubert was drawn toward villainy like the moth who rushes toward that far-off star which summons it into the flame. A villain in '68, he had California in '72, and after the greetings this morning were done, "I haven't had an audience of the Press this large in months," he said for commencement, drily, all the backed-up surly sad dignity of a man who knows he is regarded as a clown, knows he has even acted as a clown for that is the style by which he may swim, but now is trapped as a clown for that is the world's fixed estimate of him. "I open myself to your questions," he said. All the concentrations of fatigue from months of campaigning had been reduced and concealed under coatings of TV makeup thick as barnacles until there was only the hint of two small discolorations under his cheek bones, but like the worst sort of bruise they gave hint of tendrils in the injury ready to travel far. Standing in front of a shiny blue-finished cotton backdrop, he wore a blue suit with a broad light-blue silk tie, and these fabrics gleamed as he spoke of party, mission, and the needs of people. His eyes were tiny, his forehead was large as a rising orange harvest moon, and there was an old man's sadness in his downturned upper lip, the curve of a bowl turned upside down, his lower lip pinched determinedly upon it. "I believe we'll now have a free and open convention," he said, and next to him, Muriel wore a royal-blue tailored suit with a white blouse, her colors well installed between the hues of his suit and his tie. Next to them, harbinger of danger and sudden mortality, stood a sad Secret Service man in a dark green suit and dull-colored shirt, a dark somber maroon-striped tie. The Secret Service man had a great pallor as if for years he had been guarding artifacts beneath fluorescent lights.

Quickly someone asked about California. Humphrey's answer was unctuous, cynical, sincere and wicked all at once, as if the separate parts of his face were no longer flesh so much as jointed shells. He was alternately pious and full of candor, quick to insist that McGovern was inconsistent if he called for winner-take-all with the California votes when such a principle went directly against the guidelines McGovern had drawn himself, yet as quick to admit that if he had won in California and McGovern lost, he would be as concerned as George that his delegates were being taken away. "I'm sure I would have been fighting for every single delegate just like Mr. McGovern, and I don't think we ought to get uptight about it." Politics, what the hell, was politics. Uptight was the mix of morality and gamesmanship. Besides, Humphrey suggested, didn't he have the most votes in all the primaries — didn't that suggest, he left it unsaid, that any means was reasonable to stop McGovern? Of course, grumbled the Press, there were arguments as to who had the greatest number of popular votes in the primaries, face-offs as opposed to running unopposed. Humphrey went on. He was confident they would stop McGovern.

"How loyal will Muskie be in a floor fight?"

"I think," said Hubert full of twinkling clownsmanship, "that his credentials will be as solid as a Maine rock."

He drew laughter. It gave him life. He worked now for more laughter. To his claim that he had 700 solid delegate votes, "delegates with a strong preference or legal commitment to vote for Humphrey" (said Humphrey), there came the query, "If you don't get the 700 votes, won't that open a credibility gap?"

"Not a bit," he replied quickly with an old politician's tart distaste for a reporter so gauche as to prod into an obvious insincerity, a functional insincerity. That response drew a very large laugh. The mood was growing jovial. He would, said Humphrey, ask for a pledge "prior to Monday night from all candidates for loyalty to the party."

Would McGovern go along?

"He may. We talked recently on the phone — just a good friendly talk."

What did you talk about?

The sly look came back to Humphrey's make-up–battered face. "We," said Hubert, "talked politics."

The meeting ended in a jovial buzz. Only in the echo of this small event, only in the distance, did the sound of the wound linger, long-gone sound of some psychic explosion on the way to the campaign of '68. Time had glued him together with less than her usual address. Humphrey looked like a man whose features had been repaired after an accident; if the collar slipped, the welts would show. It was the horror of his career that as he came to the end of it, his constituency was real (if antipathetic to one another — what did his Blacks, old and middle-aged Jews, and trade unions have to do with one another?) but he was not real, not nearly so real as the constituency, more like some shattered, glued, and jolly work of art, a Renaissance priest of the Vatican who could not even cross a marble floor without pieties issuing from his skirt. Father Hubert. He had the look of a man who knew where the best wine was kept, but old age would have to conquer his desire to lisp when dogma was invoked.

5

As if he has formed a taste for greeting politicians, Aquarius is out again Saturday to see if he can catch the arrival of John Lindsay who is due just before McGovern comes in at Blast Site One. Lindsay is arriving without a ceremony to greet him. Lucky even to be a delegate (since the New York group in a forthright sweep of the McGovern broom has passed this year over Averell Harriman, James A. Farley, Robert F. Wagner, Meade H. Esposito and Patrick J. Cunningham among others) the Mayor of New York has been picked by Democratic State Chairman Joseph F. Crangle as a delegate-at-large. All advance word is that Lindsay is by now so unpopular with some factions of the New York caucus that he will keep a "low profile" at the convention.

He arrives in a commercial airliner with other delegates. It happens that his plane comes in by the last gate, at the end of a long passenger corridor, and there are only a few Miamians waiting to greet visitors or family. Plus one TV unit. They interview Lindsay. Out of the race, plastered with humiliating defeats in Florida and Wisconsin (where his share of the vote was as low as 7 percent), he carries his loss well at this moment — his features have the eloquence of fine-carved bone. Those features suggest he will yet have the last laugh on his enemies, for he will grow more handsome as he gets older. Even the hint of pain in his expression gives an agreeable distinction to that movie star face which has aroused so much animosity in New York.

"Do you think you have a chance at this convention?" asks the TV interviewer.

"Oh, nobody is burning down the aisles to get to me," says Lindsay.

He is altogether cut off. Having left the Republican Party to join the Democratic, he had two choices in the spring — to work for the new party but run for no national office until new credits had been established, or to enter the primaries and prove so powerful a vote-getter that his candidacy would emerge. Since he had no out-of-state cadres, nor real time for preparation, his best hope was as a television candidate. In Wisconsin he ran into all the force of McGovern's years of work at building an organization. "If Lindsay will admit he knows nothing about the grass roots, I'll agree I don't know my way around '21,' " said McGovern. And Meade Esposito, Brooklyn boss, and Lindsay's familiar enemy, sent a telegram: "Come back, little Sheba."

Of course, Lindsay violated the oldest law of politics. You don't join a fraternity and offer to become its president in the same week. The question was whether he was obsessed with the squandered virtues of the position he had not chosen. It was obvious Humphrey, Jackson or Muskie were all unable to unify the party, but Lindsay, if only he had remained out of the primaries, would now be the only Democrat who could lead a coalition against McGovern, and prove acceptable to some McGovern delegates. At the least, he would have been the most glamorous Democrat in Miami, and everyone's candidate for Vice-President. But Aquarius does not ask the question, for the answer is obvious. No politician as young as Lindsay is able to choose the prudent course when there is no final obstacle between the splendors of his personality and the Presidency — just the need to get the votes. He has to assume he will get the votes. Men are not in politics because they hold a low view of their charm.

But by the schedule, our leading man is due to be in. Quickly, the few reporters decamp from Lindsay and rush to get to Blast Site One. McGovern's arrival, however, is dramatically delayed by a tropical storm which keeps the plane circling in the air almost an hour (as if to speak of oncoming dark hours of the Republic) and then is still near to anti-climactic. The crowd, although larger than Wallace's, is not a patch on the crowd which greeted McCarthy in Chicago in '68 and that crowd, Aquarius recollected, had been too tame for him. Nor is McGovern his kind of candidate. He respects him for his political positions, admires his hard work; he more than admires his political victories (since Aquarius by his own feeble record knows what it is to get votes) but there is a flatness of affect in McGovern which depresses and the muted singsong of his conversational voice might lead one to divine he grew up in a rectory, if indeed one did not know it already. There is a poverty of spirit in the air. While it is certainly not a poverty of moral principle (for even arriving at the Blast Site with a rich suntan and a superbly tailored light-blue suit of a luminous silver sheen, McGovern is an embodiment of principles strong as steel) it is perhaps a paucity of pomp and pleasure which those very moral principles forbid — McGovern, every story tells you, doesn't even have a trusted flunky to pack his bag each morning but does it himself (shades of Henry Wallace and Abe Lincoln). It is not that he does not have a nice personality — if he is even half so decent as he seems, he is probably the most decent Presidential candidate to come along in anyone's life, and if he is not half as decent as he looks, then he is certainly a consummate actor. Still, it is all unexciting. He has come from back of the Democratic field and out of 5 percent of the polls to succeed in building a campaign organization without parallel in the grass roots, has done it all over two years of work and with the finely tuned foresight to forge a new set of principles for selecting delegates which has worked almost entirely for him, all those women, those young, those minorities giving him parts of the vote in states he could barely have entered before, he has brought the catboat of his small political fortunes into exactly the place where the winds of history were blowing for him, has put some of the air into those political breezes himself, has pulled off a feat of political appropriation which speaks of greatness — in the history of American Presidential primaries, the McGovern campaign of '72 must be a modest equivalent to the Long March of Mao Tse-tung. Yet there is no excitement. It is as if a fine and upstanding minister has moved into the empty house up the street: isn't it nice to have Reverend and the lovely Mrs. McGovern for neighbors? For certain, if McGovern's politics were more conservative, one would speak of him as the Democratic Nixon. For both men project that same void of charisma which can prove more powerful than charisma itself, although vastly less agreeable (as if one is alone in a room with a television set).

Aquarius could hardly dare to explain why he thinks it is important for a candidate to have charisma (he is much more mystical about the Presidency than fashion permits: he thinks, when all is said, it is a primitive office and inspires the tribes of America to pick up the modes and manners of their chief). While nobody he ever met seemed to be in love with the Republican President, history might yet decide Nixon was the man who forged the peace with Communism in the Twentieth Century. Yet could one measure the damage to temperament, bravado and wit which the emotional austerities of Nixon had laid on the nation? It was even possible Nixon had prepared the very toned-down climate in which a mild and quiet voice like McGovern could flourish. If that were so, and McGovern was yet to win, then what would happen to people who believed that Nixon was a chip off old Nick? Was McGovern then the second chip? All this was obvious nonsense for people who took their politics straight, and were happiest at three in the morning with a lukewarm beer and six hard issues to be discussed, but assassination was not the worst fertilizer for theories of demonology or Satanist perspectives on the seizure of history. Aquarius could travel far along these lines, but then he was forever ready to look for the devil in many a plain case: the nature of the undramatic Satan, true evil one, was to conceal himself, after all.

At any rate, cleaving to the good American principle that no successful man is ever to be completely trusted, Aquarius clung to every instant of study he could obtain of McGovern in action. Appearing the day after his arrival at the La Ronde Room of the Fontainebleau, he responded to the question "Do you think the winner-take-all principle is fair?"

"I don't. I was opposed to it. And in 1976, California will come under the same guidelines as the other states. But winner-take-all was the rule California chose for itself for '72, and while we were opposed to that rule, we played by it and we won. I submit that if you want to change the rules after a game, that is certainly permissible, but you cannot change the score of a game which is already played." It was the agreeable logic of the playing fields of Mitchell, South Dakota. "Are your agents," asked a reporter, "making any headway on the California question with Senator Muskie's people?" With a smile McGovern said, "Not to my knowledge."

"Have you had any conversations with Senator Muskie?"

"I talked to him about this matter."

"What did you say?"

Very drily. "I asked him to meditate upon it."

He did not suffuse himself in that fog of imprecision by which other politicians would bury, trap, suffocate, or slip a question, he had hardly the air of a politician, indeed he was more like a teacher dealing with a matter common to him and his students. Yet it was still not easy to know what one thought of him. If the force of his psyche was with you in the room like a fine silver blade, strong as steel, yet there was also that damnable gentle singsong prairie voice, that tight voice of a thousand restraints which sings of not a thing but its singsong resentment against the fact of its restraint — one had heard such voices on Midwestern bankers, and on athletes and bureaucrats and YMCA secretaries, on ministers, and kids selling subscriptions, and on the baby-faced killer who had always been the nice boy next door, it was the mild self-negating ripple of a life devoted to causes external to oneself and to the show of acts of Christian love. No, it was not a voice to find easily agreeable, for it spoke of Methodist beds of Procrustes where good souls and bad were bent equally into the rigor and rectitude of a bare, arduous, and programmed life. Small wonder that in his boyhood sneaking out to see a movie was mentioned by him as an example of forbidden fruit, yes, his voice gave small pleasure because it revealed so little of the man. And yet McGovern also seemed somehow reminiscent of an astronaut. It was in that sense he gave off of Christian endeavor, of total commitment of strength, of loneliness and endless stamina, of the tireless ability to bear interruption of his mood, and all of that same astronaut impersonality, professional gentleness, vaults of reserve, that subtle charisma so unlike the live hearth of conventional glamour, rather an incorruptible filament of charisma, which could be a halo if talking of a saint, but was invisible in McGovern until one became aware of it. For this charisma was not of personality but of purpose. It spoke of a bravery next to weightless — of course! That sense of a fine blade, stern and silver, was exactly what one felt when meeting certain astronauts. There too was the same sense of a psyche which had traveled already to a space beyond. "It would be nice, I suppose, to have a few more exciting personal qualities," McGovern had once said — it was a remark in the syntax of Neil Armstrong.

It gave focus, then, to think of McGovern this way. Indeed the image grew more comfortable as one wore it along, for McGovern had been a good pilot with a Distinguished Flying Cross for thirty-five bombing missions over Europe, and had, according to his biographer, Robert Sam Anson, the reputation of coming back to base "with more gas in his tank than 99 percent of the other pilots," which would be characteristic of spacemen who were noted for their passion to conserve fuel.

Seeing John Glenn at a party, his first reaction to the observation was "George? I don't think of him as an astronaut." Then Glenn hesitated. "I suppose the one quality in an astronaut more powerful than any other is curiosity. They have to get some place nobody's ever been before." So the question remained alive. "Yes," said Glenn. "It's possible George has that kind of curiosity."

326

6

There were parties in plenty. If the image of McGovern as a lonely astronaut piloting the ship of state through new moral galaxies of democracy was one million-footed mile of metaphor, the ten thousand feet of the delegates had by now come to town, all 5,114 of them with their alternates and their fractions (some 22 Rhode Island delegates would have 15/22 of a vote — an excruciating dismemberment to make 22 bodies count for 15), the working total for all to come to 3,016 votes or 1,509 for a majority, and the delegates were, of course, a bona fide new species, 80 percent never at a convention before, 14 percent Blacks, Latins and Indians at 6 percent, women at a full 38 percent. The young (under twenty-five) were 13 percent of the whole and another 20 percent were under thirty-five; professionals, teachers and housewives made up close to half the count, and 95 percent of the delegates had a year or more of college. It was a mass of hard-working citizenry, more honest, uncompromised, innocent and sober than delegate legions of the past, and the work overflowed into so many caucuses of category (Black, Latino, Women and Youth) and such immersion in state caucus that the convention became as complex as a field of tunnels and burrows, the nights of the convention set records for working hours, some delegates busy from early in the morning until early in the morning, from 8 A.M. for example to 6 A.M., and if they could hardly be a majority, the drinking parties, such as they were, had ceased by Sunday night. Yet, over the weekend, there was material to brood a little on the nature of McGovern's candidacy and the glum conclusion that his revolution was a clerical revolution, an uprising of the suburban, the well-educated, the modest, the reasonable, and all the unacknowledged genetic engineers of the future. The best of the liberal mind and the worst were his troops, all the warriors for a reasonable ecology and a world where privilege could not longer paralyze were in his army as well as all the social whips for a new state of collective mind opposed to any idea of mystery in any organism social or human — a spirit of science concentrated into pills to push behavior. If as a good Democratic voter, Aquarius thought it would be time to worry over such foes when McGovern was in, yet he noticed over the weekend celebrations that most of the fun was to be found in the polar ends of

327

the party, in the Wallace delegates whooping it up to the music of Ferlin Husky and in the warmth and faction of the Black Caucus on Monday morning; whereas the McGovern youth at the Doral, while certainly nice, had the subtly wan look (beneath Florida tan) of kids who get their kicks by replaying on tape recorders conversations they have just lived through.

The Wallace party for delegates had been a hog bath for heavy perspirers, with hard liquor, lots of gravy on the spareribs, and a sense of animal warmth coming off all those red country faces, meanness, spite, spice, loyalty and betrayal, carnal equalities all over the place like a cross between a horse auction and a roadhouse on Saturday night. Delegates with Jackson, Mills, and Humphrey buttons were there, in for a good time, and McGovern delegates also having a good time, there to show party solidarity with Wallace, all but the Blacks were there. And in the midst of all this white soul food and sexual savory there was the elucidation of a fine plot, with a Mills campaign official to drop it quietly in the ear. It seemed the Stop-McGovern forces were not without a plan — their plan was Teddy Kennedy.

"But how could he take it after McGovern is stopped? None of the kids would work for him."

"Oh, McGovern would have to call him personally and ask him to run."

"Why would McGovern do that?"

"Where else," the man said wisely, "can McGovern go? With a third party, he's dead."

"Does Teddy Kennedy know about this?"

Silence. The moment is weighed. The confession is contemplated. "He will disown us if a single word is printed," says the Mills man, baring all.

Of course, he is not talking about a plot but a scenario. This momentous secret cabal is hardly to be offered to Aquarius for the sake of his art, no, it is merely a move to create interest in Mills. And a ploy to pick up the credit later if Kennedy is ever nominated. Yet, as a scenario, it offers virtues. For if McGovern were actually stopped, only Teddy Kennedy could put the party together, and indeed could do it only if McGovern requested it of him, which was indeed a scenario to carry in one's mind so long as the issue was in doubt. At least it gave promise that this dull and quiet convention could yet burn a hole in all the plots and dramas of men.

Was it therefore with thoughts of Elizabethan tragedy and apocalyptic shift that he studied the face of Cornelia Wallace when the Governor came down in his wheelchair and from the short podium addressed the delegates in welcome, and gave his blonde daughter Lee, age eleven, to the microphone that she might give her little speech, bright and sassy was the child's speech for the folks, and practiced in oratory like her father? There were enough people in front of him to render the Governor and his daughter invisible, and Wallace's speech was benign, the king of a small castle welcoming his guests to the groaning board. But Cornelia Wallace's eyes were stellar while he spoke and, as she looked at the crowd, her rich face was animated with theatrical vitality — she could, for example, have passed convincingly as the most beautiful opera singer in the land — she was certainly the most beautiful woman he had seen in politics since Jackie Kennedy, and if Cornelia Wallace was nowhere as grand, she was certainly more vivid as she clapped her hands to the beat of Ferlin Husky. What a dramatic couple would the Governor and Cornelia Wallace yet become.

So that was a good party, the best he sensed glumly the Democrats might offer for the rest of the week, and steeped himself in parties as much as he could; it was a way, given his habits, of apprehending some modes of reality, and was bored later that evening at the Democratic Telethon — there was too much money in the back of the room, and the money was wan — comparisons might not be fair considering the compressed energy of the squeezed Wallace horde. Again that sense of being on the edge of some political revelation teased him. For twenty-four years, going back to the Henry Wallace days of 1948, he had been watching actors raise money for progressive politicians — there was an affinity between the two like red meat and red wine, or was it hot dogs and sauerkraut? Something in progressive politics believed in the forced feeding of message to the mass, and where was the professional actor who did not subscribe to the art of manipulated instruction? But this was hardly the revelation whose edge he might inhabit. With an alternating sense of melancholy and elation he felt as if he were coming close to some simple understanding of politics, clear as the simple step across a profound philosophical divide, even as once, how many years back, he had thought to himself, "The world's more coherent if God exists. And twice coherent if He exists like us." And had come to live as well with ideas of a Devil whose powers might be equal or sometimes prevail as in the bullets of assassins which found the mark (although his philosophical canon was to make no final assumption on the origins of any deadly message). Deep thoughts for a telethon — were they in

329

reaction against the bright optimism of actors whose new ideas were twenty-four years old for him? He was in a foul mood at his inability to fit the five thousand and more souls of this convention into some idea of one living creation in one bower of history.

His spirits improved with the Yippies the next night. Their role in this convention was small if McGovern were nominated; once he was stopped, they would be catalytic agents to thousands of furious young sympathizers for McGovern. But the mood in Flamingo Park was balmy on Sunday night. A feast was being provided for the old and the young — the Yippies never engaged in an action without a theory and the beauty of the new theory was that it was designed for Miami Beach since it had declared there was no real war between the young and the old. The villains were the middle-class generation between, those sons and daughters of the grandparents who were also the mothers and fathers of the Yippies; that was the middle generation which had collapsed into conformity and fear of Communism, but the old had radical memories of the Depression and the pains of forging the unions. Since this was the first time any of the young had made an overture to the old, and since the Yippies were easier to get along with than anyone had thought, some of the old citizens of Miami Beach felt ready to fraternize, and a few even came to the free feast in Flamingo Park where the face of Richard Nixon had been drawn on a field by laying out hundreds of quarters of watermelon in the pattern of his face. The thought was that the old would dive in to eat and massacre his image before the cameras of the Media; they had certainly gorged on watermelon in an earlier feast for the generations. Indeed, one Yippie cutting a watermelon had almost cut off an old man's hand because those senile fingers had plunged into the meat so fast, but this Sunday night the old were not numerous, and it was the kids who gorged on the watermelon and ate the free health food served up to hundreds, the lettuce and onion rings, the lentil salad and unpeeled carrots with the skin washed and sliced. Unpeeled cucumbers were also served, hard-boiled eggs, organic bread, plus the huge quarters of watermelon which had just lain on the field. The Yippies were dressed in every rag and feather of color, in belts and pieces of leather, in dungarees and cut dungarees, and their chests were brown from living in the sun, their hair and beards had gleams of gold, their tents were colorful in the evening. The encampment in Flamingo Park was somewhere between a love-in and an army bivouac, with pup tents scattered irregularly in the grass, and squad tents to the corners, field-size latrine trailers, and

CBS trucks near the trailers, but there were also colored balloons in the trees and a hand-painted sign: YIPPIE — TEN DAYS TO CHANGE THE WORLD.

Jerry Rubin and Abbie Hoffman appear. Since they are writing books, they have Media passes, and Rubin's declares he is working for *Mad* magazine; Hoffman has written Popular Mechanix on his. With his rug of dark hair, his big beaming nose, and his ferociously happy smile (as if he has just worked loose a rusted nut with his teeth), Hoffman has the skin of a man who has spent his life lying on his back looking up into the oil pans of a thousand jalopies, and eyes to suggest that "nobody knows the chimneys I've swept." And, yes, he is a mechanic of sorts, he and Jerry Rubin, both mad mechanics, tinkering with the Rube Goldberg traps of all the mad social machinery which fails to run the nation, and now laughing together at the Media passes, watching middle-aged people come into the park to look, Miami Beach residents suddenly confronting themselves as tourists, smelling the pot which dissipates as slowly as the odor of honeysuckle, feeling the peculiar peace of this bivouac (even though ten or fifteen of the children have eyes spaced out into the next county and Zippies with a pirate flag on their shirts stalk about — they have become the unmanageable Left to the Yippies' new center of establishment — "I'm having an identity crisis," said Rubin with his broad smile which welcomes all human phenomena including upheavals in himself), yes, across all of this peaceful Miami Beach evening, hot and placid as the streets of Flatbush in Brooklyn on a very hot July evening, the schizophrenia of the Republic is murmuring at the edges of the horizon — for this peace will not last. In August, the Republicans will be here, and the honor of the young is bound to protest the war; riots in the street will not necessarily prove a disaster for the Republicans. If legend has it that Allen Ginsberg once told a college audience he drew the line at nothing but incest, and the audience told him, "Draw the line at nothing," now Nixon was coming to draw the line.

Were the armies of the final Armageddon forming in the seed of men not yet born, or would even this calm summer end in blood?

7

But then in this hour of the night before that convention would begin which was to bring McGovern his nomination, there was doubtless a drop of blood already on the streets. For even as the feast was proceeding in Flamingo Park, a group of SDS were blocking the driveway to the Playboy Club where a party for the big sponsors of the Democratic Party was commencing, and before they were removed, a fire engine had been called to deal with a blaze outside the Bunnies' dressing room, alleged to have been started by a commando of Women's Liberation who would remind the Bunnies that they were degrading their sex even as they were being exploited. The police in full squadron, led by Pomerance, cleared out the demonstrators. But not before a number of sponsors had difficulty entering the party. The purpose of the raid may even have succeeded, for the party was spoiled. The old mood of Chicago lay over the guests, and the hours of confrontation and nightmare when the party had divided within itself returned, bringing the memory of how more than one good drinking Democrat, complacent for years with his bourbon, his special reserve of broads, and his warm appreciation of his own attention to the interests of the workingman, had exploded in rage against a thousand upstarts in the ranks of the delegates, and had come to realize in Chicago, in the ham heats of his clenched fists, that there were Democrats he would like to kill before he even tapped the nose of a Republican. Those powers of the Democratic Party which resided in the trade unions and the Mafia recoiled from Chicago and the loss of the election to Nixon with such numb stunned horror that the newest recruits to the party regarded them separately and together (how often together were the unions and the Mafia now lumped!) as the villains of the party, the corrupt and grease-impacted bottlenecks in all the arteries of Democratic progress. What made it worse was that their rage for being cast in such a position was able to burn on a true core of guilt. The union men were guilty of much. They had fattened themselves and their unions with the profits of the Cold War, had supported the scandals of Vietnam out past the time when men could turn against that war and still be called honest, and they knew they had adulterated the quality of work, and blown nonproductive air into the processes of production, they were part of the engines of pollution which squeezed the waste into the gears and skins of the products they made. They had delivered a living wage to the American workingman, but at the cost of an immersion in unneeded armaments which debauched the American economy, and had to listen to the accusations that they had left brothers on the factory line to marry the corporation. If true, it was a miserable materialistic marriage with endless bickering over what share of the benefits belonged to whom — but the corporation and the labor union chief were married to each other through every hatred. And now the labor unions had lost the party. These new delegates had come out of caucuses. They were people who had been willing to sit through weary long parliamentary evenings in order to prevail. Some would call it political intensity, but the union leader, veteran himself of a hundred negotiations in which he had worn out the softer executives who confronted him across a table, had now in his turn been ground out by the boredom of facing implacable students and teachers and hippies and clerks. By McGovern kids. Who were even worse than McCarthy kids, for some of the new ones had been fourteen years old in 1968, and had one characteristic which was calculated to drive the union leader into fever — these kids had been raised by mothers who loved them, and taught them the world was theirs to shape — so they had a complacent innocence altogether near to arrogance. The trade unionist reared more often than not by a mother who laid the frequent back of her hand on every idiot potato and onion and lemon head of a kid in her brood, could now have the immense anger of seeing his leonine powers lifted by a horde of suburban ants who had never been stepped on, and now could hardly be. Since these kids knew nothing of transcendence, he hated them. The unions had once been built by the unstated belief of organizers that they could transcend the given, the old leaders had come from the ranks, and the past was filled with legends of labor chiefs who had taken six shots from a .45 and chased their assailant as their life was pouring into their shoes; now the spiritual descendants of these men, installed here at a Thousand-Dollar-a-Plate dinner (ticket free), had to put up with women who set fires in Bunnies' dressing rooms and boys with beards who lay down on the road in front of their Cadillacs. The rage rose. Thinking of McGovern, the deposed labor leaders felt the natural hostility of sinners toward ministers. And before the evening was over, Hubert Humphrey came to the party, walking slow, naturally tired, his voice even more fatigued than his feet. The decision to pick the California delegation by majority of those eligible to vote had probably ended his chances.

8

Out of the deliberations of Larry O'Brien had the decision been made.

What a secret domain in the midst of open convention! Moving around a ring made of a strip of paper, one finds oneself first on the outside, then on the inside. Since one has not quit one's plane, it must be a twisted ring. History has moved from a narrative line to a topological warp.

McGovern had come into the last week of the California primary with his polls showing a 20 percent lead; enough for his aide, Frank Mankiewicz, to remark, "It won't be a convention, but a coronation." Somehow, nobody understanding how, McGovern on June 6 beat Humphrey by only 5 percent. Suddenly, the political air was full of lag — a sail was about to jibe. Humphrey, for whom four years have passed with one heart-pricking thought each morning — What *I* could have done with the presidency! — must have been like a young Chicano who lolls on a summer street and sees an elegant model go by. What *I* could do with her! All of that knowledge going to waste! Is there any motive more powerful? Since McGovern had had four times as much money to spend in California, it was not hard for Humphrey to find a moral victory in those close results. So he urged the Credentials Committee to overthrow the California primary: the principle of winner-take-all had denied the new guidelines. Of course, the Credentials Committee was filled with politicians kin to Humphrey, and they threw out more than half of McGovern's California delegates, giving them by proportion of their vote to Humphrey, Jackson, Muskie, Wallace and Chisholm. A Stop-McGovern coalition was thus formed. McGovern had been so close to a majority that the loss (151 of 271) was critical. The center of decision shifted from the depths of political life to the fourth dimension of the courts. A Federal District judge upheld the Credentials Committee, then the United States Appeals Court ruled against his decision. McGovern had the delegates back. And lost them as quickly to a stay of judgment ordered by the Supreme Court upon the Appeals Court ruling. "The convention itself," said the Court, "is the proper forum for determining intra-party disputes as to which delegates shall be seated." So the party chairman, Larry O'Brien, was put into the position of offering the decision which would make George McGovern the candidate of the Democratic Party, or, most probably, stop him. In a party whose incompatibilities had been equaled only by its paradoxes, the result of the most open selection of delegates in the conventions of this century had now come down to the word of the nearest man Democrats still had for a boss, Larry O'Brien, who worked as campaign manager for Jack Kennedy, Lyndon Johnson, Bobby

Kennedy, and Hubert Humphrey. Not unnaturally, he spoke of "awesome" burden.

O'Brien declared it would prove "an absolutely impossible situation if there was the remotest idea of a suggestion that O'Brien was pro or anti anyone." But what an occasion for distrust. O'Brien's first assistants were James O'Hara, a labor congressman from Michigan, and Joseph Califano who had worked for Lyndon Johnson in the White House. What a park for paranoia! Could Hubert Humphrey have planned a better terminus for the game than to have his chances judged by a party man? Of course, the McGovern strategy offered the return of an old nightmare: Chicago might be repeated. "I don't think," McGovern said, "people have fully assessed how the party could destroy itself if the reform process is denied after all that has happened in American politics these past few years."

The first and crucial decision for O'Brien was to determine how many votes were needed to establish victory. Should McGovern be required to amass 1,509 votes, an absolute majority of the convention, in order to win his challenge against the Credentials Committee, or should the 151 contested delegates be removed from the total of 3,016, and a majority of 1,433 thereby prove sufficient? McGovern could almost certainly command this latter figure. "We went over and over it," O'Brien said. "The stakes were never as high. It took us three days and nights before the light came on." They were talented lawyers with years of exploring complicated situations but it took them three days to reason that if the absolute sum of 1,509 was decided upon, then the moot 151 delegates would in effect be voting upon their own challenge. For while they would not be allowed to vote, McGovern would still have to get as many votes to win as if all 151 had been there to vote against him. So O'Brien reduced the number to 1,433. It was equivalent to giving the nomination to McGovern. The old pol had decided for the new politics.

What consternation in the coalition! Wallace's campaign manager Charles Snider asked if this was what they got after their candidate "almost died in the service of the party." Jackson's representative promised that Jackson was "triple-pissed." Humphrey's man called it a "hostile act," and Muskie's aide Sherwin Markham said he might make a move to force adjournment of the convention. There was laughter. "Don't laugh," Markham told them.

Will it be easier to understand the decision if we assume O'Brien might have preferred to give the advantage to the Stop-McGovern

335

coalition, but was compelled to accept McGovern's arguments against his inclination? (It must of course be supposed that the argument was never decided on logical merits — when the stakes are high, logic is obscene to a politician.) More natural is it to expect that O'Brien was looking for the survival of the party. A decision against McGovern was equivalent to creating a third party which could come close to getting as many votes in this next election as the Democrats themselves — probably that could kill the old party forever. Whereas if McGovern won the nomination, he might never be able to make peace with the old pols and the trade unions, nor find any real money, but at worst he would lose the election, and if he lost badly it might be easier for the old party to rebuild in '76 with old hands restored, and some of the McGovern cadres conceivably chastened. The wisdom of Solomon was O'Brien's. Such things happen to the Irish. Of course in the three days it took for the light to come on, there might have been more than one phone call to a compound near Hyannis.

9

Next morning Ed Muskie called a press conference where he read a statement. He stood there in his light-blue suit and he was knob-eared, knob-jawed, blue-eyed, knob-nosed, still gangling in his sixties, homespun (as if actually pondering whether he might have karmic ties to Lincoln), and with it all, was stately. Indeed, he looked like a gentleman of the frontier out of the Nineteenth Century — he had the dignity of simple manner, of a man who has absorbed his share of pain without brooding on the cost to his features.

Of course, such pain had come lately. Politics is not an art of principles but of timing. The principles are few and soft enough to curve to political winds. The fundamental action of politics is to gain the most one can from a favorable situation and pay off as little as possible whenever necessity forces an unpopular line. In every political profit, there is a loss somewhere — in every loss, a profit if one knows how to find it. That is all there is to politics if one considers principle. But when it comes to timing, politics is an art which makes the moves of athletes look heavy. Timing becomes as vertiginous as genius. Timing, and the power to contain huge ambitions and never lose one's temper. Since politicians make few remarks people have not heard often tested before, they are given little credit for their best remarks, and are never forgiven for their mistakes. They are not supposed to make mistakes. So they dare not lose their temper.

Muskie had made every mistake in the last few months. He had run a primary campaign with the slogan "Trust Muskie" in a year when nobody was trusted. Probably, he trusted himself. He had a slow honest bottom-of-the-barrel integrity on tough issues. He was ready to scrape the barrel of his own insides on difficult issues, searching within until he felt the authenticity of a bona fide answer. It was a good way for a politician to work so long as he was successful — people began to believe in the depth of his comprehension. Once he began to lose primaries, however, it turned inside-out. He could not recover his timing — suddenly he seemed always too strong or too weak. When his temper made him emotional at unpleasant slights to his wife in New Hampshire, the Press turned. They began to look for his nuts and bolts after Florida and Wisconsin — since they had once predicted his victory, now, unforgiving, they looked to take him apart. By now it would not have mattered if he began to do something right — they had him fixed as a man who was now always wrong. So as he read his statement, an unwilling pathos came off him, like a sound issuing through gritted teeth. He was a man of pride, he wanted no pity but it was a torture to him that he had been thought of and looked at as the next President for two years and more, and now he was without position or honor or respect in his party, the butt of jokes from the staffs of other candidates, even stories of his own staff making remarks to the effect that he needed a transplant for his vertebrae. His only crime was that he had tried to run for President in his own way, his own way had failed utterly, and nobody forgave him. Nobody forgives a favorite who loses by seven lengths.

So now he looked to regain respect. To be the statesman who bound the wounds of his party. With dignity his words issued; he was taking pleasure in the weight of his courtly rhetoric:

> We have witnessed over the last several weeks a growing polarization of our party. . . . The credentials disputes have become weapons in a battle for votes among presidential candidates. This has spawned litigation, accusations, resentments, and antagonisms. . . .
>
> Moreover, what we have had to say about each other has become increasingly strident, intemperate and accusatory. Foul has been claimed in circumstances where foul may not have been intended or administered. We have heard impugned men and women who

337

have labored long, diligently and well in an effort to ensure the openness and fairness of our convention.

In short, we have seen this convention being turned into two armed camps. . . .

Therefore, I have sent the following message, together with a copy of this statement, to each candidate for President:

I earnestly ask that you meet with me, the other candidates for our party's presidential nomination, and Chairman O'Brien at his office or a place provided by him at 1:00 P.M. today for the purpose of arriving at joint recommendations for presentation to the convention which would resolve the major disputes over credentials and procedure which now threaten to embroil us all in protracted and damaging controversy. At that time I will be prepared to present specific recommendations designed to resolve these disputes in a manner which does not finally determine the nomination.

While I have not discussed this invitation with any of the other candidates, it is my earnest hope that it will be accepted by all of them.

But once again his timing was to prove atrocious. O'Brien had decided California. So nothing was left to compromise. McGovern did not need others. Indeed only the other candidates met on Monday afternoon with O'Brien. They had to look foolish. McGovern would hardly enter a meeting where his vote would be one against five. So the Press turned again on Muskie. He was derided as pitiful and incompetent. If he had grave sins, and hell was awaiting him, he must certainly have paid a tithe in purgatory. How raw must the inside of his stomach feel.

10

O'Brien had never been chairman of a convention before — by the time he was done, many were asking if they had ever seen a convention chaired as well. It was as if he had studied the style of every man he had ever seen with a gavel, and appropriated the best of what he could use from each. Since he was a man of parts and a good deal of wit, he appeared to the thousands of delegates who were young, new, and reluctantly innocent of conventional ways, as an arbiter of manners, wise, senatorial, urbane, firm, good-humored and never pious. Since he was a representative of the old politics who had proved sympathetic to the new politics, he also possessed the essence of political sex appeal for new delegates — nobody is more attractive in politics than a formidable adversary who is now your friend, indeed, nothing gives more fortification than the powerful manners of an enemy joining the court. For witness to this principle, we need only contemplate the illimitable charisma of William F. Buckley if he ever became a liberal Democrat.

So, from O'Brien's opening speech — "The first challenge we face this week is to decide whether party reform will in fact make the Democratic Party better able to deal with our real problems, or whether party reform turns out to be an exercise in self destruction" — O'Brien had attached the interest of the delegates to himself and to his own doubt, and to their ability to convince him. He was saying, in effect, "I am here, like yourselves, a man of contradiction and confusion who wishes to discover if his love of party is justified." Since he did this with a sense of tradition — in appearance he looked like a benign version of Joseph Kennedy when the founding father was still young — the readiness of this young convention to maintain decorum found its perfect focus. "Getting here," said O'Brien, "was only half the job. Now we must go to work. The hours will be long. The job will be tough. But we must prove to the American people that the Democratic Party should again be entrusted with America's future. I think it comes down to this: do we have the guts to level with the American people? Only *you* can answer this question."

They gave him the ovation he deserved. He was a work of art. Had there been any dirty deal in the Democratic Party, over the last twenty years, he did not know about? He seemed born with the ability to walk through a barnyard on his way to the cotillion and never have to wipe his pumps. So he gave dignity to the notion that a man could be a political animal and still acquire class. Since they were all thinking of a life in politics, they admired him for it. Perhaps the measure of the best art is that it does not excite envy.

Of course, O'Brien would have need of his newly acquired status. The wars of nomination were on. It was the next irony of this convention (whose drama like some masterwork of the absurd was never so much in its proportions as in its disproportions) that the climactic event of the entire week occurred on the first vote over the first challenge (which was not even California but South Carolina) and proved to be a drama of obfuscation since the result seemed to suggest McGovern's forces were in trouble whereas in fact they now controlled the convention. To magnify such irony, the South Carolina challenge also brought McGovern's herculean labors of the last two years down to a fine point of parliamentary procedure which resided within the other fine point of O'Brien's decision to make 1,433 votes enough to

339

win the California challenge. Because it was the essence of parliamentary nuance that a chairman's ruling could not be challenged on its own direct application (or else what was a ruling worth?) but only on a parallel situation, so South Carolina was chosen by the Humphrey coalition for a test inasmuch as it had been selected by lot as the first vote on the night. The California challenge being not yet decided, all of the 151 Stop-McGovern delegates could still vote. Now, in the new situation, nine of South Carolina's seats being contested, a vote of 1,504, by O'Brien's ruling, would be enough to win. Of course, if the final vote fell between 1,504 and 1,509, then the chairman's decision would have made a critical difference in the result, and there would be legitimate ground for "controversy." Then the entire convention would be obliged to vote on the wisdom of his decision. Still retaining their 151 contested delegates, the Humphrey coalition could easily prevail on such a point. Having won, they would then be able to pass a new ruling requiring McGovern's challenge on California once again to obtain 1,509 votes, equivalent to stopping him. What a broil of maneuvers ensued! The Humphrey coalition had to win the South Carolina challenge in such a way that their final total fell into what they called — all shades of television — the "twilight zone" between 1,504 and 1,509. McGovern had to win by more than 1,509 or lose by less than 1,504. Since he had also promised the Women's Caucus that his forces would support the South Carolina challenge (which demanded, by way of the guidelines, that nine seats now held by men be delivered to women) McGovern's aides soon had to face the dilemma of taking a dangerous chance with the nomination or betraying his promise. To pose such a choice is to name the result. McGovern had hardly selected Ribicoff, Fred Harris, Gaylord Nelson, Frank Church, Phil Burton of California, Stewart Udall, Governor Lucey of Wisconsin, Gary Hart, Frank Mankiewicz, and Lt. Governor William Dougherty of South Dakota as floor leaders in order to be outmaneuvered in the pulling of votes on a parliamentary point. Halfway through, by the best estimate of Rick Stearns, the Rhodes scholar who was directing the strategy on this roll call, there was no certainty McGovern's forces could avoid the twilight zone (which they termed "the window") if they tried to go over 1,509 on South Carolina. It was going to be too close. The women would have to be dumped. Hart telephoned the Doral Hotel to give a clue. "All right," said McGovern, "I'm going to take a nap. Call me back so I can watch California." The nap would at least give him the right to say he had not intimately directed the strategy for choosing to lose on South Carolina.

"I got busy up and down the aisles," said Hart. In the California delegation, all 120 McGovern votes had gone to the women, plus 14 other delegates. The co-chairman of the delegation, Willie Brown, took 14 votes from his own pocket. California voted 120, not 134, for the minority report. It was a way of suggesting the McGovern vote was solid while Chisholm delegates were more attached to stopping McGovern than voting for the women. It was a trick which would be exposed by the next day, but Brown was working on the premise that the California challenge coming next would be over long before word would get around.

In their turn, the Humphrey coalition was trying to reduce the majority they were being given. The chairman of the Ohio delegation, Frank King, a man with the honest dogged face and silver-rimmed glasses of a bank examiner, was thrust into the massive embarrassment of looking incompetent on television for he had to pass the Ohio delegation four times. His eyes were almost crossed with the misery of seeming unable to do simple arithmetic before half of America. But one can imagine his conversations on the phone with Humphrey Headquarters. "Frank, can you up your total six? No, wait a moment, can you bring it down by nine." Groans. "Hold tight. We're not sure yet." To complicate matters, he had to deal with four Ohio counters representing other candidates, and of course nobody trusted anyone.

Through this scramble to phone circuits, the floor leaders for McGovern, better organized, kept switching votes back and forth in the Wisconsin, Nebraska and Oregon delegations until the speed of their calculations drove and dazzled the Humphrey coalition into confusion, indeed such confusion that they finally lowered their heads, bulled into a charge, and decided to win by a big margin as if this might convince the convention that McGovern could be stopped. It convinced some of the television commentators that McGovern might be in trouble, and brought suspense to the California challenge which followed, but in effect the total had landed well outside the twilight zone, 1,555.75 against 1,429.05, and the nomination was safeguarded.

Soon after, the California delegates were restored to McGovern by a vote of 1,618.28 to 1,238.22, a solid and overriding victory (which would have been a defeat if not for O'Brien's ruling), but it possessed no excitement commensurate to the results, and probably offered its most explosive moment when black Willie Brown got some of the convention to its feet by shouting "Give me back my delegation" in the debate which preceded the vote. Since Willie Brown was small and slight there was a pathos of the streets in his cry as if he were a newsboy whose papers had been stolen, but since he was also as lithe as super-cat, and young, and super-cool as a dream of Black supremacy in his creamy stay-cool-forever clothes, he was also engaging in the highest kind of Camp as though really there to say, "Listen to the Black man cause he is the wounded and the wise warrior, and he will show you how to wipe the warts." A huge campground. "Give me back my delegation!" The crowd roared. And roared again when the vote was counted. The first demonstration of the convention took place.

So, California was over. It had been won and lost in June, and won and lost and won again in July, but the damage it had done would offer no easy repair, for any period McGovern might have spent in preparing for the campaign, mending the party, studying his choices for Vice-President, and presenting an air of unity to attract the money had also been lost; the first price California would exact had already been paid in the challenge for South Carolina — more than a few of the women were storing resentment. The second was immediately on its way, and showed itself in the failure of the McGovern aides to find a compromise in Illinois which would seat both the Daley delegation and the Singer delegation which had ousted it. Singer's delegates were pro-McGovern, but hardly welcome to McGovern who needed Daley if he was to win Illinois. Still, McGovern could hardly repudiate Singer without enraging all too many delegates who had not forgiven Daley for Chicago in '68. So McGovern was ready for compromise. Singer, after a pull or two on his arm, was also ready for compromise. But Daley wasn't. He hadn't built from the first story to the second story all the way to the top story of all that larcenous Chicago politics in order to have an election half-stolen from him at the end of his career. He was not available for compromise. He did not answer calls from the McGovern staff nor did he accept visitors who were ready to mediate. "He," said a Daley man, referring to McGovern, "needs us more than we need him." There would be reverberations in other big-city machines. If McGovern were to finally lose the election by the margin of Illinois and one or other urban states, Daley might own the honor of having been the instrument of defeat for two Presidential candidates in a row.

11

On Tuesday morning, after the McGovern forces had won California on Monday night, Humphrey called a press conference, and standing with Muriel next to him, speaking in the slow and even voice one tries to maintain at a funeral when half the love of one's life now lies in the box, he read the following words:

> I have a very brief statement, and just a statement. I shall read it and there shall be, if you will indulge me, no questions.
>
> After consultation with some of my closest friends and supporters I have determined that I will not permit my name to be entered in nomination at this convention. I am therefore releasing my delegates to vote as they wish. But my withdrawal from the presidential race is a withdrawal of candidacy only. It is not a withdrawal of spirit or determination to continue the battle that I've waged all of my life for equal opportunity for all of our people, for social justice for this nation.
>
> On behalf of Mrs. Humphrey and me I wish to thank those who have worked so hard, who have given so much, who have been so steadfast in their friendship and loyalty for these many years, and particularly for these past six months. . . .

When he was done, his eyes shining with the high light that tears will take when one does not permit them to fall, he patted his wife awkwardly on the side of the cheek, as if this was something he should certainly do, and he and his wife left the room slowly. The Press followed along the hall down the red carpet and past the aquamarine chairs with their brass arms. Outside on the street, the sign at the Carillon which read WELCOME FUTURE PRESIDENT HUMPHREY has already been taken down and the marquee bills AMERICAN SCENE REVIEW FEATURING MAIN STREET SINGERS. In America, titles bounce off one another like molecules in solution.

Later in the afternoon a feeling of tenderness for Humphrey came back into the heart. It was analogous to the tenderness one used to feel for Boris Karloff in *Frankenstein*. How the dead in Vietnam still groan in the American bed.

343

12

Humphrey's withdrawal spurs him to interview Gene McCarthy. For once, there is no Secret Service about. In fact, there is no office, just a suite of three or four rooms, and in one of them a few people are gathered. They have faces which, if studied, might give insight into the nature of the loyal — it is as if they were the last handful of the millions who once were followers of McCarthy, decent faces with an inbite of the appetite as if they can put up with political penury for years. But McCarthy is looking splendid. He has never appeared more handsome, more distinguished, and more a philosopher prince — he is probably the most impressive-looking Democrat in Miami Beach. And he takes pleasure in teasing one of his total of four delegates who is a good young woman from Chicago but aware to a fault of her own lacks. "Oh, my God," she says, "I'm just the wife of a butcher. I can't put you in nomination." "Well, you may have to," he says with as much pleasure as if he were President of Notre Dame and had just told an All-American he will have to read the works of Immanuel Kant before trying to go on to the priesthood. "Yes, we're talking of nominating me," he says with a smile. "It seems as if that's the only way we can keep our floor passes and gallery seats," and the petty details of being completely out of fashion seem to interest him as much as the details of power.

Interviewing him alone, his wit flows so naturally through each topic that it is like trying to keep track of the light on water — it is easy to see one reason the Press never adored him is that he is not easy to quote. His phrases engage in extended relations with one another across long interesting sentences full of suspension: part of what they used to call his arrogance is his love of the English language — it is possible he has come to dislike politics because its tendency is to debase language, and its necessity all too often is to amputate the limbs of a thought. There is his famous remark about liberal criticism of his indifference to carrying on the fight, "They want me not only to bare my breast but go in for indecent exposure," and he recalls how McGovern accused him in the Wisconsin primary of giving up in the summer of '68. "But that isn't true," McCarthy says. "It was just," and his voice is very quiet with the memory of the frustration, "that we couldn't get anywhere. All the sources of power we needed were closed, the trade unions" — he is about to mention the Kennedy forces who gave him nothing after

Bobby's assassination — "it's all very well to talk of carrying on the fight, but that didn't give us anything to fight with." And there is a hint of sadness when he speaks of how he came to run again, "I suppose I believed the loyalty I could arouse would be greater."

A hint of the elegiac arises as Aquarius confesses his wish that it was McCarthy who would be nominated tonight. "I like McGovern," Aquarius says, "but I just wish he spoke with a little metaphor from time to time."

"Methodists are not much on metaphor," says McCarthy.

13

By Tuesday night, McGovern's nomination assured, he had still a set of delicate maneuvers to perform: politics was always delicate when one's next action was obliged to break a promise. If part of the drive of his campaign had come from women who believed McGovern would support their platform demands for abortion, from homosexuals who assumed he would go down the line with them for repeal of sexually restrictive laws and from the National Welfare Rights Organization workers who had a plan for a $6,500 minimum income for a family of four, the difficulty was that too few of his supporters understood how the dance of flirtation is always followed by the politics of withdrawal. In the mind of a political leader it is no betrayal to move away from people to whom you have made promises, provided your aim remains intact to fulfill the promise (or some part of it) when elected. The dance in between has been an employment of one another; during the period of closest attachment, stature has been given, after all, to unpopular demands. Now one might expect it would be obvious that McGovern was not going to capture the heart of America on a platform of abortion, legally free homosexuality and larger grants of welfare, not when thus hairy and wet a platform would be exposed to Nixon's oratorical gang for comment. If McGovern had been sympathetic to such causes in the first phases of his campaign, it was probably the reflection of an earlier attitude that he would not win the nomination but could at least come to Miami with a solid block of delegates to deal for position. Having far surpassed such early expectations, the time had now come to separate himself with the minimum of damage, a *delicate* political act made more difficult by the high passions of factions so new to politics they could not understand that the basic shift of emphasis going from a primary to a Presidential campaign was in getting ready to plunge into the muck of public opinion, that same public opinion which was the direct intellectual victim of fifty years of polluted reporting and vested editorial writing. Public opinion had by now a power of inertia which pulled every candidate (who wanted to win) directly toward the center of the cess as powerfully as the momentum of a spinning gyroscope will maintain the axis at vertical.

Still, McGovern's blow fell with decency and dispatch. It was an open convention. (Which by the language of politics meant it was not utterly closed.) Brutality was never employed. The gloom of late hours was successfully invoked and the more embarrassing of the platform debates took place near to dawn. At 5 A.M. delegates paraded about the floor with signs saying FREE WALTER CRONKITE, a show of good humor. Indeed, not too many delegates were coerced. Most McGovern supporters were simply told to vote their conscience. It was obvious that nearly all of the Wallace, Humphrey, Mills and Jackson delegates were going to be against anything like "ass, grass, amnesty and abortion," so just a fraction of the McGovern votes were needed to put down the planks. They were employed. Down went the planks, and could be forgotten if the questions they raised were not among the more interesting of the convention: the shape of political ideas to come was conceivably in their content.

The homosexual plank proved the measure of lag between sex and politics. To declare that there should be no legal restriction on sex between consenting adults was certainly a defensible idea of human conduct — one could even believe, if religious, that homosexuality was a mortal sin and yet see no reason for society to punish it, not when the soul would have its full impost of karma to pay. There was of course the conservative argument that legal acceptance would tend to create an atmosphere of permissiveness, but, reversed, the argument was just as conservative: legalization was more likely to reduce anything gay or exotic down to the size of marriage. Nonetheless, a plank supporting the rights of homosexuals was political suicide. For it had the power to mobilize votes against you. Out in America, far beyond Miami, lived a damp dull *wad* of the electorate. They often did not vote. It took no ordinary issue to fire their seat. But the right to condemn homosexuality (and abortion! and welfare!) was a piece of their cherished rights: woe to the politician who would deprive them of rights. Homosexuality had to go.

346

And welfare as well. Was there an issue which put more poison into the liver of the wad? It is bad to find oneself at the age of forty or fifty with monotonous work, meaningless family relations, and the cowardly fears of childhood alive again at the thought of walking the streets, but it is worse to recognize that there are healthy and insolent bodies prowling around out there who command the streets and they are living on the welfare one's taxes provide! Is there a cheap politician in America who has failed to invest this argument with all the wrath of his own fear that he doesn't have enough intelligence to be running for office?

It was not that thoughts of welfare could offer any happiness to a serious politician. One could hardly build moral equity in a society where some were paid for working and some were paid not to work — that was as basic to fouling good will as sweating the day shift in a factory to support a wife who is shacking up with boy friends in the afternoon. Every afternoon. When it comes to welfare, murderous emotions are quick. Yet who has the moral right to speak out against it? When Aquarius ran for mayor, he talked to women in some of the New York welfare organizations. They were not pitiable. They were proud. They told him, "People are always saying we're not entitled to welfare, we got illegitimate children, we got boys out there on drugs. Fuck em. We're the ones who got to raise the children. We're the ones whose apartments get robbed. Our welfare checks get stolen by the same junkies they're complaining about. Fuck em if they don't like my TV set or my rug. I'm as entitled to that as they are. I don't have too much money given me, I have too little. I want more. I'll tell you what I want, candidate for mayor, I want my share of the waste."

An incontrovertible argument. "I want my share of the waste." So long as there were wars which had no meaning and smog whose smell was equal to the excessive profits which had been derived from creating excessive desires, so long as there was massive excessive irrational earth-destroying waste as empty as the fields of Vietnam after a hundred American bombers had passed over, then anyone on welfare was entitled to their share of the waste, indeed, had title whether they would work or not, for in a society which was abstractly and ubiquitously criminal, it might be a mark of merit for a man to choose a life of crime and swindle. Certainly, it demanded more initiative and risk.

But when he had talks at this convention with workers for welfare rights, he discovered they were serious about the subject in ways he was not, and the argument that people on welfare wanted their share of the waste aroused small interest. "The problem," said a welfare organizer

347

named David Ipshin, "is that people on welfare have only the shit jobs to go to. So where is the incentive to work? The real question is whether society will ever be able to take people off shit jobs." Dark-haired, intent, his arguments moved with the force a good lineman might use in clearing a hole. "When we ask for that $6,500, we're trying to advance the idea that it's not the fault of poor people that they're poor. We're trying to get them out of that self-defeating bag where they look down on themselves because they have no money. We're looking to get them to respect themselves. And they need a little security for that. What the hell, they're just as much entitled to a chance for new consciousness as anyone else." Later, on the convention floor, on the night of the nominating speeches, he also talked to George Wiley who was head of the National Welfare Rights Organization, a tall pale Black with a full body and a Dashiki shirt. On Tuesday night the plan for the $6,500 minimum income for a family of four had been defeated 1,852.86 to 999.75.

"You didn't really think you were going to win, did you?"

"Not this year." Wiley gave a smile. "At least we made the floor and got voted on, and ran up a thousand votes." But it is the trap of the poor that they never get full measure. 999.75 votes!

Wiley had the polite and yielding manner of a man who hears the same arguments every working day, but is not prepared to yield anything other than his polite voice, since it is possible he has thought longer about the problem than anyone else. "The real perspective on welfare," Wiley said, "is exactly who will do the unpleasant work? *Shit* jobs are what it's all about. How do you solve that problem?"

"Well, how do you?"

"Maybe by letting people be paid in proportion to the disagreeability of a task." He said this softly as if not wishing to throw it away.

"A sort of existential wage? An existential economy — where money is a measure of the degree that work has invaded your existence?"

"Of course," said Wiley. "Exactly."

Was this the first new economic war-call since *Das Kapital*? It was better than "From each according to his ability, to each according to his needs," for it stayed closer to greed, ego, stamina, and desire. Aquarius' mind was racing to the convention of 1992.

14

On Monday at the Carillon, there had been a Women's Caucus, and behind the speaker's podium a large hand-lettered banner declaring WǪMEN PǪWER was attached to the curtain. Viewed from his angle off to the side, he first read it as OMEN POWER, a tribute to witchcraft in the new political cosmos.

When McGovern addressed OMEN POWER, an incident occurred. The speaker who introduced him said that one reason they were able to attend the convention in large numbers was because of McGovern's efforts to open the party to women.

McGovern rose, and said with modest humor, "The credit for that must go to Adam."

He was booed. "Should I have said Adam and Eve?" asked McGovern. But the laughter was tight-lipped. A humorless friction was in the air. Hisses continued. This cold reception was due warning. Not since militant Blacks arrived on the American scene had a political group appeared who were as threatening. But there had been a legitimacy to the ugliest Black demands, obviously still was — every injustice against a black man poisoned the root of America's existence. Whereas every injustice against a lady in Women's Liberation gave every promise of poisoning her husband's existence. But just this was the intolerable disproportion of Women's Liberation — they pretended to a suffering as profound as the Blacks, when their anguish came out of nothing more intolerable than the intolerable pointlessness of middle-class life. (Which of course was as intolerable for the men.) So Women's Liberation might be a totalitarian movement, yes, more totalitarian than not was its style. It appeared to speak for a volcano of legitimate furies but its rage was more likely to derive from boundless seas of monotony, and so a species of schizophrenia resided in some of the chillier demands. Ms., for example, spoke of the totalitarian passion for spoiling the language. Mr. at least stood for Mister. But how did one pronounce Ms.? Was it Miz or 'ims? Wherever it could create a mood, language gave life to the human condition; mood was a bed of rest for the nerves. Totalitarian was the need to inject non-words into the language, slivers of verbal plastic to smash the mood. If Aquarius had a simple idea, it was that language had been a creation of the female, first forged from the sounds of communication between herself and her young. But it was a natural mark of the Twentieth Century (perverse to the core of its historical knots) to use the representative of each human promise to defeat that promise. So any dependence of ecology upon the resonance of mood would now be shattered most quickly by women.

No surprise, then, if they booed McGovern for giving the credit to Eve. She was a comic book creation of the male chauvinist pig Jehovah; Eve was acquiescent nature with tits to pop for *Playboy*, and a sea-smelling cunt. Whereas the pride of Women's Liberation was that cunts had the right to smell as bad as any man's half-dead cigar. There was the total Twentieth-Century proposition! Of course, Aquarius' real opinion was that at the bottom of Women's Liberation was all the explosive of alienated will, a will now so detached from any of the old female functions, and hence so autocratic, that insanity, cancer, or suicidal collapse might have to be the penalty if the will did not acquire huge social power. Totalitarian power. What a fund of scientific jargon was their ideology. They spoke of the nonexistence of the vaginal orgasm (which was a way of certifying that they had never had one) since it was indeed most likely that the vaginal orgasm involved some temporary surrender of the will to something else, whether man, god, nature or some portion of the cosmos termed "It," but the vaginal orgasm was surrender just so much as the full orgasm of the man was the giving over of his will to something other in himself or in his woman or in the split vision of his fuck. So the best operative definition of a female in Women's Liberation might be that she had so little notion of vaginal orgasm she was convinced it did not exist and thereby was fortified in her contention that the clitoris was the last station on the line. But the liberator was wrong. Suicide was the terminal station. For people of outrageous and buried will, the failure to attain power is suicide. The liberator is first a woman of murderous will, but then many a suicide is an absolute murderer who is finally reduced to the absolute humiliation of killing himself.

Now, if this was his own prejudice (all because the women booed McGovern for invoking Eve), still one had to recognize that the best was usually bent like a line to the worst. So Aquarius had to contend more than once with a recurring recognition that Women's Liberation had given birth to some revolutionary ideas which he had to respect: the first was their view on abortion. If he had supported the legal right to abortion for as long as he could remember, even took an unadmitted intellectual pleasure in the way the problem buttressed his political

350

philosophy as a left conservative, it was because he found himself in favor of abortion but opposed to contraception; even, by his logic, more opposed to the pill than the pharmacological reek of the diaphragm. The latter offered, at least, a choice each night, whereas the pill removed the dignity of such choice, and so invaded the undeclared rights of the fuck whose romantic imperative is to prevail — against all odds! Something had to be lost when there was no last possibility for lovers to declare, "This fuck must be apocalyptic — why else reach in, remove the plug, and try to have a child?" Yes, upon such remote and unendurably sentimental possibilities did any larger dignity of a fuck depend, for the act of love which discharged into chemical fences of the pill bore the same relation to capital punishment as the old California gas chamber, whereas the apocalyptic fuck owed a little at least to the early Christian who survived the lions.

Of course, abortion, in its turn, was a classical curb against excesses of the romantic spirit. Embryos extinguished by abortion were more likely to be the product of extraordinary fucks than the legal infant who saw the first light in a hospital — all too often embryos who were to be aborted had been conceived in the first place by too many good things happening not to conceive them. Since it is hard to imagine an optimistic view of human nature which would not assume that those who are born out of apocalyptic fucks are more likely to be rich in potential than those conceived from a dribble, abortion is tragic. (In clear opposition, it is exactly the logical premise of the technological society that artificial insemination is the perfect equal of any great fuck, so much so that readers can recognize themselves as advocates of a technological society if they believe such a proposition.)

Seen by this perspective, there was the real possibility then that abortion killed off more than an average proportion of superb babies: if so, advocates of the Right To Live had a powerful argument. Aquarius, nonetheless, would remain in favor of abortion; he thought the argument had only been raised to a higher level. For if at its most tragic, abortion is the decision to kill the memory of an extraordinary night, and so can be cruel and unendurable, close on occasion to creating insanity in the woman, still abortion is the objective correlative of sanity. Even in the abysmal condition of much love lost, it always speaks, it says: "My nature is divided between the maximum of my romantic moments and the minimum of my daily self-calculation, too divided to permit this child to live. Finally I prefer to be loyal to my working habits rather than to the recollection of magic." Abortion is therefore an act of self-recognition (which is a step to sanity) even as the decision not to have an abortion is another kind of sanity which states, "I am committed to the best moments I have known and take my truth from that." (Which is why the pill like all other technological concepts is an insulation against sanity for it inhibits the possibility of those confrontations which might reveal a woman to herself.)

The real argument to be presented then to advocates of the Right To Live is that if a woman had the ability to begin an extraordinary conception, she had also the right to terminate it. Who could be certain that a more virulent pollution was not given to existence every time a child was born with remarkable potential and failed to fulfill it than when a soul of such potential was murdered in the womb? Nobody had a deeper sense of what could be provided for a future child than the woman who carried it. If she knew she was not ready to devote herself to such a creation, then why not assume she was in her right to deny the life? For who could ever calculate the violation left on life, or the extinction of karma, which resided in the loveless development of souls who had been conceived in love? So he thought abortion of even the most apocalyptic fuck was still the measure of a woman's right. Therefore, when it came to the question of abortion for conceptions which had never been wanted (creations emerging out of such resolute mediocrity of impulse as to shatter every romantic idea that conception was a serious product of human state), well then Aquarius could find no argument against abortion at all, not when the world was in danger of being overpopulated with a new wad who promised to be as uninteresting as the mass architecture which would house them, no, better to let abortion have its legal status and become still another social hypocrisy that it was not murder even if, indeed, it was.

The women of the liberation had come up, however, with an idea which went further than his own, and he admired it. Abortion legislation would of course be equal to giving women a new right to control what went on within their bodies. The extension of that principle was wondrous! It might give patients the right to die in peace when doctors were determined to extend, stupefy and therefore shift their last meditations before death. It might even open the idea that soldiers had first rights over their own bodies and need not go out on patrol if in their opinion there was an unreasonable or foolish chance that they might die. That was equivalent to saying soldiers could demand the right to military actions in which their death would not be in vain, an altogether stimulating idea, for in nations of one hundred million men would there then be ten thousand willing to die in an army? What a fine inhibition upon the power of mammoth countries to wage mammoth war if this became a principle of the world, which of course it would (just so soon as the Age of Aquarius arrived).

So one did not quit the thought in a hurry.

Still, this was no Age of Aquarius, but the summer of 1972, and the McGovern forces, thinking of the choleric priapism of the wad forced to contemplate all those vaginas open to abortion, had an understandable caution before the language of the plank. Mild almost to the point of being inoffensive — "In matters relating to human reproduction each person's right to privacy, freedom of choice, and individual conscience should be fully respected, consistent with relevant Supreme Court decisions," the plank would still suggest that the right to abortion was part of a proper election campaign. So McGovern's platform man, Ted van Dyk, sent out word to McGovern delegates that if they felt "strongly," they "should feel free to vote accordingly." The vote for the platform change on abortion would be free. Of course, not entirely. There were 250 whips on the floor for McGovern, each with a half-dozen delegates to contact, and some of the whips were employed to discover those delegates who would switch their vote "in an emergency" or abstain. Something like an emergency may have developed, for Rick Stearns was reported later to say, "If we hadn't sent out our word, the abortion plank would have passed." It failed by a vote of 1,569.80 to 1,103.37, and so a switch of 250 votes, or less than one McGovern delegate in six, would have been enough to pass it. The women were furious. First South Carolina, now abortion. Of course, there is always the parochial masochism of politics which is ready to welcome betrayal for the pleasure of the bitterness it provides. Some people are in politics to find a focus for all their latent bile, and nothing generates bile like betrayal. So the women were acting like women — in a fight with the husband: they were now superior to male arguments of priority and proportion. McGovern would be nominated the next day — they were not so furious as to interfere with that — but in the weeks to come when the Eagleton affair would weigh down an election special which was perhaps doomed never to ride and hardly to fly, Aquarius would think more than once of the unvoiced curses of OMEN POWER.

15

Wednesday, he gets to see Shirley Chisholm. She has doubled the
glory of her campaign overnight by telling the Black Caucus, "I'm the
only one among you who has the balls to run for President," her barb
so perfectly splitting the shaft of the last arrow she has fired into their
ranks (by accusing some of the delegates of being bought) that the
Black Caucus gives her a standing ovation. Now in her room on the
twentieth floor of the Deauville (which is guarded by a young woman in
the Secret Service, blonde and attractive) Shirley, who weighs 98
pounds, is ordering a meal, soup and meat and spaghetti and a Key
lime pie (gift of Rocky Pomerance) for dessert. It is enough to put
weight on a 200-pound man. "Oh, I burn it all off," she says. And she
would. She moves as quickly as a sparrow when she speaks and her
arguments pile out nonstop — she is as related to politics as the air is to
the wind, and she is soaring on a zephyr now: after coming to the
convention with 25.4 delegates, no more, it is obvious she is going to
gain ground. And each time Mr. Chisholm, a man whose features and
build are as round and reserved and benign as Shirley's are pert and to
the point, comes into the room, it is to tell her she is wanted again on
the phone. Shirley is having dreams as delegates keep coming to her. It
is Wednesday afternoon and she says, "McGovern is in more trouble
than he realizes. We're going to give him a surprise tonight," but it is
not as if she believes she will stop McGovern, more as if her arguments
on any subject must come from a positive base. So now, in response to a
question, she calls McGovern a decent man and says she will work for
him, "but you know he made a real error in underestimating the innocence of those gay liberationists. He should have told them he would let
them down." She nods her head. "He just assumed they'd understand
he was running for President and couldn't afford them. But they're
new to politics. Now, they're mad, and they're all flocking to me." A
white delegate obviously gives her just as much joy as a Black delegate.
"You see, I was salty with them from the start, so they trust me now. I
started talking to them about bank presidents who are homo and hide
it, and I said, 'Don't pretend you speak for your whole group, or that
homosexuals are some kind of an elite. Half your people aren't with

you, don't even want to be identified as part of your constituency.' I let them have it straight and they like it. Same with the Black delegates when I lay it on them. I don't mind getting their vote bought. They're poor people, and poor people always need the money. I just say to them, 'Take the money and run — don't let them fool you. Use them, don't let them use you,' " and when the interview is up, a film crew is moving in, and she is finishing her meal and getting ready to meet some more delegates. In her office, Helen Butler her secretary has put up a sign which is perhaps designed more for the white girls than the Black — "We left our maid in Washington, so everybody has to clean up."

16

We can pass easily over Wednesday night when McGovern was nominated. Senator Ribicoff who put him up in Chicago four years ago was here to do it again, but the occasion was quieter. No need on this night for Ribicoff to speak of "gestapo tactics on the streets of Chicago," nor was Mayor Daley there to shout "Fuck you" across the floor. The demonstration while vigorous was brief, it had been coordinated to be brief — something like a total of half an hour for nominating speech, seconding speeches, and demonstration was allotted to each candidate, and Jackson, Chisholm, Wallace, Terry Sanford of North Carolina, McGovern and Mills had all to be nominated. So the demonstrations were cut. It was a bow to the Media; for years the newspapers and TV had been mocking the sight of red-faced heavy-paunched Democrats cavorting drunkenly in the aisles as they blew their noisemakers, and McGovern with his taste for restraint doubtless agreed with such a verdict. But no convention had ever seemed more like an endless litigation before a worn-out jury of thousands, no convention had ever been more in need of the primeval hysteria of an all-out demonstration which might remind the delegates of the fires which resided beneath. A convention had always been a court of political process, but it had also been a circus — which had been part of its value — a fair measure of the American desire to move back and forth between vulgarity and justice. But the old-fashioned demonstration was too hot a phenomenon for the cool shades of TV. That depended upon a shift of narrative line controlled as carefully as the rising of yeast. TV could not bear shifts in tone which were too abrupt. No more could it tolerate a series of images which progressed to no development. Besides a scream-ing caterwauling demonstration for the candidate ruined any illusion that the event had entered the living room of the viewer; demon-strations obviously took place in somebody else's house and you were alone with the set. Media executives didn't work at giving a careful wipe to the bottom of every last viewer in TV land in order to remind them that watching TV was an essentially unsatisfactory act. So there was no brassy, wild, nor overextended demonstration. A pity. Who knows how many points the Democrats dropped to the wad by offering no circus?

Later, there was a victory party at the Doral where McGovern kids wandered happily about. The final count had been 1,864.95 for McGovern, and Frank Mankiewicz smiled happily on TV when he mentioned the sum, for it was possible he came as close as anyone at the convention to knowing how each vote was gotten. For the rest, Wallace had received 377.5, Jackson — in a fever of activity once Humphrey and Muskie dropped out — had 486.68, Chisholm 101.45, Sanford 74.5, Mills 32.8, and other votes were scattered for names not placed in nomination: McCarthy, Muskie, Humphrey, Kennedy, Hayes and Mondale. There was no move to make the nomination unanimous. Indeed it would have failed. And the streets were quiet on the way back. The helicopters had gone home, as well as the solicitors on the street. Gone were the Jesus freaks with their broken teeth, a lightning zigzag of sharp and broken teeth and lightning in their eye, but then they looked like an improbable mix of rednecks and Zippies. They sang out to every delegate "You're here to raise hell, I'm here to raise heaven." They sang on street corners. "Who does Wallace need? Jesus," they replied. "J.E.S.U.S." "Who does Humphrey need? Jesus," they replied and went by rote through each of the candidates. "What do the Democrats need? Jesus," they sang. "What do the Republicans need? Jesus! J.E.S.U.S. Go, go, go," they cheered, and cops waiting through the quiet hours while the convention inched its way into his-tory were playing card games for small stakes on the grass behind the wire fence in the cool of a banyan tree. A kid in a denim jacket carried an anti-McGovern placard. Earlier that day a crowd of several hundred had invaded the lobby of the Doral to protest a remark McGovern had made the night before that he planned to keep "military capability — in Thailand and on the seas," and the candidate had taken the danger-ous step of coming to the lobby to talk to them and say, "I'm not shifting my position on any of the fundamental stands I've taken in this campaign." Maybe the placard had been painted earlier, and now wobbled in the languid midnight air as a remnant of the afternoon action: MCGOVERN SUCKS. A Black man in a dark suit carried the morose sign DON'T VOTE '72.

Back at the Doral, however, was every incongruous mix of the McGovern kids, all there, Phi Beta Kappas with clean faces and clean horn-rimmed glasses, their presence to offer clear statement of a physiology which had little taste for liquor and much taste for good marks, as well as a horde of suburban youth with long hair and the sense of boredom of waiting on still another evening for some tribal Left wind to touch the hair of their nostrils. Out on the driveway of the Doral were kids wearing no more than white canvas shorts and copper bracelets on their biceps, their bare feet padding the asphalt to a beat which came to them out of Ravi Shankar by way of stereos in Scarsdale, and the mystery of America floated up upon Aquarius still once again. For the social phenomena of the country were as clear as the expressions on groups of faces, yet never a period of four years elapsed in which you saw the same expressions again. America kept shifting, growing more wild even as it grew programmed, more unbalanced as it became stable, the blood of the heart beating with thoughts of the frontier even as the suburbs choked the ponds and killed the trout, and now this latest phenomenon of the technological young and the drug-steeped young both out equally for McGovern, man of principle, clear-headed and altogether separate in mind and style from any vocation for drugs. It was enough to begin to brood on the nature of those reforms the Democrats had put into their party, new pockets for an old suit, but the pockets had become the cloth of the suit, and the young were wearing it. There was humor at the thought of those party bosses who had first agreed to cut the pockets in the comfortable cynicism that it would be an easy way to store the demands of minorities in the party, a sophisticated species of tokenism whose losses could be absorbed by the old pols in state-house committees. After the debacle of Chicago, it was also seen as a way of putting the party together. No old pol had seen reform as the instrument which would yet take his power away, nobody had been prepared for the possibility of a man laboring for years to set up a code of rules which would work to the benefit of his own candidacy. Nor had any old pol come close to the real meaning of the radicalization of the suburban middle classes (who were finally the parents of these children at the Doral). The country club gentry of ten thousand

357

suburbs (cognoscenti of the golf course, the paddock and the beauties of the jury-rigged spinnaker — Republican, of course, to the bone) had been replaced, or was it swarmed over, by millions of families newly prosperous, newly endowed with educations, specializations and professions, and absolutely alienated — or by their own view blissfully delivered — from the old inch-along eat-your-gut game of social advancement in country living under the inspection of one's betters. There were simply not enough betters left to go around. Nor was there anything left to respect. The war in Vietnam had done much to take away one's faith that lawn tennis, proper posting, and a nose for the shift of wind had any value in the training of leaders when the most powerful nation in the history of the world had squandered its moral substance in a war of massive bombardments, near to meaningless, a wholly cancerous war of the technological age. (Of course it is possible that the cancer cell, if possessed of a voice, would argue that it is trying to redesign a way out of the insoluble contradictions of the body.) But then if the Devil was devoted to destroying all belief in conservative values among the intelligent and prosperous, he could not have picked a finer instrument to his purpose than the war in Vietnam. If one continued to ask why America still remained in Vietnam, the final remark History might make was what exceptional power could be possessed by such a small Far Eastern land that it might preside over the slaughter of America's belief in itself, preside over it indeed to such a degree that our climate was finally prepared for peace with China and Russia, an event equal to admitting that America no longer saw itself as a hero facing two villains on a field of Colossi, but rather was ready to look upon itself as still one more corrupt and tarnished protagonist now as much in need of coexistence as any of the new-found friends. Small surprise if the newly prosperous liberals of the suburb welcomed the idea that all principles of the Establishment — God, nation, family, marriage, patriotism, and the distinction of the sexes — were wrong or nonexistent: the social contract, far from being a mystical union between God and man, was a pottage of curds whose lumps were best dissolved by disbelief. Liberal with their money, and liberal to every idea which was anathema to the Establishment: women's liberation, welfare rights, minority rights, tax reform (it was their pride, their delight, and their levitation from guilt that McGovern's tax reform would hit them hardest), they were also devoted to every right and liberty which would make humans more equal in soul and body. Of course, the center of their aesthetic was the androgynous. A wonder that McGovern was their candidate! But a small wonder so soon as the law of political sex appeal is invoked, for if there was a man in America who was more of a Wasp than Richard Nixon did it not have to be George McGovern? A joy then that the minister was ready to join the swingers! And pick up the children of suburbia as well, those children who lived in a far advancement of the ideological confidence of their parents, for the children were rid completely of the idea that one's personal development might still be measured by the ways one could perform in relation to some code handed over by the cultural lights and sneaky vested needs of the prosperous community, no, one was a child of light, and the enlightenment was new — the sanction to act came from within the body. Did streamings of energy from the body reach out to that horizon where one could join the world stream of new consciousness stirring? — then one was part of a new historical process which no one could comprehend whose body was not part of the stream. If drugs were the inner circle of the new world family and acid rock the second circle, sex the third, well politics was always on the outside circle of them all, a condition of valence with loose electrons which could be picked up or shed at amazing speed. So the suburban young would plunge into politics until the disillusionment of events would strip all outside electrons. Then they wandered, inert, passing though fluids of consciousness, waiting for the hypodermics of social action to inject a few electrons they could spend again. Be certain they were a curious force for old pols to comprehend! One could never know in which given season they would exhibit the dedication of the damned or seal themselves back to apathy again — although rare was the spring of a year for Presidential election which would not act as catalyst.

This year the suburban young had come out for McGovern, come out in all the muted arrogance of their world confidence that there on the other side of the world, unknown faces were closer to them than the compromised tissues of squalor in the faces of the old pols. And if with their much discussed tribal sense, they made a good army of volunteers, it was not surprising. Their egos were tribal. So their narcissism was for the group — therefore they could for a period immerse themselves in the absolute lack of vanity which routine political work will demand. And were joined to a cadre of hard workers on the left of the Democratic Party, a corps of schoolteachers and hard-working professionals, who together with the socially-minded, the community-minded, and the decent-minded, outraged by Vietnam, helped

359

McGovern to do well in the early primaries. After them came the money, the glory, the political technology, and the winning of the nomination at last. Now kids with long sunburned hair and bronzed bodies, wearing copper bangles and spaced-out heavy eyes, sat nodding on the steps of the Doral, kin across all the stages from Flamingo Park to the delegates to the hard-working Phi Beta cadres, holding in common a species of belief in the man, McGovern, even if they could hardly comprehend the gulf between the mindlessness of the Mind which might have brought them here, and the outraged motors overhead of helicopters looking for some wildman or freak or assassin upon whom the helicopter could charge with a beating of blades and a reduction of pressure in the great gorged military-American industrial choleric and McGovern-suffocated great American hard-fucking motorheart. Around the pool forty or fifty kids were sitting quietly on benches, only two were in the water, and off to the side a boy was playing a violin. Where was the bourbon and broads of yesteryear? Yes, every sense of power in the Democratic Party had shifted. History had become a crystal ball whose image shivered so erratically one had to wonder if a TV set was transmitting the image or the underworld of crystal balls was in convulsion.

17

On Thursday afternoon, with McGovern nominated, and only the last night of the convention still to be enacted, a final press conference was scheduled at the Sheraton–Four Ambassadors for George Wallace. Yet when the Press arrived, the Governor did not appear. At his Sheraton headquarters there were always two opposed sets of reports on his physical condition. Some officials would speak of his splendid progress, of the hours he spent in calisthenics, his prowess with a medicine ball, the development of the muscles in his arms, his zest to get well, and his unbelievable stamina in talking to visiting delegates — other officials were always taking one aside with a haunted look in their eye (as if no one could describe the scenes of pain and torture they had just witnessed) to say that the Governor had to call off all meetings because he was feeling poorly.

In any case, since this was the last opportunity to see Wallace in public, the Press was furious, and a long delay in waiting for his Press Secretary, Billy Joe Camp, and his National Campaign Director, Charles Snider, helped nothing. When they finally appeared, Snider read a Wallace statement which Aquarius reconstructed from his notes. "We came to the Democratic National Convention to carry the message of the people. We would have hoped they would accept this message from the average citizen across the country. They did not. Now we will see the results of this convention's thinking in November. We know what we have done in Miami has been good for America."

"Does this mean the Governor is starting a third party?" came the question.

"It means what it says," said Snider. He was short and very well built with blond hair and the confident close-cropped features of a man who has made his money early in construction. But Snider being called away for a few minutes, the Press Secretary, Billy Joe Camp, was left alone at the podium, and he had a gentle manner, and the unhappy look of a Ph.D. candidate who is in danger of flunking his orals. Since the drama of the arrival had ground down steadily all week, Wallace's appearance at the convention muted and far from climactic, the majority of the delegates receiving him with all the enthusiasm of marble walls, his changes in the platform rejected, and his own politicking with the delegations kept carefully away from the Press, there had been less and less to report. Wallace's absence today was the final rebuke to the Media. So they took it out on Billy Joe Camp, who stood there in his dark brown suit and brown-and-white tie, stood there with his soft and cherubic mouth hanging loose beneath his dark hair and dark horn-rimmed glasses (which looked to keep sliding down his small soft nose) and tried to field every impossible question with Southern courtesy. The questions were impossible because he had no answers to give. He did not know what the Governor thought about this. He certainly did not know what the Governor thought about that. No, the Governor had said nothing to him, no, he could not satisfy the last question, no, he was sorry he had no information on this particular topic. After much phumphering and several long silences which he could only end by declining to answer once again, a newspaperman flicked a whip. "Billy Joe, don't you ever get the feeling that you're locked out of information?"

Snider came back to help him. Snider stood in front of the podium with his legs apart, as if at parade rest, weight on the balls of his feet.

Wearing a pale cream suit, a yellow shirt, and a well-chosen light-blue-and-light-brown figured tie, he suggested the aplomb of a Marine who is wearing the world's best clothes.

"Is there going to be a third party?"

"The statement will have to come from the Governor."

"Will Wallace talk to McGovern?"

"If Senator McGovern calls Governor Wallace before we leave, I know the Governor will be polite to him because the Senator now holds a position the Governor respects as nominated candidate of the Democratic Party which the Governor respects very much."

"But do you, Charles Snider, think McGovern is a loser?"

"I, personally, do."

"Does the Governor?"

"I haven't gotten the Governor's thoughts on it."

"Will he start a third party?"

"I don't know."

"Will you advise him to?"

Snider looked back in scorn. "The Governor is the most astute politician on the face of the earth," he said in his Southern voice, "and I wouldn't presume to advise him on whether to start a third party."

"But yesterday didn't you make a statement that you wanted him to?"

"I made some remarks. A few may have been of that nature."

"Was the Governor displeased?"

"He wasn't too displeased, or I wouldn't be here right now. I don't have to go up to the twentieth floor to get the news if he don't like something. I get it right here on the third floor."

"So the Governor is thinking of a third party?"

"Now, look," said Snider, "I'm not going to answer any more questions on a third party. The Governor has more political intelligence in his little finger than I have in all of me. I wouldn't presume to speak for him. I'll just tell you this. If what happened in Maryland had not happened, and the Governor had been active through Oregon and California, I think you would have found a tremendous difference in the way we came to this convention and in the way we were received. And you all would have seen what the Governor is like in action, and there is no one who can compare to him, believe you me. He would have come in with all the power of all the people who believe in him which is a tremendous power because I believe that the Governor is the greatest messenger who has ever been on the face of this earth . . ."

"Including Jesus?" came a voice from the Press. The question was from a reporter with an aquiline nose and a beard like a Saracen.

Snider stopped as if he had just run into a pole. He bared his teeth in a good-boy grin. "I knew I could expect something like that from you and the fine magazine you work for," he said.

Hours later, catching him for a moment outside the convention, Aquarius asked if the reporter's question hadn't been legitimate. After all, Snider *had* said "the greatest messenger ever."

"Oh, I see what you mean," said Snider. "I should have said, 'the greatest political messenger.' " He shook his head. "Why," he added with shock, "I would never compare the Governor to Jesus. How can you? *Nobody* compares with Jesus."

18

There were arts to picking a Vice-President, and the first was the name. Your ticket became a company. Recognize that a man named Procter running for President would look for Gamble to go along. McGovern had the best of good monikers for a liberal since thoughts of the Conquering Celt had to be aroused in many an illiterate and reactionary head. At the least, could Mick Govern fail to give promise of Irish home rule? There was a percentage of voters (10 percent, 20, or more) who came to the secrecy of the election booth without a political thought in their head — they knew the name of the President and sometimes they knew the name of the man who ran against him. In the isolated terror of the booth, where voting was a religious act to inspire awe in the simple, God being closest to you when alone, the sound of the names on the ticket could be enough to catch your vote. The problem was a to find the name to go with McGovern. Kennedy would of course have been acceptable no matter how, Teddy Kennedy belonged to a higher order of powers than euphony or the symbol of a word, but he was not available. If it was McGovern's first act upon being nominated to receive his midnight call, it was the Senator from Massachusetts' first response to congratulate McGovern and then to refuse. "For very real personal reasons." Despite every warning, McGovern's staff had hoped in common with the candidate that the ticket would bring them together but McGovern — according to Jimmy Breslin — now

363

told his people that if he pushed Kennedy into the nomination and anything ever happened to Kennedy, he would be unable to live with himself. Faced with the loss of the best possibility, their choice was thereby reduced to Ribicoff, Eagleton, Mills, Leonard Woodcock of the UAW, Governor Lucey of Wisconsin, Mayor Kevin White of Boston, Gaylord Nelson of Wisconsin and Sarge Shriver. Plus a few others. One was Reubin Askew, a perfect name! Govern and Ask-You. However, the Governor of Florida had already said no — his ideology and McGovern's were too far apart. After a flurry with Ribicoff who also refused (out of the fine political sense, no doubt, that he had been invited to show McGovern's solidarity with the Jews but was expected to say no — McGovern and Ribicoff as a product would be reminiscent of ambulance chasers) there came the hard business of picking that Catholic, from a big city or an industrial state, who could best warm South Dakota's prairie vestments. The difficulty was that fewer people knew Eagleton, Mondale, Lucey, White or Shriver were Catholic than believed McGovern to be. So there was also talk of Woodcock of the UAW because he could help to offset the cess of old George Meany and bring the unions in. But McGovern and Woodcock was a name fit for a company which put out a special variety of Tabasco, manufactured a fine grade of bronze casket, or catered to the Queen's grounds with croquet equipment. McGovern and Lucey was worse. McGovern and Shriver had a poor sound — stationers, old pharmacists, something pinch-penny! — otherwise, why not have picked Shriver after Kennedy had refused?

Now, McGovern and Mills was a fine sound, management and manufacture well combined, an aura of industry and competence rose from the words, but the ideological gulf was still not navigable. On the other hand, McGovern and Gilligan were Irish whiskey, McGovern and Bayh were depressing (too many millions would not know how to pronounce Bayh, and when they did, nothing was gained but subliminal thoughts of farewell). There was McGovern and Nelson of course but the Senator from Wisconsin had a first name of Gaylord — help! There was talk of Frank Church as well. McGovern and Church would be the equal of Dr Pepper in the Bible Belt but could one sell it to the Jews? Besides, Church was no Catholic, alas. The list was reduced to Eagleton and White, and as between the two, White was in. Eagleton had connotations of the American eagle, a stern virtue, a modest plus. But the company of McGovern and Eagleton offered no particular ring — camping equipment! George and Tom might be fine, but both family names ended in *n,* a nugatory sound, reminiscent in the lower depths of the collective unconscious of the wad as no-no. It was down to Kevin White, Mayor of Boston, a Catholic, a jewel of a ticket to mollify the most ignorant of the Wallace voters, Govern in a White way, yessir. If you were close to Black aims in your program, then it was wisdom to choose a man named White. But calls to the Massachusetts delegation were reputed to close that choice. They threatened to revolt on the floor. Kevin White was a fine Mayor of Boston, which is to say, a Boston pol and in politics up to his neck and sheepish with the memories of a deal or two, and ready by repute to stand up and shake a hand when told to, a superb Mayor of Boston but the thought of him as President — White was the size of a mayor. The choice moved back to Eagleton who was conceivably the size of a Senator, and there were warm stories that night on TV how Eagleton had become so nervous waiting that he drank many a gin and tonic and wore two different shoes. Indeed his first appearance on TV was excessively modest — a white damp and vastly perspired face swam into focus. "Sparrow Who?" said a reporter staring at the set. But first impressions shifted. Eagleton had a nervous running humor which was sweet-tempered, then agreeable: he borrowed from the style of Carson and Cavett — sparks of wit were struck from the gait of an ongoing patter. *The New York Times* would later give him the Quotation of the Day, "Senator McGovern called me, and he said, 'This is George McGovern' — and I recognized the voice. And he said, 'Tom, I'd like you to be my running mate,' and I paused and it sounded like four seconds, and I said, 'Well, George, before you change your mind, I accept.' "

He was to do even better before the night was out. His family was seen in their box at the convention and his son who was ten or eleven had all the charm of the bright and assured, and spoke particularly well out of a delicate face. Later, Eagleton would give his speech of acceptance, and another side would show — he was a good and polished speaker, with considerably more power at the podium than in the sweat of interviews, something practiced and successful was now in his voice. That, however, did not take place until five hours later. It was two in the morning when Eagleton was nominated, and the run of bad luck for McGovern, which had begun with California in June, continued still. For the effort to win back the 151 delegates had exhausted the resources of the staff every day before the convention and through the first night, created the ill repute of the lost South Carolina challenge and the insufficiency of time to deal with Daley and Singer. Then maneuvering over the platform used up their attention and energy on the second night. By the time the nomination was won, McGovern's staff needed sleep. Not until Thursday had there been time to pick the Vice-President. Then — given the mediocrity of the choices — it took until close to four in the afternoon. So there was no opportunity to ask for an afternoon session. The best television hours of the last night were consumed nominating a number of candidates who had no chance. McGovern, ready for the occasion of his acceptance with a superb speech, was able to give it at three in the morning. America had gone to sleep. Nobody could ever calculate if the votes he might have gained that night would tally in the millions.

As the small compensation, there was some action. Given a political convention's definition of open — which is to say cracked so wide as a slit — there was *open* action. Many of the delegates' resentments broke open. Too few had heard of Eagleton, and he was a Muskie man. There was annoyance that McGovern was engaging in the old style of politics. Besides, the women, balked by failure to get the plank for abortion, were in no mood not to nominate a female, and gave their support to Sissy Farenthold after Shirley Chisholm, out of the niceties of political decorum, refused. Shirley might have done very well, but she was wise in the political values of a single clear impression; her candidacy had been a sentimental success. A second effort following immediately on the first would have to be exceptionally successful to improve the elegance of her status. So Farenthold, who had run well but unsuccessfully for Governor against Dolph Briscoe in the Texas primary, became the woman to enter the list. Against her, among others, was Stanley Arnold, the businessman who campaigned with full-face photographs of himself in horn-rimmed glasses decorating all the hotel lobbies, a comic candidate despite himself, and Endicott "Chub" Peabody who had traveled through thirty-seven states looking for delegates and talking of the need for a Vice-President who would be selected by the people and thereby armed with a mandate from the people. He had worked hard, harder than many a Presidential candiate, but had the foul fortune to be immortalized by the old Kennedy court jester Dick Tuck who declared that Chub was the only man who had four towns named for him in Massachusetts: Endicott, Peabody, Marblehead and Athol.

Then there was Mike Gravel who provided considerable excitement in the first hours of the evening, the young Senator from Alaska, good-looking enough to have played leads in B films (if the Casting Director could decide whether to cast him as hero or villain). Gravel was regarded as something of a lone gun, a wild man from the West ever since he had read portions of the Pentagon Papers (which were Classified) to his Subcommittee on Public Buildings and Grounds. It had been a direct violation of the code of the Senate which looked upon Classified — that is, secret — documents as sacramental objects. Perhaps it was the thought of endless small punishments, or some large ones like censure that weakened his composure, but as Gravel read the following lines to television cameras in the Subcommittee room: "The story is a terrible one. It is replete with duplicity, connivance against the public. People, human beings, are being killed as I speak to you. Arms are being severed; metal is crashing through human bodies" he began — to his absolute horror — to weep. He had, he said afterward, passed through the nearest experience he had known of a vision, for as he spoke it was as if those bodies he described in Vietnam were milling about him; the flesh being rent was real; before his eyes, severed arms flew across the line of sight. He was overcome.

In the Senate they lauded him for courage, he was scalded for exhibitionism; the Department of Justice worked to convene a federal grand jury to investigate any possible violation of federal statutes; since the case involved the separation of powers between executive and legislative branches, it had already gone to the Supreme Court.

This proved no check to Gravel. He had already known that sensation of political transcendence which when it comes to senators leaves them ready to run for the highest office; invited to the White House soon after election to hear Nixon discuss the ABM, "it just dawned on me that he didn't know any more about it than I did." Even to politicians who are bold, there is still an instant when they let go of the modesty that men who run the world are possessed of qualities superior to their own. Gravel was bold. Winter nights in Alaska gave a man daring: even to visit a friend who lived ten miles away took daring. For if your motor stalled in the middle of the trip, you were alone on an empty road, the cold was down to fifty below, and you were therefore soon dead if the motor didn't start.

Gravel ran. Like Peabody, he cut across the principle that the choice of a Vice-President was an occasion for the nominee to exercise his art and add those strengths which would balance the ticket, unify the party, and ideally give some sense of excitement to the years ahead, a principle, obviously, which believed in the lore of the politician, subscribed to his craft, and honored his ability to live between privilege and justice, honesty and corruption, idealism and an adroit employment of the cynical — it was finally a view to suggest that politicians should not be morally better than other men so much as more skillful. Perhaps it was a sound principle. One could begin to measure its importance to the electorate by the disfavor McGovern's choice would yet bring upon him when it became evident he had exercised no more art than the use of crude rule of thumb.

Gravel, of course, was working on the opposed notion that a Vice-President, selected separately from the President, should serve in effect as an Ombudsman. "A person of the caliber of George McGovern would realize," Gravel remarked, "that having an in-house adversary within the executive would be an asset. Not a vicious adversary. The Vice-President should be pushing for the same programs and backing up the President. But I think he could back up the President much better as an independent agent than as a vassal."

An interesting idea. Its time, of course, had not quite come. The McGovern staff, now running the convention after nomination of their man the night before, were ready for all practical purposes to treat Farenthold, Arnold, Peabody and Gravel as, precisely, vicious adversaries. How account for the phenomenon which occurs in every political campaign once victory is in? The staff immediately discloses its secret passion is to get a good glove for the iron hand. No politician was kinder or more decent than McGovern — so said all. Who could say the same of his staff? Not Gravel. On Thursday night when the vice-presidential candidates tried to raise the issue of an open convention for the nomination, their representatives could not get recognized. For to do so, they had first to phone the podium and describe their purpose. The voice of the podium replied that their motion was out of order, it could not be considered when it failed to be relevant to the business at hand. But that, they protested, was exactly the issue on which they wanted the convention to vote — whether to suspend the rules. No, replied the podium, such a motion was at the discretion of the Chairman. Where was the Chairman? He was not available to come to the phone.

In the old days, a maverick could grab a microphone and shout loud enough to get the floor. Now, the power supply for all microphones was controlled by the podium. So were passes to the floor. Eagleton's operatives had easy access, the other candidates had next to none. Gravel's workers sat outside the hall in their trailer, and were obliged to communicate by phone. Friendly delegates called in to report an anti-

Gravel movement. Why, was it asked, had Gravel voted for the ABM, Carswell, and the Alaska pipeline? He hadn't, cried his workers on the trailer phone. Pass the word — he voted against ABM! and Carswell! and the pipeline never came up for a vote at all!

A political tactic can now be absorbed: in a fluid situation, waging a quick war for delegates, it is obviously essential to have crack troops on the floor to serve up as many lies about your opponents as they are spreading of you. Access to the floor is access to that sea of prevarication where the nomination may be launched. Gravel, now aware that in an unsuccessful floor fight a man had nothing to lose but his anonymity, succeeded in the high maneuver of reaching the podium to speak for himself. His name scheduled to be put in nomination by Bettye Fahrenkamp, Democratic National Committee-woman from Alaska, the Committee-woman pretended to be faint with excitement at the magnitude of her speech. So Gravel came along to give support. Medical emergencies being always the best franchise to cross borders, they let Gravel approach the base of the podium, where, unseen by the floor, he might smile at her. But the lady's nominating speech was short. "The best way for you to judge," said Bettye Fahrenkamp, "the next Vice-President of the United States is not for me to tell you about him, but for you to hear and judge for yourself. My fellow delegates: Senator Mike Gravel."

He stood up to thank her, advanced to the podium, began to speak, and was stopped by the Co-Chairman, Yvonne Braithwaite Burke, a young Black woman who was alternating with O'Brien. For hours she had delighted the convention with her wit, her speed, and her vivacity. She had been offering an unmistakable zap to parliamentary life. Now she was annoyed. The cool of the chair had been invaded.

Burke: Thanks a lot. Sorry. We just can't do it.

Gravel: You're telling me I can't talk to the delegates of this convention on behalf of my candidacy?

Burke: I'm telling you that I'm here to follow the rules and the rules say you can't talk.

She was still saucy and confident. But when he did not step down, her charm was withdrawn. In the instant, something palpable as stone came to her skin. She was a tough lady. Her eyes were empty of expression. Clearly they said, "Kidding is kidding, but get your ass off my pillow!"

Gravel: And I'm — I'm here to correct you on the rules. The rules say — the rules say very precisely that the person who seconds does not

369

have to be a delegate. And I am therefore entitled to speak to these people.

Burke: Okay.

"You're making me look," said her expression, "like I don't know how to deal with a drunk. You have now gone and asked for it good." But she looked backstage for a legal interpretation. A general uproar had begun to rise from the floor.

Gravel: Is this an open convention? *(Cheers from the floor.)* If there is a parliamentarian let him come forward. . . . I'll be happy to hold my peace until we can get a ruling from the leadership of this convention.

Now, however, Yvonne Braithwaite Burke had gotten her signal from the rear. "Go right ahead," she said, and gave him the podium with a sidelong look, as if she had underestimated him.

He gave his speech. It was a good speech and might have been a better one. But he was perspiring from the hazards of first reaching the podium, then drilling into the formidable displeasure of Yvonne Burke's eyes. Now, as though lightly sandbagged across the kidneys, jostled just a hint in the high corner of the testes, Gravel went on with his plea to the convention:

"Select a person for the Vice-Presidency who is your choice, not a person who's been dictated to you. Pay no mind to the last-minute smears — whether against me or anybody else.

"The spirit of reform which has brought us all together will fade, this spirit will be compromised if you give in to a selection other than one of free and open choice.

"The Vice-Presidency belongs to the people of the United States."

There were cheers and boos.

"A little over a year ago, I released to the American people the Pentagon Papers." Cheers and applause. "What I did — was to give information to you, the American people, so that you could be more qualified in the exercise of your franchise.

"How can you get involved in government if you don't know what your government is doing?

"Let me paraphrase to you a dialogue between Senator Robert Dole, the head of the Republican Party, and myself. Senator Dole said when I was attempting to introduce the Kissinger Papers — said, 'Senator Gravel, you're going to have to live with what you've done.' I answered back angrily: 'Senator Dole, I'm proud of what I've done. You're going to have to live with what you have not done.' "

His point was powerful as he declared, "Secrecy is the reason we're in

Vietnam today committing genocide," but some of the juice was undeniably gone. He was, comparable to half the delegates on the floor,
still a romantic — he had grown up in the belief that a great speech
carried fortifications before it. So had Gary Cooper spoken in *Mr. Deeds
Comes to Town* and James Stewart in *Mr. Smith Goes to Washington*. But in
politics even a great speech had to raise such a wave as to wash over the
mountain, and Gravel could feel the defeat of such a possibility even as
he came to the peroration.

"George McGovern had a magic that swept this country in the spring
of this year. George McGovern can be the next President of the United
States — not by doing less of what was done in the spring, but by doing
more of what was done in the spring with George McGovern, and I
hope myself on the ticket.

"I thank you for your consideration and hope that you'll consider my
candidacy."

When he was done, well-wishers mobbed him as he descended from
the podium. The floor of the convention was alive. But it would never
last. Hours of nomination of other candidates were to follow, and the
rains of prevarication would muddy his ground. Gravel's troops, bereft
of floor passes, would molder in their trailer. No act on earth was
necessarily more difficult than to take a convention by storm. Gene
McCarthy had tried when he nominated Adlai Stevenson in 1960, and
it was the greatest nominating speech in memory; the demonstration
which followed gave promise it would never cease, and didn't for sixty
minutes. Hours later, passions ground down to common meal, Jack
Kennedy was nominated without trouble. Tonight, with just as powerful a machine, so would Eagleton get his required total on the first
ballot and Gravel finish back of Farenthold, and the incident be near to
forgotten in the agreeable force of Eagleton's speech, and the cornucopia of cheers for Teddy Kennedy when he said, "There is a new wind
rising over the land. In it can be heard many things, promises, anguish,
hopes for the future, echoes of the past, and our most cherished
prayer. 'America, America, God shed His grace on thee.' " Then came
George McGovern, speaking with animation to each roll of cheers,
calling for an entrance of democracy into the secret councils behind the
closed doors. "I want those doors opened and that war closed." Cheers
came again to him. "Let me inside the government and I will tell you
what is going on." They ended in the signs and tokens of unity, Humphrey, Muskie, Jackson, Chisholm and Sanford all holding hands with
the nominee. The mood was warm. The convention had run before

winds and beat through waves. Now they were done and the ship would be put to bed. Up came the high medieval note of the hands marching off to the strains of "Onward, Christian Soldiers."

Weeks later, Gravel would say with a grin, "The pioneering consumes you. The next guy walks on what you build."

19

Having come down now to the final minutes of the convention week with the speeches done, and the huge hall closed, the convention's aisles finally empty as if the echo of the Chairman asking the delegates and Press to clear the floor had finally taken ghostly effect, having returned down Collins Avenue in the early morning for the last time, and having come in the final hour before dawn to the entrance of the Doral where hordes of the young, half-dressed in the heats of a late Southern night, again gave an exotic sense of disarray while they lounged on the steps of the hotel (as if one were transported beyond Bombay to some future where Americans to come would sit half-naked in Lotus position before the gates of the American palaces), and having ascended the elevator and been brought and issued by the good will of Shirley MacLaine into the room of a private party in some roof garden of the Doral where McGovern was accepting the congratulations of some of the people of means who had helped to finance his campaign, Aquarius was able to take up position at last before the nominee and live in the charisma (or lack of it) his presence might convey. If there was all the warmth of a quiet and winning mood, and the sense of a vast relaxation as McGovern chatted for a few words with first a friend and then a sponsor, his tall body planted on legs which must have felt like posts of concrete after these two long years of campaigning, and these tense days of dealing and refusing to deal in Miami, the wealth of fatigue which came off McGovern now was happy and compassionate as the last rose-colored velvets of evening before the night was in, and it occurred to Aquarius that if he had stood next to many politicians over the years, he had not ever before had such a splendid sense that he was standing near a man who had a heart which could conceivably be full of love — something awfully nice came off McGovern — and that was an extraordinary gift for a politician to give. It clearly returned Aquarius to the events of the convention and restored a knowledge of why these days had been so agreeable and so boring, and why the faces of the delegates massed in ranks on the floor had been like no faces any political observer had ever seen before, not in a convention hall, for they were in majority the faces of men and women who had come to have a good and serious time, like the faces of a crowd who have gone to the most important basketball game of the year in their home state, and so felt honored to have the ticket of admission, and happy, and there to squeeze the goodness in their will and determination out across the air and into the bodies of their players — a sense of *innocence* lived in more than half these faces as if they had yet to learn of the deaths within compromise and calculation. One had to be partial to a man whose delegates had the fair and average and open faces of an army of citizenry, as opposed to an army of the pols, and Aquarius knew then why the convention was obliged to be boring. There was insufficient evil in the room. With all the evil he had seen, all the lies and deals and evasions and cracks of the open door, with the betrayals of planks and the voids of promises, still there had been so little of real evil in the room.

So one could know none of the fascination one found at other conventions, when a walk on the floor was a promenade through vales of malignity or a passage through corridors of vested bile, and a study of faces was equal to a study of American corporations and crime. There, in those old conventions, the posture of political fixes came out in the set of the hips when a deal was in, and the skill with which it was once possible to read the moves of a convention (because the faces of the leaders and the gargoyle heads of the minions had been as dead and carved and fixed and ornamented forever as the pieces in a set of chess), such skill was lost. There was now no leader to follow as he put a finger to his nose to tip the vote to the leader across the aisle. The spell of drama when an evil piece of political property was traded for a more or less equal piece of profitable position was also gone, all gone except for a delegation here and there, as old in appearance with their baffled old-pol stone-set faces as the portraits of another century, and of course one was ready to laugh as one walked down the aisle because the count was already in — there were more live faces than dead ones on the floor — so McGovern was in, simple as that, and how different a sensation and how less compelling than in the days of other conventions when it was one dead face against another, and which of the candidates for nomination was best equipped to enter the sinuosities of negotiation with evil, for evil was the law of politics and the provender of the floor.

Now there was a convention where delegates had come to work. How diffident they were at parties and how good at work — it was as if the animation of being at a party came to them on the floor — their politics was their pleasure, and the tide of those faces returning to him as he stood near McGovern now, there came to him as well the first strains of that simple epiphany which had eluded him through these days, and he realized it, and it was simple, but he thought it true. In America, the country was the religion. And all the religions of the land were fed from that first religion which was the country itself, and if the other religions were now full of mutation and staggering across deserts of faith, it was because the country had been false and ill and corrupt for years, corrupt not in the age-old human proportions of failure and evil, but corrupt to the point of terminal disease, like a great religion foundering.

So the political parties of America might be the true churches of America, and our political leaders the popes and prelates, the bishops and ministers and warring clergymen of ideologies which were founded upon the spiritual rock of America as much as any dogma, and so there was a way now to comprehend McGovern and enter the loneliness which lived in his mood, for he inhabited that religious space where men dwell when they are part of the powers of a church and wish to alter that church to its roots. For yes, the American faith might even say that God was in the people. And if this new religion, not two hundred years old, was either the best or the worst idea ever to shake the mansions of eschatology in the world beyond, one knew at least how to begin to think of McGovern; if he had started as a minister in the faith of his father, he had left that ministry to look for one larger. When it came Aquarius' turn to speak to the new candidate of the Democratic Party he felt content to say no more than that he had liked all three speeches at the end of the night. Eagleton, Kennedy, and the speech of the candidate himself, which was the best he had ever heard him give. And McGovern listened with that charisma which was finally and indisputably his own — which was to listen — for if his voice had no flaming tongue of fire, his power to listen surrounded everyone who spoke in his presence, and so had the depth to capture many a loyalty before he was done. Then the words of the speech came back to Aquarius:

"From secrecy and deception in high places — come home, America. From military spending so wasteful that it weakens our nation — come home, America. From the entrenchment of special privilege and tax favoritism — come home, America. From the waste of idle hands to the joy of useful labor — come home, America. From the prejudice of race and sex — come home, America. From the loneliness of the aging poor and the despair of the neglected sick — come home, America. Come home to the affirmation that we have a dream. Come home to the conviction that we can move our country forward. Come home to the belief that we can seek a newer world. May God grant us the wisdom to cherish this good land to meet the great challenge that beckons us home."

"I thought Ted Kennedy gave a very fine speech," McGovern said.

"He did. All the speeches were good. It was a fine mood, it was strong and tender," and McGovern nodded (as if it might be his own observation as well) and it was only after they had talked for another minute and Aquarius stepped back to listen to McGovern talk to others again that he realized he had used the word "tender" in speaking to a Presidential candidate and felt no remorse and, agog on this realization, headed slowly for the exit with the rueful admission to himself that for the days left in which to write his piece he must leave out much in order to be able to put this little in, and thought McGovern was the first tall minister he had every really liked, and so must have a chance to win the election. He kept his good mood until getting in the elevator when it happened that a dreamy McGovern kid started to approach the car ahead of a Secret Service man who gave the practiced equivalent of a karate chop with a small quick blow of his shoulder — for nothing! — and the kid bounced off to the side and the Service man, carrying his drink in his hand, went in first and stared morosely into his glass as though those waters went all the way back to the raw seed of the hurricane. And if Aquarius had been a man to pray, he might have thought of the embattled God he discovered years ago. But then who had the right to ask the Lord to let America have one election which went all the way down the rails without a wreck? He shivered. The idea next to the unexorcised nomenclatures of Oswald and Sirhan left a discomfort on his back.

TWO

POLITICIANS AND PRINCES

1

NOT TEN DAYS were gone and the derailment had occurred. With no deaths and no blood. Just a broken wheel on the election special, and the assailant proved to be one fine political fellow, Senator Thomas F. Eagleton of the railroad state of Missouri, indeed not even an assassin but a harried mechanic in a hurry to grease that golden axle on which his own wheel was going to be installed. He had neglected to mention the bit of grit in the bearing. A tortuous metaphor, but there may be torture in the idea that not all political assassinations call for death; there is also bloodless slaughter in the Media.

Once a politician used to work on his constituency to gain power in the party. Then the party worked to win election. The Press reported the result. While they led a number of the blind by editorial hand, more numerous were the legions of the unseeing carried to the polls by the party. But that was still in an age of Herbert Hoover and Roosevelt and Truman. By the time Eisenhower was first elected, the Media was beginning to make history as well as report it and Richard Nixon was its foundling. By the year of Goldwater's nomination, the Media had already become a mirror which reflected every curse back upon its sender, a Holy Ghost to intervene with every political conception. At its most palpable, the Media had *droit de seigneur* in its pocket, and had become a force between the party and the public with a license to rape

376

the candidate or his party. Media would even create giants so that it could listen to the sound of their fall. In the groans of the dungeon, Muskie might give testimony to this. It was even possible that Nixon was the gymnast of the dungeon and the only man to scale the Media wall, for Nixon had survived! He breathed a summit air the Media did not inhabit. In recompense, Media dominated the levels below. One could not give issue to an event before the Media explored the potentiality of the event. Like a doctor who overadministered to every wheeze, the Media interrupted each national symptom until the specific ill was wasted and the general malaise was general. So a clearcut discovery of buried secrets was aphrodisiac. On the instant, Thomas F. Eagleton's medical history became the best political story to come the Media way in many a month, and if one looked for a criticism of McGovern when all was done, it was to question the final acumen of a man who could assume that such a story would not engorge every issue before it and quickly become the center of the campaign.

2

Interviewing Eagleton on the afternoon of the morning of his resignation as Vice-Presidential candidate, Aquarius finds him changed from the diffident politician who perspired before the television cameras on the night of his nomination and looked too furtive, too nervous, too quick, too quick-tongued, too bright, too unsure of himself and finally too modest to be Vice-President. Now in the two weeks and more which had elapsed since nomination and through the last seven days of disclosure the nightmare of his most secret life had blazoned every breakfast table, as well as the political shame of his treatment in a mental hospital with electric shock, not once but then and again, 1960, 1964, 1966, all kept so secretly by the family and skillfully over the years that even the worst of the whispering campaigns against him hinted at drink as a serious problem — an excusable vice in a politician. But never shock. Shock spoke of incarceration, not treatment, of manacled hands and the possibility of a blasted mind. For there was the public prejudice and who to refute it? A man who drank too much could be wrestling for his soul and losing it — implicit was the idea he might yet regain it. A heavy drinker could still carry on a political life — the impost of booze spoke of a war against too much of some

377

powerful quality in oneself, too much perhaps of passion, talent, or pain. But shock treatment spoke of the irrevocable. Cures derived from a machine, when the cure itself was not comprehended, left an aversion. Nobody could argue that the cure had not come from blinding the innermost eye of the soul — so went the unspoken weight of public prejudice, and who to refute it? Not Eagleton when it was obvious he had made the choice to let rumors of drinking hang him first. (His disappearance into the Mayo Clinic had even been once announced as a visit to Hopkins for gastric disturbance.)

Now, in the last week, the secret of his life disgorged, he sat behind his desk in the New Senate Office Building, with a change in his looks. He was bigger today, heavier, stronger and more relaxed, somehow not unreminiscent of a quick and nervous boxer who has finally gotten into a punchout, been hit hard for ten rounds, and now sits around in the next week with lumps on his head, welts on his face, even a certain thickening of his wits, but manhood has come to him. He has a new kind of calm. So sat Eagleton. Yesterday, after a week of desperate campaigning to win public approval of his candidacy, crowds cheering him in Hawaii, and Jack Anderson confronting him on TV like an older brother with evidence of busts for drunken driving which Anderson didn't have, and apologized for, after a week in which half of America took Eagleton to its heart like a wounded puppy, while half of the top brass in the Democratic Party threatened to boycott the election if he wasn't dropped from the ticket, and campaign money went dry, McGovern had the fell political embarrassment of asking him to withdraw, this after making the needless remark at the first height of the disclosure that he was behind Eagleton "1,000 percent," a phrase which entered the language so quickly that 1,000 percent might yet live as the conclusive way to let someone know they must certainly not count on your word. A whole disaster for McGovern which had not been helped by Eagleton's unwillingness to withdraw — anyone familiar with politics had to know that McGovern was counting, if it came to it, on just such a voluntary withdrawal to safeguard that 1,000 percent. But Eagleton had been riding with all the energy of that cyst being lanced, a buried horror released and himself still alive, crowds cheered him, strangers (from states other than Missouri) grabbed his hand, he was a national figure for the first time in his life, and with a brand-new constituency — all of that Wallace folk who liked a candidate with a flaw they could recognize, something homey and down to rights, a skeleton in the closet at which they had had a peek, what pleasure! That threw a cunning shadow into the soap-opera light. Just as the folk loved Wallace because Lurleen had made the sacrifice to run for governor knowing it could not help her dread disease, and folk loved Wallace again for recovering from her loss and marrying a young woman — renewal was the precise salvation of which the soap opera sang — so now Wallace folk loved Eagleton because he was a rich boy with a bad secret who was going through a crisis and not giving up. (If Aquarius had any doubt of this last hypothesis, it was demonstrated to the detail while he sat in Eagleton's outer office waiting for the interview, and a file of tourists kept coming by to pay their respects to the Senator, murmuring in intense throat-filled voice to the receptionist that they sure were sorry the Senator wouldn't be running and didn't know if they wanted to express their feelings about George McGovern but leave it that they sure wouldn't vote for him now — Wallace faces, every last one of them, clear in their election plumage to a face-watcher like Aquarius, equal after such years of practice to many a bird-watcher.) Eagleton had lived in politics all his life, could smell the turn of one's luck in the sweat of the work. So he knew better than anyone else that he had become a species of new political dynamite, and he didn't want to quit — how could he? But the less he wished to withdraw, the more livid and enormous became the wrath of the party at the caper he had pulled. "Get that mother fucker out" had to be the sweetest message of the hour to McGovern from all the boss and divergent forces in the party he was trying to unite. By refusing to withdraw, Eagleton had the largest play of his life available to him — and if ever elected might just as well have served as an Ombudsman — but the odds against him were huge, and the bulk of his own party would treat him like a leper. So he met with McGovern, and they came out, Eagleton's arm on McGovern's shoulder, using the old senatorial wedge as they drove into a press conference, and Eagleton announced he would withdraw, and did this morning, and now sat back on his chair, his legs on his desk, and talked in a deep politician's voice which still vibrated with the pain of loss and the pleasure of relaxation. Of course, he was far from wholly relaxed as yet, soon jumping to his feet to read aloud an item from the *St. Louis Post-Dispatch* which had just come in, and read (in the loud throw-it-away tones of an actor picking up new lines just handed him) that McGovern was "spineless."

"Spineless," Eagleton repeated. "A little too extreme, don't you think?" he said, but he was obviously enjoying himself.

"Oh, oh," he added with mock pain as he picked up another paper,

379

"they're still misspelling my name. My God, they've called me every-thing and I don't mean dog catcher, I mean Eggleston, Eaglesworth, Eggnog, you call it." His secretary now handing him a take-out menu from the Senate cafeteria, he groaned at the familiar items, "Darn it, I'd like something more glamorous than cherry pie," he complained, as if finding his stomach convalescent, he would call for a taste tender and cozening to the palate.

Back again behind the desk, Eagleton replied to the quick question "Do you play chess?" with the answer, "No, I wish I did, why do you ask?"

"Sometimes in chess games between masters, a move comes up which is so unprecedented and therefore so good or so bad that the people who annotate the game put both an exclamation and a question mark after the move. And I thought if you had not withdrawn, it would have been such a situation."

"I see what you mean," he said heartily. "No, I must say I never learned chess, but I wish now that I might have gone in for it." It was a politician's response. Complimented the questioner, but did not answer him; took pains to praise what might be a hobby. A hobby commended is usually worth a vote.

"Granted this may not be the day to ask such a question, but wouldn't you say that on balance you're still in pretty good position? The nation is aware of you, and there are new friends . . ."

"Oh," he rumbled, "I'm not bitter. Hell, we could say it was the cheapest campaign I ever ran. They gave me a free charge for my batteries. Think of it. All that publicity, and I didn't have to spend a cent."

It was an interview which so far had persisted in remaining out of focus. Not twenty-four hours ago, Eagleton had still been running; now with the proper politician's love for a meaty role (even the role of a loser done well is fertilizer for future votes) he was already working out the tone of new lines, but it was the first day, he was probably a slow study after all this pounding and so he had to sound a fraction off on every reading. The problem was to work out how much he could speak against McGovern — which would be tonic for his blood — and how much he should support him, a professional decision which might take weeks to work out. So now he chose to get away from any suggestion of bile, and also gave up the forced and hearty gallantry he had been exhibiting of a man who is being good about his pain. Instead, he said in the voice of an absolute good guy, "I'm really not bitter — George

McGovern was wonderfully decent to me last night." This line was delivered with no more or less conviction than the others. The new role was going to take work.

"Senator, could I ask a question which might be a little presumptuous?"

"After what I've been asked these last seven days, you could bounce the worst insult off my head, and I wouldn't even know I'd been hit."

Well, one thing did confuse him, the questioner admitted. He had read the reports of Eagleton waiting for hours on the last day of the convention to find out if McGovern would pick him for Vice-President. The former candidate nodded. And it had also been reported that as he waited, his good mood naturally began to go down. Eagleton nodded again. "Well, Senator, forgive me for entering your head, but didn't there come a moment when you said to yourself, 'They're turning me down because of that electro-shock business.' "

Eagleton looked thoughtful. "Earlier in the week when my name first came up as a possibility, and there were still twenty names in the hopper, I talked about the shock treatments with my wife, and we felt it was over and done with. I don't know if you'll believe this, but I then forgot about it."

"You didn't think about it once all that long day of waiting?"

"While I can't vouch for my unconscious, it was not an element of calculation in my conscious head, no sir, strange as that may now sound."

It was preferable to believe he told the truth, that somehow it had not been in his mind when Mankiewicz asked him if there were skeletons in the closet. But who could know what was in Eagleton's mind? Probably he did not know himself. When our motive is imperfect, the flaw is whipped like a pea from mental shell to shell. We smuggle our honesty just out of our reach while keeping an eye on the other man's game. Maybe Eagleton had built so many reflexes on his ability to whip a miserable recollection from shell to shell that he had lost the power to think of the hospital episode when questions were asked, just as a murderer living in a respectable world must manage to forget his murder and feel as much indignation as anyone else at the thrashing of a cat.

Leaving, Aquarius asked, "Anyone ever told you about a resemblance to Scott Fitzgerald?" He was thinking of photographs in those late years when Fitzgerald was handsome still but growing heavy.

"I've been compared to Jack Lemmon, but never Fitzgerald." He smiled. "Do I want to look like Fitzgerald? Didn't he have a drinking problem after all? I'm in enough trouble without being told I remind people of a drunk."

"Not just a drunk. A fine Irish poet."

"Well," said Eagleton, "*The Great Gatsby* is one of my favorite books."

If he was not telling the truth now, there was a fair chance good George McGovern had just disengaged himself from a congenital teller of the worst fibs.

Walking down the hall, Aquarius felt as if he had been talking to a nice friendly reasonably hard-working good-drinking congressman who in another term would be ready to run for senator. No matter how many times it happened, it was unnerving to meet men who had been near to high office and recognize they were no more magnificent than yourself. Perhaps there were mysteries to charisma he would yet do well to ponder.

3

In McGovern's office in the Old Senate Building, the staff was digging out from their disaster. An unprecedented bout of political foul weather, it was hardly at an end, for in days to come Teddy Kennedy would again decline the Vice-Presidency, as would Muskie (while Humphrey and Ribicoff would state they were not available) before Sargent Shriver would take the ticket. The first Gallup Poll since the convention had been announced, and McGovern was riding low, Nixon ahead 58 percent to 34, but even the ripping velocity of such bad news had to be read as even worse, since McGovern's percentage had dropped as a result of the Democratic Convention, dropped! When it should have risen after four days of exposure. All those liberated faces and somewhat adenoidal voices of the articulate young telling America how to live right over the tube had obviously brought no good reaction from the Jews of the wad and the Italians, the Polish and the Irish — go through the minorities, go through the unions — the polls were terrible, they would get worse. For these last polls had been taken before the bad news about Eagleton was released; McGovern was in twice poor circumstances now — it was as if the political virus which wrecked your timing had been passing among the Democrats and he had caught Muskie's disease. The timing could not have been worse on Eagleton.

Having supported him 1,000 percent when the first reaction was negative, McGovern decided to drop him just as Eagleton began to capture America's affection. Probably it had seemed like good timing — allow three or four days for the cut-off to take place, habituate Eagleton and America to the impending change, and give time also for the breezes of ambition to stir again in prominent Democrats' hearts. Instead, there had come Jack Anderson's disclosure that he had "located photostats" of arrest records on Eagleton for drunken driving. So, it looked like McGovern was dropping Eagleton just when his troubles were at their worst. Then, it developed that Anderson's charges were false. No photostats. No arrest records. Eagleton's fortunes were now ready to zoom and climbed instead up to the low ceiling of McGovern's decision already committed to dozens of Democratic leaders that he would definitely drop Eagleton. It was worse than the worst moments in "The Short Happy Life of Francis Macomber" — once again, the protagonist was getting killed just when ready to become a man. What a direct reflection in polls to come! (A month later, Nixon would lead 64 to 30.) But then the timing and retraction of Anderson's charges had been so bad for Democratic fortunes that more than one sinister interpretation was passing around in Washington. For as political intelligence was quick to point out, Jack Anderson didn't make that kind of mistake. Aquarius, who sometimes thought it was his life's ambition to come up with evidence that the CIA was tripping on American elections, might have loved the story, but since even men like Anderson could have lapses, it was possible astrology offered as much revelation. Whether a plot, Muskie's political flu, the fine hand of the Devil giving a stir of the broth for Richard Nixodemus, or the worst zodiacal concatenation ever handed a Presidential poker player, McGovern had just managed to stop a series of haymakers by the forceful motion of his head against his opponent's glove, and, true fighter, was not yet necessarily aware how totally he had been hit. (Pete Hamill indeed had described him as reminiscent of "those old Irish heavyweights like Braddock who catch everything and still go fifteen.") Maybe McGovern would go fifteen, but no big Democrat was running up this day to second him; it would be a week until Shriver was nominated in full assembly of the Democratic National Committee.

Waiting in his Senate offices to get an appointment with the candidate, there was opportunity to talk for a while with Warren Beatty in a corner behind two file cabinets, and Beatty who had carried the reputation of being a not-altogether-manageable movie star, heir among others to that surly mix of pride, wit, benightedness, bumps, lumps, and independence which had been legend for Brando, was in the position of having been working hard for months and years for McGovern, and he spoke from that unmistakable base of centrality which sits in the chest when you are part of the team. So it was like talking to a halfback who will explain why his coach, the best coach, can still lose a game. "You got to understand, naturally. There's been work here in this place. I mean some of the people in this office were with McGovern back out there two years ago when he had 2 percent of the vote in the polls, and figure this — they were lying. It was not a *solid* 2 percent." From time to time Beatty moved his head the way an animal might, as though to take stock of sounds not heard but sensed — shifts in the ringing of mood. "People like that, back there working so long at 2 percent, think how they feel now their man's all the way up, and boom, low bridges, the newcomer, *this* newcomer has his flaw which is going to louse up the campaign, smash all the good work they've been doing for two years. People were incensed at Eagleton here. Cause you know he wasn't exactly telling the truth. He made Frank Mankiewicz look incompetent. And it isn't so. Frank didn't say, 'Ho, ho, fellow, any skeletons in Daddy-O's closet?' Frank questioned him. I was in the room. Frank asked *all* the questions. I mean, he didn't say, 'Any mental difficulties?' but he was *thorough.* The man had plenty of time to search his own mind. And that leaves Frank on the spot now. He's had to keep his lip buttoned. Cause we didn't know if Eagleton was going to stay or not." Beatty gave that hint of wry balance which was his smile, and went on in his slow, off the beat, laconic voice, not Clyde so much as some dry variant of the syncopation Brando first brought to phrasing when he played psychopaths and gave a mix of the old man's stern salts with the delinquent's softened voice, yes, the sociology of half of America was an Oriental rug, and actors were a legitimate part of the cadre. "It all," Beatty said, "goes back to California. If we'd known we were in, we could have done a full check. But the way we had to do it! Look, even the *St. Louis Post-Dispatch* had no stuff on Eagleton. That's the clue to the kind of search we couldn't make. Just think — we're back there where we don't have the nomination yet, and we're trying to make that search, poking in Rochester, Minnesota, for *medical* records? And Eagleton is still a *Muskie* man! Think of the stink."

"But when did word first get to you about Eagleton?"

He shrugged. "A couple of reporters called."

"How did they know?"

"There was a phone call to them from Rochester."

"Was it anonymous?"

He nodded.

Why bother to look for the CIA when there was always the FBI? But, as if the sense of excitement he felt at this possibility quivered across the air and was seized instantly by Beatty, the actor gave a wooden look in return. The interview was abruptly over.

"Are you sure of this?"

"No."

"Is it a secret?"

"No matter. It's not said."

"What do you mean?"

"The rain in Spain."

"What?"

"Doggerel."

Now Beatty got up. The interview was certainly over. Aquarius made small talk with the staff for a minute. Yet, before he left, Beatty tapped him. "It's okay. You can use that story. It's been in print."

He was not to get in with McGovern for an interview this day but had an opportunity to say hello as the candidate passed through his office, and it was the first time Aquarius saw fatigue on his face. The Senator had been defeated that day in the attempt to put a ceiling on the defense budget, defeated (like an index of the polls) by 59 to 33 — nineteen Democratic senators defecting to Nixon for the vote, and it had been McGovern's first important effort on the Senate floor since winning the nomination. Then, the candidate's plan to offer over nationwide television a full account of his reasons for encouraging the resignation of Eagleton had been refused for that night by the networks on the ground his remarks would not be newsworthy, not unless he could name the new Vice-President. A rebuke. For whatever the legal merits of the networks' position, it was also Media's way of telling him he had been demoted: his thoughts and emotions in coming to so agonizing a decision were without the content of real news. Obviously, he was a candidate whom the Media had concluded was not going to become President.

We may leave aside the attack on his vanity. He was in the worse frustration of not being able to present his side of the Eagleton affair for another week, just that crucial week in which opinions would be hardening. Yes, McGovern had just had the kind of news which stirred fatigue.

Next day, there was still no interview, but all the opportunity to watch him from the Press Gallery in the Senate Chamber, for there was one close vote after another on a series of amendments to a bill for military procurement. And after two hours of watching the floor and observing McGovern as he wandered around Senate desks, so could the character of any sentiment surrounding him also be observed. But the Senate Chamber was not the most cheerful place in which to make such a study, for with its inset black marble columns along the beige walls, and its colorless dingy lavender-gray carpet, the great room despite its high and noble molded ceiling still looked like one of the grimmest of grand old hotel lobbies. The sofas in the corner of the floor were of the dark brown of office leather which can only be found in the oldest banks and hotels, and the desks of the senators were as old and dark as a Havana cigar. Upstairs, the seats in the visitors' gallery were red and pink as if some small-town decorator had been called in on a change of management to warm the mezzanine and had only succeeded in firing the essential loss of connection between the heaviest habits of decoration in Establishment past and present. If, on reflection, it was not a badly designed set considering how many times it had been called the most powerful and exclusive men's club in America (ninety-nine of the one hundred senators were men), still never had the appointments of a Men's Club been more in need of Women's Fumigation; the rules of the club, as if grown in the logic of the décor, were chiseled enough to suggest that the code of senatorial manners must be filed in aisles of marble. That severity of air which arises when the banker's rights of money are preeminent to the rights of men (McGovern was later to say, "Money made by money should be taxed at the same rate as money made by men") sat in judgment over the Senate like a palisade of cigar smoke on a counting-house floor, and one had not been in the precincts of that chamber for an hour before a few new observations were clear: The fortitude of Gravel in defying Senate protocol to read the Pentagon Papers had not been rated sufficiently high; the view of other senators toward McGovern was cool. He might be running for President, but in the eyes of his peers, he was an upstart, or was it nearer to estimate that he was regarded more as a fellow who had taken the pledge and next year might even live in the fraternity but for the present his only fame was that he had won some sort of sweepstakes off the campus.

A huge simplification, but analogous perhaps to the kind of notes anthropologists might take on the goings and comings of baboons in the brush. There were flurries to the passages of senators between their desks, men they made a point to greet, others they passed with a nod, and the desks of particular senators came to seem like stations on the line. The Democrats' half of the chamber was beneath his perch in the Press Balcony, and after a period it was established that the desk of Teddy Kennedy while in the last row and to the side might as well have been the center of the floor — everybody stopped there! — not even his worst detractors would ever claim that Ted Kennedy could not become the president of any fraternity to which he belonged: one could define the prerequisites of an ideal fraternity leader in Kennedy's qualities — to be rich, hearty, handsome, cognizant of tradition, witty, and not without independence. Charisma glowed like aurora borealis about his desk.

And Humphrey, peripatetic this day, moved like the most expensive tropical fish in the tank, and was greeted everywhere and was obviously loved, and as obviously loved the Senate — he had never looked so well campaigning for President as he appeared this afternoon, younger, slimmer, the bloat gone, the career now finally in balance again — warm were the greetings they gave him as he visited from desk to desk. And warm were the greetings given to Eagleton. He remained in the seat he occupied, chatting with senators who came by, and was altogether at ease — his life, ideally, would move from club boy to club man — it was obvious after a period that the oldest and most venerable of the senators were making a point to stop and accost him, a set of avuncular buttresses to remind him that he was back in the place where he belonged and could spend his life, and it was only after a period of observing him that the realization came home that Eagleton was occupying McGovern's seat! Many of the senators could be found at strange desks, maybe more than half were not at their own, but the query which would remain unanswered was whether Eagleton's move had been accidental or chosen, and if the second, then was it a way to declare allegiance to his former running mate or just a casual means of reminding him that ghosts last longer than corpses.

And McGovern? Even though he is running for President, there is a difference between him and other senators, an absence of rich greeting, a delicate air of the cool, as if they cannot forgive him for succeeding when he has still not learned how to move in these halls. He wanders through the Senate as if he attends a somewhat strange campus function, looking perhaps like that affable and lonely graduate student who holds two jobs and gets the best marks in class, and walks on flat feet as the price of working those nineteen hours a day he can remove from the tyranny of hours lost to sleep. Now although he knows everyone here (he has worked with them on other campus functions), he does not know how to time the weight, duration, and splendor of his greeting to individuals of different merit, knows that the function of the particular job he has at this minute is to be friendly, and is of good will, but something in his manner speaks of that prairie poverty which teaches decency and good manners, yet always leaves one circling outside the intimidating pauses and rich thrusts of successful manner. If the Senate had been a roaring abbey with a blazing fire, McGovern would have been the monk who prayed in the chill at the rear — something of the transcendent passion of the poor graduate student now came clear. For out of five decades of American graduate students, he must be the one in ten million who had successfully taken the vow to rise above every closed circle of elegant establishment he would never enter. Movies had been his forbidden fruit, not country club dances. If men run for President out of a hundred motives, certainly a good one for McGovern was that it would be easier to become Commander in Chief of America than be accepted in the Senate. Aquarius wondered if part of McGovern's readiness to pick Eagleton had not come out of the simple social pleasure that he would have allied to himself the kind of man who was born to an inner club — what McGovern did not know is that poor graduate students tell the truth when questions are asked (for examinations are their Olympics and their triumph), whereas rich boys are in need of cribs and there is always some family secret to snake away with charm.

4

Next morning when he went in to have his interview, McGovern was not visible in his office. So his secretary, Pat Donovan, stayed and talked for a few minutes. If one could judge the caliber of men by the presence of their secretaries, then all the qualities already perceived in McGovern were fortified. Pat Donovan had one of those modest pleasant and turned-up faces which used to speak of the integrity of Americans, as if something in the lakes, the pine woods and the prairies bred honesty in American flesh as naturally as vitamins in grain — if she were the young teacher sent to meet a parent on the first day a child was put in school, the mother might surrender the first-born without a qualm. Still, the most honorable people are not always the easiest to talk to. Conversation worked against a certain embarrassment. "Two days ago," said Pat Donovan, continuing a fumbled set of remarks about politics which Aquarius had begun, "I even spoke to Hubert Humphrey on the phone. I could hardly believe it. There I was being pleasant to him, saying hello as if nothing had happened." She shook her head at the peculiarities of the profession she found herself in. Politicians could forgive each other, but not the women who worked for them — he could remember the ice picks in the eyes of female workers when McGovern's name was uttered in Eagleton's office.

Still he did not know why Pat Donovan, confessing how her days since the nomination were never removed from the phone, took one precious minute and then another to fill silences with sound — why did she give him this attention he did not need, and could not use nearly so well as a minute to himself the better by which to note a detail or two of the furnishings in the room.

And the answer came in a flushing of the john. McGovern's private bathroom was next to his office. Miss Donovan had simply not wanted a reporter to sit in a state of open ears while her boss had that obligatory few minutes to himself. What a delightful sense of protection she had! Aquarius wished he could have told her how, out of the depths of his own political career, he knew no candidate's bowels were ever in condition to be eavesdropped upon!

So began his interview with McGovern. They shook hands on the human ground of the Senator emerging from his bathroom door. Then McGovern took a seat some fifteen feet away, a good distance for what was only a fair-sized room, yet the distance was comfortable, for once again Aquarius felt a sensation not altogether separate from that mixture of eminence, near-levitation and dread one breathes (in the lightening of the weight of the heart) as one walks on the edge of a cliff. McGovern seemed so unlike a politician, and so much more like a man of some inestimable goodness sitting in one's living room and emitting a free current of moral decency which proved to be as strong as the agreeable sense of awe one could know at the best of times in a church. Yet the office in which they spoke now, while a nice office — no more had he observed it! — seemed to be in his own service as much as McGovern's: part of the Senator's most exceptional quality as a politician was that he did not even appropriate his own surroundings. Of course, if one sat literally in one's own living room, and was confronted by a man of such superb moral worth, there would be all the discomfort of not knowing what to offer for conversation, except that McGovern's power, perceived all over again! was in his grave and pleasant quality of attention as if all that was said could be of value. So Aquarius made the error of not interviewing but of talking for too many of his precious minutes on a theme he envisioned for the campaign, and recognized even as he spoke that these ideas were too subtle to be reported properly if ever inserted in a speech. The admission of this — his own discouraging reaction to his own ideas — seemed to come as some function of the attention McGovern offered, much as if Aquarius had been abruptly endowed with the power to apply any critical spirit he used for others upon himself. So he shelved the catalogue of these once dear ideas, and recognized that he had no real questions to ask. There was no form of inquiry on earth more unwholesome to him that a face-to-face interview — truth could emerge no more easily from that than statistics on the sum of British Guiana's arable acreage, gotten up for a test, might bring some cognition of life in British Guiana.

Since the office day was beginning, however, the phone began to ring. Between two calls, Aquarius managed to suggest that one of the obstacles to election might be the desire of China and the Soviet Union for Nixon to win; any progress achieved with Republicans would be concrete and not easily reversed, whereas fine relations with a Democratic President could always be overthrown four years later.

"Well, there may be some element of truth to what you say," McGovern offered. He pondered it. "I've never heard the question put that way before." Was this a compliment to slip away from the need to answer? "Let's leave it," said McGovern, "that while I don't necessarily have a rebuttal, we can still contend with the idea that history takes place in an *atmosphere*. The prevailing tone in the world might be somewhat different if I can win."

Once he had been described as "not modest but humble," and the phrase was comprehensible. He was certainly not modest since he obviously thought he could make a good President, but he was humble in his unstated confidence that it would not necessarily be himself who accomplished such a wonder. There were human forces powerful as waves in which he believed and they would yet carry him. It is only, his manner seemed to say, that there may not be time for people to recognize I am probably sincere.

Yes, in the silences after he spoke, something in his manner spoke again, and better.

Then the phone rang once more. When he was finished, McGovern began on his own accord to speak of Eagleton, doing this with the painful smile of a man who has always trusted his candor and now must trust it again. "I think," he said, "it may have been the hardest decision I've ever had to make in my life." He spoke in the self-removed tone a man would have to employ after an automobile accident in which he had been the driver and others had been hurt. "It was bad not to be able to give him a chance, and yet the division in the party would have been total. And the money stopped. Nothing has been coming in. And then in all this time we couldn't get to see his medical records. We still don't know how serious it was. Although, of course, no matter what the records said, they're old. He could now be more stable than any of us. There are no guides in this."

"What would you have done if he had mentioned the shock when Mankiewicz asked?"

"I don't know. Maybe we would have asked for the direct release of the records, and seen if they were the kind of thing we could announce and proceed to live with." But that could hardly be the answer. How would they ever decide at four in the afternoon on the day a Vice-President must be nominated, a monumental question whose edges were undefined?

"You picked a nice man who just doesn't give the impression that he could ever conceivably be a President. With due respect, I think it was your fault."

"Yes," said McGovern, tall and sad and brooding, "it was my fault," and Aquarius thought that if they had only talked of the mistakes he had made, and the flaws in his powers, still he had never looked more and sounded more like a President, for it was as if his error now leaned against all the wounds of that world he hoped to mend, and the wounds leaned back on him.

But, indeed, being next to McGovern was like being in a movie film next to Gary Cooper. No man could give off such an impression of strength, fine attention, and guarded concern for the vulnerability of existence itself without possessing something of those qualities. For how could any actor offer a decency in his face which was greater than the decency he might be capable of attaining at certain moments in his own life? One can simulate many an emotion altogether, but not decency. Perhaps this could explain why actors like Cooper were loved as if their roles were real. In any case, whether the nicest politician he had ever met, or the unheralded matinee idol of splendid Westerns never

391

made, Aquarius had just known the most disturbing sentiment one could feel for a politician — was it something like love? Or was McGovern the living embodiment of a principle which was only new to the Age of Technology: the clear expectation of democratic government that good and serious men of honorable will were ready to serve.

5

The calendar being never so orderly as the requirements of literary form, Aquarius had his conversation with McGovern on the day after an interview with Henry Kissinger, but in memory the occasions were reversed, as if he had shifted from observing Democrats to covering Republicans on the precise hour he crossed over the parties and went to visit Dr. Kissinger in the White House.

Since it was an interview which had been scheduled weeks in advance and confirmed the day before, with all option given to meet at Sans Souci for lunch or the White House, he had naturally picked the White House. How often did such opportunities arise? Still, it took fifteen long minutes and then five more to pass through the special police at the gate. Interrogating him through a microphone in a plate-glass façade, they claimed at first to have no record of his appointment, and then informed him he had been due at nine in the morning, only to discover they were looking through the schedule of the resident White House physician, Dr. Tkach. Kissinger! now that was better! but before they could announce him, he would have to complete a questionnaire. There was something as reductive as a steam bath in this colloquy through the glass. Already he was perspiring at the minutes being lost for the interview.

Once admitted to the kiosk, however, he was freezing in the air conditioning and fuming at the questionnaire. When he handed it back, the Sergeant who conducted the inquiry through the window scolded him. "I told you not to use abbreviations, didn't I?"

"Why don't you have a form which gives you space to write out the full word," he snapped back, and was apparently accepted at last by the Sergeant as a man of sufficient self-importance to visit the White House, for he was invited to take a chair.

Still, he had to wait while they phoned for clearance. In the meantime, he listened to the Sergeant and his assistant, a bright-eyed and wiry Southerner, who said, "I just reduced crime in my neighborhood by forty percent."

The Sergeant jeered; the other policeman, a young Black with a ramrod posture, smiled uneasily.

"Hell, yeah. The other night I talked my wife out of hitting me on the side of the head with a skillet. That's forty percent right there. But when it comes to armed robbery I'm helpless. I come home at the end of the week with my pay check and she holds me up for all fifty-one cents."

"Why," said the Sergeant, "don't you study the life of George Washington and stop telling so many fucking lies?"

"There's an example. George Washington cut down the cherry tree and they gave him ten thousand dollars a year. Why, way back then he was making more money than I am right now."

"What are you complaining about?" asked the Sergeant. "He was the first President of the U.S. What was you ever the shit first of?"

But a young Secret Service man had now come up to the kiosk, and conducted him across the North Lawn. Inside the West Lobby a receptionist apologized politely for the delay. Ushered through a door into a hallway, he was met by Kissinger who gave the greatest of broad smiles, pumped his hand, and said in a deep and gutty German accent, "Today must be my day for masochism since I dare to be interviewed by you."

Almost immediately, they were in his office, large and full of light. "We have a momentous decision to make instantly," said Kissinger. "It is: where shall we eat? I can offer you respectable food if you wish the interview here, not exciting but respectable, and we won't be interrupted. Or we can go to a restaurant just around the corner where the food will be very good and we will be interrupted a little although not very much."

Similar in height and build, it was probable they would not wish to miss a good lunch. So in much less time than it took him to enter, he left the White House (that most placid of mansions!) with Kissinger, hardly noticing the same Secret Service man who unobtrusively — it was the word! — had stopped the traffic on Pennsylvania Avenue while they crossed. If not for just such a rare American pomp, he could have had the impression that he knew Kissinger over the years. For as they walked along, chatting with no pain, it was much as if the learned doctor had been an editor of some good and distinguished quarterly, and they were promenading to lunch in order to talk over a piece.

In fact, that was the first topic — his piece. "We must, from the beginning," said Kissinger, "establish ground rules. We may make them whatever you wish, but we have to keep them. I can speak frankly with you, or not so frankly. But if I am frank, then you have to allow me the right to see what you put into my mouth. It is not because of vanity, or because of anything you may say about me, you may say anything you wish about me, in fact" — with the slyest grin — "you will probably hurt my position more if you say good things than bad, but I have, when all is said, a position I must be responsible to. Now if you don't wish to agree to such a procedure, we can do the interview at arm's length, which of course I'm used to and you need show me nothing. Either method is agreeable, provided we establish the rules."

They had by now reached Sans Souci, and Kissinger's advance to his table was not without ceremony. Since he was hardly back twenty-four hours from Paris and some talks with the North Vietnamese, the head-waiter teased him over the pains of quitting Parisian cuisine. Passing by the table of Larry O'Brien there were jokes about Watergate.

"That was good luck, Henry, to get away just before it hit the fan," said O'Brien.

"Ah, what a pity," said Kissinger. "You could have had me for the villain of the sixth floor."

And a friend intercepted him before he could take his seat. "Henry, what truth to the rumor that McGovern is picking you for Vice-President?"

Kissinger chuckled. "Twenty-two thousand people in the State Department will be very happy." He was animated with the pleasure these greetings had given him. While not a handsome man, he was obviously more attractive to women now than when he had been young, for he enjoyed what he received, and he was a sensuous man with a small mouth and plump lips, a Hapsburg mouth; it was not hard to see his resemblance to many a portrait of many an Austrian archduke and prince. Since he gave also every sign of the vanity and vulnerability and ruddy substance of a middle-aged man with a tendency to corpulence — the temptation to eat too much had to be his private war! — his weaknesses would probably be as amenable to women as his powers, and that German voice, deep, fortified with an accent which promised emoluments, savories, even meat gravies of culture at the tip of one's tongue, what European wealth! produced an impression altogether more agreeable than his photographs. So one mystery was answered — Kissinger's reputation as a ladies' man. And a difficulty was commenced — Aquarius' work might have been simplified if he liked the Doctor less. A hint of some sinister mentality would have been a recognizable aid.

Yet even the demand for ground rules was reasonable. The meal ordered, Kissinger returned to the subject — he repeated: he would obviously expect the rules to be clarified before he could go further. Nor was there much impulse to resist him with argument. Secretly, he respected Kissinger for giving the interview — there was indeed not a great deal the Doctor could gain, and the perils were plentiful, including the central risk that Kissinger would have to trust him to keep his side of the bargain. Since his position not only as Assistant to the President on National Security Affairs but as court favorite must excite the ten thousand furies of bureaucracy — "this man who can't speak English that they keep hidden in the White House" being a not uncommon remark — the medium of this interview was not without its underlying message: Kissinger, in some part of himself at least, must be willing to function as a cultural ambassador across the space of mind between the constellations of the White House and the island galaxies of New York intellectual life. So Aquarius made his own speech. Like a virgin descending the steps of sexual congress, he said that he had never done this before, but since he was not unsympathetic to Kissinger's labors, and had no wish to jeopardize his position, which he would agree was delicate . . . so forth. They set up some ground rules.

"Now what should we talk about?" asked Kissinger.

Well, they might talk about the huge contradiction between the President's actions in Russia and China as opposed to Vietnam. "You know, if not for the bombing I might have to think about voting for Nixon. Certainly no Democrat would have been able to look for peace with Russia and China. The Republicans would never have let him. So Nixon's achievement is, on the one hand, immense, and on the other ghastly." Kissinger nodded, not without a hint of weariness to show his familiarity with the argument.

"If I reply to you by emphasizing the difference in our styles of negotiation in each country, it is not to pretend that these negotiations preempt moral questions, but rather that I'm not so certain we can engage such questions properly if they're altogether stripped of context. For instance, it would be impossible to discuss the kind of progress we made with China and Russia unless I were to give you the flavor of those negotiations for they were absolutely characteristic and alto-

395

gether different. For instance, I was not unfamiliar with Russian matters, but my ignorance about China was immense on the first secret
visit, and I had no idea of how they would receive me" — a hint of the
loneliness of his solitary position now passes across the table at Sans
Souci — "nor even what we necessarily would be able to talk about. In
the beginning I made the mistake of assuming that they negotiate like
the Russians, and they don't. Not at all. With the Russians you always
know where you stand. If, for example, you are hammering out a joint
statement, you can be certain that if you ask them to remove a comma
in one place, depend on it they will ask you for a comma in return.
Whereas the character of men like Chou must emerge to a great degree
from experiences like the Long March, and so I discovered — and not
immediately — that you always had to deal with them on the real substance of the question. I remember when the President visited China,
and I was working with Chou on the joint statement we would issue
describing our areas of agreement and difference. I asked if a certain
point the Chinese had brought up could be dropped because the word-
ing would be difficult for us in America. In return I would give up a
point to them. Chou said 'Explain to me why this point causes you
difficulty, and if your explanation makes sense I will cede it to you. If it
doesn't convince me however, then nothing can make me give it up. But
I don't need or want your point. You can only give your points back to
your President, you cannot give them to us.' So he shamed me," Kissinger finished.

"And the Vietnamese?"

"They could hardly be more different. The problem is to convince
them we really want peace."

"Don't you think a million tons of bombs a year makes it hard for
them to believe?"

"No. I know this has to sound unendurably callous to you, but the
North Vietnamese are inconceivably tough people, and they've never
known peace in their lives. So to them the war is part of the given. They
are able to live with it almost as a condition of nature. But when it
comes to negotiation, they refuse to trust us on the most absurd little
points. Let them feel if they will that we are not to be relied on in the
larger scheme of things — that is not my point of view, but an argument can obviously be advanced — it is just that they refuse to trust us
on the pettiest points where it would not even be to our interest to cheat
them. So they are not easy to comprehend. On the one hand they have

a fortitude you cannot help but admire; on the other, they are near to little lawyers who are terrified of the larger processes of the law — and so cling to the most picayune items. That is one difficulty in dealing with the North Vietnamese. The other is their compulsion to the legalistic which bears no relation to reality, nor to the possibility of reality. In effect they expect us to win their war for them for they want us to write up into the peace agreement their literal investiture of the government of South Vietnam. And that obviously we can't do. There's nothing we want more than for the war to end, but they must take their chances too. They have to win their own war."

"When they began their offensive in April, why then didn't the President just let them drive ahead and solve the problem for you? Why, just at that point, did he choose to escalate the bombing?"

Kissinger did not reply. The difficulty in continuing the discussion was that they would now be obliged to talk about the character of Richard Nixon rather than the nature of the North Vietnamese; given Kissinger's position, that was hardly possible: so the character of the interview changed. If it was easy for Aquarius to have the idea that Nixon and Kissinger were more in accord on Russia and China than on Vietnam, there was no evidence for it. Kissinger took pains to express his respect. "The President is a very complex man," he said, "perhaps more complex than anyone I've known, and different from the public view of him. He has great political courage for instance."

"Yes. It was no ordinary gamble to go to China."

"And he made moves in Russia which would take too long to explain now, but believe me he showed extraordinary decisiveness."

"Still, don't you think it's a vice that he has a personality which is of no use to the country?"

"Nixon is wary of exhibiting anything personal in himself. You have to consider the possibility it's for very good cause considering the way he has been treated by the Media."

"Still his wariness creates contempt."

"And a spirit of debunking which I don't find very happy. It was like that in the Weimar Republic. Just the kind of wholesale debunking that may yet lead to totalitarianism." Kissinger shrugs. "I wonder if people recognize how much Nixon may be a bulwark against that totalitarianism."

"Can he be?"

"I'm not certain I know what you mean."

"As people grow up, don't they form their characters to some extent on the idea a President gives of his person to the public. Nixon may give too little."

"Is it your point of view then that in the presidency one needs to have a man it is worth being like?"

"Yes. Nixon offers nothing authentic of himself."

"You would argue that he is not primarily a moral leader. I do not wish to agree. But perhaps you go along with me that he has political genius," Kissinger said.

"Absolutely."

It was indeed Aquarius' opinion. Still, that was a thought he could return to. Their lunch broke up with the passing of their table by Art Buchwald who announced to Kissinger that Dobrinin was coming to his house one night soon to play chess, and schedules permitting, he thought, granting Dobrinin's status as a chess player, that they should make a date to team up against the Ambassador. Kissinger agreed.

On the way back to the White House, they talked companionably of the hazards of working life, of jet-lag and fatigue. "How much sleep do you get?" asked Aquarius.

"I am happy if I can average five hours."

"Is it enough?"

"I always thought my mind would develop in a high position. But, fatigue becomes a factor. The mind is always working so hard that you learn little. Instead, you tend to work with what you learned in previous years."

They said good-bye in the white office in the White House with its blue sofas, its Oriental rugs, and its painting by Olitsky, a large canvas in blue-purple, a wash of dark transparencies with a collection of pigment near the center as if to speak of revery and focus. "I've only come to like modern art in the last few years," Kissinger remarked.

Aquarius was to think again of focus. Because Kissinger opened to him a painful question on the value of the act of witness: lunch had been agreeable. Yet how could one pretend that Kissinger was a man whose nature could be assessed by such a meeting; in this sense, he was not knowable — one did not get messages from his presence of good or evil, rather of intelligence, and the warm courtesy of Establishment, yes, Kissinger was the essence of Establishment, his charm and his presence even depending perhaps on just such emoluments of position as the happiness he obtained in the best restaurants. If there was a final social need for Establishment, then Kissinger was a man born to be part of it and so automatically installed in the moral schizophrenia of Establishment, a part of the culture of moral concealment, and yet never was the problem so perfect, for the schizophrenia had become Aquarius' own. Kissinger was a man he liked, and in effect was ready to protect — he would even provide him with his own comments back to read. So Aquarius wondered if he had come into that world of the unendurably complex where one gave part of one's allegiance to men who worked in the evil gears and bowels and blood left by the moral schizophrenia of Establishment, but still worked there, as one saw it, for good more than ill. It was a question to beat upon every focus of the brain, and he prepared with something near to bewilderment to go down to Miami again, and see if there were moral objects still to be delineated in the ongrowing blur of his surest perceptions.

THREE

PROGRAM

HE HAS EVEN GONE DOWN early, and finds himself in Miami so soon as
Wednesday for a convention which will not begin until the next Monday, and then promises to be an exhibit without suspense, conflict, or
the rudiments of narrative line. If the selection of the Vice-President
might have offered drama, Nixon announced his choice of Agnew
much in advance and the V.P. in reply to a reporter who asked if the
Republican Convention wasn't going therefore to be dull, replied,
"Very well, then, we'll be dull," a way to point out that the values of the
Media and the values of Republicans might by now be as separate from
one another as opposed political systems.

Aquarius was early because he wanted time to think, and lie perhaps
in the sun, but in fact he was not at the Fontainebleau a day before he
was working. The Platform Committee was meeting, its subcommittees
were meeting, and already a parade of speakers had come and gone,
Senator Dole (the Republican National Chairman) and George Romney, John Ashbrook the conservative who had run for President
against Nixon in the primaries and John Gardner of Common Cause,
Senators Buckley and Javits of New York, and Frank Fitzsimmons of
the Teamsters who was successor to Jimmy Hoffa.

There was of course no need to catch much of this. Hours of reporto-
rial prospecting would pan very few grains of gold; most of the prepared statements were read in the La Ronde Room, which was so large
that one would not get near enough to see the faces (not when Platform

Committee workers occupied most of the floor). Besides, the statements would hardly matter. It was taken for granted that the platform was being written in the White House and the hearings were going on because conventions had platform committees which were bound to listen to speakers. But he could legitimately miss the pleasure of not having heard John Ashbrook's voice speaking as the spirit of the Republican Right when he called for the U.S. to restore its "clear-cut military superiority" so that it might take the lead in resisting the "spread" of Communism. (Which genius of the Right, Aquarius wondered, had divined that a cure for cancer would not be found until there was a cure for Communism?!?) Of course, Ashbrook also called for "the government to live within its means" and bring an end to interference "with the freedom and self-reliance of the average citizen." Such reasoning would not be equaled until a politician called for the absolute enforcement of absolute monogamy with no restriction upon pornography. But then Richard Nixon had once spoken in much the same way — if twenty years ago! Was this the law of historical progress? — that it took two decades for the ideas of the center to be evacuated to the Right? Well, a good healthy body plus fat-shit for a head might be the indispensable stock of a patriot. (And proceeded to play with the punnings of fascism, fetishism, and fat-shit.) Like a fighter getting mean in the last days before a bout, he was obviously ready to work, and so plunged in to witness the best hearings he could find on Wednesday afternoon, Subcommittee II on Human Rights and Responsibilities, not the worst way to spend an afternoon — his powers as a witness could even feel temporarily restored.

He had chosen II because a representative from the National Coalition of Gay Organizations was listed to speak — Human Rights and Responsibilities was his fair category! — and Aquarius had naturally looked for a confrontation between flaming youth and fierce-eyed Republicanism, an appetizer to tempt his jaded political palate! but the schedule was running behind, and there were other speakers to come first. After a time — perhaps he was just enjoying his work — he relaxed into the somnolence of an atmosphere of visiting speakers reading very rapidly from concentrated reports (fifteen minutes for statement and questions) while members of the Subcommittee read along with mimeographed copies, working with their pencils to make that diagram of trunk lines, private lines, and shunts in the brain which is called doodling. The Subcommittee was invariably bored. There was a platform to be gotten out and fifty impossibilities to be eliminated first.

So it was as if they all agreed there was a marble statue back in the barn which bats were juicing with rabies spit; the aim of the committee was to let the bats beat their wings, flare their gums, then thank them for spreading that rabid saliva. Once the bats were gone, the Sub-committeee could wipe the saliva off. In a few days, their work would be done and the statue could be unveiled. No one could say they had not worked on it. If no Subcommittee hand had guided the chisel, who was to say that Chase and Honaman, Jackson, Olson, Victor, Brake, Ramey, Hansen, Ashcraft, Sullivan, Hopkins, Weston, Babcock and Heckler had still not done their bit by holding a seat through long neon-lighted air-conditioned summer afternoons while catching spit? Counting Peter Frelinghuysen from New Jersey and Alice Perry from Mississippi, Chairman and Co-Chairman, there were four men and twelve women on the Subcommittee and the value of the sex quota was established forever since one could not begin to see how a shift in the virtues of the atmosphere would take place if there had been twelve men and four women. Doubtless it was only the title of the Sub-committee which had dictated the particular ratio of vagina to penis.

Donald W. Riegle, Jr., was the first speaker he heard, Congressman Don Riegle of Michigan, the anti-war Republican, and he was young and personable with blond hair which he wore at a generous enough length to reach his collar.

Perhaps in reply to Chairman Frelinghuysen who had opened pro-ceedings the day before by saying, "We intend to have impact on the writing of the platform [and] want to assure each witness appearing before us today that this is where the action is," Riegle gave this forthright beginning. "As you know, certain Republicans have been banned from appearing before the full Platform Committee, including Paul McCloskey, John Gardner, and myself. When I raised this issue with Platform Committee Chairman John Rhodes he said to me: 'You're crazy if you think anyone is going to appear before the full Platform Committee that would say anything that would embarrass the President.' As a result . . . full and open discussion of the issues has been denied. . . . I hope that what I say here to you will find its way back to the full committee."

The Subcommittee members were now a hint ill at ease and they studied Riegle covertly in the light of the Bonaparte Room (a most ordinary hotel meeting room, considering the weight of its name), shifting their study to other faces or back to their fingernails whenever Riegle looked up to make a point.

"Today the U.S. wages undeclared, automated war in Indochina —
using weapons technology that . . . is the most savage, brutal and
inhumane the world has ever seen. . . . In the past three and a half years
of our Republican Administration, the President, with the silent
acquiescence of the Congress, has dropped some 3.6 million tons of
bombs in Indochina — the equivalent of some 200 pounds of bombs
for every man, woman and child in both North and South Vietnam. . . .
In three and a half years of bombing under our Republican Administration some 4.5 million additional Asians have been killed, wounded or
made homeless. Over 12 million American bomb craters under Nixon
have left much of the land torn and useless. Some would respond with
the statement — 'But we're winding down the war — our ground
troops are coming home.' The truth is that we have taken our troops
off the ground and put them in airplanes. The war goes on — and our
bombing policy makes it a bigger and more destructive war than at any
previous time."

Now he tried to touch into the center of their attention. "Innocent
people are this minute being blasted and burned to bits — their families and homes are being destroyed. And these people are innocent of
any wrong doing. There has been no declaration of war — because
none is justified." Good Republican faces looked back at Riegle in the
uneasy bewilderment of bankers who listen to an attractive client apply
in well-ordered and reasonable style for a most sensible loan, but they
know they will not grant it because there is a note in the file "Do not
lend this man money!" So their attention had a tethered look. They
were obliged to listen as this articulate maverick congressman went on
with his simple unendurable facts,"200 pounds of bombs on every man,
woman, and child" (people poorer than the dirtiest Mexicans on either
side of the Rio Grande). What species of masochism to listen to an
argument when they have lost the thread which goes back all of twenty-
five years. They have married, and some of their children have married, they've gone through the meat of a life and it's all been built on
the rock of one certainty — America is the only country which can stop
the "spread"! The nation has gone through a cultural revolution in the
throes of that faith and suffered the third worst war (by casualties) in its
history and certainly the most expensive, and then their own Republican President has stopped the spread by virtually joining the spread.
China and Russia are practically our friends! And still we are massa-
cring gooks who never dropped a bomb on us. So perhaps the
contagion is not a worldwide conspiracy but a conspiracy which is

piecemeal, a rabies where even the poorest peasant is a menace. Good Americans, contemplating the national motive, had nothing to lose but their minds. (So, too, did good Germans come to believe that if Hitler was not right about the Jews, they were all mad.) Of course, Republicans had always lived with the generally unstated premise that if there was a logic to things, it was to live one's own life with decency and not try to contemplate the starving Chinese. Now, however, we weren't just ignoring the empty bellies of people we had never seen, we were burning those empty bellies. Even the thought of leaving four millions of fish or birds dead, wounded or homeless would have made the Subcommittee ill. Riegle was going to win no popularity contest here. He finished by saying: "If we wish to destroy our country, destroy its meaning, corrupt and destroy our capacity for moral leadership in the world, then we need only shut our eyes and our ears and our minds to this inhuman bombing policy. If any of you dare speak out — dare ask the President to stop the bombing — then something important will have happened here."

One of the ladies of the Subcommittee was waiting for him. Possessor of a nervous mobile face with prominent eyes, a full head of iron-gray hair, and chiseled features, she was quivering with the nearness of her anger as she announced that she was Jean Sullivan (of Alabama) the wife of Ira Sullivan, who had been a PT boat commander in the Navy — here the words coming so fast that Aquarius could only gather that her husband was the brother or close relative of the five Sullivan brothers who had all been killed in World War II (which had provided the story for a box-office movie on the family disaster) and she and her husband had three sons in the Air Force, or so Aquarius heard, and Jean Sullivan wanted to know if the witness thought maybe they were murderers, her contained wrath tightening the taut flesh a little more over the prim bones, and Don Riegle answered that he was working to end the war so her sons would not have to be overseas, and was certain they would not be happy to prosecute a war like this one. And Jean Sullivan having been answered to that point where she could rest in the momentum of her wrath — how like a flywheel must such an anger once aroused keep turning! — Riegle was queried next by C. Tucker Weston of South Carolina, a heavy-set man with the honest moon face of a farmer or a judge, and he wanted to know why nothing had been said of the atrocities of the Vietcong and the North Vietnamese upon the South Vietnamese, and Riegle gave a courteous reply which referred to the corruption of the South Vietnamese and their profits in drug traffic, and to the fact that the last man to run for the highest office in South Vietnam, and lose, had been imprisoned since 1960 for just that crime, no more, and could one conceive of what America would be like if Richard Nixon had been in jail since 1960 for the crime of losing to Jack Kennedy? And when Weston's face went suddenly thoughtful, Riegle said deftly, "I think this country was founded on the idea that we should be better than others."

They thanked him and he went out, and it was late in the afternoon, he had been scheduled late so as to keep him out of morning hearings which might get TV prime time or newspaper deadline time. Somnolently, the Republicans listened to the next speaker who was now Martha Rountree, the head of Leadership Foundation, founded "for the purpose of acting as the catalyst for organized women's groups, clubs and organizations," and she was a pale and delicate blonde, no longer young, and her body had gone toward the edges of irreversible rounding and plumping — perhaps as an insulation to her nerves. She was nervous, read nervously, droning on as she told of Leadership Foundation "waging a crusade against what we call Moral Pollution," uttering up that ongoing whine which indifferent orators make when they worry at consuming the time of others. Perhaps she had not been listened to in childhood but now she was there to speak on the issue of putting prayer back into the public schools. "Show me," she said, "one young person who has ever been harmed by acknowledging God. I cannot concede for one moment a position which will accommodate the atheistic point of view in our American society. . . . Today we are beset with drugs, with crime, with rioting and with an obvious moral breakdown. . . . Many people are comparing the problems of today with the Rise and Fall of the Roman Empire," and she was almost petulant as she said, "Will the first nation to put foot on the moon be unable to keep its feet on the ground?" The Subcommittee listened to her politely, but the word was doubtless down on this as well — forget prayer for '72 — there was no sense in stirring up liberals and getting the technicians into a crusade against even the faintest hint of hick irrationalisms in the Nixon Platform, the President was calling to Democrats this year and prayer in the schools had the smack of pure Republican piety. So the Subcommittee contented itself by showing open sympathy for Martha Rountree's nerves but had an embarrassing pause when they could find no questions to ask just as the lady finished by saying in a tremulous tone, "I am eager for your questions." She had been obviously affected by her own speech but still no questions. While they might be

Vice-President Agnew greets the Nixons upon their return from China.

Jerry Rubin argues with Miami Beach Mayor Chuck Hall.

Democratic National Chairman Lawrence O'Brien and Yvonne Brathwaite.

Senator Mike Gravel.

Tent in Flamingo Park.

Hubert and Muriel Humphrey.

Jesse Jackson with the Illinois delegation.

Eleanor McGovern.

Senator Thomas Eagleton and George McGovern.

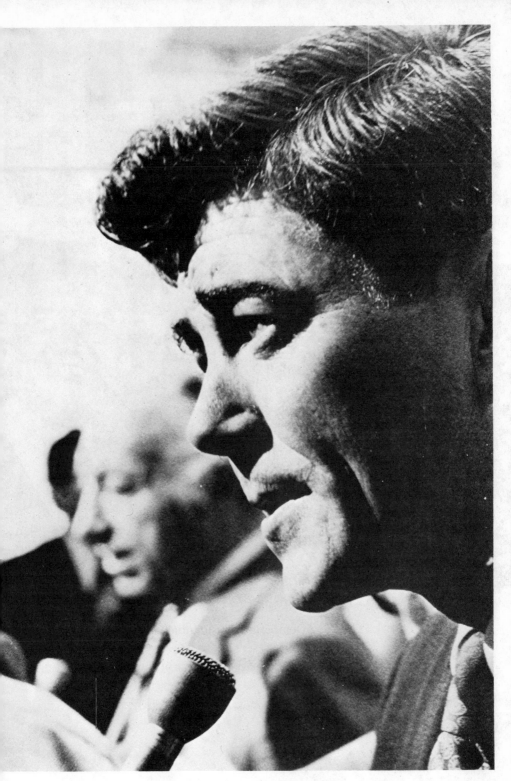
Representative Paul McCloskey.

The 1972 Democratic Presidential ticket.

Anti-Nixon protesters block the sidewalk in front of the
Fontainebleau Hotel.

Clark MacGregor, campaign manager for Richard Nixon.

Mrs. Richard Nixon arriving at Miami Beach.

Left to right: Edward Cox and Tricia, David Eisenhower and Julie, Sammy Davis, Jr.

Henry Kissinger briefs President Nixon in Washington on Kissinger's
secret Paris peace talks.

John and Martha Mitchell.

sympathetic, they were hardly suffering those wretched nerve chitterings which have one sleepless and brooding on Moral Pollution in America in the middle of the night while the distant sounds of automobile exhausts come in the window like the blasts of flame throwers and the cries of drug-heightened rapists stir a dream horizon where bestial yellow eyes glow in the awful world of all moral work undone! The pause went on until Mrs. Honoman from Pennsylvania, a substantial genial woman, thanked Mrs. Rountree and reminisced about Martha's energies and powers and kind favors as a good Republican in a bygone Rockefeller campaign, and Rountree left with hope in her eye but the wisdom on her mouth of a speaker who knows the words failed to reach the hearts they were supposed to touch — failed the Lord again! — and a minister was next, Dr. Elwyn A. Smith, the Provost of Eckerd College, speaking on behalf of the General Assembly of the United Presbyterian Church in the U.S.A., and the Provost was a dry and formal man who would have looked well in high collar and a pince nez, but he read a paper which called for "complete withdrawal from Indochina, normalizing relations with Communist governments, support of the United Nations, renewed social services, tax reform, ecological responsibility and compassionate criminal justice" among a schedule of other liberal items, and the Subcommittee listened and let his words buzz like flies passing through the stone grotto of their ears, and when Elwyn A. Smith of Eckerd had finished, Mrs. Nancy B. Chase of Michigan, a middle-aged lady with a face as stern and proper as her name, was ready to say she knew now why a Methodist member of the Subcommittee had complained yesterday about a Methodist minister who pretended in these hearings to speak for all Methodists. She, a Presbyterian, could now make the same objection. Did the speaker really think his views were representative of Presbyterians? The Provost, as gravely composed as when he read his paper, said that he had explained carefully already that the General Assembly for which he had been selected to speak was "composed of seven hundred commissioners, half ministers and half laymen elected from 188 presbyteries in all the fifty states," representing three million United Presbyterian Church members, and Mrs. Chase while silent had a face which spoke eloquently of the intrigues and trickeries of front organizations which led good church groups down the pinko drain, no, she was not impressed, and Smith had done his duty, and the next speaker, long awaited, would speak for the Gay plank.

There had been several homosexuals in the room with long shag

420

haircuts for hairdo and hip huggers for pants. They tossed their hair as if they had read all the paperbacks about faggots tossing hair, and they *minced* with good awareness of that word, and *worked* on the Subcommittee, looking for eye contests while they tingled the air with the Christmas tinkle of their love beads. Yet when the time came, their spokesman was wearing a dark business suit, a conventional haircut, a shirt and tie and introduced himself as Dr. Franklin E. Kameny who lived in D.C. and appeared "before you, with pride, as a *homosexual American citizen.* If, throughout my remarks, and in your later deliberations, you will keep constantly in mind the second and third words of that phrase — *American citizen* — instead, merely, of the first word — *homosexual* — you should have no problems at all with implementing our needs and with incorporating our concerns in the Republican Party Platform. In fact, if you keep that phrase in mind, it will be difficult indeed for you *not* to incorporate our concerns in your platform, if only because it is so outrageous that ANY group of *American* citizens, in this day and age, should still have these concerns unmet and requiring attention."

If God gives every man a bonus, Kameny's voice was not the bonus. Probably, he had not been born with it, but cultivated its character, the community tone of the didactic homosexual who speaks clearly, contemptuously and pityingly to his audience (with just enough effeminacy to establish credentials) and with just enough of the finest strain of exquisitely insinuated vulgarity to remind you that homosexuality goes back to the childhood root of the stinky pinky and, hee-hee, your asshole is showing, but now the vulgarity was reduced to a veritable dingle-berry beneath twenty mattresses of homosexual pride, born to all purple princemanship. How the Subcommittee loved Dr. Franklin E. Kameny for the way he presented his ideas! He might just as well have inserted sixteen thermometers up sixteen Republican channels of rectitude.

"I could easily devote several times my allotted quarter-hour to a full and detailed recital of those of our grievances which our government at all levels should be considering. I will not try. Even an adequate treatment of our abuses at the hands of our federal government alone would take far more time than I have, even were I to limit that, in turn, to the indignities visited upon us just by the executive branch."

It was written with all the polemical indignation of a thousand conversations over the years between his friends and himself, homosexual citizens. It was a cultural document, a recitation of woes in lofty

421

language which he read in a haughty voice, he *deigned* to address them, and all the while some wistful underpull of the human desire to vault the void put a touch of stridency into his invincible air.

"Our country's birth certificate, the Declaration of Independence, grants to us — ALL of us — the inalienable right — *in*alienable — to the pursuit of happiness. That is really what America is all about. To guarantee that right to all Americans is one of the major functions of our government. That right is one of the unique glories of our country. And, of course, that right is meaningful only if it refers to the happinesses chosen by each individual citizen for himself, not merely those happinesses granted him by his government or allowed him by society. But when *we*, as homosexuals, wish to pursue *our* happinesses — interfering with no one else in the pursuit of their happinesses — we are hounded, harassed, and presented with often insuperable obstacles at every turn. And not only do we get no redress from our various governments, but they are the most rabid zealots of all in doing the hounding, harassing, and placing of obstacles, with a singular ferocity rarely equaled elsewhere.

"Our society takes pride in its pluralism. But you had better realize just what pluralism means and where it leads. . . . In a pluralistic society, every minority group can properly say — and we do say — that for us as homosexual American citizens, this is OUR society, quite as much as it is yours as heterosexuals, and it is OUR country, and it is OUR government, and he is OUR President, and they are OUR political parties — and this is OUR Republican Party. That places an inescapable obligation upon you, as an *American* political party. We ask — we insist — that you shoulder your obligation, and do so NOW."

Was it fifteen years ago or more that Allen Ginsberg, the prophet, had written, "America, I'm putting my queer shoulder to the wheel"? On went Kameny, scolding the Subcommittee.

"And so we have come here to ask for no special favors or dispensations, for no crumbs from your table, for no condescending, patronizing, demeaning, degrading and dehumanizing compassion or pity. We are asking for — and ever more of my people would say that we are quite properly *demanding* — that which is OURS, *by right* to begin with, and which we should have been enjoying all along, not fighting to obtain."

He had read for many minutes at a great rate, but he had all his life to tell, so he moved on without pause. "And that brings me to the stuff and substance of politics: votes.

"The Democratic Party was fearful lest those Democrats who might find it offensive to cast their votes for the candidate of a party supporting rights for homosexuals, might defect and vote Republican. Nevertheless, they did include us. Therefore the Republican Party need have no corresponding fear, because a defection from the Republican ranks for this reason would gain these bigots nothing, since they would now have no place to which to defect. In any case, however, the argument is specious for either party, since there are enough of us so that every vote lost through supporting us will be offset by several gained."

Yes, his argument was specious said the faces of the Subcommittee. What he preached was *license,* the granting of franchise to sin and disease. The country was indeed in a state of advanced Moral Pollution (when poor Martha Rountree could not get her prayers into the schools) and the Republicans were here to safeguard America's spirit. So the promise of ten million votes would not sway them. Indeed the votes were not there. Let McGovern have all the political homosexuals, and in return the GOP would be pleased to pick up all the homosexuals who kept their private lives in some kind of closet and were probably more than proud of their Republican ties, high church was the party of elegance, when all was said!

"Severe limitations of time have necessarily forced this to be a somewhat superficial and simplistic presentation," said Kameny. "I have left a few minutes, and will welcome questions, comment, dialogue and discussion for as long as you may wish. I will be pleased to discuss these matters with any of the Subcommittee members who may wish, more informally later on today. We look forward to seeing a gay rights plank in the platform of the Republican Party. Thank you."

He was done, there was one question, a mild one, and then he went outside to be interviewed, not a very handsome man. His sex life may have been no accommodating bed of pleasures, for his hair was thin and graying, his nose was large and not excessively distinguished, and from the strain of having appeared before so *dim* a group with such urgency of purpose and pride of deportment, his eyes had a restrained but wild and marbleized look, staring blue eyes with raw red rims as though he had been up all night and all this morning and afternoon working on the speech and looking for support on the plank, he was perspiring profusely from fatigue and effort, and now his assistant, a quiet pleasant-faced young man also dressed in dark drab clothes (together they looked like fund-drive solicitors for some rural charity — Northern-Midwest Lutheran Orphanage Association, some such!),

423

was telling the few members of the Press ready to listen about their difficulties in trying to reach Republicans who might be sympathetic. "We expect very little from these proceedings. Why, even when we managed to reach Paul McCloskey, who is after all by reputation most liberal of the many Republican figures here, the *paragon* of Republican liberalism replied when asked if he would offer us support on the gay plank, and I repeat Congressman McCloskey's remark exactly, he said, quote, 'Oh, shit!' unquote."

2

Now the faces began to move faster, and promise arose of a convention which would be interesting after all, not for its conflict — rather, for the promise of design. Slowly, as if one were studying a huge canvas inch by square inch through the glow of a pencil light, a composition of splendid grasp began to reveal itself, a portrait perhaps of the faces tending that great and impeccable computer which measured the pulse and politico-emotional input and emoti-political output of those millions of votes which lived like algae on the rivers of history — the wad in the hour of decision!

If while speaking to Kissinger, he had called Nixon a genius, he meant it. For a genius was a man who could break the fundamental rule of any mighty sport or discipline and not only survive but transcend all competitiors, reveal the new possibility in the buried depth of the old injunction. So Nixon had demonstrated that a politician who was fundamentally unpopular even in his own party could nonetheless win the largest free election in the world, and give every promise of doing considerably better the second time! What Aquarius had not realized until this convention began however to disclose its quiet splendors of anticipation and management was that Nixon would reveal himself not only as a genius but an artist. What had concealed the notion of such a possibility for all these years is that it is almost impossible to conceive of a literary artist who has a wholly pedestrian style. It was possible that no politician in the history of America employed so dependably mediocre a language in his speeches as Nixon, nor had a public mind ever chased so resolutely after the wholly uninteresting expression of every idea. But then few literary artists proved masters of the mediocre. Nixon was the artist who had discovered the laws of vibration in all the frozen congelations of the mediocre. Other politicians obviously made their crude appeal to the lowest instinct of the wad, and once in a while a music man like George C. Wallace could get them to dance, but only Nixon had thought to look for the harmonics of the mediocre, the minuscule dynamic in the overbearing static, the discovery that this inert lump which resided in the bend of the duodenum of the great American political river was more than just an indigestible political mass suspended between stomach and bowel but had indeed its own capacity to quiver and creep and crawl and bestir itself to vote if worked upon with unremitting care and no relaxation of control. He had even measured the emotional capacity of the wad (which was vast) for it could absorb the statistic of 4.5 million civilians and 1.5 million combatants being killed, wounded, or made homeless on all sides in the three and a half years Nixon had continued the war, yes, quietly accept it as a reasonable cost for the Indochinese to pay in order that we not lose our right to depart from Vietnam on a schedule of our own choosing. Better than that — Nixon had spent more on the war than on welfare, not far from twice more — and so had taken the true emotional measure of the wad which calculated that two dollars expended on burning flesh in a foreign land was better than one dollar given to undeserving flesh at home. But if this was the major work of Nixon's intellectual life, to chart the undiscovered laws of movement in the unobserved glop of the wad, it had been a work of such complexity that it would yet take the closest study of the design he had put upon this convention, this masterpiece of catering to every last American pride and prejudice going down the broad highway of the political center. However, there were also smaller perceptions to make each day, and the growth of political excitement in a political student like Aquarius at the size of the bonanza being offered: a course in the applied art of politics by the grand master himself. That this convention would be studied for years by every political novice who wished to learn how to operate upon the insensate branches of the electorate was clear to Aquarius by Sunday when Pat Nixon arrived and certainly by convention time on Monday when the lineaments of superb design had emerged, but that was still later — his earlier days of watching Republican faces provided only the small pleasure of suspecting that a design would yet be here to find, and at times he despaired, obtaining, for instance, very little from a press conference Elliot Richardson gave, since he had gone to hear Richard Kleindienst explain his lack of relation to Watergate, but at the scheduled hour Kleindienst had been replaced by Richardson who offered himself as a bewildered substitute. Richardson was the Secretary of Health, Education and Welfare — HEW, as the initials went — and he had a face for the job. He looked somewhat like Clark Kent wearing his glasses, a fine example of a Harvard Club man on the bureaucratic hoof, tall, lithe, vigorous, awkward as a crew man, but *hew!*, he had a face as keen as the blade of an ax. While obviously a quiet wit, he first chopped down the tree assigned to him in the Democratic woods: Richardson was there to state for newspaper leads that there were 12,000,000 people now on welfare rolls, whereas under McGovern's plan, 97,000,000 would receive benefits — only Clark Kent Superman could stretch a point like that! But the Press preferred to hear about Watergate. Richardson smiled to himself. He couldn't resist suggesting (with the grin of a man who is contemplating the principals all caught in the act) that if the Committee to Reelect the President had actually pulled off Watergate, Richardson, for one, couldn't believe that they would be so inept. He used the word as if the first Republican sin was to be inept. Yet at another press conference, with Black Republican politicians now in the same room where the Platform Committee had originally met, with the same powder-blue tablecloths (now wrinkled for the Blacks), there are few of the Press and no excitement and an air of things close to the edge of the inept. Even the Black Press is a hint hostile. The first speaker, Paul Jones, Executive Director of the Black Voter Division of the Committee to Reelect the President, a pale moon-faced Negro with a worried purse of his lips and a genteel Afro, is wearing Republican clothes, dark suit, gray-blue shirt, a blue checked tie. In answer to a Black heavy-set reporter who asks what he thinks of the attitude in the Black community that Black Republicans are back-stabbers to their people, Jones says mildly that this administration has at least delivered on the promises it made to Blacks instead of offering a hundred years of rhetoric and Democratic pie in the sky. "What I'm saying is in 1972 the Black vote is not in the bag." Next is Ed Sexton, Black member of the Republican National Committee, and his rose-pink shirt and white silk tie give *statement* to his gray suit. Since he wears horn-rimmed glasses and keeps his gray Afro high on his head and shaved near his ears, he suggests a Black English barrister wearing a court wig on top of his head. But he is *crude*. It is by choice. "Our so-called Black leaders are now all in bed with McGovern. Why he had to buy a king-sized bed to get them all in! We might have fewer Black delegates here, but Republicans don't play the numbers game. We're content that we have our people in now in responsible positions whereas McGovern has the lousiest civil rights record of anyone running!" Then comes the third spokesman, Robert Brown, half bald, with silver-rimmed glasses and a white suit with large lightly indicated blue checks, a gray shirt, a maroon tie. He is substantial as he says, "Law and order is one of the biggest issues in the Black community. I don't need anybody to tell me about law and order, I got mugged last week. I can assure you the Black community is behind the President in his desire for law and order." But now the first speaker, Jones, is asked what he thinks of Haynesworth and Carswell. The Press snickers as he answers that his choice "might" have been different. "Still the background does not necessarily indicate the performance. The Supreme Court can change a man. In terms of looking at the overall track record of the President — which is what I go by — I don't know of anyone who has been better for Blacks." The cynicism in the Black Press is audible. "Better for *you*, Nigger" is the mutter.

By all estimates, Nixon will do well to get one Black vote in five. It is tokenism in action, a black face or two to pop a word for him on the tube, and yet, it is more, an elucidation of the political principle of scraping the bowl for whatever vote is there to be scraped. If Nixon had a hole in his heaven, it was in that Black hole of space where all the gravity of American patriotism disappeared with our moral worth. Long before Vietnam, we had had a species of moral Vietnam for fifty years in the Black ghetto and the South, yet this past is going to be nobody's politics if Nixon can help it. So you blow on the faintest glow of every fire, concentrate on the glow of the one coal among the dead coals which you might be about to save when election comes up. So Nixon blew on the remnants of the old ideology of the Black bourgeoisie (before sympathy in Black communities for Black militants preempted the scene) and if he blew the Black vote from 19 percent up to 22 percent, well that was half a million votes he did not have before.

Of course, if Aquarius had seen no more than Elliot Richardson or the Black press conference, he would have done well to suspect even a hint of design, but the next speaker is very much on time (probably so that the Black press conference will not go on beyond its means) and is Pierre Rinfret, the economist in residence to the White House who gives a fast hard-pounding sell on Nixon's economics as opposed to McGovern's. Rinfret who looks like a chubby British M.P. wearing a very broad gray-on-gray pinstripe with immense and elegant lapels, a broad-striped blue and white shirt with a broad dark-blue silk tie, is, despite a round face, straight gray hair, a pointed nose and a receding chin, nonetheless not bad-looking. There is something in his booming voice, utterly confident and wholly reminiscent of the autocratic child at the nanny's breakfast table, which gives him all the heartiness of a spoiled Member of Parliament; his voice resounds out of a chamber which holds no dusty files of doubt, why he could be a hard-sell television salesman for some expensive foreign make of car giving five hard real incontestable reasons why his product is superior to the competitor, yes, he says, the "economic position of Senator McGovern must be considered not free enterprise but socialist in character." It is, he virtually burps with disdain, "Alice in Wonderland economics" and has the following characteristics, five in number, wholly regrettable he would assure the Press. "McGovernomics" moves, one!, toward equality of income "the numbers-game way of getting into socialism," and he holds up a finger. "Secondly, it is the most inflationary set of proposals ever presented to the American people — there will be a 130 billion net increase in government spending." Now, in preparation, the third finger goes up — "this does not mean tax reduction but a *massive tax increase.*" Rinfret looks down at his audience, thus collaring his young first chin in the beginnings of a second. "Since stagnation and recession will prove a function of a new calculated 17 billion dollars of corporate taxation, we can be certain that point four involves nothing less than a reduction of American capital investment, which with its inevitable retardation of the rate of increase of the GNP (if not its absolute decrease), means nothing less than the fifth and fatal point — an increase in unemployment." This Walpurgisnacht of transfer from Nixonomics to McGovernomics having been delivered by Rinfret in one long oratorical breath as full of gusto as a head waiter in a heavy eatery recommending the pot roast tonight with its gravies and magnificent roast potatoes just like Mommies used to make — Rinfret loves his job!

On the other hand, here is the record for Nixon's economics. "In the last quarter of this year, we had one of the highest expansions of the last seven years. There has been a substantial increase in the private sector. If the Press would like a 'fun' statistic, this country adds on in two months what the Swiss economy adds to its GNP in twenty years. Our growth alone is equal each year to all of Canada's economy and nearly equal to Britain's. The Confidence Index of the American People is rising — 74 percent to 90 percent in the last two years according to a study at the University of Michigan. The President has defended the integrity of the dollar whereas" — he speaks loftily —

"McGovern never talks about the concern of retired people for a stable currency. And if in this picture of growth, prosperity and a controlled dollar, the 5.5 percent rate of unemployment is still too high, let me assure you the reasons for this are to be found in the winding down of the war in Vietnam and the reduction of jobs in defense industries by 1.5 million plus the fact that 1,700,000 youths join the labor force each year. So the rate of unemployment conceals the fact that the administration had actually created 3 million new jobs in the last year, a vigorous creative statistic! Nixon economics is sound, stable, dynamic and progressive economics, not Alice in Wonderland McGovern economics."

They asked him questions and he took pains each time to find a way to compliment the query — a technique he must have learned from the boss. After a while, Aquarius' mind began to wander. In their turn when the time came, the McGovern economists would speak in the same positive terms of their economics and would deride that Nixon economy which had just been praised. They would take the same figures and draw opposite conclusions. It seemed to him that economic arguments were invariably reminiscent of court disputes on sanity. On such occasions, the only certainty was that an expert for one side would always be matched by an expert for the other. Perhaps morality and money, equal mysteries, might yet prove to be mutually antagonistic systems, and much like matter and anti-matter calculated to destroy each other on contact. For morality, carried to its logical development, might have to insist that one soul was worth all the coin and credit in the world, whereas money might have to argue that nothing should finally prove alien to its measure. Since each economist, however, tainted the pure science of his economic analysis with moral weightings so subtle as to be unperceived by himself or even by his colleagues and critics, and since producers and consumers moved slowly by times and sometimes quickly through shifting moral displacements there was as yet small recognition and no units nor instruments of measure, it seemed to him that one's only legitimate confidence was that economics was famously unpredictable, and might yet prove more so since the pollution of the world's ecology had begun to invade the natural wealth of the five senses — those same five senses for which all products of consumption were finally intended. It was this thought he had tried to present to McGovern, but so poorly! — tried to say that Nixon had impoverished the real wealth of the land (by his personality first) but also by continuing the straightout pollution (by the economy) of the five senses: the sight of urban and suburban sprawl, highway glut, and bad and monotonous architecture; frozen and chemically fortified food on the palate; a touch of plastic in all of one's intimate environment; the noise of motors, electronic whine and static; and the smell of inversions and smog had taken one vast if undetected bite out of the Gross National Product, indeed had grossed out the sweet and marrow of any average good life in the second third of the Twentieth Century — part of the rage of the wad was that life did not feel as good as the sum of their earnings encouraged them to believe it was going to be. But he smiled at the thought of presenting such notions in the form of a question to Rinfret, that raging bull of the economic pampas! Long live Nixonomics. It would poison us no faster than the rest.

3

Later that day, Clark MacGregor is giving a press conference at the Doral just one hour after his arrival in Miami. A big man with straight sandy hair and dark horn-rimmed glasses, a big friendly nose, his manner is there to suggest that if only there were no Blacks, no Latins, and no slaughter in Vietnam, then America could be a country where Republicans administer government for other Republicans, and they would be superb at it, for collectively (MacGregor's presence is there to suggest) Republicans are better able to give off that necessary aura of confidence, good management and impersonal courtesy which the managers of successful corporations are also able to convey. Of course MacGregor is no corporation executive but a former congressman from Minnesota appointed recently by Nixon to run the Committee for Reelection of the President after John Mitchell has resigned, and in fact he dresses with just a little too much hint of the lost Square to work for an *Eastern* corporation, he is wearing a gray suit, baggy from travel, a pale-blue shirt *and* a black tie with little red diamonds, but these are unworthy items — what he fairly promotes is the geniality of high confidence. Behind him, reminiscent of Rinfret, are charts. "Rate of Inflation Is Down," they say; "Real Earnings Are Up"; "Total Civilian Employment Is Up While Armed Forces Man Power Is Down!" and they stand in front of the powder-blue curtain (TV-blue in every press-conference room) while underfoot is a blue-green carpet and gold-painted chairs for the Press. Mermaids and sea horses look down on MacGregor from the ornate ceiling of the Mediterranean Room as he is asked if there is any way the Republicans can lose the election.

"No," he says. A smile. "Although I think it will get closer. Let me say that we are gearing up for a close fight, and absolutely on the watch against overconfidence."

"But you think the polls are good?"

"In Minnesota, my home state, 96 percent of the Republicans are for Nixon, and that's an incredible figure if you know anything about party breakdowns."

"How many Republicans for McGovern?"

"Two percent. We're ahead in the state 58 percent to 31. Exceptional statistics for Minnesota." In 1970 at Nixon's request, he has run for senator against Hubert Humphrey, an impossible campaign and lost by 2 to 1.

"How big is your budget for the election?"

"We're aiming — the figure is not yet fixed — but we look for a total budget between 35 and 38 million." (The Democrats have announced 25 million for their budget, and nobody thinks they will reach it.)

"What about Watergate?" comes the first voice. "Will that hurt you?"

He is unflappable. "I am absolutely satisfied that the so-called Watergate caper will have absolutely no effect on the election of Richard Nixon." His doughty air suggests that he could be hired equally well as a sales manager or a police commissioner.

"In relation to Watergate," says another reporter, "is it possible you've set up your tight security in this hotel because you expect the Democrats to bug it?" There is mocking laughter, for the Press is much irritated. A security tight enough to guard the President has been installed at the Doral, yet the President won't even stay here!

To get to see even a minor Republican official, it is necessary to obtain a special folder and look up his room which is listed in it, get the official's permission by telephone for an interview, then look to obtain a pass in the downstairs lobby in order to get on the elevator. A woman reporter cries out that the Republicans call themselves the Open-Door party. "Will you please open the door of the Doral a little?"

"Well, look," says MacGregor, "I just got off the plane. Let me look into the situation."

"Will you ease it?"

"Let me see." He thinks he is done with this, but another reporter asks, "Any truth, Mr. MacGregor, to the rumor that the security is so tight because the Republicans already have the 35 million in the hotel?"

MacGregor laughs heartily. "I knew it was the dog days, but not the silly season."

Now the conference is moving to its point. If there is a single flaw in any Republican presentation of themselves, it is (except for the six million killed, wounded, and homeless) to be found in Watergate. What a mess. Five men have been caught trying to remove the bugging devices they have installed (by breaking and entering) in Democratic Headquarters in Washington, and the two leaders not only have had links to the CIA but to the Committee to Reelect the President, indeed have worked for a more important team with the modest name of "plumbers" who were set up to investigate White House leaks to the Media: the "plumbers" include members of the White House staff, and a former Assistant Attorney General, are even connected to a special counsel to Nixon. One of the plumbers, E. Howard Hunt, formerly a high official in the CIA and White House consultant, has now disappeared. Two weeks before the Watergate arrests, however, Hunt has flown to Miami to meet Bernard Barker, leader of the five men who were caught in the middle of the night at Watergate, and Barker has deposited four checks totaling $89,000 to his account, the money reputed to have come from wealthy Texas Democrats via wealthy Texas Republicans, but none of these names will MacGregor agree to divulge (at the request of the contributors, he says) and then there is still another check for $25,000 which has gone through Maurice Stans, former Secretary of Commerce, and Hugh Sloan, Jr., treasurer of the Nixon campaign (who has since resigned for personal reasons). Allegedly this check has been given to G. Gordon Liddy, a former White House staffer, who became the attorney on the Committee to Reelect the President's Finance Committee — Liddy — it is the same allegation — has converted the check to cash and given it to Barker. Liddy has been fired for refusing to respond to questions. "You know I can't answer that" is the reply everyone hears him making to his sympathetic interrogator. What a mess! Rumor in Miami, Washington, and New York suggests Martha Mitchell's last ultimatum to her husband John that he must dare to choose between the government and herself is no curious coincidence. Certainly, not since the writing of *El Cid* has such a conflict between love and duty been presented to so high an official with such perfect timing. Is it true that John has been told he could not do better than to choose Martha? Some go so far as to suggest Martha has been encouraged to be Martha. Whatever! Mac-

Gregor has replaced Mitchell as the Head of the Committee to Reelect the President and now can dodge the worst of the questions by saying that he has only been on his new job since July 1. So he has no first-hand knowledge of what has gone on before, "Although, I am convinced, let me say, that no one in the White House, or in high responsible position on the Committee to Reelect the President, has any prior knowledge of, or gave sanction to the operation generally known as the so-called Watergate caper. I will say," MacGregor stated solemnly, pushing his glasses up on his large nose, "that I have talked to the White House principals in this affair, and Mr. Stans, Mr. Mitchell and Mr. Colson have all assured me that they were not involved, and I am convinced that they are men of honor. I can only say that they have satisfied me."

"Will you agree that if any of them were lying, there was no way you could know?"

"No, I cannot agree. The word of men of honor is good enough for me. More than that, I cannot say. We have been warned by Judge Richey to employ all necessary discretion against impinging on the rights of the defendants by making disclosures which would then hurt the government's case."

"But since you were not there before July 1, you have only the word of these high officials to go on?"

MacGregor has a temper, and he is containing it now. The straight sandy hair suggests some fire at the root, for his face is getting red. "I have endeavored to be as forthright as I can, given my lack of knowledge before July 1 of the activities of the Committee to Reelect the President."

No one quite dares to suggest he is saying that he knows but he doesn't know. "In public life," MacGregor says, "you have to learn when to trust the word of other people." But what he can't know is when an honorable man has overpowering motive to lie. So, too, for motive something less or somewhat more than this, have public officials already created the highest euphemism for an official lie — the credibility gap. MacGregor gulps and reddens and his temper singes his hair, his glasses slide down his nose and are pushed up once more, the sea horses and mermaids look down on him, the Press looks up from their golden chairs and he does not move. He doesn't know and he does know, but he is a man who has been picked to weather more than one storm, and it will be no trick at all, here today, to ride this out. The

433

Judge, he repeats, wishes to restrain them from talking of the case. ". . . necessary discretion . . . you fellows are trying to get me to impinge . . . rights of the defendants. . . ."

4

Were counter-espionage and Christianity the good true poles of the party? Next day — what could possibly restrain him from going? — Aquarius attends the Sunday Worship Service of the Republican Convention. It is being held in the Carillon Room of the Carillon Hotel, a supper club room which moves in a crescent of coral curtains and gold fringe around the room, with golden seats arrayed for more than a thousand guests and these seats are filled. American flags cover the wall on either side of the stage. Sitting there, he thinks there is probably no act on earth more natural to Republicans than going to church on Sunday. That bony look which seems to lay flat white collars on ladies' clavicles, that Wasp look bony with misery (when they are merely tourists eating in some jammed Johnson's off the boiling reeking superhighway during family summer travel, the windshield shellacked with the corpses of bugs numerous as dead Vietnamese, yes, same gangling bony lonely pointed elbows) comes instead into its inheritance and stands out in all the decorous composure of characterological bone when Republicans get to church. Then their virtues live again — hard work, neat clothes, patriotism, and cleanliness become four pillars of the Lord to hold up the American sky.

This church service, however, is being held in the morning as balance perhaps to the Republican gala of the evening, a veritable panorama of worship with celebrities to pray and Mamie Eisenhower for Honorary Chairman, plus the wives of Cabinet officials to compose the Advisory Committee. Senator Tower, tough little John Tower, right-wing Republican from Texas, gave the welcome as Worship Leader. Once, when he first came to the Senate, Tower had the mean concentrated take-him-out look of a strong short welterweight, but the Chamber laid senatorial courtesies upon him — now this Sunday morning he was mellifluous and full of the order of dignity as he whipped out his reading glasses, intoned "Almighty God," and delivered the prayer written by President Eisenhower for his first inauguration, "Give us, we pray, the power to discover clearly right

434

from wrong." There was no hitch in the words for him. Tower was a hawk, and the operative definition of the hawk is that they do not have trouble with moral discernment.

Then came Frank Borman, the former astronaut, who had read Genesis on Christmas Eve as the capsule of Apollo 8 circled the moon. There were a few (liberals and Democrats in the main) to whisper that Borman read the familiar words like a grocery list, but this morning, wearing the shortest haircut still left on a good-looking American, he read the same way, comfortable before the audience — he was a man who always occupied his own volume — and it was clear that he came out of all that part of America which knows that to read with expression is suspect.

George Romney offered a prayer. "Help us to help those who most need help." Was he praying to the 12 million bomb craters in Vietnam? "A crisis of the spirit requires an answer of the spirit."

Cliff Barrows who was the Music Director for Billy Graham now led the singing of "America the Beautiful" and for once Aquarius listened to the words.

> *O beautiful for patriot dream that sees beyond the years,*
> *Thine alabaster cities gleam, undimmed by human tears!*

John Volpe, Secretary of Transportation, gave the congregational prayer "Through your goodness, the sustenance of life is always flowing," and thoughts wandered again, mindless once more, over the concrete, macadam, asphalt, sand and gravel which had poured and flowed across ecological cuts in the land since Volpe first came in to build more roads, and then spoke liberal Senator Brooke from Massachusetts. It was only in some inner suppleness which suggested the tricky reflexes of a ball player like Maury Wills that one could sense he was a Black. Otherwise Brooke looked more like a respectable young Jewish businessman as he read from Corinthians "and the greatest of these is charity," his liberal contribution to Sunday morning.

But it was left to Dr. Elton Trueblood of Earlham College, Richmond, Indiana, to give the sermon, and Aquarius later wondered if Richmond, Indiana, was looked upon as a swing vote in a swing state; in that case, local Hoosiers might be loyal to the honor that one of the town clergymen had addressed the assembled Republican mighties, loyal at least for a few hundred more votes — Aquarius had already begun to admire the thoroughness with which Richard Nixon looked

435

for such votes — quite the equal of any first-rate housewife on the hunt for ants during spring-cleaning. (It is the innocuous corners which must never be overlooked.) So, even on this nonpolitical and nondramatic occasion, this *un*political and highly Christian convocation, care had been taken to invite the President of the Synagogue Council of America, also serving as rabbi of Temple Emmanuel, Miami Beach, to offer an Old Testament meditation. Then Maryland's Junior Miss, Miss Cathie Epstein, soon offered the song "Amazing Grace" which was harsh on the ear for its amazingly tortured sounds, he thought, but the crowd gave Miss Epstein such a spontaneous whip-out of the sound "Amen" and so much hand-clapping that they had obviously heard something else — score one for Jews-for-Agnew. No, Nixon did not miss any corner with an opportunity for amazing grace, and the Reverend James A. McDonald who sang next with the deepest pleasure of the ages since Paul Robeson, was also black, blacker than Brooke, and the benediction being given by Father Ramon O'Farrill who was Cuban, his name in the Miami Beach papers would do no irreparable harm with local Cubans, no more than Rabbi Lehman, Epstein and Jeannette Weiss would offend nearby Senior Citizens. Of course, Jeannette Weiss, an alternate delegate from Michigan who read the Pledge of Allegiance, might have been German as easily as Jewish, but all the better — she could gladden both kinds of newspaper readers, and certainly would not hurt the pride of women, alternate delegates (so often ignored) and a few hundred near neighbors in Michigan. But since Jeannette Weiss proved when she stood up to be black, it could be said that Nixon was tickling every straw in the broom. Now, there was not much chance that the President had literally been able to bother with such detail as this, but of course it was not impossible he had actually put the program together for the sort of relaxation others take in crossword puzzles — it didn't matter — his hand was laid so finely upon the palpitations of this convention's breast that from the thought of his presence came all the necessary intimations of *intelligence*. Even the least of his assistants must acquire a sense of how to place each potential use in its slot. Not every evidence of harmony in the Vatican issues directly after all from the Pope, but who would say he is not the center of all its political spirit!

Along came Dr. Elton Trueblood then to give the sermon, and in fairness to him, he was there for more reasons than to swing a corner of Indiana; the Doctor was a sermonizer of invention — he fulfilled that Sunday function which requests the preacher to give the parish something to think about from Monday to Saturday for he said, "Government ought to be a holy calling, a divine vocation. We ought to speak of the ministry of politics." And he quoted Romans 13:6, "The authorities are ministers of God," and so decided that "Whatever your occupation in politics or government, you are called to be His ministers." As he spoke, his features too far away to be discerned, only his white hair and glasses, his balding head, dark blue suit and starched white shirt visible in the distance, he looked nonetheless like a compressed whole bully of faith — small surprise that Faith was his favorite word. It was as if he was the first to know that this worship service was not part of the convention so much as the convention was going to be a service of worship. Nonetheless, Trueblood touched something of confusion in the Republican heart, which he did not necessarily put to rest. No more than the good decent average Republican would admit that he loved to fuck his wife (those who did) in a voice which might ever be heard aloud — as if blight must immediately descend on the marriage — so must many Republicans have thought in private over the years that they were doing God's work and being *His* ministers in the world of corporation and government, *His* ministers to work for the salvation of this tortured and troubled Republic, as divided as two souls residing in the same heart, this Republic of order and barbarism where the young would, if given their way, yet walk with naked breasts and faces hidden by matted hair and trampled flowers, timeless droning drug-filled young with filthy feet — they would yet walk upon the heart of America. And now Aquarius knew suddenly why good Republicans would never mind the bombs, for the blood of the North Vietnamese was the smallest price to pay that America might be saved from the barbarisms beating in the young — yes, it was Nixon's genius to know that every bomb dropped somehow extinguished another dangerous hippie in the mind of the wad, evil was a plague of creeping things and the bombs were DDT to the cess-dumps of the world. It was America which had to be saved — the heart of God resided in the living life of an orderly America, and this passion was so deep, so reverential, and so in terror of the harsh light of the word, that his congregation listened to Elton Trueblood with respect but not comfortably, staying at the edge of that bolt of comprehensions he would loose, for if good Republicans might think of themselves privately as ministers of God protecting the homeland by their acts and their presence from every subtle elucidation of Satan, still they feared the loss of magic, like primitives they feared the loss of magic once the thought was declared aloud. Fierce as the fever of discipline which holds the heart in righteousness is the fear of the fire beneath — what a fire is that compressed American combustible of love and hate which heats the stock of the melting pot.

And Aquarius, carried along by the flux of some of his own thoughts, began perhaps to comprehend the certainty of these Republicans whose minds never seemed to reach beyond the circle of favors, obligation, work, courtesies and good deeds that made up the field of their life and the repose of their death. That was the goodness they knew, their field was America, and they seemed spiritually incapable of hating a war they could not see, yes, sentiment against the war had eased even as infantry had ceased coming back with tales of the horrors on the land — yes, Nixon was a genius to have put that war on the divine national elevator high in the sky where nobody could see the flowering intestines of the dead offering the aphrodisiac of their corruption to the flies. So, was it then a compact with the Devil to believe one was a minister of God and live one's life in work and deeds and never lift one's eyes from the nearest field? Or was that all any human could dare to comprehend, his own part of the patch, and leave Nixodemus to be divided by Satan and Jehovah, no, impossible! the miserable truth was that men and women, willy-nilly, were becoming responsible for all the fields of earth since there was a mania now loose on the earth, a species of human rabies, and the word was just, for rabies was the disease of every virulence which was excessive to the need for self-protection. One hundred seventy-six thousand tons of bombs had been dropped on Cambodia in the last two years, and that was more than all the bombs dropped on Japan in World War II. Cambodia! our ally! but on Laos it was not 176,000 tons but more than a million. We had in fact dropped more bombs altogether in the three and a half years of Nixon's reign than we dropped on Europe and Asia in World War II, indeed almost twice as many tons of bombs and there was no industry, military population, railroad yards, navy yards, or other category of respectable target to compare with Germany, Italy and Japan, no, finally not much more than the wet earth, the dirt roads, the villages, the packing-crate cities and the people — so the bombing had become an activity as rational as the act of a man who walks across his own home town to defecate each night on the lawn of a stranger — it is the same stranger each night — such a man would not last long even if he had the most powerful body in town. "Stop," he would scream as they dragged him away, "I need to shit on that lawn. It's the only way to keep my body in shape, you fools. A bat has bitten me!"

5

So, yes, carriers of a rabid disease the Republicans might certainly be (that same disease of the Twentieth Century which first had transported the victims to the ovens even as — a speaker in Flamingo Park would cry out — we were now bringing the ovens to the victims, Amerika!) but small evidence of the rabid was visible as he watched Senator Dole on Sunday TV after this worship service. Nothing appeared in Dole of the disease unless the rabies had been transmitted into Dole's private reserve of contumely and scorn. Dole was perhaps the best looking of the Republicans, Senator from Kansas, Chairman of the Republican National Committee, a ringer to play Humphrey Bogart's younger brother, and he had taken something of Bogart into his style, that stubbornly created manliness which scorns any other man who cannot live on the wry edge of the code, "Yes," Dole promised, "I'm going to keep an eye on McGovern in the Senate — if he ever shows up." He gave every evidence of disliking McGovern personally (which is effective politically if you have the looks to hold your audience) although, for fact, Dole might be truly jealous of a senator from a sister state as equally unglamorous as Kansas who could still win a national nomination. "Yeah," said Dole, vintage Bogart wit to the jugular, "he's always 1,000 percent certain until he changes his mind." Of the running mate, Dole was heard to say, "Shriver's always available," which was kinder than his comment on Pierre Salinger who, subject of anathema for a trip to Hanoi, was described as a man who "can never do much but smoke a cigar." Dole had all the sharp bite of the proud and crippled — a little later, greeting Pat Nixon, it was evident that his right arm was paralyzed for he shook hands with his left, and held the right to his chest like the wing of a wounded bird.

Then came Rockefeller and Reagan down the broad highway of the tube and they sat side by side, and jiggled each other in the soft inner flesh of the arm, the telltale flabby few inches above the elbow on even the most weathered old politician, teased each other for TV nearly so much as they teased the Democrats, Rockefeller and Reagan who had

439

not been able to get together in '68 to stop Nixon, their ideological differences too much to right and left. Now, they were closer. Rockefeller was blooded. He had his Right-wing dueling scars. Thirty-two convicts and eleven guards had been killed at Attica after Rockefeller refused to visit the prison and talk to the convicts about their demands, or even to be present to watch over the details of the attack to regain the prison. Something had gotten into his face since then — the look of a sour clown. Or, was it a stale hero? So that face which once had been able to win votes for him, would now lose them. His honor was gone (if not his ambition) and it was possible he knew it.

Yes, Rockefeller had paid. He had the beginnings of a high-pitched whinny, he snaffled a little as he laughed, and Reagan had him going and coming, because Reagan had never wandered out of the arena of his own imagination, whereas Rockefeller had once traveled to such strange stadiums that he even tried to capture a nomination after obtaining a divorce, bold Republicanism! Rockefeller had had more to lose, and now within must feel older than Reagan, wearier certainly, and he argued with less wit on their point of dispute (which was over the reallocation of delegates for '76 — were the big Eastern states to get them or the small and Western states?). Actually, they seemed fonder of each other's presence than with continuing the dispute because, now if they wished to try for the nomination in '76, they were indispensable to one another. By then, Rockefeller would be sixty-eight years old, and Reagan sixty-five, which is old for a presidential candidate. So the living presence of each would give sanction to the other's campaign. Indeed either one would prove a final disaster to the other if he died. No wonder Rockefeller spoke of Reagan as Ronnie. For a politician there is small distance between necessity and affection.

6

Pat Nixon arrives with her daughters at the gate of the Fontainebleau, up the driveway and into the crowd of Young Voters for the President. She disappears in a sea of white floppy hats with blue brims and straw hats with red-white-and-blue bands. A combo with red-and-white-striped jackets is playing middle-class weddings songs, pseudo Benny Goodman music (maybe the term for its category), accordion, clarinet, flute, drums and electric guitar, and George Romney has been running before her arrival — he is excited — and Dole is now down to greet her. There is a flood of cheers when she comes up in her black Cadillac — much like the on-off hysteria you hear when the team hits the field, and all the signs wave. Now, the signs painted by the YVPers all begin to wave, these Young Voters for the President who in the eyes of the liberal Press will yet look as ears of goldenrod to hayfever sufferers. Somebody has provided all YVPers with the paint, no dark secret, Republican money can be spent for Republican posters and paint, but the kids have done the work themselves and the signs say WE STAND FOR PAT; WE LOVE JULIA; TRISH YOU'RE A DISH; MIAMI LOVES THE 1ST FAMILY — there is just a hint of the slovenly in the uncertain use of capital letters. WELCOME BACK, PAT; AGNEW FOR PEACE; VOTE FOR A WINNER; NIXON GIVES A DAMN — here is one — NIXON IS FOR LOVE. Now kids are chanting "Four more years," "Hey, hey, whateya say, Nixon, Nixon, all the way." They are not the most attractive faces he has seen. Hundreds of young faces and not one is a beauty, neither by natural good looks nor by the fine-tuning of features through vitality or wit — the children in this crowd remind him of other crowds he knows well, and does not like. Of course! — they are the faces of the wad! — all those blobs of faces who line up outside TV theaters and wait for hours that they may get in to see the show live, yes, the show will be more alive than their faces. The genius of Nixon! Has he selected this gaggle of mildly stunted minds from photograph files? Or had they been handed applications as they left the theaters after the live shows? Aquarius remembers the look of the television set in his room at the Fontainebleau. It was up on a small pickled-white dais and looked like some kind of altar for a medico-religious event. Nixon may have drawn the deep significance from such a sight twenty years ago — how valuable must be the insights he could pass on to McLuhan, well, Aquarius was frothing again and so came near to missing the value of Pat Nixon's entrance.

Ergo, he went back to the opportunity to watch Pat Nixon do her work, went twice that afternoon to see her, once at her planned spontaneous tumultuous entrance with Secret Service men who quietly, gently, steadily, *politically,* forced an aisle for her up the steps and for a few hundred feet along the lobby to an elevator up to a private room in the Fontainebleau Towers while the band played (a trip which must have consumed a half hour) and there after a bath presumably — how much desire for still another shower did such waves of human flesh arouse in a First Lady? — she had changed and came down again with

441

her daughters to plunge into an orgy of hand-shaking and autograph-
ing as she proceeded along a six-foot-wide roped-off aisle to a banquet
room of the Fontainebleau where a reception party was being given for
Pat Nixon, her girls, and the Young Voters for the President.

What a rich opportunity then to study Pat Nixon, first with her
entrance to the hotel in a pink dress, then her immersion later into the
reception crowd with a royal-blue dress, long-sleeved, straight-skirted,
a light soft material vulnerable to crowds, she was able to demonstrate
that particular leathery hard-riding sense of grace she possessed which
spoke of stamina first, for she could knee and elbow her own defense
through a crowd and somehow never involve the dress, that was one of
the straight-out tools of her trade and she knew how to employ it —
that material was not going to get snagged on some dolt's ragged elbow
or *ripped* any more than a seaman would get his feet caught in a rope
he was coiling in a storm.

So, for instance, had she managed her passage through the lobby for
the reception, pointing her head at an angle up to the glare of the
Media lights poised like flaming swords over her way, the ears inured
to the sound of another brass combo (with one Black trumpeter, trombone, banjo, other trumpet, and drums), still she moves a little to it, just
a flash, as though to demonstrate that dancing is one of the hundred
and sixty-eight light occupations she can muster.

Earlier Clark MacGregor has come down the steps with his wife, he
stands close, he is proud of her like a college kid with one smash of a
keen steady! Indeed there are older people all through the lobby waiting with love in their eyes for Pat — she has worked hard and she is
better off for it — they are ready to revere her for caulking the hull of
the ship so well (it is their ship, too — the Presidency residing somewhere in the awesome fall between one's God and one's parents) and
the crowd is orderly, not pushing, the YVPers all stashed in the reception room, but Pat is still going slowly down the aisle through the older
folks in the lobby, tarrying to say hello, and before her comes Julie,
committed, determined to do a good job in a green top and white-
skirted dress, black belt, and Tricia in a white and pink dress with her
husband Ed Cox who looks gracious, as if he takes considerate care of
her which she might need for she is near to beautiful and tiny, wearing
perhaps a size 5 dress with blonde hair all pulled back and sprayed into
an immaculate pale-gold mass, but her dark eyes, nymphlike and lost,
suggest the vacant remote and yet flirtatious look of a princess who has

been told about life outside the castle. Then comes Pat. There are liver spots to perceive on her hands, and her teeth must be capped, she has obviously pinched and pushed and tightened her presentation of herself all her life, but she had ridden the beast of such discipline, she looks better now than when she entered politics. No, she has emerged as a pro, such a pro indeed with such a pride in having mastered every side of her occupation that one did not ask oneself if she liked shaking hands. Possibly the question did not exist for her, since it was a matter of indifference whether she liked it or not — she was not on earth to like things but to do them!

Still, for a politician, the love of shaking hands is equal to a writer's love of language. Ultimately that is the material with which a politician must work, yet not all politicians love shaking hands, nor with everyone, any more than Ernest Hemingway loved every word in the English language. Certain words like "gorgeous" brought out Papa's snobbery — perhaps he was in this sense equivalent to a Republican politician who preferred to grasp the hand of the clean, the neat, the precise, and the well-laundered. (Hubert Humphrey, to the contrary, was a veritable Thomas Wolfe of a politician; just as no word was too mean or out-size splendiferous for the man who could write *Of Time and the River*, so Hubert would kiss queens and scrofula victims with the same warmth.) Now, if Pat Nixon had been a writer, she would have gravitated to the commonest words that everyone used or the most functional words — she would have wanted to reach the largest audiences with ideas they could comprehend on first reading — that was how she shook hands. Like a *Reader's Digest* editor attacked a paragraph. She loved to work with the wad. Give her the plainest dullest face, no spark, no flair, just the urgency to get what it wants — her autograph, her handshake. She gave them out equally, like the bills and smiles of a bank teller. There are faces to greet, currency to handle, stay on top of the job!

In his own mayoralty campaign, Aquarius ended up by shaking hands wherever he could, had in fact to his surprise ended up liking that act more than anything else in politics, at least once he comprehended that the only way to do it was to offer as much of himself as was present with every greeting. The phenomenon was that energy came back, and the hand did not get tired. It was as if in shaking a thousand hands, six hundred may have returned a little more energy than they took, as if the generosity of a mass of people might be larger than their

443

greed, a belief which was as it should be if one wanted to become a politician, for it gave, on balance, some confidence at the thought of working for others.

But Pat Nixon had obviously come from folds of human endeavor which believed the reward for service was not to be found in the act but afterward. Naturally she gave energy and she took energy, impossible not to, and was somewhat wilted if with a glow when she was done, but it was the muscles of her arm which worked, and the muscles in her smile, her soul was the foreman of the act, and so did not reside in her muscles, but off to the side and vigilant as she worked the machine. She no longer saw faces, no, she was a heavy worker on an assembly line, and bodies came her way, there were touches and taps, a gloved rhythm to keep — she moved in some parallel perhaps to the burden of a slim tight-mouthed Negress with heavy family worries on a heavy assembly line for whom the pay was good and so she was in it until death or double overtime. So, too, would Pat Nixon have no inner guilt before trade unionists or Blacks — she had worked as hard as any of them — in her own way, she moved as well. Afterward, her fixed expression stayed in memory for she had the features of a woman athlete or the heroine of some insurmountable disease which she has succeeded in surmounting.

A man getting an autograph from her asks, "How do you stay so young?"

She smiles carefully. "With hard work," she says.

7A

If it seems to be a convention with nothing but background, arrivals, receptions and press conferences, nothing in contention and nothing to commence, still he finds it more and more interesting for it is the first sustained clue he has ever had to the workings of Richard Nixon's mind and *his* comprehension of America, and it is a mark of Aquarius' own innocence that he has never recognized until now how Nixon's vision might be conceivably more comprehensive than his own.

At the Celebrity conference in the same Mediterranean Room of the Doral, three of the five most massive celebrities are not present. Charlton Heston, Sammy Davis, Jr. (Sammy for *Nixon!* all the pastrami eaters will scream), and Frank Sinatra are somewhere else or not arrived.

444

There is only good Jimmy Stewart and good John Wayne in a dark blue yachting jacket and gray pants, his cheeks red, his dark hairpiece on, and his eyes as wide open, expressionless and sleepy as a lion digesting a meal. Later, when he makes his speech, it will be very short and he will say no more than that he wants Nixon cause he's the right man in the right office at the right time, a way of remarking that Nixon isn't his man under other circumstances, but he is also there to guard the flock — there is a herd of women, honey-blonde soft-featured animated Ruta Lee from TV who will be seen at the convention Tuesday night with Kissinger — she has converted to Nixon from the Democrats, as has Mary Ann Mobley, former Miss America, now a "card-carrying Republican," and she is animated too. Mary Ann Mobley has obviously gone to acting classes where they taught her to use her personality, and so there is the unhappy suspicion that if you asked her how to cut a carrot she might say, "I take out my *cleaver* which is shining bright, for cutlery must *gleam* in the kitchen, and I wash my carrot, and then" — flash of her eyes — "I go chop-chop, chop-chop!" So she was using her personality as she spoke about politics until interrupted by Johnny Graham, a comic and/or gag-writer, a sawed-off man in a big yellow jacket who seemed to be serving as team shepherd and Commissar — Graham got her to sit down at which point she received cheers. At a press conference! But it was now apparent two-thirds of the room was filled with Young Voters for Nixon out to see their TV stars.

Graham had the floor. He was funny. "I see where all by himself Bob Hope raised as much money on television for flood victims as all the actors who worked to raise funds for the Democratic Party on their telethon. I guess," he said with a grin wide as a barn door, "Americans are particular which disaster they give their money to."

Glenn Ford gets up to a big hand, but he is soft-spoken and very shy. He makes an inaudible speech three sentences long and goes back to his folding chair, but one of the rear legs inadvertently slides off the back of the platform, the chair collapses and Glenn falls down only to get up quickly in the middle of bales of his sheepish embarrassment.

"Get a stunt man," yells Johnny Graham.

"Glenn will do anything for publicity," says Ruta Lee.

Chad Everett, a TV star, ambles up and says, "I think if you got a big gun, shoot it. And Nixon's the man." He sits down. The YVPers scream. Somewhere in Nixon's Maxims must rest the observation that a TV star in a current series is worth two Hollywood evergreens.

Nonetheless Kathy Garver, TV star on a show called *Family Affair*, is

445

trapped by the invisible imps of her motive, for she is suddenly unable to say Nixon's name and mispronounces it. Jerry Rubin in the Press section gives her the friendliest grin out of his wild red-and-blue T-shirt and full chestnut beard, and John Wayne glares at Jerry Rubin. Kathy Garver corrects her pronunciation, Mary Ann Mobley laughs wildly. The YVPers clap.

Ethel Merman takes a bow, and none of the young in the audience even know she was the madam in *Call Me Madam*. The speeches get shorter and shorter and say less and less. Jimmy Stewart humphs and phumphs his skinny presence all the way up and says, "I'm a lifelong Republican and not about to change now." Cheers. The actors have all borne testimony to the show-biz maxim which goes, "If you're doing a benefit, and it's a nothing mood, don't be the one to try to turn it around."

Still, how reassuring will the dullest of these actors seem in memory to the dullest regions of the wad, for they have demonstrated that even if one is famous, it is possible to be utterly uninteresting. Across our continent, the yaws of one soul will offer comfort to the voids of another. Bombs are fireworks to the sleepy.

7B

On the way back to the Fontainebleau, he stops off at a Black reception. Negro doctors, lawyers, and businessmen, delegates most of them, move around with their wives who are heavy-set. There is not a jive Black in sight, no smocks, sarongs, or flaring Afros. No prime evil. Nothing carnal. The mood, if boring, is absolutely safe. He has not felt so safe among Blacks in years. The spirit is sullen, long-suffering and secure. It is as if he has been invited to a gathering of Pullman porters. Then some young Blacks come in. They are saltier in their stance for they are self-defensive. Still, there is no menace. Just safety. Will America be miserable when the streets are safe?

Later, he will hear about the Black caucus next morning. It takes place in a small pink room at the Eden Roc with wrought-iron black chairs and white plastic seat covers. Counting various whites and the Press, there are present two hundred people. Paul Jones, who had spoken at the Black press conference, walks in with Julie Nixon who is wearing a white dress with a sailor collar. Reportedly Jones has the sly look of a man who is pressing hard not to reveal that he is the first Black from his hometown to have a white lady on his arm. Of course the other Blacks look on it as a token — where is Pat? So when Julie Nixon starts speaking, they are annoyed that her speech is prepared. (Indeed, it is so prepared that next morning Julie Eisenhower will give the same speech at the Latin caucus, only substituting the word Latin for Black, etc., as she talks of the administrative appointments of Latins to high-ranking position.) "We," she says, "will do much better among Black voters," then tells them her father has ended much discrimination in the South. "Even if we had the most massive busing program ever proposed, we couldn't reach all the children." Perhaps it is her didactic manner (where spontaneous if halting remarks might have been more appropriate), but she is hardly begun before there is a strong undertone of muttering. It grows so loud that Jones from the podium is obliged to hush the audience.

When Julie is finished, the Press start to move out, and a short heavy-set woman on the podium pleads: "We would appreciate it if the Press didn't leave now." En masse, the Press goes away. They have come to see Julie. A chairwoman announces the time of departure for the bus which will take the Blacks to Convention Hall.

7C

That was Monday morning after Sunday night when the Republicans had had their Gala, one thousand dollars a ticket, and security as tight at the gate of the Ballroom in the Fontainebleau as at the elevators of the Doral. He cannot get in, and succeeds only in missing some of the street action outside, for a few of the guests have been harassed. Next day he hears of women whose dresses were spattered with eggs. A mistake, he thinks, to inflict small damage. Be able to shut a Gala down, or leave it alone — to a Republican lady, one egg on the dress can mop up the guilt of five hundred bombs. Later, that evening, he stands on a balcony and watches police twelve stories below form a wall across the entrance to the Fontainebleau. On Collins Avenue, the demonstrators, down to a few hundred, are marching off. "Back to the Park, back to the Park," a girl keeps shrieking over a radical bull horn. He wonders if she is the same girl he has seen in Flamingo Park on Saturday night, one of the leaders of one of the groups. He has been remiss about

447

preparing to cover the street action. He recognizes that he expects it to fail.

The Jefferson Airplane has been planning to perform at a big free concert in Miami the weekend before the convention and other groups have promised to come if the Plane was there. It would bring tens of thousands of kids to the area. Which would bring more thousands of government troops to stop them. But there is a military principle to public assembly. When the number of demonstrators increases from hundreds to thousands, then it hardly matters how well they are policed, nor how quickly one moves to disperse them. There comes a point of congestion where traffic cannot move at all. So if the Yippies and the SDS, the Zippies and the Vietnam Vets Against the War are to be effective in their demonstrations, they need thousands of youths to amplify their moves. But the big free concert has had to be called off. The Jefferson Airplane changed its mind. It did not wish to come. Grace Slick was supposed to have said that demonstrations are of no use after the Eagleton affair because McGovern is sure to lose. There were some who had thought the point was to embarrass Nixon and protest the war regardless of who won the election, but in any case a lesson has been taught which will not be learned. It is that one should not try to found a revolution on musicians; because the delicate instrument of their body can all too easily be damaged, they are all too prone to desert.

In any case, there have certainly been no fine musicians in Flamingo Park the night before. Hundreds of kids sat on the grass and watched movies about atrocities in Vietnam, and listened to a boy with a black beard dressed in red-white-and-blue overalls (and nothing else) sing a song called "Revolution." Indeed even as he padded up to the platform in his bare feet another boy in the grass shouted, "Watch out for the nails in the board."

"No, man, my feet are tough," the boy said, laying down his soles from step to step with inadequate caution but some kind of heavy grace. Then he sang. His voice was even flatter than his feet. "Revolution!" But the words were so poor that hardly anyone could retain them long enough to give back a chorus. The kid now made a speech about everybody staying cool and not getting grassed out so they could *work* for the demonstrations, but put-on is the law of the revolutionary young, you are nothing if your head is not living in two places at once, and therefore half a minute later he announces, "The revolution means sharing, so pass around your dope." A big laugh from the spaced-out throng. They sit there waiting in the night, an apathetic mass respectful of their own apathy, for Sunday, Monday, Tuesday and Wednesday they will be demonstrating.

Later, he walks through the park. A group called Sequoia are finishing on another bandstand. He stares at a sign near them which says PEOPLE'S INDEPENDENT MILITARY PARTY — PIMP. Yes, support your pimp. The signs are good at least. One tent has a placard over the entrance. JAIL FOR WAR CRIMINALS it reads. Beneath is a list.

1. Richard Nixon
2. Spiro Agnew
3. Richard Helms
4. Henry Kissinger
5. Melvin Laird
6. Nguyen Van Thieu
7. The Rockefellers

Now the next night, Sunday, watching the few hundred demonstrators move away from the hotel and begin the two-mile walk back to their tents and bedrolls in Flamingo Park, he thinks that Miami Beach is a splendid site for a picturesque war, but one would need an army of Mexicans to wage combat in its heat. Languorously, a few yachts are meandering down Indian Creek running parallel to Collins Avenue so they can study the demonstrators from the water. Rich and native Miamians on a sightseeing party. And he is observing from the balcony of the twelfth floor. He must have turned some corner in his life for he feels no shame whatsoever. Later he will go out and eat a good dinner and not think of the kids in the park. When the time came for the real war, if it ever came, and came to America, he would presumably be enough of a man to recognize it. If he was not, it would be his own karmic ass he fried. So, cheers to Hemingway, he thought, and a good dinner.

Still, over the meal he found himself thinking once again of Nixon's genius. Of course, it had only been common sense, no more, to pull the convention out of San Diego. The scandal of ITT would be well averted, and so would all too many groups of musicians be averted. All of San Francisco would have come down to jam San Diego. Half of the experienced college demonstrators in America lived within a few hundred miles. How many California undergrounds would have mobilized? Rumor even had it that John and Yoko Lennon had been sheepshanked on citizenship and visa applications in order to keep them

449

away. Slowly, the metastases of the totalitarian were setting up their new colonies and the Republic was kind enough to give Media a perfect seat for each non-event. What benignities might reside in the malignities to come. Muzak in the cancer ward. Tomorrow he must go to Vizcaya and study the reception for Agnew.

8A

He sees an example of typical Republican management. The strategy is excellent and the tactics moot. It is probable there is not a better place in Miami to exhibit the Vice-President than in Vizcaya since it is much too far away from Flamingo Park for the demonstrators ever to march to it. Besides Vizcaya, being an uncommonly luxurious estate situated in a mangrove jungle by the sea, proves to be a perfect setting for Agnew, yet it has been turned over by the heirs of the original owner to Dade County and is now an art museum which charges admission and even has a gift and snack bar (hidden away). Any group of one hundred people can rent the place for a private function and pay no more than $350, so the Republicans are thereby able to present a reception which will be distinguished, lavish, and symbolically resonant, yet need never be considered guilty of squandering money. The greatest single expense will probably prove to be the salaries of the Secret Service men, for a platoon, at least, must be on hand. The outlay, however, will certainly not be great for entertaining the Press: the costs here seem restricted to two bottles of whiskey, a tray of sandwiches on the patio (which will get wet in the late afternoon rain) plus a velvet rope drawn totally across the middle of the East Loggia so that reporters will not be able to touch Agnew or any of the guests whose hands he shakes, nor incidentally hear any of the conversation which is the probable purpose of the quarantine.

From Nixon's Maxims: Never make friends with the Press on a short-term basis. The sudden warming of relations will encourage their true nature which is spite. Cold relations create chilly stories whose details however remain correct since the Press is now afraid of reprisal. Then, if the office is esteemed enough, the "chilly" story may actually work to advantage since it is obliged to keep the central figure at a distance which is where he belongs. Warming relations with the Press must however only be undertaken during periods so long as a four-year administration and then should be conducted with great care analogous to the methods used in training intelligent dogs for the harsh routines of the circus. Reporters whose behavior cannot be predicted by any of the best methods once sufficient evidence is in must be maintained in a state of chilly relations.

Since Aquarius certainly had had no opportunity to work for the Prince, he could only assume that the wisdom of these neo-Machiavellianisms was coming to him as a species of spin-off from one of the more Aquarian manifestations of the century (which had to be the incalculable amount of telepathic transmission and reception now girdling the globe — a phenomenon doubtless ready to exhibit vigorous activity over Miami tonight what with the President arriving tomorrow and the young yearning the Cosmos over a little toward the vortex of their grassed-out heads in Flamingo Park). Psychotronics, the new science of the century, must be putting him on the same beam of RN Maxim Intuits that the Nixon staff was receiving. But who was serving as his antenna? It could not be Vic Gold, Agnew's press secretary, who kept a conversational Ping-Pong bing-banging over the velvet rope while reporters waited for some action to begin.

"Did *he* play tennis this morning?" a voice asked.

"Of course, you kidding? When doesn't he?" asked Gold.

"Vic, tell the truth. Where is *he* staying?"

"I don't know where he is staying, believe it or not. The Vice-President's residence in Miami is a secret even to me."

"How you holding up, Vic?" asked an old intimate.

"Lousy. Nervous. Look at these." He held out his hand and cocked the near Press a peek at his sedatives, four leaden-blue capsules, as impressive in their color as bullets. Dr. Bill Voss, Agnew's personal physician, now said, "These are Eagleton pills." Gold groaned. "Man, will I be glad when this is over? You kidding? Will I be glad!" he said, distributing his largesse of news to the ten or fifteen members of the Press who had come all the way out to Vizcaya. Abruptly, Aquarius was happy. Psychotronically speaking, his unwitting antenna must be no one other than the Vice-President himself. How else account for the authoritative language in the maxim he had received. What a bonus. He has a plug into Agnew!

Since we may be confident that Aquarius only becomes fanciful when he is frustrated, it will help to explain that Vizcaya is a palace of exceptional beauty and he would like to be able to explore its rooms and talk to the guests Agnew is receiving, instead of being grateful for the bulletins Vic Gold has been providing in the roped-off corral of the East Loggia. There is at last in this palazzo a sense of the tropics and the high style of the tropics, of sunsets turning from gold to the deepest washes in mother-of-pearl, of orange flamingos and Spanish blood and coral keys, patios which overlook the sea, even pirate chests buried in the mangroves. Vizcaya! It is an Italian Renaissance palace, planned in part by the first owner for its courtyards and galleries, its pillars, its arches and its Italian steps, its Great Stone Barge which serves as a breakwater and looks as large as Cleopatra's float, standing off the terrace, moored to the sea. Vizcaya's gardens are isolated from the visitor today, and its statues of coral. It is altogether, he senses, one of the few legitimate palaces in America, and he will read afterward about its history, discover that James Deering, the manufacturer and philanthropist, its creator, has the peculiarly American history of being born in Maine, growing up in Evanston, Illinois, where his father has founded a fortune in harvesting machines, and is, our capitalist-protagonist, a bachelor heir who dies an exotic bachelor, a traveler, a collector, and the creator of the most remarkable stage set ever arranged for an American politician since the moment Agnew comes out and stands in the loggia with his wife and daughter and the heirs of James Deering to receive his guests — a move he has made with no rush to ceremony at all — Vizcaya is transformed. There is Agnew not ten feet away on the other side of the rope in a dark near-black suit, a white shirt, and a black-and-white-figured tie, a stern mode of dress one cannot locate at first — it is not quite the costume of a banker nor an undertaker, and certainly not an executive. It is perhaps the suit a retired French hangman might wear, but he would have to be wealthy. The suit sits on Agnew with distinction. He stands there, his eyes heavy-lidded, narrowed down to slits — the writer Joe McGinnis will later describe them as looking like the slits in a tank turret — although it is possible Agnew closes them the better to pick up messages through his skin — but in any case Agnew is composed and remote as he shakes hands, a figure of distance and very well installed as he stands on an inlaid marble floor with marble busts in the niches in the walls behind him. Through the arches one can see a terrace with balustrades by the sea and the Great Stone Barge with its herms and gargoyles and nymphs of gray coral dripping in the waters of Biscayne Bay. A combo is playing on the terrace and black waiters serve drinks to the guests who have gone through the reception line and now take a buffet under a pink tent with white posts while white metal chairs and tables decorated with ornate patterns of holes seem to repeat the holes in the flagstones of the coral, the much-pocked look of a stone wall which long ago must have weathered a burst of bullets, yes the coral gives the impression that all of Vizcaya has been spattered with bullets, and then taking in at last the steel shutters cranked up high on the arches of the loggia, Agnew's suit assumes its focus. He looks, of course! he looks like he is wearing just the suit a Latin American dictator would wear in his palace by the tropical sea, and indeed has there ever been a man as high in American public life who has looked this much like the general who throws over a banana republic in a putsch?

The idea, while endlessly attractive for its sinister connotations, is nonetheless too simple for Agnew. He is a curious fellow, much more curious than Aquarius has ever realized, and not nearly so formidable as his pictures, a particularly quiet man on this occasion. As the guests go through, he shakes their hand with a peculiar impersonality much as if he is a spirit installed in some flesh-and-body machine which shakes hands. Perhaps his soul is away somewhere and his body is playing the equivalent of computer chess as it shakes hands. It is not that he has lost his soul or is a robot, it is just as if he understands this occasion so well he knows there is no need for the soul to suffer with him. An altogether unexpected reaction for Aquarius, and cheers him as nothing else could on the virtues of covering a convention in one's own body-and-flesh machine rather than watching it on television. For example, seeing Agnew come in yesterday at the airport, and be greeted on the TV set by a solid and united wad of cheering YVPers, Agnew had looked merely like Agnew. Now, ten feet away, across the untransmitted air, there was this inexplicable sense of his privacy as if no one in America knew the first thing about him. There was even — was it with the faintest hint of contempt — a suggestion that he was altogether aware of how much people would regard him as like unto a South American dictator, and therefore how much some would need him, not *him* he would know, but the symbol of his appearance. And again a suggestion arose from his presence of something so shrewd and self-centered and private, so recognizant of the possibilities life had thrust upon him, so recognizant of the instrument the whole public idea of his person had become, that it was almost profitable to wonder

453

what he thought of all that rich man's fear in all that money and power of corporate America which had settled so strongly on him as the successor to Nixon, settled on him because he was reminiscent in appearance of Mussolini, Perón, and a dozen other prognathoid promises of a man who would *run* the country and so shore up the bottomless anxiety of those tropical rich who swallow frontiers no more but live in the sun and fret — if their anxiety can be described — at the triple worry that the country is on the edge of apocalyptic violence, the wife is readying herself for a fling and if they weren't so old they'd be long gone queer. The religion of the rich, like the religion of the wad, was freedom from dread. And the reception line moved forward, Republican delegates from all of America, and Republican celebrities beginning to come, and rich men from this region of tropical gardens and treachery where revolution is an excuse for the letting of blood, and strong men are more desirable than saints.

As Aquarius departs, the cops are feasting in the wood on what is left of the sandwiches in the rain.

8B

From Nixon's Maxims: The ESSO Company is changing its name to EXXON for all of its 25,000 gas stations. We may say that there has never been a more deeply based compliment on the successful centrality of my name.

From Nixon's Maxims: Nixon-Agnew is the ticket whose sound best elicits voting response in the Silent Majority. This may be attributed to three factors. (1) The lack of specific meaning in the sounds. Explanation: Nobody can be offended in the absence of a specific statement, concept, or idea. (2) The rhythm of Nixon-Agnew, ONE-two, one-TWO, while irregular, is strong. Explanation: This tends to activate a similar sense of rhythm in the Silent Majority. (3) The sounds of Nixon-Agnew while not agreeable are also not disagreeable. Explanation: Therefore they will speak of the middle, the recognizable, the monotonous, the daily. The Silent Majority will always vote for anything which suggests the maintenance of their daily life. Let me say that the more this daily life is without interest, the harder they will vote.

9

Of the convention itself, of the formal programmed activities of the Republicans in Convention Hall, nothing need be said, and everything can be said. The President was heard to remark, "It's like no convention has ever been in the world," and he was right if the function of a convention is to infuse the candidate into that part of the American brain which watches a television set. For three consecutive days it was inevitable to find the President's face on the tube, or the face of some Republican who was speaking about the President (not unfavorably!) or thinking about him (with a smile!) and if occasionally a demonstrator in the street would also be heard stinging the Office with an indictment sharp as pepper in the nostrils, still the reference was always to Nixon, and it was a fair assumption that the demonstrator's interruption of the benign mood was worth more to the President than whatever he could lose to the words. The medium is the message, and the fundamental message of television is an electronic drone of oscillating dots. Onto that psychic vehicle of almost unperceivable nausea upon which our senses focus is installed a rider — the content of the television program — but the content is to the nausea as the size of the rider to the size of the vehicle. People who sit before their television set for hours must use it as a kind of videotronic tranquilizer, a psychic poison whose uses are also medicinal; they sit there in order to receive the nausea— yes, to receive the nausea, exactly so that something unbalanced in the play of their appetites or the swoop of their fears can be vitiated a little, worn out precisely by that imperceptible nausea of drone and dots. Something animal washes out of them and into the cosmic sea. Reduced to less over the years, they are nearer to balance, even if such balance has been achieved by polluting the dread of their soul (which may be their only guide to Heaven!) — what an unnatural distance to come from reporting a convention. But perhaps no explanation of Nixon's success may suffice which fails to consider the possibility that this public personality, once young, near to rude, and self-righteous, has become a bland drone of oscillating ideological dots. In its impact as it comes over the tube, his personality is close to the nature of the tube itself, closer than anyone else in political life. (Which may be a way of saying that while Nixon is speaking, if the set should regress down from color TV with a clear image to nothing but the bare and vibrating gray screen offering no more than the drone and the glare of the dots, shock and shift of mood would be felt less with Nixon on that screen than with anyone else!) How tempting to rephrase such a thought into one of his maxims for is it not also a way of saying that a politician of the center does well to look for a personality which will cohere to the spirit of centrality of the television tube and so be part of the cure which is found in the reducing drone of the TV atmosphere?

Still, not everyone who watches television is ill. Healthy bodies (if not too many vigorous minds) spend hours before a set and take this all-but-unperceived nausea as small price to pay for the pleasure of the content. So the art of television is to find a content which can sit agreeably with the nausea, a rider who can take the motion sickness of the machine. If we can conceive of books printed upon a paper whose texture is slimy and odor repulsive, it is evident that the fundamental art of the writer might then be to accommodate his topic and prose, so far as possible, to the paper. (Given offset printing and plastic pulp that day comes nearer.) How successful the Republicans had been at choosing a content with a high degree of nausea-accommodation may be seen in the pleasure of the President's reaction after watching much of his own gathering on TV. Complimenting Rick Reichstein who had overseen the production Nixon said, "It's like no convention has ever been in the world." We can take the existential meaning of his words, and assume he is really saying that other conventions have had their historical life confined mainly to the convention hall where their political war was being waged, and only a fraction of this history was communicated outside. Nixon, however, had conceived of a convention which would possess *no* history — since there would be no possibility for anything unsettling to happen in the hall. Therefore the *history* of this convention would exist immediately, but in the world, not the hall — the communication itself would be the convention. Whereas the happenings in the hall would have almost no legitimate existence in themselves — they could, for example, have as easily been photographed in a mammoth studio with superb mimics playing the principals, then have been edited into a spectacular. The shift in content and mood might have been minimal. Nixon had succeeded in composing an artwork with highly skilled actors who would not have to concern themselves with the perils of improvisation, ergo they could bring all of their energy, spontaneity and charm to prepared positions, an ideal situation for most skilled politicians since like professional actors they are happiest with familiar lines and a winning role. If there were also elements of opéra bouffe in the mass entrances and exits periodically of an amateur chorus, the YVPers, there was also sophisticated comprehension of how to incorporate the anti-war demonstrators outside as an element of uncontrolled improvisational cinema left to the discretion of the television networks themselves, a freedom not so large as might first be suspected, since Republican orchestration of the major events would hardly be interfered with by the networks. On that Nixon could count. Indeed he had made the elegant move of turning the Media's resources against itself. Since he offered a paucity of conflict, the means and modes of television reporting — which are interviews with embattled principals and contentious delegates — were diminished; indeed many of the interviews had been all but scripted, then choreographed, since every lack of eagerness by Republicans to trust the Media resulted in a seller's market: the television interviewers — will horrors never cease! — had to apply for interviews, and thereby be screened out of the best questions while the subjects of the interview were prepared. With desperation, the Media discovered that their little impromptu interviews were more boring than events on the podium where anti-McGovern invective was winging and zinging. So they had to cover the podium more than they cared to, for that was the only continuing action Nixon provided. Thus his own script became the one which would finally be filmed. The occasional insertion of the street action, however, didn't hurt; in fact, it helped to spark the product which emerged as a species of new TV film (in effect!) as sophisticated in its mass wad-like way as a work by Jean-Luc Godard — for if the actors virtually wore earphones through which the director could tell them how to respond to unforeseen reactions, there were also minor montages in this spectacular left open to moods of chance — yes, that is the very nature of sophistication in a highly controlled film; once in a while it is wise to put in a pinch of unlabeled herb for a classical sauce. So let us see Nixon as the first social engineer to harness and then employ the near to illimitable totalitarian resources of television. If the remark is not immediately comprehensible, its impenetrability can be reduced if we will recognize that every film director is totalitarian to the degree he exercises a near to total control over script and actors — it is

457

just that he is a totalitarian competing alone against other totalitarians — he has no troops, is merely a tyrant to a few actors. It was Nixon's fundamental achievement to recognize the possibility of a three-day spectacular of *celebration* — the most difficult sort of script one can conceive — except that Nixon had the artist's wisdom to confine himself to those themes and audiences which were compatible; he would offer the reductions of his personality, warmed and *gemütlich-*ized, to the Silent Majority of both parties. Never before in history had a prepared tide of sentiments so similar in direction been washed for so long across the American brain.

Not for small effort had Nixon become the Eisenstein of the medi-ocre and the inert. A monumental arrangement of details and the most careful timing of their sequence had gone into the Program, as well as a host of materials and a hundred artful resolutions of his problem — which was to conduct all necessary business of the convention while catering to the audience's desire for direct or symbolic representation of their favorite organizations, military forces, their fifty states and all such small and large and variegated categories as: the local Florida officials, the women, the parochial Republican organizations, the major religions, the senatorial and congressional proprieties, the police (local and national), and such unorganized groups as children, teen-agers, the young, the middle-aged and the old, Republican liberals, conserva-tives, athletes, and all hordes of Democrats who detested McGovern.

The disposal of convention business could be handled. While a bold solution might have been to show no business at all (and so turn the convention into a telethon raising money for the nation's most incur-able disease — the national vanity) Nixon was famous for caution and compromise! so he merely reduced business to a concentrated mini-mum, then employed the theatrical properties of business as a tone for his palette, industrious hues of gray-green and brown were occa-sionally established for background. The party platform was, as ex-pected, written in advance and most modestly amended by the com-mittee and subcommittees. No platform disputes reached the floor. There were none visible. On Tuesday afternoon there was a floor fight between separate liberal and conservative plans for the allocation of new delegates among the states in 1976, a matter of no importance or much importance depending on whether a liberal and conservative might be in close competition for delegates four years from now. Since no one could be certain, the rules fight finally was important, but since conservatives had more representation in this convention than liberals, it was evident they would win. Nixon permitted the matter to come to the floor where the conservatives won after a carefully limited hour of debate by a vote of 910 to 434, and this proceeding provided a thin and most useful red line of narrative strife to the afternoon activities, delayed nothing at night, and gave the delegates a half-hour of deliberation and balloting which participation accelerated their cheerful faces into greater cheer. Participating at last! And happy to laugh at themselves. The Chief was so smart.

That was convention business. For representation of all the American groups watching TV, the Jeannette Weiss Principle (discovered during Worship Service) was employed — wherever possible use a black lady with a German Jewish name doing a patriotic bit. Thus Ray Bloch, the Music Director of the Convention Orchestra, had a name which at once might please Jews and Germans as he played music which satisfied every gamut which ran from Dixieland through Lawrence Welk to Lombardo. Chad Everett, of *Medical Center,* the Special Guest, pleased TV fans, doctors and Californians; the United States Naval Sea Cadet Corps satisfied the military, the young, the patriotic, and Senior Citizens who remembered John Philip Sousa. The Pledge of Allegiance was given by Thomas Joiner of Rock Hill, South Carolina, winner of the 1972 American Legion Oratorical Contest, a choice which pleased Legionnaires, high-school debating teams, citizens with the first name of Rocky, or the surname of Hill, the state of South Carolina, and all the many Southern families for whom a name like Joiner was well regarded. When one considers that all this did not occupy more than the first fifteen minutes of the first afternoon of the convention, while audiences still adjusting their sets were also being entertained by Acting Chairman Senator Dole, the Republicans' handsome injured war veteran, engaged in his quiet understated resurrection of Humphrey Bogart, respect for Nixon begins to rise. It is the mark of great artists that they pay attention to those surfaces of the work to the rear of the niche. By Tuesday afternoon, the Jeannette Weiss Principle was being employed in full swing. Not only did Philip Luther Hansen of the American Lutheran Church give the invocation, but he was also Director of Alcohol and Chemical Dependency in a unit of Northwestern Hospital, Minneapolis, a lock thus on Scandinavians, Scandinavian Lutherans, Alcoholic Lutherans, Senior Lutherans on pills, and the formidable number of voters in America named Hansen or Hanson. But of course Tuesday afternoon was aided by a theme — it was Salute to Older Americans, and led by the Honorable Jacob K.

459

Javits (winner of pluralities of so much as a million in New York State
and obviously much beloved by Jewish voters of all ages), a double use
of the distinguished Senator since he was honored by a place on the
program and denied (or had relinquished temporarily) his position as
one of the few liberal Republicans in the Senate who were articulate
against the war in Vietnam. The super-function of the Jeannette Weiss
Principle (like double- and triple-word scores in Scrabble) not only
connects the separate properties of a speaker, but manages to convert
his negative potential to positive. To complement Javits, the salute to
the aged was fortified by a lady named Church who could thus reassure
some of the more bigoted Senior Citizens, especially since she was on
the Planning Board of the *White House* Conference on Aging! —
Tuesday afternoon had its buried arts to reveal.

So through the five sessions of Monday afternoon and evening,
Tuesday afternoon and evening, and Wednesday night did the Jewish
Rabbis, the Catholic Bishops, and Greek Orthodox Reverends give
Invocations and Benedictions, so too did the Lutherans and the
Methodists, and the Baptists. On the last night, Ms. Susan Savell gave
the invocation. She was a former Chaplain Intern of Vanderbilt, thus
delighting Liberators, youth, and the distinguished universities of the
Middle Southern Conference. Indeed all the Protestant sects, including
the A.M.E. Zion Church, were brought in but for Episcopalians, Presbyterians, Congregationalists and Unitarians. The Episcopalians and
Congregationalists were bound to be so completely for Nixon that they
could take a snobbish pride in not being called to a gang demonstration, the Presbyterians were so stubbornly divided that no one
could unify them and not worth the effort to try. The Unitarians were
long gone to McGovern.

It would be tempting to follow the order of appearance of Boy
Scouts and Girl Scouts, 4-H, the Salute to Working Youth, and the
Fellowship of Christian Athletes; to give an accounting of how often
there was a mention of each state, or a study of the flattery paid to local
officials in Florida, the honors paid to the police, liberals, athletes and
the middle-aged — Ethel Merman would sing "The Star-Spangled Banner" on Tuesday night — but finally a college course in Government
could devote a semester to the near to ninety items on the program
over these five sessions. Better to concentrate on the higher applications of the Jeannette Weiss Principle in the Keynote presentation
which produced the metamorphosis of an Eastern Black senator into a
Midwestern mayor with a resemblance to young Nixon, which then

became an attractive former Democrat from Texas who was a woman. There was thus an Eastern-Midwestern-Southwestern Black Woman Nixon giving the Keynote speech who was also white and a mayor and a Massachusetts senator. We may pass over Senator Brooke who passed over his own disapproval of Vietnam — "It is the privilege of every American to differ with his President, but it is the obligation of every American to be fair in judging a President's performance." Fairness would suggest that no mention be made of the six million Indochinese who were dead, wounded, or homeless. We may even pass over Mayor Lugar of Indianapolis who indeed looked very much like young Richard Nixon first entering the Senate, in fact, Lugar was reputedly a favorite of Nixon's and thought enough of his resemblance to the Chief to announce, "I'm hopeful I'll be considered for President of the U.S. . . . in this decade." Like an earlier Nixon, he attacked. McGovern would "cripple our Army, Navy and Air Force," be found "begging, crawling to the negotiating table," "abandon prisoners of war and friends in Saigon," and we Republicans would not permit "radical new taxation plans to flatten hard-working Americans," or "perpetuate welfare into a way of life." Lugar was as tough as a pistol; he could go fifteen rounds with his own voice. Then came Anne Armstrong who could not be passed over.

She was attractive, she was agreeable, she was relaxed. She did not show any of that fatal political screw-tight at the corner of the jaws which disfigures so many otherwise good-looking women in politics; on the contrary, Anne Armstrong looked like a good liberal Democrat from Texas, humorous and brave. The worst of it was that she had once been a Democrat, and moved over to the Republicans. If the delegation she brought to the convention from Texas had no Blacks, one Chicano, and one delegate under thirty, small matter, she now gave her third of the Keynote speech which must have been worth hundreds of thousands of votes, maybe it was even a million-dollar speech (if a vote is worth a dollar) for one could feel Democrats sliding off the party wagon as she cantered along in her easy friendly voice there to show how nice you could be when you owned a ranch.

"A small group of radicals and extremists has assumed control of the National Democratic Party, taking its name but repudiating its principles. The sudden storm of McGovern has devastated the house of Jackson, Wilson, Roosevelt and Kennedy, and millions of Democrats now stand homeless in its wake.

"We say to you millions of Democrats deserted by McGovern and his extremists, 'We are the party of the open door. That door is open to everyone. . . . Come in and join us.' "

On the Republican Party would move, with its new friends, "up the broad middle road to progress," she said, and one had an image suddenly of all the pokey finicky nervous little women and old men who crawled their automobiles in panic down narrow roads, all the drivers who should have had their licenses revoked a decade ago, and Anne Armstrong was calling to them.

10

There were calls to many a corner of the land before the first Nixon Spectacular had finished its first day. If the three elements of the production had been Business, Representation of American groups (via the Jeannette Weiss Principle) and Entertainment, it was part of the aesthetic wealth of such a spectacular to convert the high business of major political speakers into entertainment as well. In the afternoon, William Rogers, the Secretary of State, had offered a tender memoir of his recollections of Dwight D. Eisenhower and a movie followed of Mamie Eisenhower sitting in her widowed living room at Gettysburg and reminiscing about Ike.

"I want to tell you a little story about the night at Walter Reed before Mr. Nixon was inaugurated. Ike called him up to wish him good luck and, at the end of the conversation, I could see the tears in his eyes and he said, 'This is the last time I can ever call you 'Dick,' tomorrow it will be 'Mr. President.' He was very proud of Mr. Nixon and if ever Ike had a disciple, certainly it was Mr. Nixon."

Since Republicans could only play in the Key of C, be certain they played Beethoven wherever they could.

In the evening, Hugh Scott, the Senate Minority Leader, introduced Alf Landon who looked incongruously like an old labor leader. Speaking in the bland and colorless voice which had lost him every state in the union but Maine and Vermont when he ran against Roosevelt in 1936, Landon said of Nixon, "One good term deserves another," thus suggesting the symbolic value of his appearance — as FDR had done to Landon, so would Nixon do to McGovern, and the delegates gave him a standing ovation. Over and over at this convention would the delegates be like the crowd at a football game when the score for the team goes higher and higher — as it does, so rises their greed for more points. It is records they wish to set, as if only a high-scoring record can cauterize the last of their inferiority complex, and Republicans had a huge if private inferiority complex — it was that America really did not want them, not that melting-pot majority of America they had once been so foolish as to let in.

Hugh Scott being given the opportunity of introducing a man so old as Alf Landon then extracted full value from the spirit of veneration. It is but a step from veneration to awe and worship — Scott stepped from all the eighty-plus years of Landon's life into a roll call:

". . . we wish to take a moment this evening to commemorate those great Americans who gave so much to this country, and have passed from us within those same four years.

"Their past dedication will help to inspire this nation's future. Out of the temporarity of life on this planet, they have become permanent. A tribute to all of those who have left us since last we gathered is symbolized tonight by the names we call. I ask this convention for a moment of silent prayer in the memory of: Dwight David Eisenhower, John L. Lewis, Everett McKinley Dirksen, Francis Cardinal Spellman, John Steinbeck, Vincent T. Lombardi, Richard Cardinal Cushing, Richard B. Russell, Whitney M. Young, Jr., Thomas E. Dewey, Louis Armstrong, Dorothy Elston Kabis, David Sarnoff, Winston L. Prouty, Hugo L. Black, Dean Acheson, Spessard Holland, Ralph Bunche, John M. Harlan, Cary Hayden, Mahalia Jackson, Marianne Moore, Llewellyn Thompson, James F. Byrnes, J. Edgar Hoover, Allen J. Ellender."

One did not expect Hugh Scott to mention Janis Joplin, Jimi Hendrix or Jim Morrison of the Doors but where were Lenny Bruce and Edmund Wilson and Brian Piccolo? Or Sharon Tate? It was possible she was worth as much in the cosmic hall of names as Allen Ellender.

Scott's appearance and the tribute to Alf Landon had been planned originally to precede a tribute to Pat Nixon. From the dead to the aged to the living had been the implicit progression, but Barry Goldwater was the only actor in this three-day spectacular to show temperament. Scheduled for ten minutes — he had written a speech to go half an hour. Since he had also been scheduled early, much too early, scheduled before the Keynote and the Nixon film, before the tribute to Landon and the appearance of Pat Nixon — he would be buried by the number of speakers scheduled to follow him. And he would not cut his speech. He had not run for President of the United States eight years ago in order to be cut down now to ten minutes, he was not willing to

463

live with the possibility that one of Richard Nixon's favorite old Italian sayings might be "Revenge is a dish which people of taste eat cold." (Barry riding high in '64 had said of Nixon, "He's getting more like Harold Stassen every day.") Goldwater was not often right, but he had principles, and one of them was that a former candidate for the Presidency was entitled to more than ten minutes of America's time at an hour when people were still at dinner. So he objected to the order of the program, and before negotiations were over, Hugh Scott and Alf Landon had been brought in to fill his place and Barry was on toward the end of the evening, and with more than ten minutes if he still had to cut down from thirty. Nonetheless, his speech had all the Goldwater virtues. While Barry had a political screw-tight at the corner of his mouth (a manly tension which comes from the civilized inability to grind on the bones of one's dead foes and bite the hams of the living), still it did not disfigure him as it would a woman, perhaps it even added to his particular charisma, for if at his worst he was a prejudice-panderer and bias-mongerer, the sour emotional butt of the great American heart, he had at least an air of primeval ferocity (which arose from the low-slung profile of his brain long dislocated into his jaw). Barry was there! — you could see him at the end, glasses broken, hair matted, but on that field of nuclear desolation he was wielding a club, swinging at the buzzards. What a sweet speech he gave:

"I would like to call attention to what happened last month when the shattered remnants of a once great party met in this city and what I listened to and saw on my television set made me question whether I was sitting in the United States or someplace else. I was reminded when I listened to their constant complaints of the coyotes who live on my hill with me in the desert of Arizona. These coyotes, particularly on a moonlit night, just sit and bay and moan and cry over everything that exists but never suggest anything new, anything better or anything constructive to replace them. They just wait, like the coyote, until they can tear something down or destroy a part of America.

"I'm tired of hearing about what is wrong with America. I'd like for all Americans to think about what is right with America tonight and in the days ahead."

Right on. Barry had to stop more than once for the cheers. They were coming hard from the gallery where most of the three thousand Young Voters for the President were sitting tonight. "By golly," said Goldwater as they brought him to silence with their cheers. Earlier, during Mayor Lugar's speech, the children had yelled whenever Pistol

Dick uttered the word "youth." The YVPers had not spent their adolescence going to live TV shows for no purpose — they knew when a sign said APPLAUSE. By golly — this was the answer to the coyotes.

All night, Ronald Reagan as temporary chairman of these spectacular ceremonies had been sticking it into the soft belly of the Democrats, flicking their eyes with forensic jabs while introducing other speakers and giving his own speech. Rap, tap, rap, rap, tap, tap, he would go with his good lines and his good timing, and his easy voice, full of the chuckles of good corporate living.

"A few days ago McGovern announced that his economists would be presenting a program very shortly to which he would be committed. Now, if that means he'll stand behind it 1,000 percent, we will have at least a week to look it over before he dumps it.

"McGovern has promised hand-outs of such lavishness that even *he* had to offer the reassurance that if his proposals proved dangerously extravagant, we could count on Congress to restrain him."

Reagan would never beef up to a political heavyweight but he was one of the better lightweights around and gave every evidence of being managed by Bob Hope who might just as well have written Reagan's speech tonight.

"Our traditional two-party system has become a three-party system — Republican, McGovern, and Democrat. And, only the first two parties have a presidential candidate.

"The rhetoric was the high-sounding phraseology of the 'new politics.' But, their tactics were the old politics of bossism and the smoke-filled rooms — although in some of the rooms it was reported that the smoke smelled a little funny.

"They didn't complete the ticket until a few weeks later when they had time to run through the yellow pages and call central casting.

"You could imagine the high drama of that moment of decision there in Hyannis Port — surrounded by their families, two men watching the flip of a coin. Sargent Shriver lost.

"A man of the common people, Shriver understands their language. He learned it from talking to his butler."

After a while souls even so simple as Aquarius began to recognize that Republicans had not been owning and managing the biggest advertising agencies on Madison Avenue for half a century without being able to contribute to the genius of the Presidency. A film, *Portrait of a*

465

President, was shown. But we can quote a fair description from John Huddy of the *Miami Herald:*

> We do not know whether the brief glimpses of Nixon wielding this power are actual or staged, but in any instance the director and his editor have shrewdly chosen to use dialog in which Nixon scraps for the little guy (in a phone discussion apparently involving a federal funding program) and for children (in another meeting about busing).
> "Let's keep the children out of the racial fight!" a tough Nixon is heard to say, a moment no doubt intended for the ears of every parent whose child faces busing in the next year.
> The theme in the film is obvious and it is driven home at every turn: Nixon is the President. . . . Never mind the issues; he is the President! Only Nixon can understand what that means. (Not accidentally, the film begins with portraits of a long line of presidential greats: Not illogically, it ends with a freeze-frame of Nixon on the phone and the film begins.)
> *The Nixon Years* may not have a cast of thousands, but it does have Nixon with Chou in Peking and Nixon with the Russians in Moscow. And how can any competitor possibly top that?

Kissinger follows by saying: "I, like most of my colleagues, had always been opposed to him and had formed certain images about him and I found that he was really, was totally different from the image the intellectuals have of him. He's very analytical but quite gentle in his manner, and I always had a quite different view."

Then Pat Buchanan offers a recollection: "When I joined him back in 1965, I was an editorial writer for a conservative paper in the Midwest and I went over to Bellevue, Illinois, to meet him and if he had told me that day that a few years hence I would be sitting in a great hall of people in Peking, China, clinking glasses with Chou En-lai when the People's Liberation Army Band played "Home on the Range," I would have said you're out of your everloving mind."

Buchanan gave the good-drinking head-shaking grin that young executives of the middle lands of America give when they are talking of the wonders of their boss. Never had the right wing of America been taught so easily to take ten steps to the left and smile at the center.

Then Kissinger was back with a cultivated verdict: "There's a certain, you know it's a big word, but it's a certain heroic quality about how he conducts his business because he does it all in a very understated way. Of course, I can only judge foreign policy and I believe that his impact on foreign policy will be historic no matter what happens. He has provided one of the big watersheds in American international history."

There was a last shot of Nixon wearing a sport jacket and strolling along the beach with Pat. It is a deserted beach and evening is near. The voice of the narrator says, "This is a man who calls out to America to have faith in itself, to go forward without fear, to build on the foundations he has laid down. . . . America will hear him."

The evening ended with a film about Pat Nixon. She was shown as Mrs. Ambassador. Then Jimmy Stewart brought her forward to take a bow. She came up in all the happiness of a movie star receiving an Academy Award, and the convention broke loose. They were scoring again and again, but if they had been the Minnesota Vikings scrimmaging a high-school team, still they would have screamed to keep on scoring. They were ready to lift the roof for a good few minutes.

For a good few minutes. But the demonstration in the gallery went on and on. It was the YVPers. They kept yelling. After a while the smile of happiness on Pat Nixon's face began to look like the freeze-frame in the film. Her sense of TV timing must have suggested that this demonstration was going on too long for its purpose. She was only up there to receive her tribute and say hello. The yawns which accompany a fall from maximum attention were hovering in the TV ears of every antenna — she would lose her national audience if those idiots in the gallery didn't stop cheering. A successful TV show is built on the TV viewers' past experience with television. Perhaps an ovation for a speaker had three good built-in minutes, not much more. Pat Nixon grinned. She waved her arms aloft with love to the delegates and to America, she lofted the heavy gavel and made a female face, a gesture of "oh, how heavy it is even for a wiry girl like me," she used every resource available for situations such as this and she like her husband had studied every lesson of her professional life, but the YVPers were in hysteria. They, too, were on television now! So they kept screaming for ten minutes. They were screaming like a crowd of kids who pour through the school gate on the last school day before Christmas vacation, and now can yell their hatred of the teachers. The YVPers were screaming with all the pent-up energy of having paid their own way here to be shunted from function to function, they were screaming with all the hysteria of the obedient. If it went on too long, they would no longer be showing their love for the charm of Pat Nixon as the President's wife, they would be revealing the heart of their own therapy which was to yell on TV. So, subtly, the hint of an indrawn critical look came back into the mellowed political screw-tight of the jaw of Pat Nixon, and she began to show the faintest trace of the high-powered displeasure of a wife who is going to tell her husband later, "You boob, you've overdone it again."

The evening ended with Rabbi Herschel Schacter of Mosholu Center of the Bronx giving the benediction.

> *From Nixon's Maxims:* The virtue of the triple Keynote speech is that having three legs, it is an ideological stool. Brooke, Lugar and Armstrong offer sturdy legs for such a stool, since crudely speaking these three names present an image of a tranquil brook, a World War II Luger, and a fine body, which in turn will symbolize Peace, Military Might, and a Healthy Economy.

11 A

It is back to the La Ronde Room of the Fontainebleau in the morning, same room where so many press conferences have taken place, same tables and cloths are there, wrinkled even more, but there is a new turnout Tuesday morning because Paul McCloskey is using the facilities to present Daniel Ellsberg, who has a communication to divulge, and the Press have responded in the hope of some disclosure which will crack into the facial expressions of the Republicans who are running this convention.

McCloskey stands at the microphone making the opening remarks. There are strains of premature gray in his dark hair which is worn in a pompadour reminiscent of JFK but he is still young enough to look like an officer in the Marine Corps who has earned a Navy Cross, in fact, McCloskey is the only Republican militantly against the war in Vietnam who has the look of a real conservative. By every standard of neatness, he belongs more in the FBI than on a podium introducing Dan Ellsberg, yes, a personality like an Irish hero sandwich — Black Irish severity on gloom! His persona speaks of that bull-headed Irish propensity to drink which can be found in jocks who are debating whether to take priestly vows. Still there is God's own integrity in the frown on his brow. He is an impressive man as he says in his soft-spoken voice that he would have liked to bring a debate to the floor of the convention but it had not been possible, "so unfortunately we're forced to have it here."

He has had his tribulations and frustrations. Possessor of one delegate, he will still not be nominated because of a decision of the Rules Committee that one must have representation on three delegations and a certified minimum of delegates. He will not even have his own delegate, merely one Nixon man on the New Mexican slate of fourteen who will mutter his name when the time comes. Nor has the Platform Committee given him time. He has been closed out. So, now, having invited Ellsberg to fly in from California, McCloskey contents himself with saying, "We are a rich country bombarding and destroying the people and economy of a poor country," which is the true, fundamental and legitimate conservative objection, for any war which pits rich against poor is an ugly combat which must erode the moral substance of a nation. This subject, McCloskey now says quietly, is not even going to be debated on the floor of the convention. "We are creating wholesale destruction in a war we are not even willing to die in." Gloom upon him (his wife will file suit for *divorce* over "irreconcilable differences" in just a few days, after twenty-three years of marriage), McCloskey now introduces Ellsberg and turns the conference over to him.

Ellsberg is handsome and slender in build with a large well-shaped nose and large expressive eyes light in color. They stare at the Press with a look which could partake of childhood woe if it were not so grave, for his eyes seem to say, "I know you will believe me, but will you believe me enough?" So he has the manner of someone who suspects he is ready to lose, and lose seriously. On trial now for divulging the Pentagon Papers, he can spend the rest of his life in jail if found guilty; the turn in public sentiment over the last few months from disapproval of the war to a grudging pleasure in the way our airplanes have stopped the North Vietnamese spring offensive is equivalent to some future echo of a penitentiary door closing behind him. While he is a man considerably more favored in features then Eddie Albert or Eddie Bracken, that same unhappy note is struck of a modest man pitting himself against giants, and so suggesting pathos with every move. Even a touch of the tenderest comedy clings to his seriousness. Ellsberg is so serious. The Press study him with curiosity. Can he possibly be as solemn as he seems?

He is trying to advance a complex argument. It is that when Richard Nixon came to office in 1968, he asked Henry Kissinger to prepare a Vietnam Options Paper which would outline every alternative he had, and having discarded only one of the seven alternatives (which was of course complete and unilateral withdrawal of the U.S. from Vietnam), Nixon had laid out a grand plan which included invasions of Cambodia and Laos as well as a resumption of the bombing of North Vietnam and a mining of the harbor of Haiphong, all of which would be accompanied by a phased withdrawal of ground forces. So, Ellsberg suggests to the Press, it is not that the North Vietnamese have refused our peace terms so much as it is that Richard Nixon has pursued a war plan which no one would have believed credible in 1968 or 1969, and in the course of fulfilling this war plan, has carried out the heaviest aerial bombardment in the history of the world. "That is his prerogative," says Ellsberg, "and it is possible the American people would have supported such a plan, but we will never know because they were never told about it in advance."

The Press asks him questions, and he answers, but the story while large in its implications is not conclusively proved by the Vietnam Options Paper Ellsberg is releasing. There is not the shock nor bite of a big news story — there are no remarks in these new papers which sit in a journalist's mind and give him his lead, just more of the same depressing sense that yes, Nixon has planned these acts in advance, but only as possibilities — there is no way to prove he was determined to pursue the war from the beginning of his administration — and no way to believe any longer that the majority of American people are concerned about the immorality of the war.

Afterward, Irving Wallace, the novelist, offers his suite for reporters and Media men to talk with Ellsberg. Eager to communicate the living incalculable horror of the war, Aquarius and he talked of statistics. It is the only way to begin to appraise such incomprehensibility. Because by every measure, but American casualties, the war has increased in scope during Nixon's administration. 1,489,240 combatants on all sides have been killed or wounded under Nixon as opposed to 1,333,215 under Johnson. 4,789,000 civilians have been killed, wounded, or become refugees under Nixon. The number was 4,146,000 under Johnson. And these figures are from the *Congressional Record* and the Senate Subcommittee on Refugees. While we have had only a little more than half as many American casualties under Nixon as under Johnson, the South Vietnamese have suffered more casualties, one and a half times as many, and the North Vietnamese have also had higher casualties. We have dropped 3,633,022 tons of bombs between January 1969, and June 30, 1972, as compared to 3,191,417 tons for Johnson. Out in the Pacific and the China Sea, we now have the greatest air and naval armada in the history of war.

In South Vietnam we have even accepted the Phoenix program which has executed 40,994 civilians since January 1969.

"That is to say forty thousand civilians," Ellsberg says, "who've been executed without trial. Under Johnson, the comparable figure is a little over two thousand. Still, we talk of the blood bath when the Communists come in. Can they do any worse?"

No, they cannot, Aquarius says. It is possible that nobody can do any worse than we have done. He is thinking that once bombing has achieved its strategic objective which is to obliterate military sites and production sites, all further bombing lands right in the essence of the superficial which is to say against the surface of the earth and the surface of human flesh.

"Look," says Ellsberg, "Cambodia is a country with a little more than six and a half million people. It's now two years since we've gone in, and there are two million refugees. That's the fastest destruction of any country I know."

And Ellsberg, his eyes burning into the incomprehensible night of these dark statistics, has the look of a lawyer who is losing the most heartrending case of his life. "I'd like to send Martha Mitchell to North Vietnam," he says. "I think she'd tell the truth."

> *From Nixon's Maxims:* The Silent Majority, while often accused of being non-political, actually prefer to have a definite idea and will often drift at surprising speed from one position to its opposite. May I point to the shift of opinion on the war in Vietnam. The American public once ready to get out is now ready to stay in and win provided no American blood is shed.

11 B

And yet the world planner responsible for these figures of population increase in Eternity ("out of the temporarity of life they have become permanent!") is such a nice man as he steps off his United States of America plane, *The Spirit of '76,* and descends the gangplank to embrace his family. The YVPers are waiting for him to arrive in Miami, and they give a lusty cheer as he walks across the tarmac to talk

471

to all several thousand of them sitting in temporary stands erected by an airplane hangar. Perhaps it is because they have been waiting for considerably more than an hour and in the rain! — like troops they are transported about in a great hurry in order that they may wait — or it may be the quality of his presence, but there is, considering it is the YVPers, almost no hysteria; rather, they cheer him as if he is the most popular high-school principal they have ever had. Still a principal does not excite hysteria. Or have their section leaders warned them to avoid the excesses of the night before? A sign stands out. I'M NOT A DALEY 6TH WARD SEWER WORKER. During one of their demonstrations from the gallery, John Chancellor of NBC had said, "At Democratic conventions we have seen Mayor Daley pack the hall with members of the 6th Ward sewer workers. What we have seen tonight seems to be the Republican equivalent," a remark for which Chancellor will yet have to apologize, but the epithet together with the benign presence of the President seems to have quieted the crowd.

The cast of the celebrity press conference is also on hand, John Wayne and Ethel Merman and Ruta Lee. Stan Livingston of *My Three Sons* is there and Mary Ann Mobley and Kathy Garver. Johnny Grant has done his best to entertain the crowd with his patter in the rain. Speaking of Agnew, he says, "I love that guy. Know why? He really knows how to give 'em oral karate."

There is an image! Swimming just out of reach we see the head of a liberal politician stuck onto some sort of pus-filled penile shaft (black presumably) and wham! go Agnew's teeth. What a karate chop! The head of the liberal has just been clipped off its Black backing.

Well, such an image is not near to Nixon. At the foot of the plane he embraces his wife and kisses his daughters but with appropriate reserve — they are being watched after all. The embrace is suggestive of five million similar such greetings each evening as commuters get off at a suburban stop and go through the revelation, and the guard they throw up against revelation, of their carnal nitty-gritty. A good game for a face-watcher, and Nixon's is not different from many another man who pecks a kiss in public. But as he walks toward the Young Voters for the President and salutes and smiles and grins, preparing to stop before them and raise both his arms (for they are now no longer just cheering him as the principal, but are off on all the autoerotics of thrusting their own arms in the air four fingers up while screaming "Four more years, four more years"), so Nixon promenading toward them exhibits again that characteristic gait which is his alone and might have provided thought for analysis in even so profound a student of body movements as Wilhelm Reich, for Nixon has character-armor, hordes of it! Several schemes of armor are stacked all on top of one another, but none complete. It is as if he is wearing two breastplates and yet you can still get peeks of his midriff. He walks like a puppet more curious than most human beings, for all the strings are pulled by a hand within his own head, an inquiring hand which never pulls the same string in quite the same way as the previous time — it is always trying something out — and so the movements of his arms and legs while superficially conventional, even highly restrained, are all impregnated with attempts, still timid — after all these years! — to express attitudes and emotions with his body. But he handles his body like an adolescent suffering excruciations of self-consciousness with every move. After all these years! It is as if his incredible facility of brain which manages to capture every contradiction in every question put to him, and never fails to reply with the maximum of advantage for himself in a language which is resolutely without experiment, is, facile and incredible brain, off on a journey of inquiry into the stubborn refusal of the body to obey it. He must be obsessed with the powers he could employ if his body could also function intimately as an instrument of his will, as intimate perhaps as his intelligence (which has become so free of the *distortions* of serious moral motivation), but his body refuses. Like a recalcitrant hound, it refuses. So he is still trying out a half-dozen separate gestures with each step, a turn of his neck to say one thing, a folding of his wrist to show another, a sprightly step up with one leg, a hint of a drag with the other, and all the movements are immediately restrained, pulled back to zero revelation as quickly as possible by a brain which is more afraid of what the body will reveal than of what it can discover by just once making an authentic move which gets authentic audience response. Yet he remains divided on the utility of this project. Stubborn as an animal, the body does not give up and keeps making its disjunctive moves while the will almost as quickly snaps them back.

Yet when he begins to talk to the crowd, this muted rebellion of his activities comes to a halt. Like an undertaker's assistant who fixes you with his stare and thereby gives promise that no matter the provocation, he will not giggle, Nixon has made a compact with his body. When the brain stops experimenting with its limbs, and takes over a cerebral function (like manipulating an audience), then the body becomes obedient to the speaker's posture installed on it.

473

Now, hands clasped behind him, Nixon begins. "I was under some illusion that the convention was downtown," he says.

It takes a while for the kids to get it. YVPers are not the sort of hogs who grab the high IQs. But when they realize he is not only complimenting them for the size of their numbers but on their importance, they come back with all the fervor of that arm in the air and the four fingers up in the double V. Nixon has appropriated the old V for Victory sign; better! he has cuckolded all the old sentimental meanings — V for Victory means liberalism united and the people in compact against tyranny. Et cetera. It is his now, and doubled. Up go the double horns of the kids. "Four more years."

One thing can be said for the Presidency — it gives every sign of curing incurable malaise. Nixon is genial! Now, he jokes with the crowd. "I think I'm going to be nominated tonight. I *think* so," he says charmingly. It is the first time he has ever spoken with italics in public. "And so is Vice-President Agnew," he adds. "He's going to be nominated too." They cheer. Ever since they arrived on Saturday, the YVPers have been cheering, on the street, at receptions in the gallery, in the lobby of each hotel they visit, and here at the airport they exhibit all the inner confidence of a Fail-Safe. When in doubt, cheer.

Once again Aquarius is depressed at the sight of their faces. It is not only that all those kids seem to exist at the same level of intelligence — which is probably not quite high enough to become Army officers — but they also seem to thrive on the same level of expression. They have the feverish look of children who are up playing beyond the hour of going to sleep; their eyes are determined, disoriented, happy and bewildered. So they shriek. With hysteria. The gleam in their eye speaks of no desire to go beyond the spirit they have already been given. Rather, they want more of what they've got. It is unhappy but true. They are young pigs for the President. He thinks of all the half-nude sclerotic pirates of Flamingo Park, over whom America (which is to say Republicans) are so worried. Perhaps America has been worrying about the wrong kids.

"I've been watching the convention on television," Nixon says through the microphone. "I want to thank you for the tribute you paid my wife." Now for the first time he puffs his chest up, which — given the mating dance he performs whenever addressing a crowd — has to signify that a remark of portent is on its way. "Based on what I've seen on television, and based on what I have seen here today" — Four more years! — "those who predict the other side is going to win the young voters are simply wrong." Deep breath. Solemn stare. Now comes the low voice which backs the personality with the Presidential bond of integrity: "We're going to win the young voters." Shrieks. Squeals. Cheers. Four more years! They are the respectable youth and they are going to triumph over fucked-up youth.

Back at the convention, the delegates are watching this arrival on the three huge screens above the podium — it is being televised live both to the convention and to America. Only the galleries are empty this afternoon, but that is because the YVPers are not present to fill their seats — they are here!

Nixon takes them into his confidence. He knows they are interested in politics, or they would not be in Miami, he says. And maybe one of them someday will be President. "Maybe one of your faces that I now am looking at will be President. It is possible. One thing I want you to know. That is that we want to work with the trust and faith and idealism of young people. You want to participate in government and you're going to." Cheers. He smiles genially. "However, let me give you a bit of advice. To succeed in politics, the first thing you want to do is to marry above yourself."

They do not begin to comprehend the seismographic profundity of this advice. They only yell, "We want Pat. We want Pat."

"Well, you can't have her," Nixon says. "I want to keep her."

Yes, he had wanted her and he had wanted to keep her. Back in Whittier, before they were married, he would drive her to Los Angeles when she had a date with another man. Then he would pick her up and drive her back to Whittier when the date was done. That is not an ordinary masochism. It is the near to bottomless bowl in which the fortitude of a future political genius is being compounded. It had made him the loser who did not lose.

But how many years and decades it must have taken before he recognized that in a face-off with another man, he would be the second most attractive. Once he had made the mistake of fighting Kennedy man to man, and wife to wife. Jack had beaten Dick, and Jackie had certainly taken Pat — Nixon cried out with no ordinary bitterness over what America could not stand. But now he had learned that the movies were wrong and the second most attractive man was the one to pick up the marbles, since losers (by the laws of existential economy) had to be more numerous than winners.

"Some public men," he had said in an interview, "are destined to be loved, and other public men are destined to be disliked, but the most important thing about a public man is not whether he's loved or disliked, but whether he's respected. So I hope to restore respect to the Presidency at all levels of my conduct.

"My strong point, if I have a strong point, is performance. I always do more than I say. I always produce more than I promise."

It was as true for Vietnam as for China. And now here was this nice man talking to children. Aquarius stood in that stricken zone of oscillating dots which comes upon the mind when one tries to comprehend the dichotomies of the century. Here is this nice man who has the reputation of being considerate about small things to the people who work for him, this family man married so many years to the same wife, possessor of two daughters who are almost beautiful and very obedient. He is a genius. Who would know?

Yes, the loser stands talking to all of his gang of adolescent losers who are so proud to have chosen stupidity as a way of life, and they are going to win. The smog of the wad lies over the heart. Freud is obsolete. To explain Nixon, nothing less than a new theory of personality can now suffice.

11C

Convention Center is a compound of buildings and parking areas which runs for several city blocks on every side, and is surrounded by a wire fence. On Tuesday night, in one of the deserted side lobbies of the main convention hall, a company of Miami Beach police are dinging their riot clubs in rhythm on the composition floor of the lobby. It is a peculiar operation. They stand in ranks, swaying and chanting and about every fourth beat they bounce the end of their long riot clubs off the floor. Then as the tempo increases, they begin to bounce the club faster and faster, chanting all the way. Soon they are bouncing the club on every beat. It is the war dance of the Miami Beach police and one hardly knows if they do it to get ready for battle, or to cool off after the frustration of early evening. Street tempo has picked up all day. Between the afternoon session and the evening, delegates had gone to eat in restaurants near the Convention Center. On their way back, there was trouble. Delegates were harassed by demonstrators, and called "war criminals." Windows were smashed and some red-white-and-blue bunting outside Convention Hall was set on fire by a bare-breasted girl who shinnied up a light pole. The cars of some delegates were stopped and protesters had pounded on their roofs, or jumped on the hood. One Continental panicked and jerked forward. A girl on the hood fell off; the limousine ran over her leg. In another place fifteen demonstrators were picked up by police when they tried to disconnect distributor caps from automobiles which were waiting at traffic lights. A brick was thrown through the window of the Pan American Bank, a display case at the Gaiety Burlesque was smashed. The police had finally made over two hundred arrests, and Rocky Pomerance, the Chief of Police, was in gloom. He had been trying through two conventions to keep from making busts. He had had consciousness-raising sessions with his cops on the psychology of dissent, and colloquys all these summer weeks with spokesmen for the contingents at Flamingo Park. It was said that he was even in walkie-talkie communication with some of the street leaders. He must have seen *Man of La Mancha* for he has been embarked on the impossible dream of trying to take Miami Beach through its convention days without any violence. During all of the Democratic Convention and until this night, he has been able to keep incidents at a minimum. He has not even made any arrests until Monday. Now, on Tuesday, there are two hundred. Tomorrow is going to be worse. For Nixon will give his acceptance speech and the demonstrators have announced they will try to create havoc so that delegates will be delayed and the convention not start on time.

Aquarius has wondered about the police chief. He could conceive of a cop who desired to show that some police could handle difficult situations with subtlety, but how had this police chief been able to control his troops? These troops who are moaning now in the rhythms of their war chant as they wait in the deserted lobby. But the answer proves simple once he meets Pomerance. Rocky is a tribute to the Jews. He has blue eyes, a friendly face, and is immense enough to be a Sumi wrestler. He has to be the strongest man on the force. The answer is very simple. All the other cops in Miami Beach are afraid of him. It opens a perspective on the way to achieve good police forces. One has only to find police chiefs who are strong, inspired, and benevolent. "The police can't win," Pomerance says. "They just can lose as gracefully as possible." Back of him in the lobby, the cops are still dinging their riot clubs.

11D

Calculating that a three-day spectacular was going to be in need of a basic set which should be impressive yet responsive to changes in mood, and symbolic of the epic it presented, the Republicans had designed a formidable podium. It was built high up over the deck the Democrats had used and it was painted white instead of blue, an immense podium — sixty-four feet wide and ninety-two feet deep. It looked like the bastions of a castle and the battlements of a medieval fort, it looked like some huge white ship in the sky. Speakers at the altar of that high and immense podium spoke as if from the heights of the white knights of Christendom. Blue curtains rose to the heavens of the ceiling, red-and-blue carpet lined the aisle, and American flags were hung in a row along the full length of a wall. The country was the religion. Once again America was readying for a crusade which no one was ready to name, but the heads were tiny upon that podium, and the faces were huge on the three white screens. After a while it became part of the viewer's logic to look from the tiny head to the huge face.

It was Rockefeller who put Nixon in nomination, ". . . brought us to the threshold of a generation of peace . . . skilled management and leadership . . . *we need this man*. We need this man of action, this man of courage. We need this man of faith in America. It is my great honor. . . ."

He gave the speech almost perfunctorily. There was no drama in his symbolic relinquishment of the role of Nixon's oldest party competitor, nor any drama to the fall of liberal Republicanism. Nixon had gone farther to the Left than Rockefeller might ever have dared, Nixon had gone farther to the Right. Rockefeller had come to politics almost by accident — what else could a man of his wealth, ambition, and lack of specific talent do with his life? Nixon had lived with politics as Michelangelo had lived with pigments. So even if he did not know how to move his body, Nixon knew how to move to his right and to his left. Nixon knew how to occupy the center. Kings, presidents of corporations, and *don capos* of the Mafia look to be installed by the man they deposed. So Nixon was nominated by Rockefeller.

The nomination was seconded by eleven speakers. It is a happy number in craps and full of good connotation for football. Since the number of nominating speeches in all, however, counting Rockefeller's, was twelve, it could also be said that Nelson was the first of the twelve apostles and Nixon was the twelve hours of the clock. It is precisely the kind of symbolic hyperbole which will do no harm to the unconscious of the electorate and might even convert one voter in a hundred while it sways another five.

One of the seconding speeches was given by Walter J. Hickel — two years ago, he had been dismissed from the President's Cabinet after talking out against the war. But the Republican Godfather was good and he was gracious. The guilty could return. Manuel Lujan, Jr., who had had the disgrace of fielding the only delegation to cast a vote for Paul McCloskey, stood up to second the President. So did Senator Buckley the Conservative and John McCarrell, a Democrat and president of Local 1544 of the UAW. The Conservative Irish and the labor union Irish were in for Nixon; so too was a Vietnam war veteran, John O'Neill of the Texas Irish. There was Representative Edward Derwinski, a Polish-American Republican, and Anne Smith Bedsole, a housewife from Mobile, an Alabama delegate for the Wallace folk; and there was Frank Borman. An hour after he gave the seconding speech his face was still shining with happiness on the floor. Mrs. Henry Maier, the wife of the Democratic Mayor of Milwaukee, was the Co-Chairman of Democrats for Nixon, and she said, "I am here because I am more nervous and frightened for America than for myself." They cheered her with delight. The Democrats were making better speeches for the Republicans these days than the Republicans. That was living, politically speaking, off the real fat of the land. The people sitting on the floor of the convention were sophisticated enough to know. Two-thirds of the Republican governors of America were here as delegates, and half of the Republican senators, a good quarter of their congressmen, and many Republican mayors. Only 19 percent of McGovern's delegates had ever held elective office. In contrast the figure was 84 percent for Republicans. So they could show their appreciation for the boss, they knew how good he was. Of course only 3 percent of the delegates were black where the Democrats had had almost 15, but that merely expressed the real quota of politics since the Democrats could count on four-fifths of the Negro vote. No more than 7 percent of the delegates were under thirty years of age, and the Democrats had had 27 percent, but maybe that was why the average income of the convention Republicans was so much higher than the Democrats!

Aquarius was hardly however in need of such statistics. A walk down these wide and comfortable aisles was all anyone needed to comprehend the divisions of the nation. For there was probably as much difference between Democratic and Republican faces as between the French and English, or the athletic and the intellectual — there is no need for a list of opposites. The point is that Democrats and Republicans belong on such a list, they are different, more different certainly than New Yorkers and Californians, and if one would look for the center of that difference it had been expressed probably on the night before when Reagan said, "This nation will do whatever has to be done so long as one American remains in enemy hands." It was the fetishism of American blood. Conservative Aquarius, Left-conservative Aquarius, could know at that moment he was wholly a Democrat, for in the midst of the roar of the deepest sentiments rising up in one animal growl from the happy Republican throng, he felt only the cold observation that Ronald Reagan was a moral fathead. It was not that Aquarius could never comprehend how the country was the secret of one's strength if only one believed in it. Then the blood of a countryman was different in kind, more valuable in the existence of the cosmos than a foreigner, especially if you insisted on it. (Indeed the cosmos might only comprehend the unities of human endeavor — and compromise, therefore, quota, and the absence of distinction, all fell away like mud.) The clearest and the most powerful emotions might even travel the farthest through space. No, Aquarius was not one to believe that a modern interfaith prefabricated meeting hall had more to offer one's survival than a quick view of Notre Dame from across the Seine. Nor did he think that order was to be debased before the virtues of the slovenly. He had had enough of the slovenly forever, including its swamp-like effusions in his own mind. And indeed he had regard for many a Republican face. There were distinguished faces on that floor. He saw faces which were models of discipline, or of elegance, or orderly style, faces which spoke of fire and pride and the idea that character was the only ceramic to hold human fire and pride; there were dry Republican faces which proved models of crystallized wit, and kindly urbane gentlemen whose minds were rich with concept when they thought of the commonweal. One could even say that if there was a drop of common but immortal belief in every Republican, it might be over that drop of American blood. It was where they would have their sacrament. Not in the numbers, no, never in the numbers game (although they played it too) but in the idea that the life of nations lay like a clear view across the horizon from past to future, and one drop of American blood also contained the rights of assembly for three centuries and fifty years, and so was linked to all the other blood which had been shed, a transubstantiation of the nation's blood which would believe that no, not all blood was equal, and American blood was worth more. It was a passion he might even appreciate, although he never felt it, and he could see that passion in the common denominator of Republican faces. They were practical to the last muttering of the last clause, but only because they also believed that the spark of every Christian light was concealed in each good clause. So the best of the Republicans had fine faces, a few had faces which were even splendid, for they knew that flesh was never so noble as with its hint of such a light, and a few of the Republican ladies looked wise or passionate or bold or pleased with the private knowledge that beauty and style were part of a life which did not have to cease.

There were even Nixon's daughters. They had had the most impossible assignments for starlets — they were obliged to be smiling, pleasant, happy with the team and radiant; no starlet in the memory of any living moviegoer had ever come close to performing that slavish assignment well through an entire role. It could be said the Nixon girls came as close as any starlets he had seen.

But once that was said, how much worse was the rest. "So long as one American remains in enemy hands" the power to avoid all responsibility is also at hand, including the failure to recognize that total faith in one's country might be as dangerous as total faith in one's own moral worth, even worse, for with total patriotism, one's own soul was no longer there to be lost; rather, America could be lost. So as he worked the measure of his comprehension along the rows of faces, all Republican here, there came to him after a time some large detestation of their average. The average Republican face was as selfish or stingy as it was ingrown, and often it was squeezed together with the ferocity of the timid. Worse. So many of these faces were dead to experience they did not already comprehend. They were closed to any face which was not near to their own, or any style of dress. Many lived in the dread of the undeserving rich, that thick-throated dread which always awaits some disaster from the side (since they have confronted nothing directly in years). So, yes, there was something unformed in these Republican faces, half at least, some refusal to face into the pressure of living in a world where moral questions do not by the end of ten seconds provide an answer. There was a glisten of stupidity in the gleam of the eye — all too many of them had been called pigs and not for nothing. They were kin to the worst expression of a cop — that particular stupidity which reflects all of moral damage, as if the sneaks of childhood are covered now in twenty layers of emotional lard, laid in by the living choice to be mediocre. Bad enough. The Republican women were worse. Did they have a mouth and jaw like the claw of a lobster? — so, too, did they have bodies suggestive of the backs and limbs of old stuffed chairs, Republican woman! Until the years of Liberation, they had been called frigid — now they were freed of the need to search for v*g*n*l org*sm; the Liberation had declared them free. One look at their faces and, truth, they had not searched hard! The totalitarian will of the Democratic Liberator was easily equaled by the frigidity of the Republican lady. So their faces brought to mind a picture of the patients in the sex clinics of Masters and Johnson — those hard-bitten unforgiving women who never had one at all until their guide at Masters and Johnson could show them how and then the lady let go a machine gun of belted sex — fifty rounds of clitoral fire.

Now the nominations droned on. "Florida," said a voice thick with the emotion of its offering, "casts its votes for the greatest President since Abraham Lincoln."

There was a fear in these frozen Republican faces which could be equal only to the woe of their inability to comprehend the size of our acts in Vietnam.

And now Nixon was over and nominated and the giant screens above the podium burst out, NIXON IS NOMINATED, NIXON IS NOMINATED, said a display of signs as they blinked on and off; the scoreboard in a new kind of stadium was celebrating a score. And in that hall like a temple where thousands of lights in every variety of metal reflector and cylinder high overhead blazed down out of a heaven of girders and spotlights, crates of balloons began to open, thousands of red-white-and-blue balloons came cascading out of great crates overhead and descended toward the floor. And as the balloons tumbled down, a band of middle-aged musicians came marching out to play "As the Saints Come Marching In," and Young Voters for the President were storming center stage from the wings carrying large plastic bags which they opened to release more red-white-and-blue balloons which ascended up to the girdered heavens, the Young Voters in with such a rush of stampede that older delegates were in a horror to get out of their way for the YVPers might trample them. Anything to reach those balloons which were coming down! Young Voters were there to devour balloons, burst them like bits of meat thrown into a pond of piranhas, balloons exploded in a cacophony of small arms fire. And the Young Voters waved American flags they carried on small sticks, waved them violently. The fins of piranhas were in on a new kill. It was as if a celebration of all the murder you could shake loose in America. "Four more years," they screamed, and the sticks vibrated in the air, and the red of the flags was like a foaming of the froth.

11E

Nixon had been on his way to a Youth Rally in Marine Stadium of Miami. Since his limousine had the newest and best of radio equipment, he timed his arrival to enter just as he was being nominated back in Miami Beach. We are about to witness the record application of the Jeannette Weiss Principle. Nixon is embraced by a Black Jew who sings for the young, does imitations for the old and has turned from Democrat to Republican. The scene is shown on the great screens above the podium, and excites the war dance of the Young Voters to vibrate even faster. "Four more years."

11F

From Nixon's Maxims: Phineas T. Barnum was a sucker.

12A

"Welcome to Flamingo Park." It said, "The liberated zone of revolutionary living, organizing and non-violent direct action. Here we shall work to expose, confront and defeat the oppressive Nixon Administration."

Thus enlightened the elderly couple moved through the gates, turned left on the Ho Chi Minh Trail and walked past:

The women's tent
The Free Berkeley Booth
The Neo-American Church
The Free Gays

The Jesus Freaks
The Society for the Advancement of Non-Verbal Communication
The Yippie Headquarters, arriving finally with no little sense of wonderment at
The People's Pot Park.

— *New York Times,* August 22

Sunday, 20th. Dishonor Amerika Day . . . The Zippies present . . . THE SECOND COMING. Jesus in a Zippie T-shirt will descend and lead a march to Convention Hall bearing a cross with Billy Graham on it. At the hall, there will be a piss-in on objects of honkie culture, we'll destroy a welfare Cadillac (to be burned previously but impounded), apple pies will be fed to running dogs, eggs tossed at a huge picture of Martha Raye (America's mom), flags burned, and a compulsory o.d. program for delegates, followed by an Om-out at which Jell-O will be served. . . .

— Youth International Party

The kid . . . sat on his yellow blanket beneath the banyan tree, snorting defiantly from a clear plastic baggie. The small cloth inside the baggie was soaked with paint thinner. . . . "Man," said one of several self-appointed Flamingo Park peacekeepers, "take your death trip somewhere else. You don't understand that a lot of us don't dig what you're into. Go off the park, man." . . . "Yeah," said someone else . . . "die somewhere else, man. If you die on this park, man, you're putting a bad number on all of us."

— *Miami Herald,* August 19

Six Yippies resorted to a "puke-in" and vomited on the sidewalk outside the Fontainebleau to show that "Nixon makes us sick." A network TV producer was there but ordered no film, turning away in disgust.

— *Miami Herald,* August 21

The name of the operation is The Last Patrol. Pat Pappas, 22, an Army medic at Chulai during 1970, explained why he was heading for Miami Beach.

"It's just a moral obligation, simply, and that doesn't help the cause very much. I don't expect to change anything much, I just want people to remember us."

— *Washington Post,* August 19

The Flamingo Park campsite was gassed several times during the night — once, reportedly, from a helicopter.

— New York Times, August 25

A committee of "religious observers" from local churches and synagogues watched the campsite and the demonstrators and issued detailed daily reports.

— New York Times, August 25

Four girls in Vietnamese costumes stood outside the hall today holding disemboweled dolls and moaning funeral chants.

— New York Times, August 23

This afternoon, the Rev. Carl McIntire, the Fundamentalist preacher, visited the park and was met with hoots, jeers, and shouts of "to the lions with him." He left, trailed by a band of youths chanting "kill for Christ."

— New York Times, August 19

Members of the Vietnam Vets Against the War destroyed two fused Molotov cocktails, three wrist rockets, two lead-weighted arrows, 200 marbles and 100 sharpened bolts Sunday after surrendering a man they said had them in his possession to Miami Beach police.

. . . Det. Sgt. Richard Procyk, liaison officer between the non-delegates . . . and police said police permitted the weapons to be destroyed in an act of "good faith" and symbolic non-violence by six regional coordinators of the VVAW.

. . . VVAW members . . . destroyed the weapons with knives and sledge hammers.

— Miami Herald, August 21

"We have a lot of sore throats here," said a VVAW medic who would be identified only as "Bill" because of possible repercussions when he returned to his full-time job as a member of a fire department rescue team somewhere in Florida. . . . Bill said he could use at least a thousand more pills to treat the sore throats. Dr. David Spiegel, Massachusetts Mental Health Center, blames the passing around of canteens, cups and eating utensils for the spread of throat infections. . . .

— Miami Herald, August 22

Bill Wyman, 21 . . . stepped on a land mine while on patrol in Phy Bai . . . has been as active as anyone . . . despite loss of both his legs. Monday he was back in a wheelchair, victim of the next most common complaint among non-delegates — blisters. Bill had been wearing artificial legs . . . because of heat or too much walking the stumps of his legs became chafed and swollen.

— Miami Herald, August 22

Mayor Chuck Hall ordered Matt Koehl, American Nazi Party Leader, arrested for displaying the swastika. . . . Koehl met with Hall to protest treatment of the American Nazi party members by Republican Convention protesters at Flamingo Park, and refused to remove the arm band. . . . It's against the law to display the swastika in Miami Beach. . . .

— New York Times, August 24

"Oh, can I see my picture?" Tina Hill, 20, of Los Angeles begged as she was put into a van. A trooper obliged. . . .

Once inside the yellow vans, though, the protesters seemed to come back to life, pounding gleefully the sides, singing "God Bless America," and perhaps appropriately, "We All Live in a Yellow Submarine."

The five rental Deatrick vans carrying male prisoners drove to the east side of Dade County Jail.

Steam came out of the hot unventilated van when the first doors were opened. A few youths had fainted and lay on the floor. The others stood.

At Flamingo Park, Zippies began taking up a collection to post bond for other protesters.

— Miami Herald, August 23

"We like to sleep on the ground, because 'The Land' (the protesters' name for their encampment) belongs to the people."

— New York Times, August 23

MIAMI NONVIOLENCE PROJECT PROPOSAL

"THAT THE PARTY GO ON RECORD AND SO INSTRUCT THE SERGEANT OF ARMS TO KEEP ALL MURDERERS, WAR CRIM-INALS, AND INTERNATIONAL OUTLAWS FROM ENTERING THE CONVENTION HALL. . . .

Richard M. Nixon happens to be a straight white man. A recent study shows that San Francisco is governed by a group who represent but 8½% of the population — married white men. This is no coincidence! Need we say more?

— *Unconventional News*

The oppression of sexism makes it hard for us to survive — and we don't want to just survive — we want to create. We struggle against the death dreams of Nixon and other men's power in the government and also against the male attitudes we find among leftist movement people and others who want to live in alternative ways to American society. We try to support all women in the effort to end male supremacy. The vision we have of a revolutionary society is not one where men continue to dominate. We urge men to *come out* into revolutionary consciousness. We think that men should become effeminate to learn to live and work collectively and to leave space free of male influence, for sisters.

— *Unconventional News*

PLACENTA RECIPE

1 placenta from self or friend
1 onion (2 if placenta is large)
½ cup of melted butter or ghee

Steam the placenta until it can be ground in a meat grinder without drippings. Sauté the onion until light brown. Grind fine together and pour in butter or ghee. From this mixture form one or more attractive mounds and garnish with whatever you have around. Serve with crackers, tortillas, chapati.

— PEOPLE'S ALMANAC

Men who are asked to leave the women's tent or women's meetings should be no more offended than they would be if they were asked to leave a Black caucus. . . .

— Miami Women's Coalition

. . . At Flamingo Park . . . we organized a Women's Anti-Rape Squad (WARS) — groups of 3 to 5 women who patrolled the campsite from 9 P.M. to 5 A.M. to deal with the harassment of women.

Many of the women in MWC want to make sure that the group continues after the conventions. Sisters, please send us your ideas,

487

comments, photographs, poems, money, support, strength, creativity, and love. A fresh wind is blowing against the empire.

— Miami Women's Coalition

The YIP gathers for resistance and change. We are the direct descendants of a freedom and justice seeking people which links us with every century, with every decent cause, with every plant and mammal that ever lived.

We stand at the barricades of decency and beauty.

We want change!
We want to change the environment!
We want to change the economy!

Change the government!
Change the culture! Change your spirit!
Change your diet! Change your sex!
Ex-change everything!

— Youth International Party

From Nixon's Maxims: Franklin Delano Roosevelt spoke of the four freedoms. There is only one freedom looked for by the American voter who votes for Nixon — it is freedom from dread.

12 B

Compared to the demonstrations of Berkeley and Oakland, the March on the Pentagon, or May Day, the week in Flamingo Park has been a failure. The number of protesters has never increased to more than a few thousand, and they are divided by every idea but one: that Richard Nixon is a war criminal. It is not enough. Other divisions are too numerous. They quarrel about sexism and revolution, about the merits of violent demonstration as opposed to peaceful sit-ins; before they are done, every old argument about revolutionary tactics from the paving stones of the Paris Commune to the grass of Flamingo Park has been recapitulated, and brother is hung up with brother, and sister hoots them out both because they are too doctrinaire or too ego trip, too heavy, too sexist, too liberated, too irresponsible or too fucking chicken to get their shit together. They even argue whether there should be a single loudspeaker system or many. Their common enemy, the pigs, are no longer common, for the pigs are not acting like pigs. So still another ideological dispute is laid on the babel — they divide whether to trash or cooperate. Since the police are not vicious, the threat of brutal arrests no longer draws them together nor gives the dignity of combating large fear. Since the danger is less than they have anticipated, they cannot even know after a time if they are serious or have become video-swingers who do the dance of the seven veils for Media men — it is possible they have become no more than actors — just so much as the politicians they despise. Television pollutes identity, and television cameras are about them all the time. So the most serious cannot even finally know if they protest the war or contribute to the entertainment of Nixon's Epic — across the screens of the nation they flurry, cawing like gulls in adenoidal complaints, a medieval people's band of lepers and jesters who put a whiff of demonology on the screen, or lay an entertaining shiver along the incantations of their witches. Did that hint of a gay demented air now serve only to dignify the battlements of the white knights of Christendom up on Nixon Heights?

Even their true show of revolutionary strength for the Media — Vietnamese Veterans Against the War — is a strength now sliced, for the Viet Veterans have six of their members on trial in Gainesville for conspiracy to cause disorder and rioting in Miami Beach during the Republican Convention — what jurisprudential coincidence! — and so must keep their deportment proper while in Miami: trashing by the Vets would hurt the men on trial. Yet they have to wonder if real fear of the war might be inspired more by the Vets of Vietnam getting violent in the streets — that might dig deeper into the nature of national distress than the wilder fringes of suburbia screaming up the tube.

Of course, it is possible that nothing would have worked. It was even likely. For the greater their numbers, and the more complete their disruption, greater was the likelihood that they would merely contribute to Nixon's consensus. So the troops of the Miami Convention Coalition and the People's Coalition for Peace and Justice, the Miami Women's Coalition, and the Vietnam Veterans Against the War, the People's Pot Party, the Coalition of Gay Organizations and the SDS, the Yippies and the Zippies, have all possibly headed into the worst trap of them all which is to attack the Godfather in a Media war. Benefactor of the American corporation, spiritual leader of the military industrial complex, and only *don capo* ever to have survived the tortures of the Media, he is learned in the wisdom of wise leaders, and knows how to put a foot in front of your ankle as you go forward and a knee in your seat as you back up, a ring in your nostrils to lead you and a hook in your ear for sit down! The art of Media war is to benefit whether your adversary does well or fails. In a strategy session at the Doral, it has already been decided that if the demonstrators ever succeed on Wednesday night in getting things out of control, then the Republicans will issue a call to McGovern and ask him to call off the kids.

So the protesters cannot win. They are doomed to be the most ineffectual of all the major demonstrations against the war in Vietnam. Yet, they are probably the most interesting, for their ideas are pioneer, and they have led a private demonstration beneath the public exhibition to show that they can live in the field like an army, house every private war, police themselves, feed themselves, drug themselves, and even with a variety of vigilante justice (which stops well short of anybody hanging — merely confiscates weapons and ejects Nazis) they govern themselves. They keep the park in some relation to order, and the tourists and sightseers who come through are sometimes welcome and never molested. They entertain themselves and share their goods and sleep on the ground. They are an area of liberty free to some great extent of civic law — they function as a community of consent — separate from the city about them. There will be others to follow. For the atmosphere is different in the park, different from the air of other communities, just as there are regions of the skin where the flesh is not like other flesh. In Flamingo Park the mood does not speak precisely of a bruise which has begun to heal nor of the pleasure beneath a piece of one's sexual skin; it is more, he supposes, like something of the air of a rain forest. He has never been in such a forest but has been told that deep in the jungle, the shade is cool and has the tenderness of any atmosphere which is never free of danger. Senses come alive. One steps out of the pressure of habit, lays down one's habits like a back pack — there is a limit to how long some live without their load. The tourists enjoy Flamingo Park but leave before too long. So does he. It is too separate from everything in the Republican Convention, too sweet, contentious, hassled, frayed, tawdry, boring, comic, comfortable, menacing, and the faces are always in opposition, so direct and so spaced out, so handsome, so full of acne, so innocent, so open, so depraved, so freaky, so violent, so gentle that first one's senses are alive as one is alive before the sight of a painting and then are fatigued, as in a museum where there is too much great painting and too much stale air. The air is also stale in Flamingo Park, stale with the butt end of dead souls all over the grass, washed out, leached out, processed out, souls dead with the consumptions of their own drug-fired awareness, and the vision is always at hand of the American Left disappearing in the vortex of the great cosmic hole of the drug while Nixon speaks from the Heights of the White Knights and says, "I will destroy 200,000,000 Asians before I let American youth go over to drugs." Audiences will cheer because nothing is worse than American Youth on drugs (and they are right!) (even if the South Vietnamese with the sanction of the CIA are sending their smack on that Bob Hope road which leads from Saigon to Miami). What a world and what knots! The devil has tied them with fingers of steel.

So Aquarius never remains in Flamingo Park too long at a time, or he might be tempted to stay and do a book about communities of consent. He is not ready for that. He is in Miami of his own desire to study Republicans — such opportunities do not come much more often than every four years. He does his duty, therefore, and breathes that other air of listening to Republican concepts which have never been illumined by any drug, or indeed any breeze which does not pass through the vaults of a bank. He does not care to state which is worse. Left meets Right at the end of ideology, and the smell of dead drugs is like the smell of old green bills. Fungus in the cellar is growth in the damp.

12C

By Wednesday afternoon, however, he could bear the Republicans no longer and so went out to the streets around Convention Center to watch the demonstrations but they were divided and disorganized and he never found the major confrontation for which he looked, and indeed only found out in the following days and by reading the papers (which is the true humiliation for a journalist!) that plans to block traffic and delay the convention had been shifted at the last minute. The police had brought in a number of old buses and parked them bumper to bumper across certain intersections but so tightly pressed against one another, and so touching the buildings on either side of the street that they made a wall, and the police had set these walls at strategic positions to create the sides of a funnel through city streets down which the buses of the delegates could pass and enter convention gates protected all the way by police on the inside. The sight of these buses divided the demonstrators into three camps (which as Napoleon has been known to remark is the first military error of them all). A majority now decided that Security had been changed to the *highest level* around the hall, and too many demonstrators would be hurt; so Miami Coalition leaders Rennie Davis and Jeff Nightbyrd urged protesters who were non-violent to accompany them up Collins Avenue to the Fontainebleau, a march of two miles which was joined by five hundred people, some of whom later broke up to trash, while others went on to sit down before the Doral, there to be arrested for blocking the street. It was a peaceful demonstration. Of those who were left in Flamingo Park, perhaps so many as another five hundred stayed in their tents and never went out at all, and two hundred of the VVAW left at 5:30 in the afternoon for Gainesville where their six members were scheduled for arraignment on Thursday. Some hundreds more went down to the Convention Center and milled about on a street or two held open for them until a sufficient number of scattered episodes finally brought attacks of tear gas by the police which increased in intensity until even the air conditioning of Convention Hall began to suck it in and the cooling system had to be turned off. Scattered groups trashed where they could on Collins Avenue and buses of the Mississippi and South Carolina delegation were halted by protesters who yanked wires off the engine and flattened their tires, forcing the delegates to walk six or eight blocks to the hall. The Illinois bus had its windshield sprayed with black paint right after it was forced to come to a stop because a platoon of demonstrators lay down before it. Then the tires were slashed and an American flag was put on fire and thrown into the engine. When the delegates rushed out, some protesters pushed them while others worked to protect them; policemen finally brought the delegates through. Delegate LeRoy Stocks of Whiteville, North Carolina, was quoted as saying, "If they want to act like dogs, they should be treated like dogs. I think next time they should issue every delegate and alternate a submachine gun." A delegate from Mississippi caught a blob of red paint on his new green-striped suit. He was in a group of twenty-five Mississippians who were taken in convoy by police after their bus was stopped; then ran a "gauntlet of curses, spit, tear gas and flying eggs." Delegate Sharon Kelly from South Carolina, reported to be an "attractive blonde," said, "Twenty hippie girls surrounded me. They bounced me around like a Ping-Pong ball. One of them screamed, 'You sure smell pretty, you blonde bitch!' It was disgusting." Perhaps the number was less than twenty. Southern belles are notorious for the ability not to do arithmetic under pressure.

So it went, and there were other scattered incidents. Later in the night protesters would march through hotels, and light trashing took place in the street; arrests continued; but the demonstrators were defeated, although Aquarius hardly knew it for he spent two hours promenading the streets around the convention, waiting in his ignorance like the others for the possible arrival of delegates, and since the main promenade was on a closed-off block of Washington Avenue, the same wide street which ran by the front of the Convention Center, there was every intimation of action to come, and hundreds of kids prowled back and forth, stalking like adolescents on a boardwalk, waiting for the encounters which will forge the character that carries them into the future, back and forth they prowled, a panoply of protesters' faces, the girls almost without exception exhibiting bodies more beautiful than their heads, which were fierce in expression, female pirates, bandanas about their hair, bandanas about their breasts, wearing hip-hugger pants with their navels out for all the police to see, as if the eye of the revolution to come was here in the navels of the women. And the boys had beards, or long hair, or both, and many wore glasses. Many were students and many were bright — it was in the complacent rest of their head on their neck, as if the head had been told from childhood it was the center of value, and these were the boys who were usually non-violent, out of ideology more than fear, since some had the smug fearlessness of the unblooded, and others were ready to bleed if it came to it (they saw themselves as blood of atonement) and indeed their fear was in their responsibility: there were protesters and provokers, and they were fearful of the second — one incident which was ugly enough and Nixon would win the headlines again. So they did their best to placate and to serve as police, and those college voices, just a little thin with the tremor of exercising an authority they did not wholly possess, would cry out in a whine of exasperation, "Come on, we're here to protest the war, not to trash the police," and some listened, some did not. Some of the non-delegates were handsome and in for the action, athletes, off a surf board, hip and with an edge, they carried themselves the way Robert Redford might if playing a protester, floated on the edge of the action, assessing it and moving on,

493

and there were kids no gang of bikers would ever accept, hyena eyes and the odor of yesterday's dead drug came off them on the reopening of yesterday's old sweat now riding on the perspiration of their new charge. With the jolt, their attention went up like a column boring into the electric core of space, out in space were their heads (and still the look of the hyena to rip off some little prey), and others, mired down on downers but still mugged in the skull with all the low lowering pressures of violence that shoved them forward, fear which pulled them back. They were holding rocks in their fists, and now one of them, half in stupor, throws it over the wire fence which borders Washington Avenue, over into the loose-spaced ranks of the cops on the other side of the fence and a girl in a bandana shouts, fearless of his wad of congested violence, "Hey, you asshole — don't throw rocks. You bring a bust on all of us." But the rocks go on. They are being thrown from time to time. Every five minutes a rock goes over the fence, and once or twice a cop throws one back. Protesters pass near the fence and give the cops a finger. "Eat the rich," they cry, and the cops lift squirt cans and give them Mace. A dwarf stands in the crowd. He has powerful forearms near to normal in length and they are held behind him. He is concealing a weapon. A couple of steel balls are wrapped in a red rag and slung from his wrist — his bare forearm looks like a phallus with two maroon testicles attached. He merely stands there waiting, a grin on his dwarf's mouth.

"One, two, three, four," the kids shout at the cops. "We don't want your fucking war." Signs are walked back and forth, one shows a host of skulls. THE SILENT MINORITY it says. Another displays a Vietnamese child with a scandalous wound of open flesh across her face. OUR GROSS NATIONAL PRODUCT says the sign. Yes, it is a fair exchange. We are bombing Vietnam, and the drugs of Indochina are bombing our young.

After a while he tries to circle around to other sides of the Convention Center, but the walls of buses make him detour. The odor of tear gas is beginning to collect in pockets on the side streets, and the old who are sitting on the balconies and patios of their cheap apartments in the cheap white stucco buildings of this part of Miami Beach are beginning to suffer, here and there. Only in Miami Beach would old people go out on their second-story porch to watch a war. Like the Orange Bowl parade, it is full of interest for them. A long-haired boy who lingers near a stoop finally antagonizes the old lady who occupies it, and seeing a cop across the street she is bold. "Stop staring at me," she says, "or I'll pour some water on you," her voice cracked with the violence that her life has almost been lived and justice has not necessarily been done. On one corner, a kid, aimlessly, hardly knowing why, sets fire to a heap of newspapers. A cop yells, "Hey," moves in, kicks out the fire, but does not arrest the boy. Another fire is burning in a wire basket at a street corner, and a fire truck comes tolling and pealing its bell, cream-green police cars with their blue lights turning and their sirens wailing, come up, crawl by, and now cruise Washington Street in front of Convention Center. He sees the buses of delegates go by, and a lost patrol of six delegates being guided by two cops passes along the porch of a hotel; the ladies are helped over the balcony when they have to jump down in order to go around a bus. The demonstrators ignore them, and the delegates are silent and proper. They have the we-are-here-to-make-no-trouble look of white tourists in Harlem.

Then, for reasons he never learns, there comes a point when the cops start clearing Washington Street and Seventeenth Street, and a battle starts, very one-sided, with the crowd advancing down Seventeenth Street, Aquarius among them, moving they don't know quite why nor for which reason in this direction only to be halted by a line of cops and then before long to be dispersed with the firing of canisters of tear gas. The crowd slips back and away at the edge of the gas, and retreating to another corner, he finds an intersection held by an impromptu guerrilla patrol of protesters who have removed a police barricade from one street and put it on another. Now — perhaps there is some last notion of disruption in all of this — they signal the occasional car which comes up to go by another route, and obligingly open the barrier to let an ambulance through; they stand stony-faced as two cops come up in a patrol car, and do not change expression as one cop gets out, removes the barricade, waits for the other to drive through, restores the barricade, says, "Thanks fellows" — sarcastically — "for helping me," gets back in the patrol car, and the police drive on. The guerrillas laugh shamefacedly. They were frightened when the cops first came.

It is the lightest kind of war, easier than maneuvers in basic training, part of the correspondent's good life — Aquarius is almost nostalgic that he has missed the good wars of other eras, and now knows why Hemingway loved to cover a war with even the thought of liquor to taste so good, he even loves this evening in Miami and the softness of the approaching tropical night, the pop of tear-gas canisters around

495

the corner, the wail of an ambulance, all the sounds of action in a city, but now intensified, as if part of the sorrow of his lost adolescence is tied up in the memory of games played in the hurry to finish before it got too dark on the city streets: the action which is going on is sad and absurd and pointless and lost and will not save a life in Vietnam, and yet he loves it, loves Miami Beach to his amazement, this crazy city of permissions and symbolic wars, and now watching the action from the vast roof of a vast parking garage, sees the rising full moon look misty as if obscured by tear gas. Is the day actually coming when there will be real battles in the cities and true smoke over the moon? Americans play many games and enjoy them well; they cannot really understand how airplanes lay death in strings of defecation on the earth. But he hates the sound of the helicopters surveying the scene from above, the noise of the blade-like chops of instruction to the back of the ear. And the wind is shifting and more canisters falling. He is trapped in tear gas at last, more now than the smarting of his eyes and the souring of his nose and throat like a catarrh upon him, this is more, and now is abruptly the end of two hours of promenading, for he can no longer see, the gas has come all around him, he has finally had enough, and good obliging war with an exit visa stamped and ready to leave, he has finally and most certainly had enough of the tear gas, and eyes screwed into the searing sorrow of bereavements he has not suffered, goes blinded with weeping like any other victim into the Convention Center for refuge, and there honored by his Press card is given a healing solution by a fireman on duty to take care precisely of all the delegates and Press who come through, the fireman saying to each of the stumbling victims as they approach, "This won't hurt you, I promise. Will you accept it? Please open your eyes." And considerate as a saint he laves gouts of solution into the fiery stream of the tears — eyes relieved, Aquarius goes on into the convention and hears a security guard in the men's room (where he has gone to wash his eyes again) say that it was the hippies who were throwing the gas. That was great. It was good to know cops were still liars — a security was left in your knowledge of the world — and Aquarius went in to the temple of politics and listened to Agnew and Nixon give acceptance speeches, and was struck with Agnew's use of metaphor. "A President lives in the spotlight, but a Vice-President lives in the flickering strobe lights that alternately illuminate or shadow his unwritten duties. It is sometimes uncomfortable. It is sometimes ego-diminishing. But it is also . . ." and even if Agnew said, "rewarding," still it was the first time in twelve years of listening to Republican Presidents and Vice-Presidents that he had heard a metaphor and a good one, and perhaps it was no more than the relief and merriment of having had his light touch of combat, but he was in a good mood as he listened to Nixon and was struck again with the knowledge that the Godfather could manipulate much in politics and do even more as a sculptor (to the fecal emotions of the American electorate) but he could not give a good speech — God had at least denied him that — and so after three days of the most consummate spectacular in the history of television (considering how modest in content was the original material) the climax was Nixon whose voice dependably lay like Bromo Seltzer upon the pumping of the heart.

"Speaking on behalf of the American people, I was proud to be able to say in my television address to the Russian people in May, we covet no one else's territory, we seek no dominion over any other nation, we seek peace, not only for ourselves, but for all the people of the world.

"This dedication to idealism runs through America's history. During the tragic war between the states, Abraham Lincoln was asked whether God was on his side. He replied, 'My concern is not whether God is on our side but whether we are on God's side.' "

"May that always be our prayer for America.

"We hold the future of peace in the world and our own future in our hands.

"Let us reject, therefore, the policies of those who whine and whimper about our frustrations and call on us to turn inward. Let us not turn away from greatness.

"The chance America now has to lead the way to a lasting peace in the world may never come again.

"With faith in God and faith in ourselves and faith in our country, let us have the vision and the courage to seize the moment and meet the challenge before it slips away.

"On your television screens last night, you saw the cemetery in Leningrad I visited on my trip to the Soviet Union where 300,000 people died in the siege of that city during World War II. At the cemetery, I saw the picture of a twelve-year-old girl. She was a beautiful child. Her name was Tanya. I read her diary. It tells the terrible story of war. In the simple words of a child, she wrote of the deaths of the members of her family — Zhenya in December, Grannie in January, then Leka, then Uncle Vasta, then Uncle Lyosha, then Mama in May.

"And finally these were the last words in her diary: 'All are dead, only Tanya is left.'

"Let us think of Tanya and of the other Tanyas and their brothers and sisters everywhere in Russia and in China and in America as we proudly meet our responsibilities for leadership in the world in a way worthy of a great people.

"I ask you, my fellow Americans, to join our new majority not just in the cause of winning an election but in achieving a hope that mankind has had since the beginning of civilization.

"Let us build a peace that our children and all the children of the world can enjoy for generations to come."

12D

FROM THE DIARY OF T'NAYEN EN DHIEU:

> For the last five weeks the airplanes have been coming over.
> On the first day Uncle Nguyen was killed. Three days later, my brother Nang Da.
> Last week Aunt Vinh Tan was killed together with my baby sister Minou.
> Yesterday Papa bled to death.
> Today Mama burned to death.
> All are dead. Only T'Nayen writes this.

12E

From Nixon's Maxims: Politics is effrontery.

12F

Nixon has a wife who gives every evidence she is fond of him. Her arm goes around her husband now that his speech is done, and with their free arms they wave to the audience who is near. Aquarius is part of that near audience down on the floor, and can see the dimensions of a diamond in the sparkle of a ring on her finger. Encouraged thereby to experiment, Aquarius looks hard at the diamond as her hand goes around her husband's back. Pat Nixon may feel his eyes on the diamond. She removes her hand. Diamonds! Basic life material is carbon, and diamonds are their hardest form. Is that why they receive our thoughts?

The Spectacular ends. The band plays "God Bless America." Nixon stands at one end of the Convention Hall and shakes hands with each of the delegates as they walk by in file. Aquarius wonders if he should try to stand in line himself, and fulfill the last duty of this week's long job by going all the way up to the man so that he will be able to bear witness to the historic feel of his skin, but Aquarius is not a delegate and they will probably not let him make the line, and besides he does not want to shake hands with the nice man. Even in politics, some hands are not yours to shake.